Corporate Income Taxation in Europe

Corporate Income Taxation in Europe

The Common Consolidated Corporate Tax Base (CCCTB) and Third Countries

Edited by

Michael Lang, Pasquale Pistone, Josef Schuch, Claus Staringer and Alfred Storck

Institute for Austrian and International Tax Law, WU, Austria

Edward Elgar

Cheltenham, UK • Northampton, MA, USA

Published by
Edward Elgar Publishing Limited
The Lypiatts
15 Lansdown Road
Cheltenham
Glos GL50 2JA
UK

Edward Elgar Publishing, Inc.
William Pratt House
9 Dewey Court
Northampton
Massachusetts 01060
USA

A catalogue record for this book
is available from the British Library

Library of Congress Control Number: 2013938968

This book is available electronically in the ElgarOnline.com Law Subject Collection, E-ISBN 978 1 78254 542 2

FSC
www.fsc.org
MIX
Paper from
responsible sources
FSC® C013056

ISBN 978 1 78254 541 5

Typeset by Columns Design XML Ltd, Reading
Printed and bound in Great Britain by T.J. International Ltd, Padstow

Contents

Contributors

Krister Andersson is Head of the Tax Policy Department, Confederation of Swedish Enterprise. Since 2005 he has been the Chairman of the Tax Policy Group of BUSINESSEUROPE in Brussels. BUSINESSEUROPE represents some 20 million companies from 35 countries. Mr Andersson is associate professor in Economics at Lund University. He is on the Board of the Swedish branch of the International Fiscal Association (IFA) and the Swedish Association of Corporate Treasurers (SACT). Between 1999 and 2008 he was a board member of the Swedish National Tax Authority, and is currently on their Advisory Board. Previously, he worked for the IMF in Washington, DC and he was Chief Economist of the Riksbank, the Swedish central bank between 1991 and 1996. He has served as vice chair for the Tax Commission of the ICC and is currently vice chair with responsibility for Tax Policy in the BIAC Taxation and Fiscal Policy Committee to the OECD.

Katharina Becker is currently deputy head of the international tax policy division of the Federal Ministry of Finance in Berlin. She worked for the Task Force on the Common Consolidated Corporate Tax Base at the general directorate for taxes and customs of the EU Commission in Brussels in 2008. Until 2008, Ms Becker headed several units at the Federal Central Tax Office (FCTO) in Bonn, at the exchange of information unit for direct taxes and the unit for mutual agreement procedures and advance pricing agreements. In 1995 she worked for the Inland Revenue, International Division in London and from 2000 to 2003 for the Centre for Tax Policy and Administration at the OECD in Paris.

Yariv Brauner is a Professor of Law with the Levin College of Law at the University of Florida. He joined the Florida faculty in 2006, after teaching at NYU, Northwestern and ASU. He has been a visiting professor or a guest speaker in various universities in the United States and abroad. He is the author of several articles published in professional journals and law reviews, and a co-author of *U.S. International Taxation – Cases and Materials* (with Reuven S. Avi-Yonah and Diane M. Ring), now in its 3rd edition.

Joachim Englisch studied law at the universities of Saarbrücken, Salamanca and Köln. After completing his PhD and habilitation theses at Köln University, he was appointed to a chair for tax law and public law at the University of Augsburg. Since 2010 Dr Englisch has held a chair for tax law and public law at Münster University. He also serves as a visiting professor at the European Tax College of Tilburg University and at the Institute for Tax Law of Köln University. Dr Englisch has published and lectured extensively on VAT issues and is serving as acting vice-president of the German VAT Forum.

Daniel Gutmann is professor of tax law at the Sorbonne Law School (University Paris-1), where he is director of a Master in Business and Tax Law programme and of a research centre in taxation (Sorbonne-Fiscalité). He also acts as partner for CMS Bureau Francis Lefebvre. He is a member of the Scientific Committee of the French branch of the International Fiscal Association (IFA). He is the author of a book on business tax law (Droit fiscal des affaires, Lextenso, 4th ed., 2013) which was awarded the Legal Book Special Prize by the French Constitutional Court and the 'Club des juristes'.

Charles-Albert Helleputte is a visiting lecturer of tax law at the Catholic University of Louvain (Belgium) and counsel at Mayer Brown. He is active in international taxation, with a focus on policy work in the field of direct and indirect taxes. He is a member of the American Chamber of Commerce to the EU Tax taskforce and chairs the VAT sub-group at the same organization.

Walter Hellerstein is the Francis Shackelford Professor of Taxation and Distinguished Research Professor at the University of Georgia Law School. He is co-author (with Jerome R. Hellerstein) of *State Taxation*, vols. I & II (3rd ed., 2013 rev., updated tri-annually); *State and Local Taxation* (9th ed., 2009); *Streamlined Sales and Use Tax* (2008/2009); and *Electronic Commerce and Multijurisdictional Taxation* (2001), as well as more than 100 journal articles. Hellerstein has practised extensively in the state tax field and has been involved in numerous state tax cases before the US Supreme Court (including successful arguments in *Hunt-Wesson, Inc. v. Franchise Tax Bd.* (2000) and *Allied-Signal, Inc. v. Director, Div. of Taxation* (1992)). He serves as an academic advisor to the OECD's Working Party No. 9 on Consumption Taxes. In 2008 Hellerstein was awarded the National Tax Association's Daniel M. Holland Medal for outstanding lifetime contributions to the study and practice of public finance.

Christiana HJI Panayi is a senior lecturer in tax law at Queen Mary, University of London. She is also a research fellow at the Institute for Fiscal Studies. Christiana studied at Oxford University for a BA in Jurisprudence and for the BCL. She also has a PhD from the London School of Economics. Christiana is a solicitor in England and Wales and an advocate of the Cyprus Supreme Court. Before joining Queen Mary, she worked for Allen & Overy. She is also a member of the Law Society and the Cyprus Bar Association. Christiana has published extensively in the area of EU and International Tax Law. She speaks regularly at tax conferences and teaches abroad.

Christian Kaeser is the Global Head of Taxes at Siemens AG. He is responsible for the worldwide tax community of the Siemens Group. He started his professional career at a German-based tax advisory firm after several years as assistant professor at the University of Mainz. He frequently takes an active role in local and international tax conferences. He is member of the supervisory board of World Tax Services AG.

Mitchell A. Kane is Professor of Law at New York University. He previously held a permanent appointment at the University of Virginia School of Law and visiting appointments at Columbia Law School, Harvard Law School, and the University of Pennsylvania School of Law. He formerly practised international tax law as an associate with the law firm of Covington & Burling.

Theo Keijzer is chairman of the Taxation Commission of the International Chamber of Commerce in Paris. He is also a member of the Netherlands Government Commission and of the BIAC Tax Committee in Paris. He was vice chair of the EU Joint Transfer Pricing Forum. Before retiring in mid-2010 he was Vice President Tax Policy at Shell International B.V. in The Hague. He has recently founded Dorean Global Tax Policy B.V., a company providing tax policy advice to governments, international organizations and taxpayers operating internationally. He is a regular contributor to the international tax policy debate on a variety of issues.

Eric C.C.M. Kemmeren is a professor of international tax law and international taxation at the Fiscal Institute Tilburg of Tilburg University, the Netherlands. He is also a member of the board of the European Tax College, deputy justice of the Arnhem Court of Appeals (Tax Division), and counsel to Ernst & Young Belastingadviseurs LLP in Rotterdam, the Netherlands.

Richard Lyal is a member of the Legal Service of the European Commission, where he has for several years been responsible for tax issues. He has been agent for the Commission in more than 500 cases before the EU courts, the EFTA Court and the European Court of Human Rights, mainly in the fields of competition, State aid and taxation (both direct and indirect). He is the co-author (with Paul Farmer) of *EC Tax Law* (OUP 1994, new edition in preparation).

Guglielmo Maisto is a professor of international tax Law at the Catholic University of Piacenza and founded Maisto e Associati in 1991. He has acted as a consultant to the Ministry for European Community Affairs, as a member of the EU Joint Transfer Pricing Forum and as the Chairman of the delegated Board of Trustees of the International Bureau of Fiscal Documentation (IBFD) in Amsterdam. He represents the Italian Association of Industrics at thc OECD Busincss Industry Advisory Committee in Paris. He is a member of several law societies and of the editorial board of various Italian and foreign tax legal journals. He is a member of the Permanent Scientific Committee of the International Fiscal Association and has acted as general and national reporter at several of its annual congresses.

Pasquale Pistone holds the Ad Personam Jean Monnet Chair on European tax law and policy at the WU Vienna University of Economics and Business (Austria); Associate Professor of Tax Law at the University of Salerno (Italy). He is a member of the Junge Kurie of the Austrian Academy of Sciences; member of the Editorial Board of *Intertax*, the *World Tax Journal*, *Diritto e Pratica Tributaria Internazionale* and of other distinguished international tax journals. He is author and editor of numerous publications on European and international tax law published in various languages around the world.

Roman Seer is a professor at the Ruhr University of Bochum (RUB) since 1996 and the holder of the chair 'Tax Law'. From 2006 to 2011 he served as the chairman of the German Association of Tax Lawyers (Deutsche Steuerjuristische Gesellschaft e.V.). He is the director of the Institute of Tax Law and Tax Procedure Law of the RUB and the Tax Law Section of the German Academic Institute of Tax Consultants (Deutsches Wissenschaftliches Institut der Steuerberater e.V. – DWS). Since 2012 he has been the Chairman of Tax Conferences of Berlin (Berliner Steuergespräche e.V.). He has published many monographs and articles on different topics of national, European and international tax law and is also the editor of several leading commentaries, tax books and journals.

Daniël S. Smit first studied classical piano at the Royal Conservatory of The Hague. After that, he attended Erasmus University Rotterdam, where he studied Netherlands Law and Netherlands Tax Law and graduated cum laude. He currently teaches European and international tax law and is employed as a faculty staff member at the Fiscal Institute of the University of Tilburg; he also works as a tax advisor at Ernst & Young Belastingadviseurs LLP in Rotterdam. Furthermore he completed the post-graduate course in European Fiscal Studies at the Erasmus University Rotterdam in 2006. He is also the author of various national and international publications in the field of European tax law. Daniel Smit is a regular guest speaker at national and international seminars, courses and lectures.

Christoph Spengel is a professor of international taxation at the University of Mannheim. He is member of the Scientific Council of the Federal Ministry of Finance in Germany, Research Associate at the Centre for European Economic Research (ZEW), International Research Fellow at Oxford University, Saïd Business School, and Academic Director of Mannheim Master of Accounting and Taxation at Mannheim Business School.

Jan van de Streek is assistant professor at the Amsterdam Centre for Tax Law (University of Amsterdam) and is employed by Ernst & Young as a member of both the Tax Knowledge Centre in Amsterdam and the EU Tax Law Group.

Edoardo Traversa is a professor of tax law at the Catholic University of Louvain (Belgium) and of Counsel at Liedekerke Wolters Waelbroeck Kirkpatrick (Brussels, Belgium). He holds a joint PhD from the University of Bologna (Italy) and the Catholic University of Louvain (Belgium), and was a visiting researcher at the Institute of Austrian and International Tax Law of the Vienna University of Economics and Business in 2007. His areas of interest cover International and European tax law, including VAT, as well as comparative and constitutional tax law.

Dennis Weber is a professor of European corporate tax law. Furthermore, he is director of the Amsterdam Centre for Tax Law (ACTL) (University of Amsterdam), head of the Loyens & Loeff European direct tax law team and deputy judge in the regional court of appeals of 's-Hertogenbosch.

Preface

The European Commission is considering a fundamental change to the tax system for companies with taxable operations in the European Union. The new system is called the Common Consolidated Corporate Tax Base (CCCTB). Companies that are eligible for and opt in to the CCCTB would be taxed on their consolidated taxable profits across the participating Member States. Those profits would be allocated between the participating Member States based on a formula apportionment and taxed in each of the states at the corporate tax rate applicable in that state. This would replace the existing system where each Member State, based on its own rules, taxes the profits of companies with a taxable nexus in that country.

Given that a significant European investment comes from third countries, the CCCTB regulations and their relationship to those third countries require more analysis and careful thought. So far, not much thought has been given to how the CCCTB affects companies based outside Europe. Accordingly, the main purpose of this book was to fill this gap and to take the first steps toward research in that field. In a total of nine chapters, issues such as the taxation of EU and EU non-resident companies are dealt with. Great attention is also given to the issues of withholding taxation and the deductibility of expenses. Questions regarding the transfer of assets to third countries or the treatment of transparent entities are also of high importance.

This project was carried out by an international team based at the Institute for Austrian and International Tax Law of the Vienna University of Economics and Business (WU), composed of the editors, and several researchers, in particular Markus Seiler and Daniel Fuentes Hernández, whom the editors warmly thank for their enthusiasm, initiative and support. The editors would also like to thank the authors and commentators of every chapter. They have patiently revised their chapters in order to enhance the quality of this book. All chapters have been linguistically edited by Margaret Nettinga. Finally, special thanks to Renée Pestuka, who brought the whole team together and enthusiastically supported this project.

This book was supported with funds from the Oesterreichische Nationalbank (Anniversary Fund, project number: 14676).

Vienna, November 2012

1. Taxation of EU resident companies under the current CCCTB framework: Descriptive and critical approach to selected 'extraterritorial' aspects

Edoardo Traversa and Charles-Albert Helleputte

1.1 WHAT THIS CHAPTER IS AND IS NOT ABOUT

The Common Consolidated Corporate Tax Base (the 'CCCTB') is probably the most controversial and often-discussed topic in European direct tax circles in the last decade. Intensively prepared at EU Commission level, firmly opposed by some Member States whilst more or less mildly endorsed by others, commented on by academics and lobbied by business organizations, much has already been said regarding which characteristics such a system should have and about its alleged benefits. The proposal for a Council Directive on a Common Consolidated Corporate Tax Base issued by the EU Commission in March 2011[1] (the 'CCCTB Proposal') is discussed at Council level and it is not a secret to disclose that political agreement is far from being reached. However, recent Eurozone crises and the dissemination of the idea of European economic government suggested by the Sarkozy-Merkel couple have reinforced the political commitment for such a system to be adopted rapidly, even at a non-EU wide level, whether in the form of enhanced

---

[1] Proposal for a Council Directive on a Common Consolidated Corporate Tax Base (CCCTB) COM(2011) 121/4.

cooperation or even using bilateral or multilateral mechanisms outside the European Union framework.[2]

The CCCTB is far-reaching and complex. The purpose of this chapter is to provide both a descriptive and, more importantly, critical approach to selected aspects of the CCCTB Proposal. Whilst we will recall, very briefly, the background and main characteristics of CCCTB, this chapter only addresses the extraterritoriality aspects of CCCTB, i.e., the treatment (and possible issues) of income from non-EU sources earned by resident taxpayers.[3] We only focus on some aspects of the three categories of exempt income, namely, profit distributions, proceeds from the disposal of shares and income of third-country permanent establishments, as well as interest and royalties, which seem to bring together most of the questions from a third-country perspective. We do not comment on the treatment of EU-source revenues nor on outbound payments or revenues (such as withholding taxes) made or earned by resident taxpayers to third countries.[4] Further, discussions of anti-abuse provisions are kept to a minimum.

---

[2] One could think of the Sarkozy-Merkel letter dated 17 August 2011 on the alignment of the French and German tax systems ('For the celebration of the 50th anniversary of the Elysée Treaty, we have asked our Finance and Economic ministers to prepare joint proposals with a view to an enhanced convergence and competitiveness of our economies'. [...] 'We have specifically asked them to prepare a proposal to create a common corporate tax between, our two countries, including harmonised tax base and rates, which would be implemented as of 2013'), joined by other EU leaders, such as the Belgian Finance Minister in an interview dated 7 September 2011 in *Le Soir*, a Belgian newspaper, who proposed that the Benelux join the race (Pierre-Henri, 'Reynders pour un impôt européen des sociétés' (see http://archives.lesoir.be/reynders-pour-un-impot-europeen-des-societes_t-20110907-01KHNE.html, accessed 18 September 2012). The matter is further developed with the publication of a joint Franco-German Green Paper on convergence in business taxation in February 2012. The Paper was presented on 21 February at the 3148th meeting of the Council of the European Union (Economic and Financial Affairs), see OJ/CONS 9, ECOFIN 158. For a study on the need for fiscal integration with the EU area, please see Taxation Paper No. 28/2011, Taxation reforms in EU Member States, Tax Policy Challenges for Economic Growth and Fiscal Sustainability, European Commission, amongst other papers, pp. 66 et seq.

[3] As defined in Art. 4(1) of the CCCTB Proposal.

[4] This is an equally important and, probably, less commented aspect of the CCCTB Proposal. For some views of the potential issues raised by such flows, please see C.H. HJI Panayi, 'The Common Consolidated Corporate Tax Base and the UK Tax System, TLRC Discussion Paper No. 9, The Institute of Fiscal Studies' (2011) 65 et seq.

Even for these limited and selected topics, we do not pretend that our chapter is exhaustive but merely point out some issues that may be considered to be of importance in third-country relations. We hope that some of the more controversial statements will be an aid in fostering debate and in participating in a successful implementation of the CCCTB Proposal.

1.2 THE CCCTB PROPOSAL IN A NUTSHELL

The CCCTB Proposal is the current answer to what the EU Commission considered in 1967 to be a key area in the harmonization of direct taxes, namely the need for a uniform definition of taxable corporate profits. The current content of the CCCTB Proposal is, however, likely to be different from what was viewed in the late 1960s as an ambitious and far-reaching project. For the last 10 years, the CCCTB project has been considered more an important aspect of the proper functioning of the internal market,[5] aiming at reducing distortions amongst Member States and providing a way of attracting foreign investments by reducing tax uncertainty.[6]

1.2.1 From the Neumark Report to the EU Commission Proposal

One of the three lines of action proposed by Neumark in his report, back in 1962, was the harmonization of corporate tax bases and rates.[7] This was followed, in 1967, by the Commission confirming, in its tax harmonization programme, the need for a uniform definition of taxable

---

[5] The work towards the introduction of CCCTB is one of the key recommendations in the area of coordination of tax policies made by Mario Monti in his report (M. Monti, 'A New Strategy for the Single Market at the Service of Europe's Economy and Society, Report to the President of the European Commission' (2010) 81–83).

[6] K Andersson, 'A Common Consolidated Tax Base in Europe' (2005) Svensk Skattetidning 5, 12 et seq. For a descriptive work of the distortion applicable to group taxation within the EU, see, for example, W Schön, 'Group Taxation and the CCCTB' (2007) 48 *Tax Notes International* 11, 1060–1080.

[7] F. Neumark (chair), The EEC Reports on Tax Harmonisation: the Reports of the Fiscal and Financial Committee and the reports of sub-groups A, B and C, Amsterdam, IBFD, 1963. For more details on other lines of action proposed under the Neumark report, please see M. Vascega and S. van Thiel, 'The CCCTB Proposal: The Next Steps towards Corporate Tax Harmonization in the European Union?' (2011) 51 *European Taxation* 9/10, 374 et seq.

corporate profits and a certain approximation of corporate tax rates.[8] In 1975 the Commission proposed to introduce a (partial) imputation credit system and to harmonize tax rates. At the time, the proposed tax rates ranged between 45 per cent and 55 per cent for corporate income tax and, interestingly, with a 25 per cent dividend withholding tax rate.[9] Progress was slow in part because the European Parliament, which wanted to harmonize the corporate tax base as well, refused to provide an opinion, adding another element of difficulty to the discussions.[10] In 1990 the Commission withdrew its 15-year-old proposal in an attempt to reshape its tax policy. Indeed, instead of a comprehensive approach to corporate taxation at the EU level, a decision was taken to focus on much more targeted measures aimed at addressing obstacles to the internal market concerning double taxation, mergers[11] and cross-border loss relief.[12]

The 1992 Ruding Committee Report,[13] providing for corporate tax rates of between 30 per cent and 40 per cent and common rules for a minimum tax base, did not receive much support in the Council and the

---

[8] Tax harmonization programme – Commission Memorandum to the Council of 8 February 1967, supplement to Bulletin 8 (1967) of the European Economic Community.

[9] European Commission, Proposal for a directive on the harmonisation of corporate income tax systems and arrangements for withholding taxes on dividends, OJ C 252.

[10] See Report from the Commission to the Council on the scope for convergence of tax systems in the Community [1980] COM(80) 139 final. See also, Commission communication to Parliament and the Council, Guidelines on company taxation [1990] SEC(90) 601 final.

[11] Council Directive 90/434/EEC on the common system of taxation applicable to mergers, divisions, transfers of assets and exchanges of shares concerning companies of different Member States [1990] OJ L-225/1.

[12] Proposal for a Directive of the Council on the Harmonization of the Laws of the Member States Relating to Tax Arrangements for the Carry-Over of Losses of Undertakings [1984] COM(1984) 404 final, OJ C-253/5, withdrawn in 1996. Proposal for a Council Directive Concerning Arrangements for the Taking into Account by Enterprises of the Losses of their Permanent Establishment and Subsidiaries Situated in Other Member States [1990] COM(1990) 595 final, OJ C-153/30, withdrawn in 2001.

[13] Conclusions and recommendations of the Committee of Independent Experts on Company Taxation (Luxembourg: Office for Official Publications of the European Communities 1992) ('Ruding Report').

Commission did not raise the need for a more general approach again until 1996.[14]

In December 1998 the Council invited the Commission to produce a study on the effects of tax base differentials on the effective tax burdens of the Member States. Since then, however, it has been relatively clear that for any progress to be made in the area, the harmonization of tax rates should be put aside. With that in mind, the Commission released a study in 2001, paving the way for preparatory work on a more comprehensive approach of a common consolidated corporate tax base (CCCTB) for larger companies and the origin principle of taxation for smaller companies (Home State Taxation).[15]

After 10 years of preparatory work and discussions both in the Commission working party and in the Council, and three years later than in its initially anticipated agenda,[16] the Commission finally adopted the CCCTB Proposal on 16 March 2011.

1.2.2 Main Characteristics of the CCCTB under the CCCTB Proposal

The CCCTB Proposal sets out a single set of rules to determine the EU-wide tax base for companies that opt into the system ('common tax base') and, with respect to corporate groups, to determine the amount of taxable profits of the group as a whole, i.e., after offsetting profits and losses against each other ('consolidated tax base').

Taxable profits would then be allocated amongst Member States in which the group is active on the basis of a fixed apportionment formula and taxed at national tax rates.

---

[14] Discussion paper by the European Commission for the Informal meeting of ECOFIN Ministers 'Taxation in the European Union' [1996] SEC(96) 487 final.

[15] See Commission communication, Towards an Internal Market without tax obstacles: a strategy for providing companies with a consolidated corporate tax base for their EU-wide activities, COM(2001) 582 final, as well as Commission communication, Tax Policy in the European Union – Priorities for the years ahead, COM(2001) 260 final.

[16] See keynote speech of EU Commissioner L. Kovàcs at the 62nd Congress of the International Fiscal Association, 31 August 2008, reported in Tax Analysts (2008 WTD 171-13). Also see L. Sheppard, 'EU Tax Commissioner Puts CCCTB Proposal on Hold', reported in Tax Analysts, 5 September 2008 (2008 WTD 173-1).

The main characteristics of the proposal can be further summarized as follows:[17]

(i) Optional participation: the proposal allows resident companies (i.e., in the current shape of the CCCTB Proposal, EU-resident companies) or companies active in the European Union (EU permanent establishments (PEs) of third-country-resident companies) to opt into the CCCTB system for a minimum period of five years[18] or remain subject to national corporate tax systems. Essentially, any incorporated company (not necessarily a group of companies) that is subject to corporate tax in a Member State may opt into the system.[19]

(ii) A common tax base: any company (or group of companies) that opts into the CCCTB regime must calculate its tax base in accordance with a single set of EU rules that are likely to coexist with the 27 national systems. Interestingly, the EU rules override the traditional OECD 'separate accounting' system under which profits are calculated separately for each group unit (branch or subsidiary) according to the rules of the jurisdiction in which the unit is established (destination principle). The CCCTB proposal shares general principles with the tax systems of the Member States but does not follow the rules of any specific Member State.[20]

---

[17] M. Vascega and S. van Thiel, 'The CCCTB Proposal: The Next Steps towards Corporate Tax Harmonization in the European Union?' (2011) European Taxation, 374 et seq. Amongst the criteria that are considered by businesses to be decisive for the success of CCCTB the optional character and the consolidation seems to perform best (see, for example, AmCham EU, 'AmCham EU Position Paper on Commission Working Papers on CCCTB' (2008), http://www.amchameu.eu/?tabid=114, accessed 18 September 2012.

[18] Art. 105 of the CCCTB Proposal.

[19] Eligibility is defined in Chapter I of the CCCTB Proposal (Arts. 1–3) and Chapter III (Arts 6–8) provides the rules for opting into the CCCTB system. The detailed rules on the treatment of certain assets and liabilities where a company (or a group of companies) transitions into or out of the CCCTB are laid down in Chapter VIII of the CCCTB Proposal (Arts 44–53), which includes specific entry and exit rules for characterization of fixed assets for depreciation purposes, long-term contracts, provisions and deductions, pre-entry losses and losses incurred under the rules of the CCCTB. Chapter X (Arts 61–69) builds on Chapter VIII and details the rules on the tax treatment of underlying (unrealized) gains and trading losses when transitioning either into or out of the CCCTB.

[20] The general rules for calculation of the tax base, including exempt revenue, deductible and non-deductible items, charitable bodies and expenditure incurred for the benefit of shareholders, are provided in Chapter IV of the

(iii) A consolidated tax base: the CCCTB would provide for the EU-wide consolidation of all profits and losses of a group that (through its main company) opts into the system, so as to arrive at a single net profit or loss for all group activities within the European Union. According to the 'all-in' principle,[21] a company can only opt into the CCCTB regime together with all of its PEs and subsidiaries that are resident in Member States, including the PEs of qualifying subsidiaries located in Member States.[22]

(iv) Apportionment: once the consolidated tax base is determined according to the common rules, it would be shared (apportioned) between all Member States in which the company and its qualifying subsidiaries and PEs are active, and taxed in accordance with the respective national tax rates. The tax base would be apportioned on the basis of a single and fixed apportionment formula[23] that relies on three, equally weighted, factors:[24]

   (a) Assets: all fixed tangible assets, including buildings, airplanes and machinery would be covered. The costs incurred for R&D, marketing and advertising in the six years prior to a company entering into the CCCTB are also to be included as a proxy for intangible assets for five years;

   (b) Labour: two factors would be taken into account under the heading of labour: 50 per cent of the payroll costs and 50 per cent of the number of employees;

---

proposal (Arts. 9–16 of the CCCTB Proposal), while Chapter V (Arts 17–31) focuses on the more-detailed elements of calculating the tax base, including accrual of revenues, deductible expenses incurred, costs related to non-depreciable assets, stocks and works-in-progress, valuation, trading book, long-term contracts, provisions, pensions, bad debt reductions, hedging, insurance undertakings and transfers of assets to a third country. Depreciation of fixed assets is provided for in Chapter VI (Arts 32–42), while Chapter VII (Art. 43) deals with losses and provides for an unlimited loss carry-forward.

[21] Art. 55 of the CCCTB Proposal.

[22] Chapter IX (Arts 54–60) of the CCCTB Proposal provides for a two-part test for consolidation, which is based on control (more than 50 per cent of voting rights) and ownership or entitlement to profits (more than 75 per cent of capital or profit). It also deals with insolvency of a CCCTB group member, elimination of intra-group transactions (transfer pricing) and the absence of withholding taxes and source taxation within the group.

[23] Chapter XVI (Arts 86–103) of the CCCTB Proposal lays down detailed rules on the formula and also provides specific formulas for the treatment of financial institutions, insurance undertakings, oil and gas, as well as shipping, inland waterways transport and air transport.

[24] Art. 86 of the CCCTB Proposal.

(c) Sales: sales would be calculated on the basis of where the goods are dispatched to/destined for. For services, this would be where the service is physically carried out.[25]

(v) One-stop shop: the proposal provides that, essentially, all the administrative procedures on behalf of the CCCTB group should be performed by the principal member[26] of the group with its own tax authority. This one-stop shop would cover the notice to opt for the regime,[27] the filing of the tax return and the assessment by the tax authority,[28] audits[29] and appeals.[30]

Within the European Union, the uniform tax base for a group supersedes many of the current frictions or weak points of international group taxation and is likely to reduce compliance costs that are triggered by differences in content between the national profit determination systems.[31] Amongst the benefits identified, the following are worth pointing out:

---

[25] See Art. 96 of the CCCTB Proposal. It is interesting to note that proxies used are of a different nature than proxies used in other tax area; one can think in particular to those used for indirect taxation in the VAT Directive (Council Directive 2006/112/EC). Further, the specific proxy used for sales to third countries is by far the most problematic issue in terms of distortion of revenues in a CCCTB or non-CCCTB situation. Indeed, Art. 96 (4) of the CCCTB Proposal states that 'if there is no group member in the Member State where goods are delivered or services are carried out, or if goods are delivered or services are carried out in a third country, the sales shall be included in the sales factor of all group members in proportion to their labour and asset factors'. This means that a Member State having in place tax policies or any other instruments favouring sales to third countries may see a significant drop in the tax revenues it is authorized to collect from a CCCTB taxpayer resident of its country compared to a non-CCCTB situation.

[26] As defined under Art. 4 (6) of the CCCTB Proposal.

[27] Arts 104 and 107 of the CCCTB Proposal.

[28] Arts 109, 112 and 114 of the CCCTB Proposal.

[29] Art. 122 of the CCCTB Proposal.

[30] Arts 124–126 of the CCCTB Proposal.

[31] Commission communication, Towards an Internal Market without tax obstacles: a strategy for providing companies with a consolidated corporate tax base for their EU-wide activities, COM(2001) 582 final. See also J. Mintz, 'Company Taxation and the Internal Market – European Company Tax reform: Prospects for the future' (2011) International Tax and Public Finance.

(i) Double taxation of the subsidiary's profits with the parent company is likely to be avoided because of a suspension of the limitations between the companies involved.[32]
(ii) Losses can – by all means in the case of a consolidation within the group – be consolidated throughout the European Union.[33]
(iii) The problem of the adequacy examination of contractual relationships is resolved, because obligations within the group can no longer influence the profit in fully consolidated tax balance sheets.
(iv) The restructuring within the group or shifting of assets can no longer provoke any profit realization.
(v) The choice of financing (equity capital or debt capital) between group companies has no fundamental influence on the attribution of revenue between the Member States (if one avoids that the financing capital is one of the relevant allocation factors). This means that special rules about controlled foreign companies, within the CCCTB perimeter, could become superfluous.[34]

1.3 KEY CCCTB CONCEPTS OF RELEVANCE FOR EXTRATERRITORIALITY SITUATIONS

Amongst the variety of defined terms in the CCCTB Proposal, it is essential, for the purpose of this chapter, to briefly describe two key concepts that are relevant for extraterritoriality situations,[35] namely the notion of resident taxpayer[36] and the notion of tax base.[37]

---

[32] See Kahle, 'Harmonisierung der Konzernbesteuerung in der EU', *Die Wirtschaftsprüfung 2006* (2006) 1408.

[33] M. Gérard and J. Weiner, 'Cross-border Loss-Offset and Formulary Apportionment: How do they affect multijurisdictional firm investment spending and inter-jurisdictional tax competition?' (2003) CESifo, Working Paper No.1004, www.cesifo-group.de/DocDL/cesifo1_wp1004.pdf, accessed 18 September 2012.

[34] W. Schön, 'Group Taxation and the CCCTB' (2007) 48 *Tax Notes International* 11, 1060–1080.

[35] For more details on the concepts, please refer to other chapters in this book, such as Chapter 3 by G. Maisto.

[36] Arts 4 and 6 of the CCCTB Proposal.

[37] Arts 10 et seq of the CCCTB Proposal.

1.3.1 The Notion of 'Residence' under the CCCTB Proposal

The CCCTB Proposal applies, under certain conditions, to (EU) resident and non-resident companies in respect of a permanent establishment maintained by them in a Member State, provided they have opted to be treated under the CCCTB.

Eligible companies are those which are listed in Annex I to the CCCTB Proposal and which are subject to corporate income taxes, or similar subsequently introduced taxes, listed in Annex II. The option for CCCTB is open both to residents in a Member State and to permanent establishments maintained by non-residents in a Member State.[38] The CCCTB defines what a resident is supposed to be and, more importantly, provides for some forms of tiebreaker rule.

For the purpose of the CCCTB, a company is considered resident if it 'has its registered office, place of incorporation or place of effective management in a Member State and is not, under the terms of an agreement concluded by that Member State with a third country, regarded as tax resident in that third country'.[39] This definition has two merits: (i) it captures both place of incorporation and place of effective management and we know that this is important given the difference in approaches that may exist amongst Member States and (ii) this provision is the first in the CCCTB Proposal that refers to a third-country situation. Further, it is interesting to note that compared to existing EU corporate tax directives, no reference is made to the fact that in order to be eligible, those companies should be subject to corporate income tax in their country of residence 'without the possibility of an option or of being exempt'.[40] The latter seems logical given the purpose of the CCCTB: to adopt a new system of corporate income taxation and not merely coordinate the tax treatment, under different corporate tax systems, of particular cross-border transactions.

The definition as it stands means, *de facto*, that some EU-resident companies or bodies will not be affected by the CCCTB, either because they do not meet the requirements imposed or because they have not opted for being treated under the CCCTB.

---

[38] Art. 6 (1) and (2) of the CCCTB Proposal.

[39] Art. 6 (3) of the CCCTB Proposal.

[40] See, for example, Art. 2 (c) of the Council Directive on the common system of taxation applicable in the case of parent companies and subsidiaries of different Member States (90/435/EEC), OJ L-225/6, as amended from time to time.

Finally, it is worth remembering that, at this stage, a situation in which the CCCTB will be implemented in all Member States is unlikely to happen. In the event that CCCTB is to move forward based on an alternative institutional basis, such as enhanced cooperation, it would require further amendment to the definition, distinguishing between CCCTB EU-resident taxpayers, non-CCCTB EU-resident taxpayers and non-EU-resident taxpayers. Such a situation will, more importantly, trigger a range of questions on treatment to be reserved to intra-EU dealings not falling with the CCCTB. Third-country mechanisms may not apply *mutatis mutandis*, as any possible solution will have to cope with other primary and secondary EU law provisions.

1.3.2 The Taxable Base Question: Which Revenues are to be Included?

The CCCTB Proposal broadly defines revenues. This broad definition reflects the intention to avoid loopholes in the CCCTB Proposal (i.e., non-taxable items of income), while at the same time keeping a general and synthetic concept. This intention is clearly expressed in the 10th recital of the CCCTB Proposal, where it is stated that 'all revenues should be taxable unless expressly exempted'.

This is further stated in the CCCTB Proposal confirming that a company resident in a Member State which opts for the system must be subject to corporate tax under that system on all income derived from any source, whether inside or outside its Member State of residence.[41] Whilst 'income' is used in a number of provisions, the definition of the tax base refers to 'revenues'. Indeed, the tax base is to be calculated as revenues less exempt revenues, deductible expenses and other deductible items.[42]

'Revenues' are defined as:

> proceeds of sales and of any other transactions, net of value added tax and other taxes and duties collected on behalf of government agencies, whether of a monetary or non-monetary nature, including proceeds from disposal of assets and rights, interest, dividends and other profits distributions, proceeds of liquidation, royalties, subsidies and grants, gifts received, compensation and ex-gratia payments. Revenues shall also include non-monetary gifts made by a taxpayer. Revenues shall not include equity raised by the taxpayer or debt repaid to it.[43]

---

[41] Art. 6 (6) of the CCCTB Proposal.
[42] Art. 10 of the CCCTB Proposal.
[43] Art. 4(8) of the CCCTB Proposal.

At first sight, the mixed used of 'income' and 'revenues' does not seem to have a significant legal relevance. The Commission's earlier working chapter distinguished 'revenue' (arising in the ordinary course of the business activity) and 'gain' (defined as 'increases in economic benefits arising from assets which have been capitalised');[44] there is no sign of this distinction in the CCCTB Proposal. Both notions fall within the above-mentioned definition of 'revenues'. This seems in line with the position adopted in accounting, where it is generally considered that gains as such are no different in nature from revenue.[45]

This definition may come as a surprise given the constitutional traditions of some Member States where tax rules tend to be interpreted rather restrictively and where only the items of income expressly defined in the legislation may be taxed. However, even in those countries, tax rules tend to take as a starting point the profits as defined under accountancy law, an area where tax law principles do not generally apply. In that regard, CCCTB follows a general principle that is also to be found in accounting, i.e., the fact that income is defined as the difference in net equity.[46] The existence of profits therefore implies that net equity is maintained and income only arises if inflows of assets exceed the amount necessary to maintain capital at the beginning of the period.[47]

Further, Article 11 defines what elements are to be exempt from corporate tax. We only point out some of them that are relevant for our purpose, i.e., received profit distributions, proceeds from a disposal of shares and income from a permanent establishment in a third country.[48]

---

[44] European Commission, Working Document 'Taxable income' CCCTB\WP\017, 7 September 2005, 4.

[45] See IAS Framework Para 74, quoted in European Commission, Working Document 'Taxable income' CCCTB\WP\017, 7 September 2005, 5.

[46] And, to that extent, is, *in fine*, in line with international accounting standards, although no reference or incorporation of such a principle is proposed under the CCCTB Proposal. See, J. Freedman and G. Macdonald, 'The Tax Base for CCCTB: The Role of Principles' in M. Lang, P. Pistone, J. Schuch and C. Staringer (eds), *Common Consolidated Corporate Tax Base* (Linde 2008) 219–270.

[47] C. Spengel and C. Malke, 'Comprehensive Tax Base or Residual Reference to GAAP or Domestic Law' in M. Lang, P. Pistone, J. Schuch and C. Staringer (eds), *Common Consolidated Corporate Tax Base* (Linde 2008) 71.

[48] Art. 11 (c), (d) and (e) of the CCCTB Proposal.

1.4 DOES THE CCCTB PROVIDE FOR WORLDWIDE OR TERRITORIAL TAXATION?

From the start questions were raised about whether the CCCTB provisions should be a system promoting worldwide or territorial taxation.[49] This is a rather theoretical discussion, complicated by the different definitions given to such terms.[50] It is admitted that territorial source taxation refers to a system where a taxing country taxes only income from sources in the country but not foreign-source income; whilst under a worldwide taxation regime a taxing country will tax its domestic corporations on worldwide income. Worldwide taxation goes hand-in-hand with relief mechanisms from double taxation in the form of exemption or credit.[51]

The CCCTB Proposal appears to be a compromise between worldwide and territorial taxation.[52] If the principle of worldwide taxation is clearly worded in the proposal, as it was in the Commission's working document,[53] the exclusions from the bases of permanent establishments and some forms of passive income (profit distributions and capital gains on shares) tend to restrict the scope of the proposal to the CCCTB territory.

Moreover, the treatment of expenses and losses incurred as regards a permanent establishment located outside the CCCTB territory by EU-resident companies makes the CCCTB look more like a territorial system, as these would not be deductible. There is also the case of the denial of taking into account the losses in the computation of the income of the foreign companies that will be incorporated in the CCCTB tax

---

49 See, for example, the comments of the UNICE CCCTB Tax Force on European Commission, Working Document 'The Territorial Scope of the CCCTB' CCCTB\WP\026, 17 February 2006.

50 For an illustration, please refer to the definition provided by the Court of Justice in Case C-250/95 *Futura Participations and Singer* [1997] ECR I- 02471, para 22.

51 See, for example, L.L. Bravenec, 'Corporate Income Tax Coordination in the 21st Century' (2000) European Taxation, 450 et seq.

52 For a description of the challenges that were ahead of Member States in compromising on the features of CCCTB, especially in third-country relations, please see, for example, U. Schreiber, 'Consolidation, Allocation and International Aspects' in W. Schön, U. Schreiber and C. Spengel (eds), *A Common Consolidated Corporate Tax Base for Europe – Eine einheitliche Körperschaftsteuerbemessungsgrundlage für Europa* (Springer 2008) 118 et seq.

53 European Commission, Working Document 'CCCTB: Possible Elements of a Technical Outline' CCCTB\WP\057, 26 July 2007.

base.[54] Nevertheless, some EU countries such as Germany, having adopted a worldwide corporate tax system, consider the circumstance that losses of foreign permanent establishment cannot be deducted by the head office if the income is exempted by virtue of a double tax treaty does not alter the worldwide character of the tax system.[55]

In a pure EU context, this situation has not been considered by the Court of Justice of the European Union (hereinafter: Court of Justice) as a violation of the freedom of establishment and is therefore unlikely to cause any difficulties, even if the CCCTB were to be adopted through the enhanced cooperation mechanism. Indeed, as the Court held in the *Lidl Belgium* case:

> Article 43 EC does not preclude a situation in which a company established in a Member State cannot deduct from its tax base losses relating to a permanent establishment belonging to it and situated in another Member State, to the extent that, by virtue of a double taxation convention, the income of that establishment is taxed in the latter Member State where those losses can be taken into account in the taxation of the income of that permanent establishment in future accounting periods.
>
> It is true that such a tax regime involves a restriction on the freedom of establishment, since the tax situation of a company that has its registered office in one Member State and has a permanent establishment in another Member State is less favourable than it would be if the latter were to be established in the first Member State. By reason of that difference in tax treatment, a resident company could be discouraged from carrying on its business through a permanent establishment situated in another Member State.
>
> Nevertheless, such a tax regime can, in principle, be justified in the light of the need to safeguard the allocation of the power to tax between the Member States and the need to prevent the danger that the same losses will be taken into account twice which, taken together, pursue legitimate objectives compatible with the Treaty and thus constitute overriding reasons in the public interest, provided that the regime is proportionate to those objectives.
>
> With respect to the need to safeguard the allocation of the power to tax between the Member States, the Member State in which the registered office

[54] CFC losses may only be carried forward (see Arts. 82 and 83 of the CCCTB Proposal).

[55] On this matter and on the specifics of the German situation, see K. Vogel, *Klaus Vogel on Double Taxation Conventions, A Commentary to the OECD, the UN and US Model Conventions for the Avoidance of Double Taxation on Income and Capital with a Particular Reference to German Treaty Practice* (3rd edn, Kluwer Law 1997) Art. 23, mn. 72 and 73. See also, A. Bal, 'New Case Law Developments in Germany: Finality of Foreign Permanent Establishment Losses' (2012) European Taxation, 46–48.

> of the company to which the permanent establishment belongs is situated would, in the absence of a double taxation convention, have the right to tax the profits generated by such an entity. Consequently, the objective of preserving the allocation of the power to impose taxes between the two Member States concerned, which is reflected in the provisions of the convention, is capable of justifying the tax regime at issue, since it safeguards symmetry between the right to tax profits and the right to deduct losses. In that connection, where a double taxation convention has given the Member State in which the permanent establishment is situated the power to tax the profits of that establishment, to give the principal company the right to elect to have the losses of that permanent establishment taken into account in the Member State in which it has its seat or in another Member State would seriously undermine a balanced allocation of the power to impose taxes between the Member States concerned.
>
> As regards the danger that the same losses will be used twice, it is possible that a company might deduct, in the Member State in which its seat is situated, losses incurred by a permanent establishment belonging to it and situated in another Member State and that, despite such offsetting, the same losses might be taken into account subsequently in the Member State in which the permanent establishment is situated, when that establishment generates profits, thereby preventing the Member State in which the principal company has its seat from taxing that profit.[56]

In the international context there might be a conflict with double taxation conventions (DTC), providing for deduction of foreign losses and recapture mechanisms such as, for example, the double tax convention concluded between Belgium and the United States. Under this treaty, in the case of a prior deduction of losses of a US permanent establishment of a Belgian resident in Belgium, a subsequent recapture mechanism is introduced, allowing Belgium to indirectly tax the profits of the US permanent establishment.[57] This might have a negative impact on investment.

1.5 SELECTED FOREIGN INCOME UNDER THE CCCTB

After having briefly discussed general principles laid down in the CCCTB Proposal such as the absence of consolidation for dealings with associated enterprises that are not within the CCCTB perimeter, the

---

[56] Case C-414/06, *Lidl Belgium & Co. KG*, ECR [2008] I-03601.

[57] See Art. 22(1) of the Belgium-United States DTC dated 27 November 2006.

treatment of deductible expenses as it relates to foreign-source income, the description of the exemption mechanism and switch-over clause as applied to given categories of foreign exempt income and certain other anti-abuse provisions, specific attention is paid to (i) the treatment of two categories of exempt income, namely third-country permanent establishment income and profit distribution from foreign subsidiaries and (ii) the treatment of foreign-source royalties, patents and interest income that follows a completely different path. The tensions with existing international tax policy frameworks, such as the OECD MC and existing EU coordination instruments (such as the Interest and Royalty and the Parent-Subsidiary Directives) are also briefly highlighted.

1.5.1 General Principles Laid Down under the CCCTB

1.5.1.1 Business income from dealings with foreign-based associated enterprises

The CCCTB will not eradicate transfer pricing issues, at least not for EU-based group dealing with non-resident associated enterprises. Indeed, if one may argue that transfer pricing questions might be less relevant in an intra-group context because of the implementation of the CCCTB[58] (as it ignore profits and losses arising from transactions directly carried out between members of the group),[59] non-resident taxpayers will be kept outside of group formation.[60] This basically means that revenues from such dealings will not be consolidated and enter the tax base and, even more importantly, that such dealings will still have to meet the arm's length test. The OECD Transfer Pricing Guidelines and the continuous

---

[58] See, for example, J. Barenfeld, 'A Common Consolidated Corporate Tax Base in the European Union – A Beauty or a Beast in the Quest for Tax Simplicity?' (2007) Bulletin for International Taxation, 258–271. Even if this statement can be supported, it is important to note that requirements imposed by the CCCTB Proposal to properly document such dealings should not be underestimated as they will imply compliance costs even in an intra-group situation (see Art. 59 (3) and (4) of the CCCTB Proposal).

[59] To some extent, within the CCCTB water's edge, the apportionment of the taxable base could be put in parallel with the long-standing discussion on the future of the arm's length standard (see OECD Transfer Pricing Guidelines for Multinational Enterprises and Tax Authorities, (OECD 2010) 1.16 et seq and R.S. Avi-Yonah and I. Benshalom, 'Formulary Apportionment – Myths and Prospects – Promoting Better International Tax Policy by Utilizing the Misunderstood and Under-Theorized Formulary Alternative' (2011) *World Tax Journal*, October 2011, 371 et seq.

[60] See the definition of Art. 55 of the CCCTB Proposal.

work of the EU Joint Transfer Pricing Forum may prove to lead to viable solutions or offer pragmatic approaches.[61] Some of the work of the EU Commission may, however, offer examples of classical interpretation issues of such soft-law mechanisms. Indeed, in one of its working papers, the Commission suggested that the arm's length principle be for loan transactions both on the level of the interest rate charged and, more surprisingly, as a test for the principal amount.[62]

Further, the existence of a double threshold, one for group formation and consolidation[63] and one for the trigger of transfer pricing matters,[64] has materialized in the CCCTB Proposal irrespective of implementation issues and concerns that have been raised in preparatory work.[65] The deviation of the CCCTB definition from the general criteria set forth under Article 9 of the OECD MC as to what qualifies as an associated enterprise transaction may represent an issue when implemented in existing treaty arrangements with third states. Further conflicts or difficulties may occur in an enhanced cooperation situation.

Amongst the variety of questions that this provision raised, the situation of transfer pricing disputes is an important one. Indeed, will transfer pricing disputes currently handled under the arm's length principle of Article 9 OECD MC and the mutual agreement procedure of Article 25 OECD MC continue to be dealt with as a bilateral issue between the specific EU Member State and its third country treaty partner?[66] If so, will this involve only the competent national authorities, i.e., the national authorities of a Member State which by adopting the directive have lost the normative competence to modify the criteria on which corporate taxation is based, or should officials from the EU Commission be allowed to take part in this procedure? Only the EU Commission may indeed approve a reconciliatory interpretation of the

---

61 M. Bourgeois and E. von Frenckell, 'Relation to Taxpayers outside the Group' in M. Lang, P. Pistone, J. Schuch and C. Staringer (eds), *Common Consolidated Corporate Tax Base* (Linde 2008) 203.

62 European Commission, Working Document 'CCCTB: Possible Elements of a Technical Outline' CCCTB\WP\057, 26 July 2007, points 44–45.

63 Art. 54 of the CCCTB Proposal.

64 Arts 78 et seq. of the CCCTB Proposal.

65 M. Bourgeois and E. von Frenckell, 'Relation to Taxpayers outside the Group' in M. Lang, P. Pistone, J. Schuch and C. Staringer (eds), *Common Consolidated Corporate Tax Base* (Linde 2008) 201.

66 M. Bennett in W. Schön, U. Schreiber and C. Spengel (eds), *A Common Consolidated Corporate Tax Base for Europe – Eine einheitliche Körperschaftsteuerbemessungsgrundlage für Europa* (Springer 2008) 140.

directive and the double taxation convention or propose a modification of the directive.

Preventing improper profit shifting outside the application of the water's edge for the CCCTB purposes requires maintaining, and even supplementing, anti-avoidance rules. The CCCTB Proposal contains four mechanisms: (i) the possibility for pricing adjustments in associated enterprises relationship,[67] (ii) a general anti-abuse mechanism aimed at ignoring for the purpose of calculation the tax base artificial transactions carried out for the sole purpose of avoiding taxation,[68] (iii) disallowance of interest deduction paid to an associated enterprise,[69] and (iv) the introduction of a controlled foreign corporation mechanism aiming to capture non-distributed income of a third-country resident.[70]

1.5.1.2 Deductible expenses and rollover reliefs

The Commission's proposal defines deductible expenses as follows:[71]

> Deductible expenses shall include all costs of sales and expenses net of deductible value added tax incurred by the taxpayer with a view to obtaining or securing income, including costs of research and development and costs incurred in raising equity or debt for the purposes of the business.[72]

The expenses incurred abroad are therefore not excluded *a priori* from deductibility. However, a close link to exempt income is made when listing non-deductible expenses as costs incurred by a company for the purpose of deriving income, which is exempt pursuant to Article 11, and

---

[67] Art. 79 of the CCCTB Proposal (although the absence of any arbitration mechanism and lack of international harmonization may increase cases of double taxation).

[68] Art. 80 of the CCCTB Proposal. For a recent comment of this provision, see, for example, M. Lang, 'The General Anti-Abuse Rule of Art. 80 of the Draft Proposal for a Council Directive on a Common Consolidated Corporate Tax Base' (2011) European Taxation, 223–228.

[69] Art. 81 of the CCCTB Proposal.

[70] Art. 82 of the CCCTB Proposal. For a discussion of CFC rules, see, for example, G. Kofler, 'CFC rules, in Common Consolidated Corporate Tax Base' in M. Lang, P. Pistone, J. Schuch and C. Staringer (eds), *Common Consolidated Corporate Tax Base* (Linde 2008) 725 et seq.

[71] Art. 12 of the CCCTB Proposal.

[72] For more comments on the background of such definition, please see, for example, G. Alarcon Garcia, 'Deductible and Non-Deductible Expenses' in M. Lang, P. Pistone, J. Schuch and C. Staringer (eds), *Common Consolidated Corporate Tax Base* (Linde 2008) 349 et seq.

considered to be non-deductible expenses.[73] Such costs have to be fixed at a flat rate of 5 per cent of that income unless the taxpayer is able to demonstrate that it has incurred a lower cost.

With regard to third-country income, this means, for example, that costs related to income derived from a foreign permanent establishment, from a profit distribution or from a disposal of shares of a company located in a third country would not be deductible. Concerning the exemption of permanent establishment income from non-EU sources, the method of computation of the permanent establishment income could have a direct impact on the amount of non-deductible expenses. As we will discuss below, the income to be taken into consideration is the permanent establishment net income, i.e., taking into account all the expenses related to the permanent establishment (or made by the permanent establishment). This raises several questions not addressed in the CCCTB Proposal, such as what the criteria for connecting an expense to the income of a non-EU permanent establishment are, or the methods to be used for attribution of profits to the exempt permanent establishment (and the possible discrepancies between the CCCTB and the third-country tax systems). Concerning the latter problem, one solution could be to apply, by analogy, Article 74 of CCCTB Proposal referring to the computation of permanent establishment income for the purpose of the application of the switch-over clause. Such a provision provides that 'where Article 73 applies to the income of a permanent establishment in a third country, its revenues, expenses and other deductible items shall be determined according to the rules of the system provided for by this Directive'.

Another issue to be considered is the tax treatment of investment outside the EU. In particular, the question could be raised as regards the rollover relief for replacement assets of Article 38 of the CCCTB Proposal, according to which:

> where the proceeds from the disposal of an individually depreciable asset are to be re-invested before the end of the second tax year after the tax year in which the disposal took place in an asset used for the same or a similar purpose, the amount by which those proceeds exceed the value for tax purposes of the asset shall be deducted in the year of disposal.

It is unclear whether such relief could be granted if the asset is used abroad. Nothing seems to prevent it, except perhaps if the asset is connected to exempt income (since in this case, the cost of the asset

---

[73] Art. 14 of the CCCTB Proposal.

could be considered to be non-deductible and therefore the re-investment could be ignored).

In the EU context, the Court of Justice has held that Member States may not limit the benefit of tax incentives to investment, whether by implementing an investment tax premium for assets used in a domestic place of business and excluding vehicles leased to foreign businesses[74] or an investment tax credit denied for capital goods physically used in the territory of another Member State.[75] Although this case law should not affect the tax treatment in the CCCTB system of investment in third countries in general, it could probably apply in the case of enhanced cooperation to other Member States, or to EEA countries.

From a political standpoint, one could also wonder whether it would be desirable to encourage EU businesses to invest, whether within or outside the CCCTB territory. Some Member States, like France, have implemented specific schemes with this objective for their overseas territory (which are nonetheless included in the EU territory),[76] which would no longer be available to an EU company opting for the CCCTB regime. If the EU considers that such measures should be maintained, they should either be included in the Proposal, or Member States should be authorized to continue to grant these aids under forms compatible with the common base. In the first hypothesis, a more precise definition of the CCCTB territorial scope, which could exclude some territories enjoying a specific tax regime within the Member States, as is the case in the area of VAT, may be needed.[77]

1.5.1.3 Exemption method and switch-over clause

The CCCTB Proposal features most of the characteristics of capital and labour import neutrality (CIN), which best serves the internal market and

---

[74] See, for example, Case C-330/07, *Jobra Vermögensverwaltungs-Gesellschaft mbH v Finanzamt Amstetten Melk Scheibbs* [2008] ECR I-09099.

[75] See, for example, Case C-287/10, *Tankreederei I SA against Directeur de l'administration des contributions directes* [2010] ECR I-14233.

[76] The system of overseas investment aid which enables businesses, subject to certain conditions, to deduct an amount equivalent to the sum of their productive investments, less the fraction of the cost price of these investments which is funded by means of a public subsidy if the investments in question are made overseas in operations within certain priority sectors of the economy, particularly in tourism and industry (European Commission, Taxes in Europe (2011); see, Code general des impôts, Art. 199*undecies* B).

[77] On the VAT definition of the territorial scope of the VAT Directive, please see Council Directive 2006/112/ES on the common system of value added tax [2006] OJ L 347/1, Articles 5–8.

the relations with third countries.[78] Political economic considerations mainly determine the magnitude of the tax jurisdiction of a state. It is commonly accepted that taxation should not influence the efficient allocation of production factors of labour and capital or, at least, should do so as little as possible.[79] Applying CIN, it comes as no surprise that the right to tax third-country permanent establishment income and profit distribution income in the CCCTB is left to the source state with the CCCTB providing for an exemption (with progression)[80] and that the CCCTB contains anti-abuse mechanisms, such as the CFC rules.[81]

The CCCTB Proposal contains a switch-over clause, meaning that a credit method will come into play to relieve international double taxation *in lieu* of the exemption in a given circumstance, primarily in cases of erosion of the taxable base.[82] In practice, the switch-over is more a protective measure aiming to combat low or non-taxation of profits originating in a source state than an anti-abuse provision.[83] Indeed, although abuses might be caught by the mechanisms, other situations could occur where the granting of an exemption, combined with low-source taxation, would result in overall (too) reduced taxation. The CCCTB Proposal provides for alternative criteria for the clause to be triggered: (i) the tax on profit, under the general regime in the source state taxation, is lower than 40 per cent of the average statutory corporate tax rates applicable in the Member States *or* (ii) a special regime in that third country allows for a substantially lower levels of taxation than the general regime.[84] The least that can be said is that both provisions raise a

---

[78] See, for example, E. Kemmeren, 'Source of Income in Globalizing Economies' (2006) 60 *Bulletin of International Taxation* 11, 438–441.

[79] See, for example, Ruding Report (FN 13).

[80] Art. 72 CCCTB Proposal. Although this is in line with internationally accepted exemption method, the implementation of such measures for countries applying flat tax will not lead to any material adverse consequences.

[81] E. Kemmeren, 'CCCTB and Exemption Method for PEs and Major Shareholdings' in M. Lang, P. Pistone, J. Schuch and C. Staringer (eds), *Common Consolidated Corporate Tax Base* (Linde 2008) 703.

[82] On the compatibility of switch-over clause with EU laws, see D. Weber and A. Russo, 'The Switch-Over Clause' in M. Lang, P. Pistone, J. Schuch and C. Staringer (eds), *Common Consolidated Corporate Tax Base* (Linde 2008) 767–768.

[83] D. Weber and A. Russo, 'The Switch-Over Clause' in M. Lang, P. Pistone, J. Schuch and C. Staringer (eds), *Common Consolidated Corporate Tax Base* (Linde 2008) 756.

[84] Art. 73 (a) and (b) of the CCCTB Proposal.

significant number of questions, both from a legal and an economic perspective.[85]

As for the computation of an average rate, the reference to such a rate as applicable in (all) Member States is questionable. Although it provides, at least in principle, a simple approach, one may wonder whether the average rate should not be compiled based on the Member States in which the group operates or where the corporate tax base will be apportioned. Further, many, if not all, of European Member States apply a range of rates, e.g., depending on the nature of the income (with passive income being subject to reduced rates or existing reduced rates for SMEs). This might lead to discriminatory computation of this absolute number that is supposed to be the 'average statutory corporate tax rate'.[86]

The question of what constitutes a special regime will inevitably be raised. Should the EU State aid criteria, providing for selectivity to exist for a measure to constitute a State aid, be invoked and used as reference point?[87] Should the case law of the Court of Justice be preferred? Should this be triggered only in abuse situations, as defined by case law?[88] To some extent, this might prove to be a more obvious choice, provided one agrees to apply intra-EU solutions to third-country situations.[89] In the current context, such a matter will need to be assessed on a case-by-case basis, which does not serve legal certainty. Further, practical application of such a clause may cause difficulties in the context of double tax conventions.

---

[85] M. Gerard and E. Traversa, 'Supplementing Consolidation and Apportionment with Anti-Abuse Provisions' in M. Lang, P. Pistone, J. Schuch, C. Staringer, A. Storck, M. Zagler (eds), *Tax treaties: Building Bridges between Law and Economics* (IBFD 2010) 183–210. In addition, many of the triggering events for such a switch-over to apply as well as the categories of income affected remain disputed; see, for example, recent amendments proposed by the European Parliament (2011/0058(CNS)).

[86] D. Weber and A. Russo, 'The Switch-Over Clause' in M. Lang, P. Pistone, J. Schuch and C. Staringer (eds), *Common Consolidated Corporate Tax Base* (Linde 2008) 758.

[87] See, for example, Advocate General Cases C-72/91 and C-73/91, *Solman Neptun* [1993] ECR I-887, point 47.

[88] M. Lang and S. Heidenbauer, 'Wholly Artificial Arrangement' in Luc Hinnekens and Philippe Hinnekens (eds), *A Vision of Taxes within and outside European Borders, Festchrift in honor of Prof. Dr Frans Vanistendael* (Kluwer Law International 2008) 597.

[89] The *Siat* case may provide for some elements in this respect (see Advocate General Case C318/10, *Siat* [2012] n.y.r.).

1.5.2 Specific Attention to Defined Categories of Income: Income from a Third-Country Permanent Establishment

Foreign permanent establishment income is exempt under the CCCTB Proposal. Such an exemption does not come as a surprise but this does not mean that the rules, as provided for in the current CCCTB Proposal, would not have unexpected effects when interacting with some international, including European, tax policies.

1.5.2.1 The CCCTB framework: definition of permanent establishment and computation of permanent establishment income

The CCCTB Proposal incorporates a definition of what should constitute a permanent establishment[90] that is deemed to be based on the OECD framework.[91] Indeed, and with the exception of mere numbering and language items, Article 5 of the CCCTB Proposal is a copy/paste of the existing Article 5 of the 2010 OECD MC language. The definition is deemed to cover two alternate sets of very different realities as it will affect (i) permanent establishments of tax residents situated outside the CCCTB jurisdictions and (ii) permanent establishments of tax non-residents situated on the territory of the CCCTB jurisdictions even though these are different, since early in the process the understanding has been that the same definition should apply to both situations.[92]

Whilst intra-EU permanent establishments and, in particular, the question of whether or not their income should either be exempt or benefit from the consolidation mechanism was widely debated across the years,[93]

---

[90] The argument for the project to incorporate definitions of key terms such as 'permanent establishment' that was made by many authors in the frame of the preparatory work (see, for example, the comments of the UNICE CCCTB Tax Force on European Commission, Working Document 'The Territorial Scope of the CCCTB' CCCTB\WP\026, 17 February 2006) has been taken into account by the EU Commission, although not fully satisfactorily (for example, no definition of 'royalty', no clear definition of 'interest' or 'dividends' and so on.).

[91] European Commission, Working Document 'CCCTB: Possible Elements of a Technical Outline' CCCTB\WP\057, 26 July 2007. Interestingly, reference is made to the fact that detailed definition and guidance will be developed.

[92] European Commission, Working Document, 'CCCTB: An Overview of the main issues that emerged at the second meeting of the subgroup on International Aspects (SG4)' CCCTB\WP\033, 24 May 2006, p. 4.

[93] See, for example, Communication from the Commission to the Council, the European Parliament and the European Economic and Social Committee, Implementing the Community Lisbon Programme: Progress to date and next

the allocation of income to third-country permanent establishments, although not ignored, was not subject to many considerations in CCCTB preparatory work[94] and it is largely absent from the CCCTB Proposal. From the absence of specific rules in the CCCTB Proposal, it follows that the rules and provisions of the Member States apply with regard to profit attributions deriving from dealings as covered by Article 7(2) of the OECD MC.[95]

The CCCTB Proposal, however, contains some provisions, other than the definition in Article 5, that are relevant to income of foreign-based permanent establishments, namely the switch-over clause in Article 73 and Article 78 relating to transactions between associated enterprises.

When the switch-over clause comes into play, Article 74 provides that the revenues, expenses and other deductible items must be determined according to the rules of the system provided for under the CCCTB Proposal. Practical consequences of what is meant by this provision remain unclear at this stage.

In Article 78, the CCCTB Proposal has been greatly inspired by the recent reshaping of Article 7(2) of the OECD MC entailing the separate and independent enterprise fiction. However, to some extent, Article 78 may be seen as having too far-reaching effects, similar to the ones that were described under the OECD MC revised framework.[96]

1.5.2.2 Conflicts with international tax policy

Given its similarity to the OECD MC definition, in essence the definition of permanent establishment under the CCCTB Proposal may display many of the difficulties of its 'model'. Definitional issues are likely to arise in a number of cases; just to name a few:

---

steps towards a Common Consolidated Corporate Tax Base (CCCTB), COM(2006)157/7.

[94] European Commission, Working Document 'CCCTB: Possible Elements of a Technical Outline' CCCTB\WP\057, 26 July 2007, point 15.

[95] See, for example, M. Bennett in W. Schön, U. Schreiber and C. Spengel (eds), *A Common Consolidated Corporate Tax Base for Europe – Eine einheitliche Körperschaftsteuerbemessungsgrundlage für Europa* (Springer 2008) 139. This is the option that was lobbied to the EU Commission by many organizations (See, for example, Policy Statement, An optional Common Consolidated Corporate Tax Base in Europe: implications for businesses worldwide (ICC 2007) 2).

[96] On the impact of the new provisions of Art. 7 (2) of the OECD MC with Art. 9 of the OECD MC, see OECD Commentaries (2010 version) Art. 7, paras 29 *et seq*.

(i) The CCCTB Proposal contains the same catch-all provision as the OECD MC;[97] conflicting or interpretative issues on the significant test may develop in third-country relationships, as they exist in the OECD context.
(ii) Article 5 of the OECD MC is under scrutiny,[98] and although developments are slow in this area, this means that potentially there is a room for deviation between the two sets of rules.
(iii) The CCCTB Proposal does not encompass the reference to the service permanent establishment that the UN Model does and which was introduced in the last version of the OECD Commentaries to the OECD MC.
(iv) The relevance of the reference to permanent establishment in the CCCTB Proposal has even been questioned, with some authors preferring the introduction of a 'substantial entrepreneurial activities' test.[99]

In addition to definitional issues, tax base exemptions are under attack in many countries around the world, especially in Europe, with more cases being scrutinized by the Court of Justice. Although not fully assessed by case law, such as in the *Stahlwerk Ergste Westig*[100] or *Columbus Container Services*[101] cases, it could be argued that the choice, in the CCCTB Proposal, to apply a tax base exemption to third-country income from permanent establishments should meet the case law test.[102]

---

[97] See, Art. 5 (3) (f) of the CCCTB Proposal.

[98] See the OECD Discussion Draft issued by the OECD on the Interpretation and Application of Article 5 (Permanent Establishment) of the OECD Model Convention (2011).

[99] E. Kemmeren, 'CCCTB and Exemption Method for PEs and Major Shareholdings' in M. Lang, P. Pistone, J. Schuch and C. Staringer (eds), *Common Consolidated Corporate Tax Base* (Linde 2008) 687–688.

[100] Case C-415/06, *Stahlwerk Ergste Westing v Finanzamt Düsseldorf-Mettmann* [2007] ECR I-151.

[101] Case C-298/05, *Columbus Container Services BVBA & Co. v Finanzamt Bielefeld-Innenstadt* [2007] ECR I-10451.

[102] E. Kemmeren, 'CCCTB and Exemption Method for PEs and Major Shareholdings' in M. Lang, P. Pistone, J. Schuch and C. Staringer (eds), *Common Consolidated Corporate Tax Base* (Linde 2008) 693–694.

Further complications will probably arise when not all EU Member States adhere to the CCCTB.[103] In this case, third-state issues within the EU are likely to arise because of the difference between the uniform CCCTB approach and the traditional separate accounting, which will differ among EU Member States. Fundamental freedoms contained in the EU treaty may come into play.[104]

1.5.3 Specific Attention to Defined Categories of Income: Dividend Income and Capital Gains

The treatment of dividend income from third-country sources and of capital gains are the items probably receiving the least attention in the CCCTB Proposal with no, or almost no, definition of the conceptual framework; this does not mean that the mechanisms provided by the CCCTB Proposal were obvious or that the CCCTB Proposal does not raise a range of questions when assessed against international tax policies.

1.5.3.1 The CCCTB framework

Dividend income and capital gains are specified in the definition of revenues in the CCCTB Proposal. They are further referred to in the exemption provision of Article 11. In a previous working document,[105] the Commission proposed that only dividend income from major shareholdings would be exempt income. Under such a proposal, major shareholdings were defined on the basis of the criteria of shareholding percentage and holding period. A 10 per cent shareholding (of either capital or voting rights) and an uninterrupted period of at least 12 months were proposed. These thresholds were very close to those set out under

---

[103] For an illustration of potential issue to arise in an inbound investment situation, please see, for example, Christiana HJI Panayi, 'The Common Consolidated Corporate Tax Base and the UK Tax System' in C. Franklin (ed.), *The Institute for Fiscal Studies, Discussion Paper No. 9* (2011) 66.

[104] W. Schön, 'Group Taxation and the CCCTB' (2007) *Tax Notes International* 1060–1080. See, also E. Kemmeren, 'CCCTB and Exemption Method for PEs and Major Shareholdings' in M. Lang, P. Pistone, J. Schuch and C. Staringer (eds), *Common Consolidated Corporate Tax Base* (Linde 2008) 701. For CJ case law that could be relevant to consider, please see, for example, Case C-293/06 *Deutsche Shell v Finanzamt für Großunternehmen in Hamburg* [2008] ECR I-1129.

[105] European Commission, Working Document 'CCCTB: Possible Elements of a Technical Outline' CCCTB\WP\057, 26 July 2007.

the Parent-Subsidiary Directive,[106] except that the latter authorizes Member States to require a holding period of up to 24 months. This solution is reversed in the CCCTB Proposal, which does not currently contain any reference to such a factor.

As is the case for other exempt income, the switch-over mechanism of Article 73 will come into play. The application of the switch-over criteria to capital gains may be difficult to apply in practice; are domestic exemptions of such income to be covered by Article 73(c) or (d) of the CCCTB Proposal? Should this not be the case, this may lead to double non-taxation.

The CCCTB Proposal does not provide for sharing dividend withholding tax at source. This is the only solution possible for withholding taxes imposed by third-country states, and also seems reasonable in intra-EU situations, as dividends are after-tax payments. The CCCTB Proposal expressly provided this for withholding taxes imposed on outbound payments.[107]

1.5.3.2 Conflicts with international tax policy

Given the broad scope of exemption, and taking into account that the CCCTB Proposal has abandoned the distinction between major shareholding and portfolio shareholding, frictions with international tax policy in inbound situations should be relatively limited. The fact that interest on loans taken for the acquisition of shareholdings would remain deductible, even if generating exempt income, represented an important policy choice, aimed at promoting the CCCTB for EU groups with foreign subsidiaries.[108]

The general exemption of profit distributions is consistent with the idea that economic double taxation should be removed in order to facilitate investment between the EU and the rest of the world, whatever the structure and the importance of the investment.

---

106 Council Directive 2011/96/EU on the common system of taxation applicable in the case of parent companies and subsidiaries of different Member States [2011] OJ L-345/8.

107 See CCCTB Proposal, Preamble (18).

108 This policy choice is not aligned with the origin principle. It finds some support in the case law of the Court of Justice (such as Case C-168/01, *Bosal* [2003] ECR I-09409 and Case C-471/04, *Keller* [2006] ECR I-02107) but will likely lead to inconsistencies when applied in practice (on the matter, see, E. Kemmeren, 'CCCTB and Exemption Method for PEs and Major Shareholdings' in M. Lang, P. Pistone, J. Schuch and C. Staringer (eds), *Common Consolidated Corporate Tax Base* (Linde 2008) 690).

The question remains whether the Proposal offers sufficient clarity on the distinction between the concepts of profit distributions and interest. Indeed, the main area of uncertainty is definitional, as the CCCTB Proposal does not contain its own definition of key concepts such as dividend income or profit distribution, but the definitions are merely in line with other European-based legislation such as the Parent-Subsidiary Directive. This leaves room for potential interpretation issues that a reference to OECD framework[109] could have mitigated.

As to non-definitional types of issues, it is worth noting that the CCCTB Proposal does not address the consequences of existing or to-be-agreed tax-sparing clauses. Although less frequently applied in an international context,[110] one may question how a CCCTB member will be entitled to benefit from a dividend tax credit granted under a DTC. Should this lack of clarity on DTC benefits have an effect on a taxpayer's choice to opt, or to not opt, for the CCCTB? Moreover, if such a credit were deemed to enter the sharing mechanism,[111] it is unlikely to achieve its objective. Indeed, such a fictitious credit, which corresponds to a specific policy of a given Member State, would potentially reduce taxes in other Member States that did not necessarily agree with the advantages of such a policy.[112]

Further, according to some authors, the CCCTB may open a new and even more complex era of non-discrimination case law.[113] This could

---

[109] See OECD MC, Art. 10 (3).

[110] On the relevance of tax-sparing arrangements in tax treaties, see, for example, K. Brooks, 'Tax Sparing: A Needed Incentive for Foreign Investment in Low-Income Countries or an Unnecessary Revenue Sacrifice?' (2010) Colloquium in Tax Policy and Public Finance, New York University School of Law, http://www.law.nyu.edu/academics/colloquia/taxpolicy/ECM_PRO_064235, accessed 18 September 2012.

[111] A situation that could have easily occurred should the distinction between major shareholding and portfolio dividends have been translated in the CCCTB Proposal, *quod non*.

[112] See, for example, J. Malherbe and D. Garabedian, 'Credit Method for Portfolio Dividends, Interest and Royalties' in M. Lang, P. Pistone, J. Schuch and C. Staringer (eds), *Common Consolidated Corporate Tax Base* (Linde 2008) 721.

[113] Christiana HJI Panayi, 'The Common Consolidated Corporate Tax Base and the UK Tax System' in C. Franklin (ed.), *The Institute for Fiscal Studies, Discussion Paper No. 9* (2011) 64.

mean that CCCTB Member States providing relief for domestic dividends would have to provide equal relief for CCCTB-sourced dividends[114] or even to non-EU sourced dividends.[115] This matter could be even more relevant if not all Member States adopt CCCTB.

1.5.4 Specific Attention to Defined Categories of Income: Royalties, Patents and Interest and Other Income

The CCCTB Proposal provides for the absence of withholding tax at source within the CCCTB boundaries, the opportunity to apply (but with sharing of revenues) withholding tax at source for outbound payments and for a shared deduction, not to say credit, of the tax liability incurred by a taxpayer on third-country source income.

1.5.4.1 The CCCTB framework

Interest, patents and royalties and other passive income follow a path distinct from profit distribution under the CCCTB. Indeed, under the CCCTB, interest, royalties and any other income that did not qualify for exemption would be taxable and shared between the CCCTB group.[116] This goes hand-in-hand with a credit for source taxes. Article 76 provides for an ordinary tax credit.[117] The credit is shared according to the sharing formula. The tax credit of Article 76 is available with respect to income derived by the taxpayer which has been taxed in another Member State or

---

[114] See, for example, Case C-35/98 *Verkooijen* [2000] ECR I-4071 and more recently the Case C-436/08 *Haribo* [2011] n.y.r.

[115] Although arguably more difficult to apply, for example, in the absence of exchange of information provisions, given existing case law (see, for example, Case C-72/09 *Etablissements Rimbaud* [2010] n.y.r.).

[116] European Commission, Workshop, 'CCCTB: Transactions and Dealings between the Group and Entities Outside the Group' CCCTB/RD/003, 1 September 2010.

[117] Although the language used in Art. 76 of the CCCTB Proposal refers to a 'deduction from the tax liability of the taxpayer' rather than a credit, this is unlikely to represent a paradigm shift as the CCCTB Preamble further contains a reference to credit (CCCTB Proposal, Preamble 12 which reads as follows: 'Income consisting in interest and royalty payments should be taxable, with credit for withholding tax paid on such payments. Contrary to the case of dividends, there is no difficulty in computing such a credit'). We share the view of these authors considering that this language probably aims at reinforcing the (controversial) fact that there could be no carry-forward of the source taxes levied on this type of income (see, e.g Christiana HJI Panayi, 'The Common Consolidated Corporate Tax Base and the UK Tax System' in C. Franklin (ed.), *The Institute for Fiscal Studies, Discussion Paper No. 9* (2011) 62).

in a third country, provided such income is not exempt under Article 11(c) (received profit distributions), (d) (proceeds from a disposal of shares), and (e) (income of a permanent establishment in a third country). This generally includes interest and royalties, but also income from real estate abroad[118] and income that is not exempt as a result of the switch-over clause.

The tax credit is calculated per type of income and per country.[119] It is limited to the Member State's tax on the income reduced by related deductible expenses. The related deductible expenses are deemed to be 2 per cent of the income, unless the taxpayer proves them to be lower.[120] Such a deduction aims to tackle discrepancies occurring from the fact that withholding taxes are levied on gross amounts and that the taxation of profits under the CCCTB is based on net amounts.[121]

The CCCTB Proposal does not provide for the carry-forward of third-country tax if this exceeds the tax due in the respective Member State, unless, however, tax treaties concluded with the Member State of residence and the third country provide otherwise.[122]

---

118 To the extent not stated otherwise, for example, under a tax treaty with a third country.

119 European Commission, Workshop, 'CCCTB: Transactions and Dealings between the Group and Entities Outside the Group' CCCTB/RD/003, 1 September 2010, para 13.

120 The deduction of 2 per cent deemed expenses is considered a 'pragmatic or appropriate way' (see, European Commission, Workshop, 'CCCTB: Transactions and Dealings between the Group and Entities Outside the Group' CCCTB/RD/003, 1 September 2010). It is interesting to note that proposed amendments by European Parliament would reduce the 2 per cent to 0.5 per cent. Questions on the threshold may be raised in comparison to the ones provided under other EU legislation, such as under Art. 4 (2) of the Parent-Subsidiary Directive.

121 European Commission, Workshop, 'CCCTB: Transactions and Dealings between the Group and Entities Outside the Group' CCCTB/RD/003, 1 September 2010, para. 14.

122 Art. 76(5) of the CCCTB Proposal. It should be noted that European Commission, Working Document 'CCCTB: Possible Elements of a Technical Outline' CCCTB\WP\057, 26 July 2007 and European Commission, Workshop, 'CCCTB: Transactions and Dealings between the Group and Entities Outside the Group' CCCTB/RD/003, 1 September 2010 indicated that only tax treaties pre-dating the directive would have precedence over the tax credit rules of Art. 76. However, the exception in Art. 76 (5), to the effect that tax treaties with third countries have precedence over the tax credit rules of Art. 76, is not limited to tax treaties pre-dating the Directive.

The tax credit is shared among the members of a group according to the sharing formula.[123] The background is that as the income received is shared, the burden of the tax credit is also to be shared. The tax credit is shared according to the sharing formula in the year in which the tax credit is granted. This is the year in which the (withholding) tax was charged, which in general is the year in which the respective income was paid.

Finally, specific anti-abuse rules are provided in the CCCTB Proposal to target deductions of interest paid to associated enterprises in a third country. They take the form of disallowing interest deductions, using criteria very similar to those triggering the switch-over clause to apply.[124]

1.5.4.2 Conflicts with international tax policy

As is the case in other matters, tensions are likely to arise and could originate both from definitional or other kinds of issues. Amongst the latter, inefficiencies of the CCCTB Proposal as it stands today should be pointed out.

The term 'interest' is defined in Article 81(2) of the CCCTB Proposal. Although there are no cross-references between Articles 77 and 81(2), one may argue that the definition could be used in both situations. This, however, creates uncertainty from the outset. Further, the term 'royalty' is not defined, which seems to imply that it is to be defined according to the definition in the domestic tax law of the Member State imposing the withholding tax.[125] Given the absence of international consensus on the definitional framework for intangibles, as highlighted by recent OECD work,[126] this also leaves room for interpretative questions.[127]

---

123 For an interesting illustration on how the sharing mechanism could work in practice J. Malherbe and D. Garabedian, 'Credit Method for Portfolio Dividends, Interest and Royalties' in M. Lang, P. Pistone, J. Schuch and C. Staringer (eds), *Common Consolidated Corporate Tax Base* (Linde 2008) 710.

124 Art. 81 of the CCCTB Proposal.

125 Although one may argue that other sources should be used to provide for more consistency, such as the definition of 'royalty' in the Interest and Royalty Directive.

126 See, for example, Transfer Pricing and Intangibles: Scope of the OECD Project, Document Approved by the Committee of Fiscal Affairs on 25 January 2011, www.oecd.org/dataoecd/10/50/46987988.pdf, accessed 18 September 2012.

127 Note that J. Malherbe and D. Garabedian consider that given the rationale for the tax credit (in other words, avoidance of double taxation), the absence of definitions is not problematic in so far as credit is granted wherever income included in the CCCTB has been subject to tax in the hands of the CCCTB

The intended balance, which is to share the income received and the tax credit, may not always be fully realized, as the income may partly accrue in a year other than the year in which the (withholding) tax is paid. This may lead to situations where the burden of the tax credit is thus not always shared according to the same formula as the income is shared.

The definitional issues highlighted in the triggering of the switch-over clause equally apply to the triggering of the anti-abuse provision.

It is difficult to assess the pros and cons of a country-per-country limitation, as opposed to an overall limitation.[128] The former is likely to trigger a greater administrative burden than the latter. However, the per-country limitation will likely have little effect on tax credits covering withholding tax on passive income, as it is unlikely for the withholding tax at source to be higher than the EU corporate tax on the relevant income.[129] Nevertheless, it cannot be ignored that tax credit may be subject to taxpayer manipulation.[130]

1.6 CCCTB AND DOUBLE TAX TREATIES

As many authors[131] and extensive Commission preparatory work[132] have demonstrated, the interaction between CCCTB and double tax conventions is to be characterized as a troubled relationship. Despite several

---

taxpayer (J. Malherbe and D. Garabedian, 'Credit Method for Portfolio Dividends, Interest and Royalties' in M. Lang, P. Pistone, J. Schuch and C. Staringer (eds), *Common Consolidated Corporate Tax Base* (Linde 2008) 716–717).

[128] See, E.A. Owens, *The Foreign Tax Credit* (first published 1961, 295–311), reprinted in M.J. Graetz, *Foundations of International Income Taxation* (Foundation Press 2003) 169–175.

[129] J. Malherbe and D. Garabedian, 'Credit Method for Portfolio Dividends, Interest and Royalties' in M. Lang, P. Pistone, J. Schuch and C. Staringer (eds), *Common Consolidated Corporate Tax Base* (Linde 2008) 718.

[130] For US case law example, see, for example, *Compaq Computer Corp. v Commissioner*, 113 T.C. 214, 215 (1999), reviewed 277 F.3d778 (2001).

[131] See, for example, P. Baker and I. Mitroyanni, 'The CCCTB Rules and Tax Treaties' in M. Lang, P. Pistone, J. Schuch and C. Staringer (eds), *Common Consolidated Corporate Tax Base* (Linde 2008) 650; E. Kemmeren, 'CCCTB and Exemption Method for PEs and Major Shareholdings' in M. Lang, P. Pistone, J. Schuch and C. Staringer (eds), *Common Consolidated Corporate Tax Base* (Linde 2008); Christiana HJI Panayi, 'The Common Consolidated Corporate Tax Base and the UK Tax System' in C. Franklin (ed.), *The Institute for Fiscal Studies, Discussion Paper No. 9* (2011); W. Schön, 'Group Taxation and the CCCTB' (2007) 48 *Tax Notes International* 11, 1060–1080.

references in the preparatory works to the interaction between the CCCTB and DTCs, and also the Commission's commitment to accommodate such an interaction, the CCCTB Proposal does not comprehensively address this very important issue. Moreover, some provisions seem to go against the principle stated: that DTCs with third countries should not be affected.

1.6.1 The CCCTB Framework Applicable to Tax Treaties

On the interaction with double tax conventions, two situations should be differentiated: the impact of the CCCTB for DTCs concluded between Member States, and collateral effects for third countries and that for DTCs concluded with third countries.

As to DTCs between Member States, the Proposal clearly states that 'the provisions of this Directive shall apply notwithstanding any provision to the contrary in any agreement concluded between Member States'.[133] The CCCTB Proposal, contrary to other EU directives in the area of corporate taxation, also directly concerns aspects that are regulated by DTCs concluded with third countries. Therefore, every issue concerning the originally bilateral application of one DTC involving one Member State is transformed into a multilateral issue having potential consequences for 26 other Member States and 26 other DTCs. However, the primacy of the directive may impact third countries, for example, in triangular situations involving two Member States and a third country. For these reasons, it would not be proper to leave to the judiciary the difficult task of solving possible compatibility problems, since the Court of Justice or a national court could only intervene *ex post* and in a controversy between only one taxpayer and Member State at the time.

Member States are also restricted by commitments they have vis-à-vis third countries deriving from tax treaties they have entered into, which in

[132] European Commission, Working Document 'The Territorial Scope of the CCCTB' CCCTB\WP\026, 17 February 2006; European Commission, Working Document 'An Overview of the main issues that emerged at the first meeting of the subgroup on International Aspects' CCCTB\WP\029, 2 March 2006; European Commission, Working Document 'CCCTB: Possible Elements of a Technical Outline' CCCTB\WP\057, 26 July 2007; European Commission, Workshop, 'CCCTB: Transactions and Dealings between the Group and Entities Outside the Group' CCCTB/RD/003, 1 September 2010.

[133] Art. 8 of the CCCTB Proposal.

turn are normally intended to take precedence over national legislation.[134] The CCCTB Proposal contains some mechanisms aimed at alleviating this. For example, on the credit granted for taxes paid abroad, the CCCTB Proposal states that 'the deduction for the tax liability in a third country may not exceed the final corporate tax liability of a taxpayer, unless an agreement concluded between the Member State of its residence and a third country states otherwise'.[135] In other words, if a DTC provides a full credit, the Member State is obliged to grant a full credit. This provision may not always ensure that the DTC will be correctly and fully applied; it depends indeed on whether the Member State concerned has to grant a full credit limited to the amount which has been attributed to it according to the formula, or if on the contrary it has to grant an effective full credit, i.e., also compensating the amounts that have not been deducted in other Member States that had not signed a DTC with the third country in question stating that a full credit had to be granted.

Concerning the treatment of the transactions between the group and entities outside the group, the Commission, in the impact assessment accompanying the Proposal, states that 'tax treaties with third countries will override conflicting rules of the Directive, meaning that a MS will not be hampered from fulfilling its commitment vis-à-vis a third country'.[136] This position was also stated in the preparatory Commission work, which gave the following example:

> A Member State may conclude a Double tax convention (DTC) which allocates revenues to an EU-located permanent establishment (PE) owned by a company resident in a third country according to the arm's length principle. Given that the DTC is concluded prior to the Directive, the arm's length rule will override the apportionment of revenue by formula, as regard the obligation of the third country to give relief for double taxation. In practical terms, a third country which relieves double taxation by a credit method will have to give a credit only up to the level of an arm's length allocation of revenues to the PE.

This example casts more shadows than light on the Commission's intentions and on the real effect of the Directive on DTC signed with third countries. It seems indeed obvious that no act adopted by the

---

[134] European Commission, Working Document 'International Aspects in the CCCTB' CCCTB\WP\019, 18 November 2005, point 17.

[135] Art. 76 of the CCCTB Proposal.

[136] Commission Staff Working Document Impact Assessment Accompanying document to the Proposal for a Council Directive on a Common Consolidated Corporate Tax Base (CCCTB) [2011], SEC(2011)315 final 21.

European Union or by a Member State could have an extraterritorial application, so as to apply also to a country located outside the EU. Further, EU primary law principles apply and reference to Article 351 TFEU, although not always supportive, is likely to be helpful in many situations.[137] Therefore, it might well be that this example only serves to illustrate the obvious territorial limitation to tax sovereignty.

1.6.2 Why Is the CCCTB, on Its Face, Problematic for DTCs?

The CCCTB is, in essence, trying to accommodate diverging ambitions, especially in third-country matters. Tax residence remains one of the basic tests for identifying entities that are part of the boundary group under the CCCTB. This is further strengthened by the use of permanent establishment required for creating the relevant nexus for consolidation of non-residents. However, a group taxation system involving a consolidated and apportioned common base cannot be implemented without drawbacks, as the allocation of income under formulary apportionment, in essence, functions independently of source/residence principles. Overall, the EU is inadequately integrated to accommodate a CCCTB without entering into DTC re-negotiations.[138]

1.6.3 Possible Conflicts with Third-Countries: A 360° View

Amongst the areas of contention that are likely to occur in third-country relations, we may mention: (i) conflict because of (non-tax) international rules, (ii) definitional issues because of friction with international tax rules, (iii) specific difficulties in properly applying relief provisions in existing DTCs, and (iv) miscellaneous items.

1.6.3.1 Non-tax international rules

In preparatory work, the Commission acknowledged that the CCCTB Directive was to include authorizations for Member States to temporarily derogate when such derogations were necessary in order to fulfil their obligations under DTCs with third countries.[139] This might not be enough

[137] For the case law application of the principle, although not in the taxation area, please see Case C-203/03, *Commission v Austria* [2005] ECR I-954.

[138] See, for example, P. Baker and I. Mitroyanni, 'The CCCTB Rules and Tax Treaties' in M. Lang, P. Pistone, J. Schuch and C. Staringer (eds), *Common Consolidated Corporate Tax Base* (Linde 2008) 650.

[139] European Commission, Working Document 'CCCTB: Possible Elements of a Technical Outline' CCCTB\WP\057, 26 July 2007, points 30–31 and 35.

under the existing international non-tax framework, such as the Vienna Convention on the Law of the Treaties (VCLT). Under the VCLT, no conflict with third countries will be acceptable, as a Member State is bound by a treaty in force and must perform in good faith. Entering the CCCTB will not justify failure by a Member State to comply with its obligations under a DTC.[140] Further, this is likely not in line with EU primary law, in particular Article 351 of the TFEU.

1.6.3.2 Definitional issues

As iterated above, the CCCTB Proposal as it stands today will raise a number of definitional issues, simply because either (i) existing mechanisms will attract identical issues as existing instruments (an example being the catch-all provision in the permanent establishment definition under both the OECD MC and the CCCTB), or (ii) in the absence of alignment of concepts, interpretative issues may develop (amongst others, with respect to potential conflict in the definitions of dividends or interest, issues with countries recognizing service permanent establishments, etc.).

1.6.3.3 Relief and credit-sharing issues

The CCCTB Proposal may also lead to relief-type issues. The availability or effectiveness to be given to existing tax sparing clauses is one example we have highlighted. Amongst the other relief issues that are likely to arise is an existing DTC providing for the credit method for dividend distributions, as CCCTB provides for the exemption.[141] Article 74 may also trigger some issues when stating that the computation of the income of a foreign permanent establishment for the purposes of the application of the switch-over clause must occur according to the 'rules of the system provided by this directive'. This provision is certainly coherent with the intention of tackling abusive practices and of discouraging the location of activities and assets in low-tax jurisdictions, which may be seen as one of

---

[140] For more highlights of underlying principles, see, for example, E. Kemmeren, 'CCCTB and Exemption Method for PEs and Major Shareholdings' in M. Lang, P. Pistone, J. Schuch and C. Staringer (eds), *Common Consolidated Corporate Tax Base* (Linde 2008) 657.

[141] In an EU context, the Court has already considered that a Member State could use a different mechanism of double taxation relief for domestic and cross-border dividends. See Case C-446/04 *Test Claimants in the FII Group Litigation v Commissioners of Inland Revenue* [2006] ECR I-11753; Case C-201/05, *The Test Claimants in the CFC and Dividend Group Litigation* [2008] ECR I-2875.

the consequences of the application of the arm's length principle. However, no distinction between whether the foreign PE is established in a treaty country or a non-treaty country is made, which means that in the first case the CCCTB will override the rules affecting the computation of the PE profits included in the DTC (usually based on the arm's length principle).

For passive income, the sharing of credit amongst the group should not lead to DTC incompatibility. However, the source state may object or have concerns in situations where income benefiting from a reduced withholding tax rate based on the DTC with one Member State is flowing in part to an entity resident in another Member State with which it has no bilateral arrangement, or a less generous arrangement.[142] Most of the DTCs signed between Member States and third countries provide for a withholding tax on dividends, which rate may vary depending on the level of participation. Since the CCCTB Proposal exempts profit distributions, this means that the withholding tax levied by the third country of source would not be deducted/credited according to the mechanism in Article 76. Therefore, depending on the effective tax rate in the profits of the receiving company and on the rate of the withholding tax in the third country, the CCCTB could provide a disadvantage in comparison with the previous situation.

1.6.3.4 Miscellaneous items

Amongst the other aspects one may identify, disputes regarding income derived from immovable property situated in a third country could be problematic: since there is no specific exclusion in the CCCTB Proposal, this category of income may *a priori* be included in the consolidated tax base, although taxing rights are generally exclusively given to the country of source.

Other issues will arise in the likely event of enhanced cooperation. In this case, the CCCTB Proposal would probably take precedence over the DTCs, at least when applied by a participating EU Member State. From the perspective of the non-participating Member State, other EU primary and secondary law would continue to be applicable, and may conflict with existing DTCs, for example for intra-group interest, dividends and royalties. In the case of enhanced cooperation, it would be wiser to include a provision on the relations between EU participating and

---

[142] P. Baker and I. Mitroyanni, 'The CCCTB Rules and Tax Treaties' in M. Lang, P. Pistone, J. Schuch and C. Staringer (eds), *Common Consolidated Corporate Tax Base* (Linde 2008) 650.

non-participating Member States, which would also concern the application of DTCs.

1.6.4 Possible Solution: Towards an EU DTC?

Amongst the possible ways to mitigate the above-mentioned risks, the promotion of a European Union-wide DTC, or at least an accepted model, that could replace existing tax treaties signed by Member States could be a promising way forward. The EU might even be allowed to conclude such agreements alone, as is the case of the agreement in the area of savings taxation,[143] or in the form of mixed agreements featuring the EU and Member States.

According to the doctrine of implied powers developed by the Court of Justice, the EU is allowed to exercise its international competence in all areas covered by (domestic) EU law, even if the latter does not make reference to the international capacity of the EU in those areas.[144] It could even be argued that the replacement of existing bilateral tax treaties would be mandatory whenever their application would hinder the correct application of CCCTB rules.[145]

---

[143] See, for example, Agreement between the European Community and the Swiss Confederation providing for measures equivalent to those laid down in Council Directive 2003/48/EC on taxation of savings income in the form of interest payments [2004] OJ L-385/30.

[144] Case C-22/70, *AETR* [1977] ECR p 263; Opinion 2/91, *ILO Convention safety in the use of chemicals at work,* [1993] ECR I-01061, para 7; Opinion 1/03, *Lugano Convention* [2006] ECR I-01145, paras 114–133.

[145] On external competences of the EU in direct tax matters, see, for example, E. Traversa, 'National report: Belgium' in P. Pistone and M. Lang (eds), *EU Direct Taxation and Third Countries* (Linde 2007) 147–176, as well as the general report by P. Pistone and the other national reports.

Commentary

Krister Andersson

Obstacles to cross-border business transactions deriving from corporate taxation are a real problem and cause significant costs for promoting growth and employment. The lack of cross-border loss relief constitutes a major obstacle to achieving a functioning Single Market. The large number of disputes in the transfer pricing area is another example of tax obstacles to an efficient Single Market. The proposed directive on a Common Consolidated Corporate Tax Base could provide a lasting solution to these problems at least between participating countries, thus making it very important to businesses engaging in cross-border activities.

The question of how to find a constructive way to split the tax cake is long overdue. There is an on-going debate about corporate tax payments and their allocation across countries and regions. In these discussions it is crucial to uphold the principle of single taxation, not international double taxation. The slices must not exceed the size of the cake. How to split the tax cake should be a contest between governments – not between a company or a group of companies and the government of a country.

The authors make an interesting historical exposé running from the Neumark and Ruding reports to the present CCCTB Directive proposal. They also give a good summary of the many features contained in the proposal.

Their chapter deals with the extraterritorial aspects of the CCCTB. It raises some very interesting issues regarding international tax policy consequences when some Member States decide to introduce the CCCTB, allocating taxable profits according to a formula and at the same time having tax treaties and applying OECD principles in international taxation. Is it sufficient that transfer pricing disputes with third countries – countries not introducing an optional CCCTB – are handled bilaterally under the arm's length principle and mutual agreement procedure, impacting the taxable profit of the group in that country, or does this invoke elements of extraterritorial taxation?

It seems that the main issue in their chapter is whether business profits calculated under CCCTB rules for those companies that opted for the CCCTB should be subject to the same treatment according to tax treaties and international tax agreements as those companies that do not apply the CCCTB. According to the authors, the residence principle and definitional aspects could raise issues of extraterritorial taxation.

Given the need to respect subsidiarity, bilateral tax agreements and international tax principles it is not obvious how the directive could have been structured differently. It does not mean that extraterritorial taxation may not arise, but such taxation effects were not actively sought when the CCCTB was outlined. However, the Commission has designed a tax proposal deliberately entailing extraterritorial taxation: the proposal of a Financial Transaction Tax (FTT proposal). There the residence principle of the taxpayer is designed also to tax transactions in countries not adopting the tax. This will be a deterrent to international trade and economic activities. The Commission should definitely refrain from such policies since they will impose undue burdens on the free trade of goods and services. Yet still, it has to be seen whether the FTT proposal ever becomes law in the EU. A proposal increasing the cost of capital for investments, reducing GDP, and eroding pensions of European workers, ought to have a difficult time and it should of course be discarded. If implemented, it would bring tax competition and extraterritorial taxation to a new and unacceptable level.

The following remarks on the chapter will be limited to a more detailed analysis regarding the issue of worldwide versus territorial taxation, the exemption method and the switch-over clause. A minor comment on relief and credit-sharing issues will also be made.

WORLDWIDE OR TERRITORIAL TAXATION

The authors rightly point out that the CCCTB proposal seems to be a compromise between worldwide and territorial taxation. By excluding permanent establishments and certain types of passive income, such as profit distributions and capital gains on shares, the CCCTB proposal seems to embrace the principle of Capital Import Neutrality (CIN). From a business perspective this is positive, since it will result in a tax treatment independent of the nature or residence of its shareholders.

To achieve economic efficiency, taxes should not distort investment decisions. The most important issue is that corporations must only be taxed on their net income and that double taxation or lack of recognition of costs or losses must be avoided. CIN would provide for a level playing field with respect to businesses located in third countries. This is particularly important in making European businesses competitive in the global economy. Furthermore, this will likely strengthen the position of head offices in Europe.

In contrast, a CCCTB based on the credit method would be extremely difficult to apply as it would reflect the actual tax rates of the various Member States. It could also impose significant complications with respect to the application of double tax treaties with exemption provisions. The concept of international taxation as outlined in the draft directive is therefore the right one.

The Exemption Method and Switch-Over Clause

The CCCTB proposal provides for a switch-over clause from exemption to a tax credit in the case of low taxation of the entity or permanent establishment in a third country. The clause is triggered if the tax on profits under the general regime in the source state is lower than 40 per cent of the average statutory corporate tax rates applicable in the Member States or a special regime in that third country allows for substantially lower levels of taxation than the general regime.

It should first be stressed that a properly designed switch-over clause is a good way to address the prevailing different levels of taxation in the world without interfering too much with *bona fide* business activities. A switch-over clause in the CCCTB adds pressure on tax havens and provides an effective incentive for them to adopt a tax rate that most would find acceptable. Such a mechanism could be designed to cover all kinds of transactions, as opposed to having various additional complicated anti-abuse measures in the CCCTB, e.g. CFC legislation.

However, the authors rightly point out that the proposed criteria for the clause to be triggered can be questioned.

Therefore, the switch-over clause should be combined with an escape clause giving the taxpayer the opportunity to provide evidence of any commercial justification. This would also apply with respect to transactions falling below the threshold. Such a rule would offer a reasonable level of predictability and contribute to a CCCTB that is both attractive and competitive. Furthermore, to ensure simplicity and predictability, it should be clarified that the special regime criteria must apply in exceptional cases only and should be defined using some sort of ‘black list’. In addition, some consideration should also be given to regimes adopted in developing countries aiming at attracting foreign direct investment.

The authors question whether a threshold of 40 per cent of the average rate of statutory corporate tax rates applicable in Member States is appropriate. Perhaps the threshold would seem fairer if based on the average rate in the countries where the group operates or where the corporate tax base will be apportioned.

Since the switch-over clause is a protective measure against low or non-taxation situations, the method chosen in the draft directive is preferable. By including all countries when calculating the threshold, a clear and important signal is sent to tax havens and low-tax jurisdictions. This rule is likely to put an upward pressure on the statutory tax rate in such countries. The difference between countries with very high tax rates, 'tax hells', and countries with very low tax rates, 'tax havens' will decrease. Such a development is likely to have a very positive effect in creating a level playing field as well as in promoting tax cooperation yet it would retain the right of countries to engage in tax competition. The Commission should be commended for developing such a mechanism in the CCCTB proposal.

Relief and Credit-Sharing Issues

The authors point out that by exempting profit distributions, as opposed to taxing the income and providing a credit for the withholding tax levied, the CCCTB could remedy a disadvantage with the current situation. That is true if the current situation is such that the country in which the company receiving the profit distribution applies a system of full tax credit or has a pooling system, i.e. an overall tax credit. The problem is that very few countries are willing to give full credit for foreign taxes. However, certain countries, e.g. Sweden, allow an overall tax credit. The fact that all foreign taxes (high and low) are pooled would normally result in a more favourable tax credit than a system based on per-item and per-country limits.

For this reason, and also from an administrative point of view, at least for businesses, an overall tax credit would be preferable to the proposed system in the CCCTB Directive of calculating the tax credit per type of income and per country. To make the CCCTB more competitive and to ensure that more businesses opt for the CCCTB, a change to an overall tax credit system should be introduced.

Last but not least the many features of the CCCTB Proposal that would help to create an efficient Single Market should be pointed out. One area which is not covered in the draft directive is the implicit bias in favour of debt financing over equity financing. Since the CCCTB is a classical corporate tax system, albeit with a lot of new features, it would result in double taxation of equity capital, unless mitigated at the shareholder level.

Even with a CCCTB, Member States must exercise restraint in the area of capital income taxation at the investor level. Since economic double taxation is implicitly assumed in the proposal, there will be a need to impose low tax rates on dividends and capital gains to counterbalance the corporate tax treatment.

Some have expressed concerns that the deductibility of interest payments in the CCCTB is too generous and that the tax base is not sufficiently protected. However, the anti-abuse measures included are prudent and should be seen as a compromise between an effort to make the CCCTB competitive and the need to raise revenue in the Member States. In this regard, corporate tax revenues should not be seen in isolation. In Europe, in particular, where labour income is heavily taxed, through the imposition of high taxes on wages and salaries, payroll taxes and high excise and value added taxes, the total revenue effect is much more dependent on the allocation of production to Europe than aggressively denying deductions for interest payments in the corporate sector. In this regard, the European situation is different from the one in the United States and Japan, where wage taxation is lower and excise taxation relatively low. The Commission has struck a sound balance in this regard, both from a competitive aspect and in view of using the revenue-raising capacity of the CCCTB.

Such an element of international competitiveness is of course not directly linked to extraterritorial taxation, but it is likely to lead to some criticism from other economic powers in the world. This is understandable. The calls for less competitive rules regarding interest deductions coming from individual Member States are harder to understand, at least from a total revenue perspective. However, no tax rule or tax regime, old or new, should allow for open arbitrage schemes nor accept wholly artificial arrangements to avoid taxes being collected. For policy-makers, it is a challenge to combine all these aspects.

Commentary

Katharina Becker

INTRODUCTION

The CCCTB is no doubt one of the most challenging and contentious directives that the EU Commission has ever launched in the field of direct taxation. Its rules provide for a considerable reduction of tax barriers such as transfer pricing compliance obligations and denials of group loss compensation in the internal market. This reduction would, in line with the Lisbon goals,[146] encourage investment and innovation, competitiveness and growth.

On the other hand, the implemented CCCTB would deprive the EU Member States of control over fiscal policy in relation to corporate tax, with the effect that EU Member States would lose tax sovereignty. The very controversial discussions taking place in the Council working group on the CCCTB are thus of no surprise.

One of the main benefits often linked with the CCCTB is consolidation, which implies that EU companies will also be freed from compliance with intra-group transfer pricing rules. Since MNEs and tax administrations have been subject to increasing compliance and verification work with respect to transfer policy documentation, country differences and multi-country filings, the EU Commission believes that the introduction of the CCCTB will be a major step to reducing compliance costs.[147] Traversa and Helleputte, however, pose very important and challenging questions on transfer pricing and the CCCTB: how transfer pricing disputes have to be dealt with under the directive and how cases have to be handled, where, under a DTC, the arm's length rule will

[146] EU-Commission, The Contribution of Taxation and Customs Policies to the Lisbon Strategy COM(2005 532 final.

[147] Algirdas Šemeta, 'EU tax coordination and the financial sector' (2012), http://europa.eu/rapid/pressReleasesAction.do?reference=SPEECH/12/109, accessed 18 September 2012.

override the apportionment of revenue by the formula.[148] This chapter intends first to examine whether the CCCTB will in fact reduce transfer pricing compliance and documentation burdens and second, whether the directive is likely to affect the application of DTCs for CCCTB taxpayers so that the question of transfer pricing disputes has to be addressed.

CCCTB TRANSFER PRICING COMPLIANCE AND DOCUMENTATION BURDENS

Transactions inside a CCCTB Group

Article 59 section 1 of the draft CCCTB Directive provides that profits and losses arising from transactions directly carried out between members of a group must be ignored in calculating the consolidated tax base. This means that there is no longer any need for the determination of arm's length prices between group members. It implies that all EU groups that comply with the definition of a group (75 per cent voting rights/shareholding) and that opt into the CCCTB are not subject to transfer pricing rules any more. In principle, this sounds like good news for the EU groups that strive for simpler rules for their inter-company transactions.

Transactions between CCCTB Group Members and Other Entities of the MNE

Associated enterprises in general have to comply with transfer pricing rules in the EU if they are connected by shareholding or voting rights that are not lower than 10–25 per cent.[149] Thus, all EU MNEs that are not exclusively 75 per cent groups have to comply with both CCCTB rules and transfer pricing rules. In addition, in all cases where shareholding or voting rights of a CCCTB group member fall below the threshold of 75 per cent, transfer pricing obligations re-emerge, maybe after several years without transfer pricing obligations.

The question is how the resulting complex questions on CCCTB group transactions, on the one hand, and transactions between CCCTB group members and other entities of the MNE, on the other hand, will be handled.

---

148. Edoardo Traversa and Charles-Albert Helleputte, section 1.5.1.1.

149. Transfer pricing, country profiles, see http://www.oecd.org, accessed 18 September 2012.

The directive does not contain an answer, even though several commentators and the OECD have already outlined the consequences. Andrus, Bennett and Silberztein[150] state that in the United States, mispricing of such transactions has led to a reduction in the tax base to be apportioned and thus to a loss of revenue in the taxing jurisdiction.

The OECD, in its Transfer Pricing Guidelines, states the same concern:[151]

> Unless global formulary apportionment includes every member of the MNE group, it must retain a separate entity rule for the interface between that part of the group subject to global formulary apportionment and the rest of the MNE group. Global formulary apportionment could not be used to value the transactions between the global formulary apportionment group and the rest of the MNE group. Thus, a clear disadvantage with global formulary apportionment is that it does not provide a complete solution to the allocation of profits of an MNE group unless global formulary apportionment is applied on the basis of the whole MNE group. … The MNE group would also be required in any event, to maintain separate accounting for corporations that are not members of the MNE group for global formulary apportionment tax purposes but that are still associated enterprises of one or more members of the MNE group. In fact, many domestic commercial and accountancy rules would still require the use of arm's length prices, so that irrespective of the tax provisions a taxpayer would have to book properly every transaction at arm's length prices.

For illustration, please see the following example:

> Example 1:
>
> *A, B and C are entities of an MNE group in Europe. A holds 50 per cent of B and B holds 100 per cent of C. C is an R&D entity and provides R&D services to B. B is a producer ('contract manufacturer') and sells its produced goods to A. For transfer pricing purposes the three entities apply the following system: C charges B with a cost plus for its R&D services. B, again, charges A with a cost plus for its goods produced, A, the 'entrepreneur', absorbs the residual profit or loss.*

An MNE group would not benefit from CCCTB rules in this situation, where B and C may form a CCCTB group. The reason is that B would

[150] J.L. Andrus, M.C. Bennett and C. Silberztein, 'The Arm's-Length Principle and Developing Countries' (2011) *BNA Tax Management Transfer Pricing Report* 495–503.

[151] OECD Transfer Pricing Guidelines for Multinational Enterprises and Tax Administrations, para 1.31.

have to charge A arm's length prices for its goods produced, which implies that B's arm's length prices have to include the prices for the services charged by C. Thus, B needs to know the arm's length price for the services provided by C to B in order to include it in B's price calculation. It follows that C would have to keep the books and the necessary documentation for transfer pricing purposes, even though C belongs to a 100 per cent CCCTB group.

The example shows that even in easy and 100 per cent group situations the CCCTB group will have to comply with transfer pricing obligations for its group transactions in the case of additional transactions with other members of the MNE. For these cases and for all other cases with more group members than three and more complex transfer pricing transactions, the directive does not contain a clear-cut line between CCCTB transactions, where transfer pricing documentation is not necessary and CCCTB transactions, where transfer pricing documentation has to be maintained.

However, such an overview is needed to provide the MNEs with clear guidance on their documentation obligations. In addition, it would be worthwhile to find out how many European MNEs are pure CCCTB groups and how many are hybrids. Such an overview would provide an estimate of the benefit of the CCCTB for transfer pricing reasons. For the time being and without any further analysis, it has to be concluded that in all cases of transactions between CCCTB group members and other entities of the MNE group, transfer pricing documentation requirements have to be fulfilled. This does not seem to imply that the CCCTB is of major benefit for MNEs with respect to transfer pricing purposes.

TAX TREATIES WITH THIRD COUNTRIES, ARTICLE 9 OECD MC

Concerning the treatment of transactions between the CCCTB group and associated entities outside the group, the authors refer to a statement in the impact assessment to the CCCTB Directive[152]: 'tax treaties with third countries will override conflicting rules of the Directive, meaning that a MS will not be hampered from fulfilling its commitment vis-à-vis a third country". Traversa and Helleputte also give the example of a preparatory Commission work.[153]

---

152 Edoardo Traversa and Charles-Albert Helleputte, Section 1.6.1.
153 Edoardo Traversa and Charles-Albert Helleputte, Section 1.6.1.

> A Member State may conclude a Double tax convention (DTC) which allocates revenues to an EU-located permanent establishment (PE) owned by a company resident in a third country according to the arm's length principle. Given that the DTC is concluded prior to the Directive, the arm's length rule will override the apportionment of revenue by formula, as regard the obligation of the third country to give relief for double taxation. In practical terms, a third country which relieves double taxation by a credit method will have to give a credit only up to the level of an arm's length allocation of revenues to the PE.

Irrespective of whether a group consists of corporations and/or permanent establishments, imagine the following example for transactions between CCCTB group members and a foreign associated entity:

Example 2:

Before consolidation (at arm's length result with a TNM of 2%):

US parent	EU sub 1	EU sub 2
	+ 20	+ 100

After consolidation:

US parent	EU sub 1	EU sub 2
	+ 100	+ 20

The two EU CCCTB group members of the US parent will, before consolidation, be remunerated with a Transactional Net Margin (TNM) of 2 per cent resulting in a profit of 20 for sub 1 and a profit of 100 for sub 2. All parties agree that this is an arm's length result.

After consolidation, the allocation of the profits may change and sub 1 will be attributed a profit of 100 and sub 2 a profit of 20. The question is whether these results comply with Article 9 of the US-EU 1 and with the US-EU 2 DTC.

It is to be assumed that the US-EU 1 DTC follows Article 9 OECD MC, which, in paragraph 1 states the following:

> Where … and in either case conditions are made or imposed between the two enterprises in their commercial or financial relations which differ from those which would be made between independent enterprises, then any profits which would, but for those conditions, have accrued to one of the enterprises (US parent), but, by reason of those conditions, have not so accrued, may be included in the profits of that enterprise and taxed accordingly.

The situation after consolidation raises the difficult question whether the conditions made between the US parent and sub 1 are different from those between independent enterprises. At first glance, they are not, because the prices have been charged according to arm's length principles and the US parent's profits are apparently not affected by the change of profits between sub 1 and sub 2 according to the CCCTB allocation.

At second glance, and looking at the cases separately, the US parent is affected. With respect to sub 1 the parent would, after consolidation, be asked to grant a tax credit on a profit of 100, whereas under Article 9 of the bilateral treaty, the parent would only be obliged to provide for a tax credit on a profit of 20. The tax credit on a profit of 100 would reduce the profit of the US parent for reasons of the non-arm's length result of sub 1. Accordingly, under Article 9 of the bilateral treaty, the US does have the right to reduce the tax credit with respect to sub 1 to the tax applicable on a profit of 20. The US would ask EU 1 to make a corresponding adjustment of 80 to relieve double taxation.

With respect to sub 2, the bilateral treaty between the US and EU 2 does not provide for rules for a US adjustment that would lead to a higher relief. This is caused by the one-sided construction of Article 9 OECD MC that starts with the check, whether the profits of the first enterprise are too low for reasons of incorrect transfer prices. Accordingly, it is necessary that domestic legislation, such as the German transfer pricing rules, allow for an adjustment in cases where transactions with an associated entity result in taxable profits that are lower than under arm's length conditions. Since Article 9 OECD MC mirrors the international consensus, the consistent application of the adjustment rules leads generally to arm's length transfer prices for MNEs.

In the case that EU 2, in order to compensate for the corresponding adjustment made with respect to sub 1 in EU 1, makes an adjustment of 80 for sub 2, the CCCTB would end up in the arm's length situation before consolidation: sub 1 would report a profit of 20 and sub 2 would report a profit of 100.

This second example shows that the consolidation rules of the CCCTB, when it comes to transfer pricing, contradict Article 9 OECD MC (and Article 7 in the same way). This contradiction can only be solved by a set of rules with respect to international dispute resolution. If, under example 2, the competent authorities of the US, EU 1 and EU 2 would be asked to discuss the case in a common mutual agreement procedure, the US tax authorities could be convinced to refrain from adjustments. Such procedures would have to be institutionalized for all consolidation cases that lead to non-arm's length results.

The questions posed by Traversa and Helleputte (how transfer pricing disputes have to be dealt with under the directive and how cases have to be handled, where, under a DTC, the arm's length rule overrides the apportionment of revenue by the formula) need to be answered. There are many more and more complex transfer pricing cases than the one described, that might incur losses for MNEs that form a CCCTB and thus to tax losses of EU Member States. To address this problem and to protect the tax base of the CCCTB, the directive needs to be amended by dispute resolution rules that have to be negotiated with the treaty partners of the European Member States. Several difficult questions such as the following will have to be answered:

- How will the mixed commission be composed, i.e. must all affected EU Member States participate?
- Who will be responsible for the final agreement?
- Should the EU commission take part in the negotiations?
- What happens if affected third countries refuse to participate in the CCCTB dispute rcsolution procedures?

CONCLUDING REMARKS

The chapter shows that the overlaps between the CCCTB and transfer pricing rules do not yet seem to be resolved in all aspects. There are questions on documentation and the relationship to Article 9 (and Article 7) OECD MC that need to be studied in more detail and for which answers have to be found to avoid possible losses in tax revenue. These issues should be of highest importance in the negotiations taking place in the European Council working group on direct taxation.

2. Taxation of EU-non-resident-companies under the CCCTB system: Analysis and suggestions for improvement

Eric C.C.M. Kemmeren and Daniël S. Smit

2.1 INTRODUCTION

Ever since its establishment the European Union has sought to create a level playing field for companies operating in Europe, so that European multinationals can compete successfully with their foreign counterparts. However, it is common knowledge that the existence of 2 different company taxation regimes within the Union distorts intra-Union trade and investment. It is true that the Court of Justice of the European Union (CJ) has already removed a large number of company tax distortions by interpreting the Treaty freedoms in a rather extensive fashion. The CJ, however, has its limits and cannot abolish all the existing distortions resulting from 2 different company taxation regimes existing side by side. The removal of tax obstacles, such as double taxation resulting from transfer pricing mismatches or the lack of cross-border loss relief, ultimately requires action by the Union legislator. However, up until now, only a modest degree of harmonization in the area of company taxation within the Union has been established.[1] Since Member States have been reluctant to give up much sovereignty in taxation matters, company tax

[1] Some degree of harmonization has been achieved through the implementation of Council Directive (EEC) 90/435 on the common system of taxation applicable in the case of parent companies and subsidiaries of different Member States [1990] OJ L225, 6; Council Directive (EC) 2009/133 on the common system of taxation applicable to mergers, divisions, partial divisions, transfers of assets and exchanges of shares concerning companies of different Member States and to the transfer of the registered office of an SE or SCE between Member States [2009] OJ L310, 34; and Directive (EC) 2003/49 on a common system of

systems of the 27 Member States nowadays still show substantial differences as a result of which patterns of investments between the Member States may still easily be distorted.

In 2004, however, the European Commission launched an ambitious project which seeks to introduce within the Union a Common Consolidated Corporate Tax Base and on 16 March 2011, the Commission has published its proposal for a Common Consolidated Corporate Tax Base (CCCTB).[2] The main goal of this ambitious proposal is to tackle some major tax obstacles resulting from the 2 different corporate income tax systems that currently exist within the European Union. It essentially says that groups of companies that opt for the CCCTB regime would have to apply only one single set of tax rules and deal with only one tax administration within the EU. According to the Commission, the proposal is expected to provide considerable benefits for companies operating in the EU as it eliminates transfer pricing formalities, provides for the possibility of cross-border loss relief and tax-free intra-group reorganizations and reduces tax compliance costs.

The CCCTB will only be applicable within the European Union. That is to say, non-EU Member States will not take part in the CCCTB project. Hence, companies established outside the Union (EU-non-resident companies) will not be able to benefit from the proposed regime in their state of residence. This does not mean, however, that the CCCTB is completely of no relevance for EU-non-resident companies, rather the contrary. A large number of non-EU-based enterprises are carrying on business in the European Union through the operation of branches or subsidiaries established in one or more EU Member States.[3] The overall

taxation applicable to interest and royalty payments made between associated companies of different Member States [2003] OJ L157, 49.

[2] See Proposal for a Council Directive on a Common Consolidated Corporate Tax Base (CCCTB), COM(2011) 121/4. Time constraints did not allow to also include in this paper the Presidency Note to the Working Party on Tax Questions – Direct Taxation on a *Proposal for a Council Directive on a Common Consolidated Corporate Tax Base (CCCTB)*, dated 16 April 2012, document 8790/12, which document was partially made accessible to the public on 11 May 2012. It contains some Presidency comments on the compromise proposal. A quick scan taught the authors that some of the suggestions produced and discussed in an earlier draft of this paper may have influenced the Presidency comments. The authors refer, for example, to the comments made in respect of Articles 4, 5, 14a, 31, 79, and 81.

[3] More in particular, the share of the Union in world foreign direct investment outflows was 34 per cent in 2006 whereas the Union had approximately 20 per cent of world foreign direct investment inflows in 2006. See, for

benefits of these investments into the Union are well-established, as recognized, for instance, by the European Commission, notably in relation to the role of such investment in creating jobs, optimizing resource allocation, transferring technology and skills, increasing competition and boosting trade.[4] Accordingly, in the relationships with non-EU Member States, 'economic openness' is key. Economic openness is also stressed, for instance, by the European Commission in its 2006 Communication 'Global Europe: Competing in the World'. According to the Commission, European economic openness is vital for creating jobs and growth in Europe and for Europe's international competitiveness. European protectionism, on the other hand, raises prices for consumers and business, and limits choice.[5] Given this, the following questions are justified:

1. To what extent does the proposed CCCTB apply to EU-non-resident companies investing within the European Union?
2. How can the CCCTB, in this context, be improved, taking into account the principle of international tax neutrality?

These questions are dealt with in this chapter.

When answering the above question, two basic case scenarios will be discussed. In the first scenario, an EU-non-resident company invests in the EU through one or more EU subsidiaries. In the second scenario, an

---

example, Eurostat, 'European Union Foreign Direct Investment Yearbook 2008' (2008) 11 and 14.

[4] See, for instance, Communication from the Commission to the Council, the European Parliament, the European Economic and Social Committee and the Committee of the Regions, 'Towards a comprehensive European international investment policy', COM (2010) 343 final, 3. Conversely, also a large number of EU-based enterprises maintain a diversified range of investments outside the Union. These outward investments are perceived to make a positive and significant contribution to the competitiveness of European enterprises as well, notably in the form of higher productivity; *ibid.* See also: Copenhagen Economics, 'Impact of EU outward FDI' (2010) 11. The latter study shows that no measurable negative impact on aggregate employment has so far been identified in relation to outward investment.

[5] Communication from the Commission to the Council, the European Parliament, the European Economic and Social Committee and the Committee of the Regions, 'Global Europe: Competing in the World', COM (2006) 567 final, 4. See also the 2005 renewed Lisbon strategy which *inter alia* highlights the need to ensure open markets around the world; Communication from President Barosso to the Spring European Council, 'Working together for growth and jobs', COM(2005) 24 final.

EU-non-resident company invests in the EU through one or more EU branches. In both cases, the question is whether the CCCTB regime can be applied to the European subsidiaries and branches of the EU-non-resident company. The outcome will subsequently be assessed in the light of the benchmark of international tax neutrality, as defined in this chapter.

The outline of this chapter is as follows: In Section 2.2, the benchmark of international tax neutrality as it is understood in this chapter will be presented. In Sections 2.3 and 2.4 the above two scenarios are dealt with in detail. Finally, Section 2.5 provides the authors' conclusions and recommendations.

2.2 THE BENCHMARK OF INTERNATIONAL TAX NEUTRALITY

As was established above, 'economic openness' is key in the relationships with non-EU Member States. In this respect, tax neutrality should prevail, i.e., taxation should not influence an efficient allocation of the production factors of capital and labour or, at least, should do so as little as possible.[6] The concept of efficiency is based on the assumption that productivity will be highest when the production factors are distributed by a market mechanism without public interference or, at least, with as little interference as possible. A given economic arrangement is efficient if there can be no rearrangement that will leave someone better off without worsening the position of others.[7] Economic considerations, not

---

[6] See, for example, Hugh J. Ault, 'Colloquium on Corporate Income Tax: Corporate Integration, Tax Treaties and the Division of the International Tax Base: Principles and Practices' (1992) 47 *Tax Law Review* 565, 572; Gary Clyde Hufbauer and Joanna M. van Rooij, *U.S. Taxation of International Income, Blueprint for Reform,* (Institute for International Economics 1992) 50; Albert Raedler and Jens Blumenberg, 'Harmonization of Corporate Income Tax Systems within the European Community' in *Report of the Committee of Independent Experts on Company Taxation* (Ruding Committee) (European Commission 1992) 441; Stephen G. Utz, 'Taxation Panel: Tax Harmonization and Coordination in Europe and America' (1994) 9 *Connecticut Journal of International Law* 785; S. Cnossen, 'Om de toekomst van de vennootschapsbelasting in de Europese Unie' (1996) *Weekblad voor Fiscaal Recht* 876 and 889–890; Sijbren Cnossen, 'Tax Policy in the European Union, A Review of Issues and Options' (2001) Valedictory Address, Erasmus University Rotterdam 3.

[7] See, for example, Richard A. Musgrave and Peggy B. Musgrave, *Public Finance in Theory and Practice* (McGraw-Hill Book Company 1989) 60.

tax motives, should determine the behaviour of economic operators.[8] Complete neutrality is probably not possible but, from an efficiency perspective, the highest possible level of neutrality should be pursued. Other values, like equity, may justify a deviation from this rule in specific situations.

In the scholarly literature, various approaches to international tax neutrality can be identified. Traditionally, the focus is either on an optimal allocation of savings (under capital import neutrality), an optimal allocation of production (under capital export neutrality) or an optimal allocation of ownership (under capital ownership neutrality).[9] The problem of these neutrality benchmarks is, however, that they focus on one element of transnational investment only (savings, production or ownership). It is difficult to see, however, how neutrality could be achieved when focussing on one element only.[10] In the authors' opinion, the benchmark of international tax neutrality should therefore be approached in a different fashion. In the authors' opinion, international tax neutrality implies that the *relation between taxes (burdens) and public goods (benefits)* should not be disturbed to the disadvantage of transnational investment. This is because the effect of taxes cannot be isolated from the overall effects of all other state-induced transaction and production costs and benefits.[11] Under this condition, fair competition between foreign and domestic enterprises which carry on the same genuine economic activities under the same market conditions and using the same public

---

[8] See, for example, Otto Gandenberger, 'Der Einfluß der Einkommen- und Körperschaftsteuer auf die internationalen Wirtschaftsströme' in Klaus Vogel (ed.), *Grundfragen des Internationalen Steuerrechts* (Dr. Otto Schmidt 1985), 36–37; Richard Doernberg, *International Taxation in a Nutshell* (West Group 1999) 3–6 and US JCT (Joint Committee on Taxation), 'Reports on International Taxation' (1999) Tax Notes International 92. Disagreeing: for example, D. Juch, 'Internationaal fiscaal (verdragen)recht' (1999) MBB 116. Considering some reports on harmful tax competition, some states seem to pursue a policy deviating from this concept of tax neutrality. See for example OECD, *Harmful Tax Competition, An Emerging Global Issue,* (OECD 1998) and the EU report from the Code of Conduct Group (Business Taxation), Brussels, 23 November 1999 (SN4901/99) to ECOFIN Council on 29 November 1999.

[9] See, for example, OECD, 'Taxing Profits in a Global Economy' (1991), 39 (as concerns CIN and CEN) and M.A. Desai and J.R. Hines, 'Evaluating International Tax Reform' (June 2003) *National Tax Journal* 487–502 (as concerns CON).

[10] Compare: K. Vogel, 'Worldwide vs. source taxation of income – A review and re-evaluation of arguments (Part II)' (1988) *Intertax* 313.

[11] K. Vogel, *Taxation of Cross-border Income, Harmonization, and Tax Neutrality under European Community Law* (Kluwer 1994) 26.

goods in that state to the same extent is promoted. Taxation on the basis of residence is incompatible with such a neutrality approach since no state can ensure that foreign investments made by its residents are subject to the same transaction- and other state-induced costs and benefits. International tax neutrality therefore implies adherence to a system of source state-based taxation. That is to say, income should be taxed only in the state where that income has been generated. This is because the public facilities provided by that state contributed to the operation of the profit-making activities.[12]

The subsequent question that must be addressed is how one should determine in which state a source of income is situated. In the authors' view, the case law of the CJ in the context of the freedom of establishment provides practical guidelines in this respect. From this case law, one can infer that the concept of establishment is essentially an economic concept and implies a genuine economic link with the territory of a Member State through the exercise of a genuine economic activity.[13] The notion of economic activity under EU law could be characterized by an activity, not being of a purely marginal or ancillary nature, which is usually carried out, on a continuing basis, by a private undertaking on a market with a business or commercial purpose, in particular the wish to maximize returns from capital invested.[14] A company can carry on a genuine economic activity directly. However, a company which, owning controlling shareholdings in another company, actually exercises that control by involving itself directly or indirectly in the management

---

12 See also, more elaborately, Eric C.C.M. Kemmeren, *Principle of Origin in Tax Conventions, A Rethinking of Models*, Dissertation Tilburg University (Eric C.C.M. Kemmeren/Pijnenburg vormgevers·uitgevers 2001) 177–181 (also available on: http://www.tilburguniversity.edu/nl/webwijs/show/&anr=304239&lang=en?anr=304239&lang=en, accessed 13 September 2012); K. Vogel, *Taxation of Cross-border Income, Harmonization, and Tax Neutrality under European Community Law* (Kluwer 1994).

13 *Cf.* Opinion of Advocate General Case C-81/87 *Daily Mail and General Trust PLC* [1988] ECR 5483, point 3 and point 5.

14 See, for example, Case C-176/96 *Lehtonen* [2000] ECR I-2681, paras 42-44; Cases C-180/98 to C-184/98 *Pavlov and Others* [2000] ECR I-6451, para 75 and Opinion of Advocate General Case C-77/01 *EDM* [2004] ECR I-4295, points 44-46. See more elaborately: D.S. Smit, Freedom of investment between EU and non-EU Member States and its impact on corporate income tax systems within the European Union (dissertation Tilburg 2011) 46 et seq.

thereof must be regarded as taking part in the economic activity carried on by the controlled undertaking.[15]

Such a source-based taxation is in substance taxation based on the principle of origin. An origin-based taxation justifies taxation of income by a state if the income is created within the territory of that state, i.e. the cause of the income is within the territory of that state. That state makes the yield or the acquisition of wealth possible. Whereas the causal relationship between production of income and the territory of a state is predominant under the principle of origin, it is of minor or no importance under the principle of source. Therefore, the principle of origin and the principle of source are not necessarily identical. If the income is not generated in a state but, nevertheless, physically appears to be from that state, tax jurisdiction may be allocated to that state on the basis of the principle of source, but not on the principle of origin.[16] Nevertheless, for the purposes of this chapter the authors will use the term 'source' since it is commonly used, but it will be used as meaning 'origin'. Furthermore, it should be noted that an activity of a person who only hops in and out of a state and produces income in that state generally lacks a sufficient nexus, a sufficient economic relationship with that state to justify taxation. For the allocation of tax jurisdiction on income from activities, a substantial relationship between the activity and the state concerned is required. Such a sufficient relationship should be considered present if a substantial income-producing activity is exercised in the state concerned. An income-producing activity is considered to be substantial if such an activity forms an essential and significant part of the activity as a whole.[17]

The EU law concept of establishment may find expression in the form of (the setting-up of) agencies, branches or subsidiaries.[18] It furthermore

---

[15] *Cf., inter alia*, Case C-222/04 *Cassa di Risparmio di Firenze and others* [2006] ECR I-289, paras 109–110.

[16] Therefore, in the authors' view, it is not self-evident that the principle of source, as used generally, may serve as a justification for a tax on income, since the income may be produced or the property may be established and preserved in another state than where the person from which the income has been received or the property concerned is physically situated. See also, more elaborately, Eric C.C.M. Kemmeren, *Principle of Origin in Tax Conventions, A Rethinking of Models*, Dissertation Tilburg University (Eric C.C.M. Kemmeren/Pijnenburg vormgevers·uitgevers, Dongen 2001) 33–35.

[17] See also, more elaborately, Eric C.C.M. Kemmeren, *Principle of Origin in Tax Conventions, A Rethinking of Models*, Dissertation Tilburg University (Eric C.C.M. Kemmeren/Pijnenburg vormgevers·uitgevers, Dongen 2001) 35–45.

[18] Case C-55/94, *Gebhard* [1995] ECR I-4165, para 24.

involves a sufficient degree of independence and a sufficient degree of management and control within that Member State.[19] In the case of companies, this implies that a company's essential decisions concerning the general management of that company and the functions of its central administration are carried out in that Member State.[20] The concept of branch under EU law, in addition, implies a place of business which has the appearance of permanency, has a management and is materially equipped to negotiate business with third parties.[21,22]

It follows from the above that a clear relationship appears to exist between the benchmark of international tax neutrality, on the one hand, and the prerequisite of a genuine economic link under the freedom of establishment, on the other. International tax neutrality implies that income should be taxed only in the state to which that income can economically be linked. In the context of this chapter, this means in basic

---

19 Case C-221/89, *Factortame Ltd and others* [1991] ECR I-3905, para 34.

20 Case C-73/06, *Planzer* [2007] ECR I-5655, paras 60–62. Although this case concerned the interpretation of the concept of business for the purposes of Article 1(1) of Council Directive 86/560/EEC of 17 November 1986 on the harmonization of the laws of the Member States relating to turnover taxes, the factors listed by the CJ are remarkably similar to those as listed by Advocate General Darmon in his Opinion in the *Daily Mail* under the freedom of establishment; in addition, given the fact that the CJ also refers to the concept of letter box companies as mentioned in *Cadbury Schweppes*, there is little doubt that this ruling can be generalized and may be applied in the context of the freedom of establishment under the Treaty as well.

21 Case 33/78, *Somafer* [1978] ECR 2183, para 12.

22 In this context and in the context of a source-based taxation, the authors think that only individuals can create income and things in themselves cannot. The intellectual element is the key component for the production of income. Through the action of an individual, with or without using a device, in other words, a capital component, value may be added to things. We believe that, in a lot of cases, the person of the recipient and the originator of the income will coincide. However, it is also possible that they do not coincide. If the income received is produced to a substantial extent through activities of an independent person, in other words, he is the person who adds the intellectual element, and the benefits from such activities do not regard this person, but are passed on to another person, in other words, the income recipient, then the income does not originate with the recipient but with that independent person, in other words, the originator. We think that such an independent person with respect to the income passed on can in substance be put on a par economically with a person dependent on the income recipient, for instance an employee. See also, more elaborately, Eric C.C.M. Kemmeren, *Principle of Origin in Tax Conventions, A Rethinking of Models*, Dissertation Tilburg University (Eric C.C.M. Kemmeren/Pijnenburg vormgevers·uitgevers, Dongen 2001) 37–40.

terms that the CCCT-Base should include EU-sourced income derived by EU-non-resident companies and, conversely, exclude non-EU-sourced income derived by EU-resident companies. As said before, the focus in this chapter will only be on EU-non-resident companies investing in the EU. It will be examined in the subsequent sections the extent to which the CCCTB regime can be applied to European investments by those EU-non-resident companies and whether this is in line with the benchmark of international tax neutrality.

2.3 FIRST SCENARIO: EU-NON-RESIDENT COMPANY INVESTS IN THE EU THROUGH ONE OR MORE EU SUBSIDIARIES

2.3.1 EU-Non-Resident Company Holds First- and Second-Tier EU Subsidiary

The first case scenario can be split up into three main sub-categories. In the first sub-category, an EU-non-resident company holds a first- and second-tier EU subsidiary in different Member States. This situation can be depicted as follows:

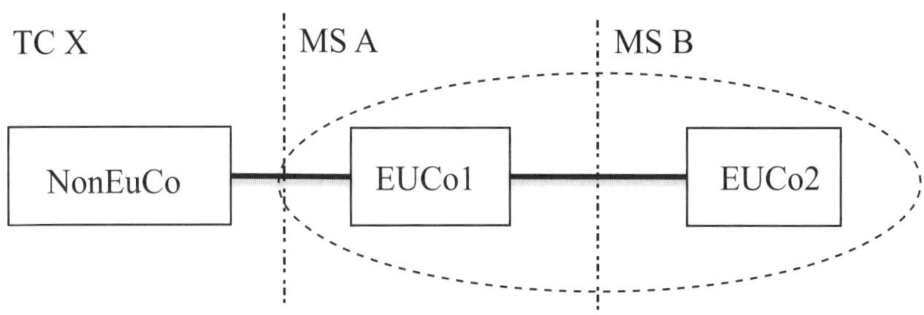

Figure 2.1 Scenario 1

It is assumed that both the first-tier (EUCo1) and the second-tier EU subsidiary (EUCo2) qualify as eligible companies within the meaning of Article 2 CCCTB. That is to say, both companies are tax resident in a Member State under the tax laws of that Member State, take one of the forms listed in Annex I of the proposed Directive and are subject to one of the corporate taxes listed in Annex II of the proposed Directive. The question is the extent to which EUCo1 can opt for the CCCTB regime given that this company is ultimately held by a non-EU parent company (Non-EUCo).

2.3.1.1 Tax residence of first-tier EU subsidiary

The question is whether EUCo1 can opt for the CCCTB regime. As a general rule, this question must be answered in the affirmative. Hence, the fact that EUCo1 is ultimately controlled by a non-EU parent company is immaterial in this regard. This is fully in line with the freedom of establishment and the CJ case law. The freedom of establishment may not be made dependent on satisfying further conditions concerning the nationality of the shareholders or directors of EUCo1.[23] It is true that a proposal to that end was put forward during the negotiations of the EC Treaty in order to prevent companies from third countries from having access to the right of establishment simply by setting up 'letter-box' companies. This proposal was, however, rejected.[24]

Article 6(3) CCCTB puts beyond doubt that a company that has its registered office, place of incorporation or place of effective management in a Member State must be considered resident for tax purposes in that Member State, unless such company is regarded as tax resident in a third country under the terms of an agreement concluded by that Member State with that third country. This tie-breaker rule may be relevant when the EU-non-resident company is not merely exercising its shareholder rights over its EU first-tier-subsidiary EUCo1, but is in substance involved in the key management and commercial decisions of this subsidiary. In such a case, the place of effective management of EUCo1 may be in Third Country X. Assuming that a tax treaty exists between Member State A and Third Country X and that it contains a tie-breaker rule similar to Article 4(3) of the OECD Model Tax Convention (hereinafter OECD Model), EUCo1 is considered to be a third-country tax resident for purposes of the CCCTB in such a case. As a result, it will not be able to benefit from the CCCTB rules, unless a permanent establishment (PE) remains in Member State A.[25]

---

23 See Case C-299/02 *Commission v. Netherlands* [2004] ECR I-9761, para 19 and Opinion of Advocate General Léger Case C-299/02 *Commission v. Netherlands* [2004] ECR I-9761, point 38.

24 *Cf.*, for example, J. Wouters, *Het Europese vestigingsrecht voor ondernemingen herbekeken*, Dissertation Leuven (1996–1997) 127; Opinion of Advocate General Léger C-299/02, *Commission v. Netherlands* [2004] ECR I-9761, point 39.

25 This scenario is further elaborated on in Section 2.4.

It is also conceivable that the managerial activities of non-EUCo do not transfer the place of effective management of EUCo1 to Third Country X, but that these management activities nonetheless constitute a PE of EUCo1 in Third Country X.[26] The question is whether EUCo1 can still opt for the CCCTB in such a case. This question must be answered in the affirmative. Based on Article 4(4) CCCTB, EUCo1 qualifies as a resident taxpayer. Pursuant to Article 55(1)(c) CCCTB, a resident taxpayer forms a group with all its qualifying subsidiaries resident in one or more Member States. It is immaterial that the resident taxpayer has a PE in a third country. Hence, EUCo1 should be able to benefit from the CCCTB regime. However, income which is attributable to the management PE in Third Country X should be exempt pursuant to Article 11(e) CCCTB[27] or, alternatively, based on the applicable tax treaty between Member State A and Third Country X.

One can conclude that in the above scenario no peculiarities arise. It can be established that the idea of economic openness is leading under the CCCTB proposal, meaning that, as a general rule, the CCCTB regime should normally apply to first- and second-tier subsidiaries established in different Member States, irrespective of the fact that these subsidiaries are ultimately held by a non-EU parent. This is also in line with the benchmark of international tax neutrality. However, the fact the ultimate parent is in a non-EU Member State may, under circumstances, raise issues on the place of management of the first-tier subsidiary.

2.3.1.2 Intra-group payments and withholding taxes

In the previous section, the focus was on the application of the CCCTB regime on first- and second-tier subsidiaries held by a non-EU parent company. In this section, the focus is domestic withholding taxes on dividend, interest and royalty payments between the said companies.

2.3.1.2.1 Relationship between non-EU parent and first-tier subsidiary Firstly, the relationship between the non-EU parent and its first-tier subsidiary is examined. In this regard, Article 77 CCCTB is relevant. This provision stipulates that interest and royalties paid by a taxpayer to a recipient outside the group (outbound payments) may be subject to a withholding tax in the Member State of the taxpayer according to the applicable rules of national law and any applicable

---

[26] *Cf.* Article 5(2) OECD Model and Article 5(1)(a) CCCTB on the basis of which a place of management may constitute a permanent establishment.

[27] This provision stipulates that income of a PE in a third country is exempt from corporate tax.

double tax convention (DTC). Based on the same provision, the withholding tax must be shared among the Member States according to the formula applicable in the tax year in which the tax is charged pursuant to Articles 86 to 102 CCCTB. In other words, in the case scenario at hand, Member State A is allowed to levy withholding tax on interest and royalty payments made to its parent in Third Country X, but it has to share the tax withheld with other Member States. Interestingly, Article 77 CCCTB is not concerned with dividend payments. Does this mean that Member States are completely disallowed to levy any withholding tax on dividend payments to third-country parents? That would mean that Member States would unilaterally abolish their withholding tax regimes in their relations with third countries under the CCCTB regime. In the authors' view, it is difficult to believe that this is really intended. The more plausible interpretation would be that Member States are also free to levy withholding tax on outbound dividend payments, but that the sharing mechanism does not apply to those payments. This interpretation also makes sense if one realizes that dividend payments are, unlike interest and royalty payments, non-deductible under the CCCTB regime. Hence, the deduction of interest and royalty payments affects the CCC tax base – which justifies the sharing mechanism for withholding taxes – whereas dividend payments do not. In the authors' view, the CCCTB proposal is simply silent on outbound dividend payments, as a result of which each Member State should remain entitled to levy withholding tax on outbound dividend payments.

2.3.1.2.2 Relation between EU first- and second-tier subsidiaries Now let us focus on dividend, interest and royalty payments between the first-tier and second-tier subsidiary. Can these payments be subject to withholding tax by the Member States? The answer is no. Firstly, Article 60 CCCTB provides that no withholding taxes or other source taxation shall be charged on transactions between members of a group. Hence, in the case scenario under consideration, dividend, interest and royalty payments between EUCo1 and EUCo2 should be free of withholding tax. This is even so if these Member States were to be allowed to levy withholding tax under the applicable tax treaty. This is because Article 8 CCCTB provides that the provisions of the Directive override existing agreements between Member States.

The ban on intra-Union withholding taxes within the CCCTB regime is fully understandable. In the absence of such a provision, Member States could have a possibility to frustrate 'through the backdoor' the functioning of the CCCTB by the levy of an income tax in the form of a (non-harmonized) withholding tax on intra-group payments parallel to

CCCTB tax on items of income which are part of the (harmonized) CCC tax base at the same time.[28] The question is, however, what the impact is of Article 60 CCCTB in the following situation. Assume in the current case scenario that Member State A does not levy any withholding tax on outbound dividends and that EUCo1 was solely interposed to circumvent withholding tax which would have been due if the non-EU parent had invested directly in the second-tier subsidiary EUCo2 established in Member State B. A number of Member States, such as Spain[29] and Germany,[30] have anti-tax avoidance provisions in force in such cases under which the interposed company is effectively ignored. The question arises whether Member State B is allowed to apply its anti-tax avoidance rules in such a case under the proposal. A second question that may arise

---

[28] Assuming, of course, that these withholding taxes would not be in conflict with the TFEU freedoms, the Parent-Subsidiary Directive and/or the Interest & Royalty Directive.

[29] Under Spanish law, a specific anti-directive-shopping clause applies on the basis of which the exemption for withholding tax under the Parent-Subsidiary Directive is denied where the majority of voting rights in an EU parent are directly or indirectly held by non-EU residents. The withholding tax exemption is nevertheless granted where the taxpayer can prove that: i) the business of the parent company is directly linked with the business of the Spanish subsidiary; or ii) the purpose of the parent company is management of the Spanish subsidiary through the organization of human and material means; or iii) the parent company is incorporated for sound economic reasons and not to unduly benefit from the exemption. See in more detail: D.S. Smit and C.A.T. Peters, 'Report on the 1st Conference on Recent Tax Treaty Case Law, European Tax College, the Netherlands' (2011) *Intertax* 227–228.

[30] K. Nakhai and T. Wagner, 'Germany Amends Anti-Treaty-Shopping Rules' (December 2011) *Tax Notes International* 773–776. These authors report that from 1 January 2012 a foreign company that receives a payment subject to German withholding tax will be entitled to withholding tax relief to the extent (i) the company is owned by shareholders that would be entitled to a corresponding benefit under a tax treaty or an EU directive had they received the income directly; or (ii) the foreign company's gross receipts in the relevant year are generated from its genuine own business activities. If the foreign company fails both tests (that is, if the foreign company is not owned by shareholders that would have benefited from the same relief had they earned the income directly and if the company did not earn the gross receipts in connection with its genuine own business activities), the company would be entitled to withholding tax relief only if it meets the following two additional tests: (i) *Business purpose test*: There are economic or other relevant (that is, non-tax) reasons for the interposition of the foreign company in relation to the above-mentioned receipts; (ii) S*ubstance test*: The foreign company has adequate business substance to engage in its trade or business and participates in general commerce.

is whether the anti-avoidance provisions included in the tax directives, notably Article 1(2) of the Parent-Subsidiary Directive[31] and Article 5 of the Interest & Royalty Directive,[32] can be applied in the context of the CCCTB. These questions are open to debate. On the one hand, the wording of Article 60 CCCTB is formulated in a rather absolute fashion. It does not allow for exceptions based on anti-abuse considerations, even though the draughtsmen of the Directive must reasonably speaking have been aware of the above possibility of abuse. On that basis, one could argue that the first question must be answered in the negative. In addition, on the basis of Article 7 CCCTB, domestic provisions required for the prevention of abuse which are allowed under the Parent-Subsidiary Directive and the Interest & Royalty Directive cannot be applied either, because they are part of the Member States' national corporate tax arrangements in the meaning of Article 7 CCCTB.[33] In addition, based on Article 8 CCCTB, agreement-based provisions required for the prevention of abuse which are also allowed under the Parent-Subsidiary Directive and the Interest & Royalty Directive cannot be applied either.[34] It is also debatable whether the general anti-avoidance clause of Article 80 CCCTB[35] can be applied. This is because this provision only aims at combating tax avoidance under the harmonized CCCTB, i.e. artificial transactions can only be ignored for the purposes of calculating the tax base of the CCCTB. By analogy to the CJ's

---

[31] This provision stipulates that this directive does not preclude the application of domestic or agreement-based provisions required for the prevention of abuse.

[32] This provision lays down that this directive does not preclude the application of domestic or agreement-based provisions required for the prevention of abuse, and that benefits of this directive may be refused or withdrawn in the case of transactions for which the principal motive or one of the principal motives is tax avoidance or abuse.

[33] Article 7 CCCTB provides that a CCCTB company ceases to be subject to national corporate tax arrangements of all matters regulated by the CCCTB Directive unless stated otherwise.

[34] Article 8 CCCTB provides that the CCCTB Directive shall apply notwithstanding any provision to the contrary in any agreement concluded between Member States.

[35] This provision states that artificial transactions carried out for the sole purpose of avoiding taxation shall be ignored for the purposes of calculating the tax base, unless genuine commercial activities are carried out and the taxpayer chooses the most tax-efficient transaction to realize a commercial result which could also be realized through less tax-efficient transactions.

decision in *Zwijnenburg*[36] it is therefore questionable whether this provision can be relied on to combat the avoidance of another tax, such as withholding taxes on dividend or interest and royalties. On this basis, one could defend the position that the second question must be answered in the negative as well.

On the other hand, one could also argue that the scope of protection provided by the norms of an EU tax directive is, by itself, restricted as not to cover abusive practices. Van Kesteren, for example, submits that the norms laid down in an EU directive intrinsically possess the eminent quality of not being available for abusive practices going beyond the goal of the directive.[37] This position finds support in *AUER*. This case concerned the interpretation of the Capital Duty Directive 69/335,[38] which does not contain any specific anti-abuse provision. In this case the CJ acknowledged that the directive at issue does not contain any rule specifically designed to prevent the risk of tax avoidance. It nonetheless ruled that:

> the formation of a company in a Member State under wholly artificial arrangements which do not reflect economic reality, with the aim of avoiding the tax normally payable, goes beyond the protection which Directive 69/335 must afford to the companies to which it applies.[39]

An additional argument can be found in the *Kofoed* case. The principle that the abuse of rights is not allowed also has its impact on directives in the field of direct taxation. A claim to the benefits of a directive will be refused if this claim results in an abuse of rights laid down in the directive concerned. The general principle that abuse of rights is not

---

[36] CJ C-352/08 *Zwijnenburg* [2010] ECR I-4303.

[37] H.W.M. van Kesteren, *Misbruik van recht in de omzetbelasting*. Inaugural address Tilburg (Kluwer 2004) 10. Van Kesteren illustrates this position by submitting that general principles of law, including the principle that the law should not be abused, can be seen as a sort of DNA which forms part of each rule of primary and secondary EU law. This is because one can reasonably assume that the European legislator took these principles into account as guidelines when drafting EU legislation. The general principle of abuse of law thus evaporates as an independent legal source, but not as a source of law because it becomes inherent part of the genetic material (or DNA) of each rule of EU law.

[38] Council Directive 69/335/EEC relating to the approximation of the laws of the Member States concerning indirect taxes on the raising of capital.

[39] Case C-251/06 *Firma ING. AUER* [2007] ECR I-9689, paras 40 et seq.

allowed may also be explicitly reflected in a specific directive provision, like Article 15(1)(a) of the Merger Directive. In the *Kofoed* case, the CJ ruled:

> Thus, Article 11(1)(a) Directive 90/434 [now Article 15(1)(a) Directive 2009/133/EC] reflects the general Community principle that abuse of rights is prohibited. Individuals must not improperly or fraudulently take advantage of provisions of Community law. The application of Community legislation cannot be extended to cover abusive practices, that is to say, transactions carried out not in the context of normal commercial operations, but solely for the purpose of wrongfully obtaining advantages provided for by Community law (see, to that effect, Case C-212/97 *Centros* [1999] ECR I-1459, paragraph 24; Case C-255/02 *Halifax and Others* [2006] ECR I-1609, paragraphs 68 and 69; Case C-456/04 *Agip Petroli* [2006] ECR I-3395, paragraphs 19 and 20; and Case C-196/04 *Cadbury Schweppes and Cadbury Schweppes Overseas* [2006] ECR I-7995, paragraph 35).[40]

On that basis, one could argue that the above questions must be answered in the positive. In other words, Member States would remain free to apply their domestic anti-tax avoidance rules in order to combat the circumvention of their domestic withholding taxes on dividend, interest and/or royalty payments as long as they meet the above-mentioned EU law standards.

In the authors' view, the second approach is preferable. Otherwise, companies that fall under the CCCTB regime would be better off than their competitors that fall outside the scope of the CCCTB. This result would be undesirable and would also contravene the benchmark of international tax neutrality. Nonetheless, the authors submit that for the sake of clarity a specific anti-tax avoidance rule should be included in the CCCTB proposal aiming at combating the above type of tax avoidance schemes. Based on the international tax neutrality benchmark, Member States should be allowed – or preferably even required – to levy withholding tax in the above scenario if the receiving company EUCo1 qualifies as an establishment which does not carry on any genuine economic activity in the territory of Member State A, or which carries on a genuine economic activity, but with which the income derived is not connected or to which it is not incidental. Consequently, the right of

---

[40] Case C-321/05 *Kofoed* [2007] I-5795, para 38.

Member States to levy withholding tax on outbound dividend, interest and royalty payments would not be jeopardized.[41]

2.3.1.3 Miscellaneous: interest payments from first- or second-tier EU subsidiary to EU-non-resident company

In the case scenario under consideration, it is conceivable that the non-EU parent company will provide funds to its EU first- and/or second-tier subsidiaries by providing a loan. The question is whether interest payments paid on such loans are deductible under the CCCTB regime. The proposed directive provides for a specific rule for the deductibility of interest payments made to an associated enterprise resident in a third country under Article 81. In brief, this provision stipulates that such interest payments are non-deductible if the creditor is not sufficiently taxed in its third country of residence. The ban on interest deductions only applies if the creditor is established in a third country which has not concluded an agreement on the exchange of information comparable to the exchange of information on request provided for in the Mutual Assistance Directive[42] with the Member State where the debtor is established.[43] Consequently, interest deduction is not denied if the creditor is established in a third country that is under a treaty obligation to exchange information on request with the Member State involved.[44] This condition should be placed in the light of the case law of the CJ concerning the free movement of capital under Article 63 TFEU, which right extends to the relationships with third countries as well. From this case law one can infer that Member States are allowed to refuse a certain tax benefit in the relations with third countries if such a third country is under no international obligation to exchange information with the Member State involved.[45] The Commission has indicated that the 'no exchange of information' condition is included in order to comply with

---

[41] See in greater detail: D.S. Smit, 'Freedom of investment between EU and non-EU Member States and its impact on corporate income tax systems within the European Union', Dissertation Tilburg (2011) Chapters IX and X.

[42] Council Directive 2011/16/EU on administrative cooperation in the field of taxation and repealing Directive 77/799/EEC, OJ 2011 L 64, 1-12.

[43] See European Commission, Workshop 'Anti-Abuse Rules in the CCCTB' CCCTB/RD\004\, 30 August 2010, p. 5.

[44] See in more detail on the minimum standard for exchange of information Section 2.4.4.3.

[45] See, for example, Case C-101/05, *Skatteverket v. A* [2007] ECR I-11531, point 63.

this case law.[46] However, the Commission seems to infer from this case law *by analogy* that a specific ban on interest deduction is not allowed at all once the creditor is established in a third country with which there is an agreement on the exchange of information comparable to the exchange of information on request provided for in the Mutual Assistance Directive. In the authors' view, this is too restrictive an interpretation of the above-mentioned case law. One could therefore legitimately wonder whether this requirement renders the application of Article 81 CCCTB illusory. This is because interest deduction will not be denied as long as the creditor is established in a low- or non-tax third country which is under a treaty obligation to exchange information on request with the Member State involved.[47] This holds all the more if one realizes that the number of information exchange agreements concluded by third countries has increased dramatically over the past years. It is therefore submitted that the inclusion of the 'no exchange of information' condition should be reconsidered.

In principle, interest deduction is disallowed if the creditor is, under the general regime in the third country, subject to a low statutory tax rate in its third country of residence or if the creditor is subject to a special regime in that third country which allows for a substantially lower level of taxation than that of the general regime. A general low tax rate is present where a statutory corporate tax rate applies in the third country which is lower than 40 per cent of the average statutory corporate tax rate applicable in the Member States. The effective tax rate is therefore not relevant. This approach has the benefit of foreseeability, but one could wonder whether adherence to the statutory rather than to the effective tax rate only fully meets the objective of Article 81 CCCTB (i.e. to combat tax base erosion through excessive debt financing). The second test of a special regime must be placed in this light. This is a more substantive test which shows substantial similarities with the definition of state aid under the Treaty and the definition of potentially harmful tax measures under the Code of Conduct for Business Taxation.

However, notwithstanding the fact that the creditor is low taxed or benefits from a special regime, interest deduction is still allowed if the creditor meets the stock exchange test, as defined in Article 81(3)(a) CCCTB or the business activities test, as defined in Article 81(3)(b) CCCTB. The same holds true if the interest receivable is already included

---

46 See European Commission, Workshop 'Anti-Abuse Rules in the CCCTB' CCCTB/RD\004\, 30 August 2010, p. 5.

47 In the same vein: D. Weber, 'Note to Article 81' (2011) *Highlights & Insights on European Taxation Year* 4, No 6, 59.

in the CCC tax base through the mechanism of the CFC rule of Article 82 CCCTB. As far as the first two safe-harbour tests are concerned, one could wonder whether these tests are really suitable in the light of the rationale of Article 81 CCCTB. After all, artificial or excessive debt financing could also occur if the creditor is a listed company or if the creditor is engaged in an active conduct of a trade or business.

It follows from the above that Article 81 CCCTB has some weaknesses. In the authors' opinion, Article 81 CCCTB would be more effective if it were drafted as a general anti-tax avoidance clause, stating that interest deduction is denied if the principal aim of the loan arrangement was to reduce the CCC tax base.[48] If the creditor is established in a 'suspect' third country, in particular a third country in which a generally low corporate income tax rate applies or which is not under any international obligation to exchange information with the Member State concerned, the taxpayer should prove that the principal aim for the loan arrangement was not to reduce the CCC tax base. Hence, under these circumstances, the threshold for interest deduction should be raised by introducing a presumption of abuse. In addition, interest deduction should be denied if the creditor is established in a third country where a special tax regime applies for financing activities that would qualify as state aid under the Treaty provisions. This is because in an intra-Union context, the benefits of such a tax regime would be neutralized under the state aid procedure, notably by means of a mandatory repayment of the benefits received. In a third-country context, the state aid rules do not apply. As a consequence, it should be acceptable that the benefits of a special tax regime applicable in the third country where the creditor is established are neutralized by a ban on interest deduction at the level of the debtor.[49] In this way, not only a tailor-made solution can be provided, but also the benchmark of international tax neutrality is better served.

---

[48] The underlying assumption of this rule is that the interest deduction creates a problem. However, it could be argued that the interest deduction is not the problem, but not taxing the interest income in the hands of the creditor in the state of origin. See further, for example, E.C.C.M. Kemmeren, 'Renteaftrek is niet het probleem in de vennootschapsbelasting; wel het niet-belasten van rente!' (2009) 138 *Weekblad Fiscaal Recht* 6806, 401–411.

[49] See also: D.S. Smit, 'Freedom of investment between EU and non-EU Member States and its impact on corporate income tax systems within the European Union', Dissertation Tilburg (2011) 629 et seq.

2.3.2 EU Sister Companies commonly held by EU-Non-Resident Company

In this section, the second sub-category of the main case scenario is discussed. Under this scenario, an EU-non-resident company holds two first-tier EU subsidiaries in different Member States. This situation can be depicted as follows:

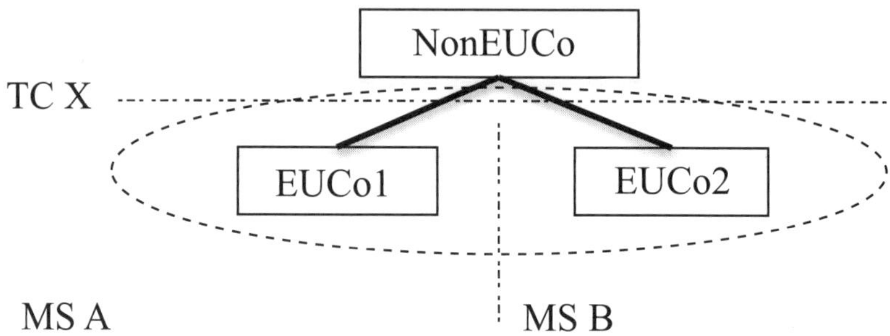

Figure 2.2 Scenario 2

The question is whether the EU subsidiaries can benefit from the CCCTB regime given that their ultimate parent is established in a third country. From Article 55(1)(d) CCCTB it follows that this question must be answered in the affirmative. Based on this provision, a resident taxpayer must form a group with other resident taxpayers which are qualifying subsidiaries of the same company which is resident in a third country. This is, however, under the condition that the third-country company has a similar form to one of the forms listed in Annex I of the proposed Directive. Under this condition, the fact that the European sister companies EUCo1 and EUCo2 are ultimately controlled by a non-EU parent company is immaterial. Hence, the CCCTB regime is territorially oriented in this regard. In the authors' view, this is fully in line with the benchmark of international tax neutrality.

For the sake of completeness, it is observed in this respect that a related issue is being currently examined by the European Commission in an infringement procedure against the Netherlands. In this procedure, the Netherlands fiscal unity regime is under scrutiny. Like the CCCTB, this regime provides for group taxation on a consolidated basis. However, the Netherlands fiscal group consolidation rules exclude fiscal unities between two Netherlands subsidiary companies in the same group, held by a foreign parent company. The European Commission takes the view that this constitutes a restriction of the freedom of establishment provided for by the Treaty on the Functioning of the European Union and the European Economic Area Agreement.[50]

2.3.3 'Papillon' Investment: EU-Resident Company holds First-Tier Non-EU Subsidiary and Second-Tier EU Subsidiary

In this section, the third sub-category of the main case scenario is discussed. Under this scenario, an EU-resident company holds a second-tier EU subsidiary through a first-tier non-EU subsidiary. This situation can be depicted as follows:

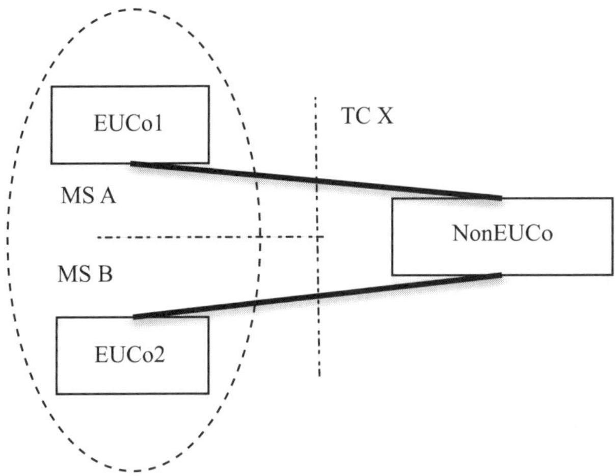

Figure 2.3 Scenario 3

The question is whether the EU parent and the EU second-tier subsidiary can benefit from the CCCTB regime, given that the intermediate company is established in a third country. From the technical outline published by the Commission on 26 July 2007, one could infer that this situation would also fall under the scope of the CCCTB regime.[51] However, the wording of Article 55 CCCTB could raise some doubts whether this situation is also governed by the proposal. The only provision that could cover this situation is Article 55(1)(d) CCCTB. As

[50] See Press Release IP/11/719, 16 June 2011.

[51] European Commission, Working Document 'CCCTB: Possible Elements of a Technical Outline' CCCTB\WP\057, 26 July 2007, p. 23.

stated in the previous section, this provision stipulates that a resident taxpayer shall form a group with other resident taxpayers which are qualifying subsidiaries of the same company which is resident in a third country. As was explained in the previous section, this provision governs the situation of two EU-sister companies held by the same third-country parent. One could debate, however, whether the above '*Papillon*' situation is governed by Article 55(1)(d) CCCTB as well. In any case, the authors submit that there are at least two good reasons that the above situation *should* be governed. Firstly, by allowing consolidation between the EU parent and the EU second-tier subsidiary in the above scenario, the CCCTB regime would be more territorially oriented which would be more in line with the benchmark of international tax neutrality. Secondly, exclusion of the above situation would be at odds with the *Papillon* case.[52] In this case, the CJ ruled that a French parent company and a French second-tier subsidiary company should be able to form a French fiscal unity, despite the intermediate subsidiary being situated in another Member State. Although the CJ recognized that there was a risk that the losses of the second-tier subsidiary could be taken into account twice (once directly through the consolidation and once through a devaluation of the shares in the first-tier subsidiary), the CJ held that this risk did not justify a categorical exclusion from the French consolidation regime. France had to provide for a more proportionate case-by-case solution in this regard.

The question is whether this risk of double loss deduction would also exist under the CCCTB regime if it were to allow for consolidation between EUCo1 and EUCo2. As far a loss incurred by EUCo2 would not indirectly materialize through devaluation by EUCo1 of its shares held in Non-EUCo, this question must probably be answered in the negative. So, it must be determined whether or not a risk of double loss deduction exists under the CCCTB proposal. Pursuant to Article 11(d) CCCTB, proceeds from a disposal of shares are, as a general rule, exempt from corporate tax.[53] In addition, Article 40(b) CCCTB provides that financial assets are not subject to depreciation. Lastly, the CCCTB regime does not provide for a possibility of devaluation of shares held in a third-country subsidiary. In the authors' view, it is therefore safe to conclude that in the scenario at hand, a possible loss incurred at the level of EUCo2 would normally be taken into account only once through the consolidation. It is

[52] Case C-418/07 *Papillon* [2008] ECR I-8947.

[53] These proceeds may nonetheless be taxable if the switch-over clause of Article 73 CCCTB applies.

true that under exceptional circumstances, a decrease in value of the shares held in Non-EUCo could be taken into account by the parent company EUCo1. This could be the case if, for example, the switch-over clause of Article 73 CCCTB applies. In the authors' view, however, this does not justify an automatic and categorical exclusion of the CCCTB regime in the case at hand. A possible risk of double loss deduction should be combated through specific measures.

However, it is also conceivable that the EU parent company provides a loan receivable to its first-tier non-EU subsidiary. The value of this loan could decrease in value due to losses at the level of the EU second-tier subsidiary. Also in such a case, the result of the second-tier subsidiary would, from an economic point of view, be taken into account twice: once by virtue of the fiscal consolidation and once through a devaluation of the loan receivable. This would not be avoided under the current CCCTB regime. Article 27(1)(b) CCCTB provides that bad debt deductions are allowed if the debtor is not a member of the same group of the taxpayer. In the above scenario Non-EUCo would probably not qualify as a member of the same group of the taxpayer.[54] Hence, bad debt deduction would be allowed. This conclusion is probably not contradicted by Article 40(b) CCCTB, which stipulates that financial assets are not subject to depreciation. It can reasonably be assumed that the adagium *lex special derogat lex generalis* applies here, meaning that Article 27(1)(b) CCCTB takes precedence over Article 40(b) CCCTB. In the authors' view, it is, however, questionable whether the risk of double loss deduction justifies a full exclusion of the CCCTB regime in the case at hand. A more proportionate approach would be that the possibility of bad-debt deductions of Article 27(1)(b) would be excluded in the scenario here.

2.4 SECOND SCENARIO: EU-NON-RESIDENT COMPANY INVESTS IN THE EU THROUGH AN EU BRANCH

The CCCTB is also open for an EU-located branch of a non-resident third-country company, both on its own and as part of group, as the case

[54] Following Article 4(7), a 'group member' means any taxpayer belonging to the same group, as defined in Articles 54 and 55. Non-EUCo is a qualifying subsidiary under Article 54 CCCTB, but it seems to be excluded from the definition of a group in Article 55 of the directive. This would be different if the Non-EUCo were to maintain a EU-based PE.

may be. Hence, here too, economic openness is leading under the CCCTB proposal. The second basic scenario is depicted as follows:

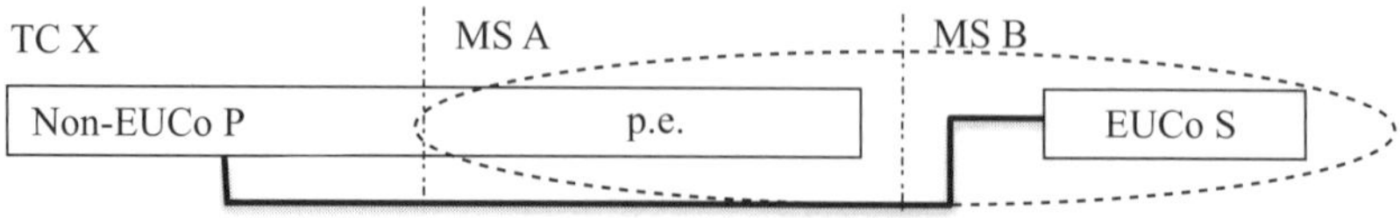

Figure 2.4 Scenario 4

The idea is that with respect to these branches CCCTB provides rules to compute each branch's individual tax results, the consolidation of those results, when there are group members, and the apportionment of the consolidated tax base to each eligible Member State. Allowing the immediate consolidation of profits and losses for calculating the EU-wide taxable bases will reduce over-taxation in transnational situations. Consequently, tax neutrality conditions between national and transnational activities will be improved. As a result, the potential of the Internal Market will be better exploited.[55] Business competes with business, not owners with owners.[56] Therefore, in principle, it should not matter whether business activities are carried out through a separate legal entity or through a branch without legal personality. In the context of taxation of business profits, legal form neutrality should prevail. From this perspective, it is consistent to open up the CCCTB not only to EU-subsidiaries of third-country companies, but also for EU branches of these companies. In this way, investments of third-country companies in the EU can also benefit from reduction of over-taxation, of double taxation, of unintended non-taxation and of tax compliance costs (e.g., in the context of transfer pricing), and tax-free business restructuring which are assumed to be the most striking benefits of the CCCTB.[57] Opening up the system to branches of third-country companies contributes to fair

55 See, for example, Explanatory Memorandum, Proposal for a Council Directive on a Common Consolidated Corporate Tax Base (CCCTB), COM(2011) 121/4, p. 5.

56 See, for example Eric C.C.M. Kemmeren, 'CCCTB and Exemption Method for PEs and Major Shareholdings' in Michael Lang, Pasquale Pistone, Josef Schuch and Claus Staringer (eds), *Common Consolidated Corporate Tax Base* (Linde 2008) 669–672.

57 See, for example, Explanatory Memorandum, Proposal for a Council Directive on a Common Consolidated Corporate Tax Base (CCCTB), COM(2011) 121/4, pp. 9-10.

competition, and therefore to the further establishment of the Internal Market. It enhances international tax neutrality. The CCCTB should contribute to making the EU a more competitive location for investments internationally.[58]

It is beyond the scope of this chapter to discuss all issues. A selection had to be made. In this section the authors will discuss aspects of eligibility of non-resident companies for the CCCTB system (2.4.1), the influence of consolidation on intra-group transactions and withholding taxes (2.4.2), the definition of PEs included in the directive including the interaction with the PE definition under DTCs (2.4.3), and finally aspects of the attribution of profits to an EU-based PE of a non-resident company, including the issue of a sub-PE and the interaction with attribution rules under DTCs (2.4.4).

2.4.1 Eligibility for CCCTB Regime

In this section, the authors will discuss the position of third-country companies, non-resident companies and the group of a non-resident taxpayer.

2.4.1.1 Third-country companies

To have access to the CCCTB, third-country companies and their EU-located branches must meet two cumulative conditions.[59] A third-country company must:

- have a form similar to the European Company (SE), the European Cooperative Society (SCE) or the legal forms of Member States as listed in Annex I to the CCCTB Directive;
- be subject to one of the Member States' corporate income tax as listed in Annex II to the CCCTB Directive.[60]

The Commission will hand down annually a list of third-country companies which must be considered to be similar to the listed SE, SCE or

---

[58] See Preamble, point 4 of the Proposal for a Council Directive on a Common Consolidated Corporate Tax Base (CCCTB), COM(2011) 121/4.

[59] See Articles 1, 2(2–3), 3(1–2), 4(1), (5–7), (22), 6(2–7), 116, and Annexes I-II CCCTB.

[60] The Commission may adopt delegated acts in accordance with Article 127 CCCTB to take into account changes to the Member States' laws on company forms and corporate taxes. Such amendments will also have an impact on the eligibility of third-country companies.

legal forms of Member States. Assuming that the listed third-country companies are deemed to be similar, this list will be very helpful for tax practice.

It is not required that the third country involved has concluded a DTC or a tax information exchange agreement (TIEA) with a Member State. In principle, this is sound, because a company incorporated under the business laws of non-DTC or non-TIEA countries may also be subject to tax in a Member State, as a resident or a non-resident, as the case may be. However, in such a situation, it may be not easy, in practice, to verify the relevant information in respect of the comparison test, because exchange of information with the third country involved has not been facilitated.[61] However, an automatic exclusion of companies from non-TIEA countries would, in the authors' view, be disproportionate.[62] In any case, the authors believe that the burden of proof is initially on the company which claims to qualify for the CCCTB system if its form has not yet been listed.

The subject-to-tax condition covers not only residence taxation, but also source taxation. This is logical from the perspective of further developing the Internal Market. Not only a resident taxpayer but also a non-resident taxpayer must have access to the CCCTB system, because both contribute through their business activities to the development of the Internal Market in a similar way. In order to assess whether the

---

[61] See, also, for example, Guglielmo Maisto, in this book, section 3.3.

[62] See in more detail: D.S. Smit, 'Freedom of investment between EU and non-EU Member States and its impact on corporate income tax systems within the European Union', Dissertation Tilburg (2011) 593–594. Hence, the focus is – rightly – not so much on the question of how the information required by the competent authorities of the Member State is obtained – through a mechanism of international exchange of information or by documentary evidence voluntarily supplied by the taxpayer directly – but rather on the question of whether the authorities of that Member State are able to assess whether access to the CCCTB regime should be allowed on the basis of the information supplied. This approach, which is essentially about the evaluation of the proof provided by the taxpayer, allows third-country companies investing in the EU for sound commercial reasons to benefit from the CCCTB regime without being 'punished' for the fact that they are established in a third country which did not commit itself to exchange information with the Member State concerned, something which is beyond the control of the company. See in a comparable vein: Veronika Dauer and Karin Simader, 'Justifying Restrictions on the Free Movement of Capital under the Rule of Reason in Third-country Relationships: Anti-abuse, Harmful Tax Competition, Effectiveness of Fiscal Supervision and Tax Collection' in Sabine Heidenbauer and Birgit Stürzlinger (eds) *The EU's External Dimension in Direct Tax Matters*, (Linde 2010) 38–39.

subject-to-tax condition is met, one has to take into account not only a Member State's domestic tax law, but also the DTC concerned. Both instruments must allocate taxing rights to the Member State concerned. Otherwise, a company will not be subject to a corporate income tax of a Member State. However, the authors do not believe that the subject-to-tax condition can (theoretically) be met *only* if a company is subject to tax under a Member State's domestic tax law and DTCs, because it receives income from a PE in that Member State.[63] *Any* source of income that leads to tax liability in a Member State is sufficient.

Transparent entities have been addressed separately under the CCCTB system.[64] If an entity is treated as transparent in the Member State of its location, a taxpayer holding an interest in such an entity must include its share in the entity's income in its tax base. If an entity is not located in a Member State but in a third country, the question whether it is transparent must be determined according to the law of the taxpayer's Member State. If more than one group member holds an interest in the same entity located in a third country, a common agreement among the relevant Member States should provide the answer to the question whether an entity is to be treated as transparent. If there is no agreement, the principal tax authority must decide.[65] However, the authors believe that these rules are not relevant for answering the question whether the subject-to-tax condition is satisfied. That question must be answered based on the domestic tax law and the DTCs of the Member State concerned. Articles 84(1) and 85 CCCTB are only relevant when a company has opted in, has become a taxpayer as a consequence thereof,[66] and, subsequently, income must be attributed to that taxpayer when applying the CCCTB system. The subject-to-tax condition is part of the test whether a company has access to the CCCTB system at all. Therefore, this test precedes the attribution rules of Articles 84(1) and 85 CCCTB.[67]

The issue of whether a company is subject to tax must be separated from the question of which income a non-resident taxpayer could opt to include in the new CCCTB system. A non-resident company will only be a taxpayer if it has opted to apply the CCCTB system. It can only opt for

---

63 Dissenting, for example, Guglielmo Maisto, in this book, section 3.3.2.1

64 See Articles 84 and 85 CCCTB.

65 The 'principal tax authority' is the competent authority of the Member State in which the principal taxpayer is resident or, if it is a PE of a non-resident taxpayer, is situated. See Article 4(22) CCCTB.

66 See Article 4(1) CCCTB.

67 See also, for example, Guglielmo Maisto, in this book, section 3.3.3.

the system in respect of income from an activity carried out through a PE maintained in a Member State.[68] This means that the scope of the CCCTB system for non-resident taxpayers may be more limited than the scope of non-resident tax liability under a Member State's domestic corporate income tax law. For example, income from immovable property leading to non-resident tax liability, but not creating a PE under Article 5 CCCTB does not give a non-resident company access to the CCCTB system.[69] If a non-resident taxpayer under a Member State's domestic tax law and tax treaty law can and may be taxed not only in respect of income from a PE in that Member State, but also on, e.g., income from immovable property situated in that Member State, but not attributable to that PE, the non-resident company can only apply the CCCTB system to the income from the PE and must apply the domestic tax laws of that Member State to the income from immovable property.[70] It can easily lead to over-taxation and such a result is inconsistent with one of the CCCTB aims. The authors believe that this split in taxation is not desirable either from the perspective of enhancing international tax neutrality or from the perspective of reducing the compliance burden.

2.4.1.2 Non-resident companies: Third-country and Member State companies

The CCCTB proposal makes a distinction between resident taxpayers and non-resident taxpayers. Quite remarkably, however, the dividing line between resident and non-resident taxpayers is not clear cut. Pursuant to Article 4(4) CCCTB, 'resident taxpayer' means a taxpayer that is resident for tax purposes in a Member State according to Article 6(3) and Article 6(4) CCCTB. Article 6(4) CCCTB contains a tie-breaker rule for dual tax-resident companies within the EU, which is not relevant for this chapter and which is therefore not discussed further. Article 6(3) CCCTB, on the other hand, is of relevance. This provision stipulates that a company that has its registered office, place of incorporation or place of effective management (POEM) in a Member State is considered resident for tax purposes in that Member State, unless such company is regarded as tax resident in a third country under the terms of an agreement concluded by that Member State with that third country. Pursuant to Article 4(5) CCCTB, 'non-resident taxpayer' means a taxpayer that is not

---

[68] See Article 6(2) and (7) in conjunction with Article 5 CCCTB.

[69] See also, for example, Guglielmo Maisto, in this book, section 3.3.2.1.

[70] See also, for example, J.A.R. van Eijsden, J.L. van de Streek, and S.A.W.J. Strik, *Common Consolidated Tax Base (CCCTB)* (Kluwer, Deventer 2011) 32–34.

resident for tax purposes in a Member State according to Article 6(3) and Article 6(4) CCCTB. Hence, Article 6(3) and Article 6(4) CCCTB provide the criteria for allocating tax residence in a Member State. If a company is not a tax resident on the basis of these criteria, it is automatically characterized as a non-resident taxpayer.

It follows that the three criteria used for the allocation of tax residence to a Member State (registered office, place of incorporation, POEM) appear to be exhaustive. In the authors' opinion, this is rather awkward. This is because it may very well be that the national laws of a Member State consider a company to be tax resident on the basis of other criteria. The wording of Article 4(4) read in conjunction with Article 6(3) CCCTB implies that such a company must then be seen as a non-resident taxpayer under the CCCTB regime. A notable example in this regard is the United Kingdom. Based on case law of the United Kingdom, a (non-UK incorporated) company resides where its real business is carried on and the real business is carried on where the central management and control actually abides.[71] The concept of central management and control (CMC) is 'understood by reference to criteria which are more economic than legal',[72] and can be contrasted with the (civil law) concept of place of effective management.[73] If one is to apply the above set of rules, the conclusion is inevitable that a company that is seen as a resident taxpayer by the UK based on the place of its central management and control must be seen as a *non-resident* taxpayer under the CCCTB! However, such a company is also an eligible company that may opt for the CCCTB system, because it satisfies the conditions of Article 6(1) CCCTB: it is a company which is resident for tax purposes in the UK. In the authors' view, this outcome is rather difficult to understand, especially if one realizes that the economic nexus with a Member State under the concept

---

[71] See, for example, *De Beers Consolidated Mines Limited v. Howe* (Surveyor of Taxes) [1906] AC 455, 458. It must be considered in this respect (i) what the attributes of central management and control are; (ii) to whom those attributes attach; and (iii) where that person exercises those attributes; *cf.* D.S. Smit and C.A.T. Peters, 'Report on the 1st Conference on Recent Tax Treaty Case Law, European Tax College, the Netherlands' (2011) 39 *Intertax* 4, 223.

[72] *Cf.* Opinion of Advocate General Darmon Case 81/87, *Daily Mail and General Trust PLC* [1988] ECR I-5483, point 5 with further references.

[73] *Cf.* R. Couzin, *Corporate Residence and International Taxation* (IBFD 2002) 26; OECD, "The Impact of the Communications Revolution on the Application of 'Place of Effective Management' as a Tie Breaker Rule", Draft Discussion Paper (OECD 2001), 6 et seq.; I.J.J. Burgers, 'Some Thoughts on Further Refinement of the Concept of Place of Effective Management for Tax Treaty Purposes' (2007) 35 *Intertax* 6/7, 384.

of CMC may be much stronger compared to the economic nexus under the concept of POEM. It is therefore submitted that Article 6(3) CCCTB needs to be revised. In the authors' opinion, determination of tax residence in a Member State should not be restricted under reference to the above three criteria only. Instead, tax residence under the national laws of a Member State, irrespective of on which criterion it is based, should constitute tax residence under the CCCTB regime, unless an agreement is in place between that Member State and a third country which allocates tax residence to that third country.

If the place of effective management of shipping group member or of a group member engaged in inland waterways transport is aboard a ship or boat, it is deemed to be a resident in the Member State of the home harbour of that ship or boat. However, if there is no such home harbour, the company is deemed to be a resident in the Member State of residence of the operator of the ship or boat.[74] In the – possibly rather theoretical – case that the home harbour is in a third country and that the residence of the operator is there as well, the special shipping provision does not provide the answer to the question as to in which state the company is a resident. In such a case, the general rule will apply. However, this rule may result in a multiple residence, because of the fact that the effective management is carried out aboard a ship. It is likely that the effective management is carried out not only in more than one Member State, but also in one or more third countries. If not all Member States and third countries involved have concluded a DTC with each other, it is likely that the multiple place of residence is not reduced to a single place of residence. In this context, it seems that Article 6(5) CCCTB needs to be supplemented. For example, it could be stipulated, in line with the rules already included, that if no home harbour is situated in one of the Member States and the operator does not have its residence in one of the Member States either, the company will be deemed to be a non-resident. However, this does not automatically mean that such a company is outside the scope of the CCCTB system. If it maintains a PE within one

---

[74] See Article 6(5) CCCTB. This provision seems to be inspired by Article 8(3) OECD Model. However, the function of the latter provision is different. It is not a provision to determine the residence of a person, but to allocate income to a contracting state. See for complex triangular situations in this context, for example, Guglielmo Maisto, 'Shipping, Inland Waterways Transport and Air Transport (Article 8 OECD Model Convention)' in Michael Lang, Pasquale Pistone, Josef Schuch and Claus Staringer (eds), *Source versus Residence, Problems Arising from the Allocation of Taxing Rights in Tax Treaty Law and Possible Alternatives* (Kluwer 2008) 50–51.

or more Member States as defined under Article 5 CCCTB, it may still have access to the system as a non-resident.

2.4.1.3 Group of a non-resident taxpayer: EU-based PE is not a 'group member'?

A non-resident taxpayer can also be obliged to form a group.[75] This group must include all its PEs located in Member States and all its qualifying subsidiaries *resident* in one or more Member States, including the PEs of these subsidiaries located in other Member States.[76] If the conditions are met, it is not possible to leave some of the PEs or qualifying subsidiaries outside the group. The option system is an all-in-all-out system.

It should be noted that not all PEs maintained in a Member State by a qualifying subsidiary can be part of a group of a non-resident taxpayer. For example, a non-resident taxpayer maintains a PE in a Member State and one of the assets to be attributed to that PE is a 100 per cent interest in the shares of *third-country resident* subsidiary which itself also maintains a PE in a Member State. Given that the qualifying subsidiary is not a resident of a Member State, it does not satisfy the conditions of Article 55(2). Only a PE located in a Member State of a qualifying subsidiary that is *resident* of a Member State can be included in the group of a non-resident taxpayer. On the other hand, a PE maintained in a Member State of a qualifying subsidiary that is a resident of a third country must be included in a group of a *resident* taxpayer, based on Article 55(1)(b) CCCTB. The authors do not see any good reason for excluding PEs of a qualifying third-country resident subsidiary from the group of a non-resident taxpayer, not only from the perspective of international tax neutrality, but also from the perspective of the compliance burden. It should be taken into account, of course, that it is possible under the proposed CCCTB system that the qualifying third-country

---

[75] See Article 55(2) in conjunction with Articles 54 and 4(7) CCCTB.

[76] A qualifying subsidiary is an immediate or low-tier subsidiary in which the parent company holds a right to exercise more than 50 per cent of the voting shares *and* an ownership right amounting to more than 75 per cent of the company's capital *or* more than 75 per cent of the right giving entitlement to profit. For calculating the thresholds, rights in companies resident in third countries are taken into account.

resident subsidiary opts for the application of the CCCTB system on a stand-alone basis only in respect of this PE.[77]

In respect of a group of a non-resident taxpayer, a 'principal taxpayer' must be identified. In the context of third-country resident taxpayers, the following principal taxpayers can be distinguished:

> A resident taxpayer which is the qualifying subsidiary of a parent company resident in a third country, where that resident taxpayer forms a group solely with one or more PEs of its parent.
>
> The PE designated by a non-resident taxpayer which forms a group solely in respect of its PEs located in two or more Member States.[78]

This means that a PE cannot be designated as principal taxpayer if the third-country resident taxpayer not only maintains a PE in a Member State, but also holds a qualifying subsidiary which is a resident of a Member State. This subsidiary is by statutory requirement the principal taxpayer, despite the fact that the shares in this subsidiary may be allocated to the PE of the non-resident parent company, where they are effectively connected with the business carried out through that PE. As a result, these rules seem to deviate from economic reality. The authors believe that it should also be possible to designate a PE as principal taxpayer in case the shares in the subsidiary are effectively connected with a PE of a parent company, because in such a situation a genuine economic link exists between the PE and the subsidiary. Now, a PE can only be a principal taxpayer if the group only includes PEs and no subsidiaries. This does not contribute to international tax neutrality.

Furthermore, the principal taxpayer rules above do not cover, for example, the situation where a non-resident taxpayer holds shares in two or more qualifying subsidiaries which are residents in two or more Member States and, in addition to them, maintains one or more PEs in one or more Member States. This situation does not seem to be covered by the other provisions of Article 4(6) CCCTB either. Paragraph (a) only

---

77 If so, it must send a notice to the competent authority of the Member State in which its PE is situated. See Article 104(1), first sentence in conjunction with Article 4(22) CCCTB.

78 See Article 4(6)(c–d) CCCTB. In the case of a group with a resident qualifying subsidiary and PEs of the non-resident parent company, the notice to opt for the CCCTB system must be sent to the principal tax authority, in other words, the competent authority of the Member State in which the subsidiary is resident. In case a PE is the principal taxpayer, the notice must be sent to the competent authority in which the PE is situated. See Article 104(1), second sentence in conjunction with Article 4 (22) CCCTB.

covers PEs of qualifying *subsidiaries* resident in a third country of a resident parent company and paragraph (b) covers only the situation where the group is composed *only* of two or more resident qualifying immediate subsidiaries of a non-resident parent company, thus not including any PEs. Therefore, it seems to be necessary to supplement the rules of Article 4(6) CCCTB in order to identify a principal taxpayer. The situation where a non-resident taxpayer holds shares in two or more qualifying subsidiaries which are residents in two or more Member States and, next to them, maintains one or more PEs in one or more Member States could be solved by having the group designate one of the resident subsidiaries as principal taxpayer or (one of) the PE(s), as the case may be.

Another issue is whether a PE of a non-resident taxpayer is to be identified as a separate 'group member' under Article 4(7) CCCTB. A:

> 'group member' means any *taxpayer* belonging to the same group, as defined in Articles 54 and 55. Where a *taxpayer* maintains one or more permanent establishments *in a Member State* other than *that* in which *its* central management and control is located, each permanent establishment shall be treated as a group member. [Emphasis added]

A PE is not a 'taxpayer' as defined under Article 4(1), because it is not a company, but a part of a company. The non-resident company is the relevant taxpayer. Therefore, the PE of a non-resident taxpayer is not covered by the first sentence. It is also more than questionable whether it is covered by the second sentence. This sentence seems to cover only those PEs of companies of which the central management and control is located in another Member State, and not the situation where the central management and control of company is located in a third country, which may easily be the case in respect of a non-resident company. If this reading is correct, a PE of a non-resident company does not constitute a separate 'group member'. The non-resident company as such with all its EU-based PEs as a whole does so. Article 55(1)(b) CCCTB provides that a resident taxpayer forms a group with '*all* permanent establishments located in a Member State of its qualifying subsidiaries in a third country' [emphasis added].

Therefore, a non-resident qualifying subsidiary with all its EU-based PEs is a 'taxpayer belonging to the same group, as defined in Articles 54 and 55'.

This may hinder, for example, the application of formula for apportionment, because this formula stipulates that the consolidated tax base must be shared between the group members.[79] If a non-resident taxpayer maintains PEs in two or more Member States the apportionment cannot be allocated to each individual PE of the non-resident company, but only to the non-resident taxpayer as such.[80] This is inconsistent with the apportionment of the tax base to PEs of resident companies. They are treated as individual group members. In order to make the CCCTB system coherent, the authors believe that Article 4(7) needs to be adjusted: each PE of a non-resident company should also be treated as an individual 'group member'.

---

[79] See Article 86(1) CCCTB.

[80] It may also create problems in respect of the application of the more detailed rules concerning the application of the formula, such as: Article 91(1) and (2)(b): employees of the *group member* must be included in the labour factor; Article 95(1): the sales factor consists of the total sales of a *group member*; Article 96(4): if there is no group member in the Member State where goods are delivered or services are carried out, or if goods are delivered or services are carried out in a third country, the sales must be included in the sales factor of all *group members* in proportion to their labour and asset factors; Article 98(3) in respect of financial institutions: If the borrower or the person who pays fees, commissions or other revenue cannot be identified or if the Member State in which the security is situated or registered cannot be identified, the sales must be attributed to all *group members* in proportion to their labour and asset factors; Article 99(3) in respect of insurance undertakings: Other sales must be attributed to all *group members* in proportion to their labour and asset factors; Article 100 in respect of oil and gas: Notwithstanding Article 96(1), (2) and (3), sales of a group member conducting its principal business in the field of the exploration or production of oil or gas must be attributed to the *group member* in the Member State where the oil or gas is to be extracted or produced. Notwithstanding Article 96(4) and (5), if there is no group member in the Member State of exploration or production of oil and gas or the exploration or production takes place in a third country where the group member which carries on the exploration or production of oil and gas does not maintain a permanent establishment, the sales must be attributed to that *group member*; Article 101 in respect of shipping, inland waterways transport and air transport: The revenues, expenses and other deductible items of a *group member* whose principal business is the operation of ships or aircraft in international traffic or the operation of boats engaged in inland waterways transport must not be apportioned according to the formula referred to in Article 86 but shall be attributed to that *group member*. Such a *group member* must be excluded from the calculation of the apportionment formula.

2.4.2 Influence of Consolidation on Intra-Group Transactions and Withholding Taxes: A Loophole?

The basic rule is that the tax bases of the members of a group are consolidated.[81] Intra-group transactions are eliminated, i.e., in calculating the consolidated tax base, profits and losses arising from transactions directly carried out between group members are ignored.[82] Furthermore, no withholding taxes or other source taxation will be charged on transactions between group members.[83] On the other hand, the CCCTB provides explicitly that interest and royalties paid by a taxpayer to a recipient outside the group may be subject to a withholding tax in the Member State of the taxpayer according to the applicable rules of national law and any applicable DTC. The withholding tax must be shared among the Member States according to the formula applicable in the tax year in which the tax is charged pursuant to Articles 86 to 102 CCCTB.[84]

The question may arise as to the impact of these provisions if, for example an EU-based parent company pays a royalty to its third-country-resident qualifying subsidiary which itself maintains an EU-based PE, the EU-based parent and the EU-based PE form a group, and the intangible involved can*not* be attributed to the EU-based PE. This situation can be depicted as follows:

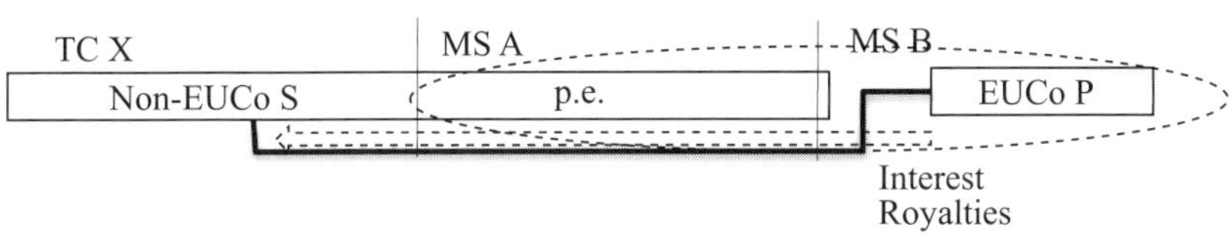

Figure 2.5 Scenario 2.2

Can a withholding tax on the royalty payment from the EU parent to the non-EU subsidiary be avoided? Indeed, the authors believe that this may be the outcome of application of these provisions. The profits and losses arising from using the intangible by the parent put at disposal by the

[81] See Article 57(1) CCCTB.
[82] See Article 59(1) CCCTB.
[83] See Article 60 CCCTB. It must be assumed that 'transactions' also cover 'payments'. See also, for example Joachim Englisch, Chapter 4 in this book, section 4.2.2.2.
[84] See Article 77 CCCTB. See also section 2.3.1.2.1 of this chapter.

subsidiary must be ignored for calculating the taxable base, because it is a transaction between group members. As discussed above, the qualifying non-EU subsidiary with all its EU-based PEs may qualify as a 'group member', whereas its individual EU-based PE does not.[85] Ignoring the profits and losses in itself does not prevent levying withholding taxes, because the rule of Article 59(1) CCCTB can only affect the taxable base of the individual group members.[86]

Both the EU-resident parent and the non-resident qualifying subsidiary qualify as group members. As a consequence, in the given example Article 60 CCCTB seems to prevent the levy of a withholding tax or any source tax.

It is very questionable whether this outcome is prevented by Article 55(1)(b). It is the non-resident qualifying subsidiary that is the 'taxpayer belonging to the same group, as defined in Articles 54 and 55', and which forms a group with its EU-resident parent company with all its PEs.

Article 60 CCCTB reads as follows:

> No withholding taxes or other source taxation shall be charged on *transactions between members of a group*. [Emphasis added]

The transaction – putting the intangible at disposal and the connected royalty payment – is a transaction between '*members* of a group'. However, only the PEs of the non-resident qualifying subsidiary belong to the 'group' of the EU-resident parent, based on Article 55(1)(b). Based on Article 57 in conjunction with Article 6(7) CCCTB, it is only the income from activities carried on through EU-based PEs that are consolidated. However, this does not prevent the conclusion that the requirements of Article 60 CCCTB are satisfied as well. Despite the limited group consolidation of the qualifying non-resident subsidiary's profits, putting the intangible at disposal and the connected royalty payments taken together remains a transaction between '*members* of a group'. Therefore, the authors believe that the currently proposed CCCTB rules will not allow a withholding tax or any other source taxation in respect of the royalty payment. The same would be true for interest or any other

---

[85] See Section 2.4.1.3, where the authors suggested amending the proposed rule.

[86] The result seems to be that the royalty payment will not be deductible at the level of the group. This conclusion does not seem to be desirable, since the royalty payment will not be included in the CCCTB taxable base, because the intangible is not attributed to the EU-based PE of the subsidiary.

income on which a Member State levies a withholding tax or any other source taxation. As a result, it may also be true that an effective application of, for example, the Interest and Royalty Directive may be frustrated.[87] One of its aims is a circulation of intra-group interest and royalty payments free from withholding taxes within the EU. The proposed Article 60 CCCTB seems to open the door for a flow of intra-group interest and royalty payments free from withholding taxes or any source taxation to large parts of the world. This cannot be the Commission's aim.

Therefore, the elimination of withholding taxes under Article 60 CCCTB should be restricted. The question is: how should this be done? If the elimination of withholding taxes and any other source taxation were to be allowed as far as the income from the intra-group transactions is part of the consolidated tax base, i.e., both the proceeds and the costs are included, then a loophole may remain in place, if such a rule were not to be supplemented with a kind of branch profit tax. For example, if a royalty paid by an EU-resident parent company to its qualifying non-resident subsidiary with an EU-based PE and the royalty must be attributed to this PE, no withholding tax would be allowed. If, subsequently, the payments received are transferred from the PE to the non-resident head office, normally, no withholding tax will be levied either, since, as rule, Member States do not levy a branch profit tax. Therefore, the authors believe that the introduction of a kind of branch profit tax is desirable if the Commission believes that intra-group payments should only be free from withholding taxes or any other source taxation as long as they circulate within a EU Member State's tax ambit. Such an approach would also be consistent with the principle of international tax neutrality, at least to the extent that the income covered has originated within an EU Member State's territory.

Of course, it should be noted that DTCs with third countries should be amended as well. As a rule, these DTCs remain valid as they are.[88] The Directive only overrides DTCs concluded between Member States.[89] It would, of course, be an infringement of international law if the Directive

---

[87] See Council Directive 2003/49/EC on a common system of taxation applicable to interest and royalty payments made between associated companies of different Member States [2003] OJ L157/49.

[88] See Article 351 of the Treaty on the Functioning of the European Union, and Commission Staff Working Document, Impact Assessment, Accompanying Document to the Proposal for a Council Directive on a Common Consolidated Corporate Tax Base (CCCTB), COM(2011) 121, Sec(2011) 316, p. 21.

[89] See Article 8 CCCTB.

were to override DTCs with third countries.[90] Most of the current DTCs with third countries will not allow such a branch profit tax. Consequently, it will not be easy to effectively repair the potential loophole.

2.4.3 Definition of PE

A third-country company only has access to the CCCTB in respect of its EU-situated branches.[91] In order to have access, these branches must meet the conditions of the PE concept laid down in Article 5 CCCTB. This provision has been inspired to a large extent by Article 5 OECD Model.[92] For example, the general definition of a PE is more or less identical in both provisions: a PE is 'a fixed place of business [...] through which the business is wholly or partly carried on'.

As result, the same issues that arise under Article 5 OECD Model will also arise under Article 5 CCCTB. It is clear that the Commission did not adopt the suggestion of one of the authors not to include the OECD PE concept because it sets unnecessary conditions. The PE concept is out of date. It was suggested that the concept of a branch be included, which means that it is sufficient that an enterprise carries on or has carried on a substantial entrepreneurial activity in another state. This is the case if that activity, carried on by individuals attributable to the enterprise, in itself forms or has formed an essential and significant part of the activity of the enterprise as a whole.[93]

---

[90] See Articles 26, 27, and 31–33 of the Vienna Convention of the law of treaties, concluded in Vienna, 23 May 1969. National constitutional law may stipulate otherwise, but the authors believe that such national constitutions are infringements of international law in themselves.

[91] See, for example, Explanatory Memorandum, Proposal for a Council Directive on a Common Consolidated Corporate Tax Base (CCCTB), COM(2011) 121/4, p. 5.

[92] Compare, for example, European Commission, Working Document 'CCCTB: Possible Elements of a Technical Outline' CCCTB\WP\057, 26 July 2007, p. 7. Detailed definitions and guidance will be developed under the comitology procedure of Council Decision 1999/468/EC as amended by Council Decision 2006/512/EC. See also, for example, J.A.R. van Eijsden, J.L. van de Streek, and S.A.W.J. Strik, *Common Consolidated Tax Base (CCCTB)* (Kluwer, Deventer 2011) 37–39 and Edoardo Traversa and Charles-Albert Helleputte, Chapter 1 in this book, section 1.5.2.1.

[93] See Eric C.C.M. Kemmeren, 'CCCTB and Exemption Method for PEs and Major Shareholdings' in Michael Lang, Pasquale Pistone, Josef Schuch and Claus Staringer (eds), *Common Consolidated Corporate Tax Base* (Linde 2008) 687–689. For example Claus Staringer, 'Requirements for Forming a Group', in Michael Lang, Pasquale Pistone, Josef Schuch and Claus Staringer (eds),

As a consequence of adopting of the OECD PE concept, the OECD Commentary to Article 5 OECD Model may also be highly relevant for the interpretation of the CCCTB provision. However, it should be emphasized that the authors believe that for the interpretation of Article 5 CCCTB, the OECD Commentary is not decisive.[94] A court should interpret independently the OECD provision taking into account the OECD Commentary as a supplementary means of interpretation in the sense of Article 32 of the Vienna Convention of the law of treaties.[95] The Commentary is only one of the relevant sources of interpretation. In the context of interpreting Article 5 CCCTB, the OECD Commentary should play a similar role.

The CCCTB provision includes a list which is identical to the list included in Article 5(2) OECD Model. The provision stipulates: "A taxpayer shall be considered to have a 'permanent establishment' [...], including in particular:" a place of management, a branch, an office, a factory, a workshop, and a mine, an oil or gas well, a quarry or, any other place of extraction of natural resources. The wording 'including in particular' may suggest that the listed items are deemed PEs. However, taking into account the OECD Commentary as a benchmark, this is not likely. In this context, all items have to satisfy the conditions of the general PE definition in order to constitute a PE.[96]

The text of the CCCTB project's PE provision is almost identical to Article 5(3) OECD Model. It only uses the words 'shall constitute' instead of 'constitutes'.[97] The authors believe that the CCCTB provision expresses much better that a project PE only and always exists if the project lasts more than 12 months and that if the project lasts for a

---

Common Consolidated Corporate Tax Base (Linde 2008) 123–125 supported the adoption of the OECD PE concept.

94 See for a more in-depth discussion, for example Eric C.C.M. Kemmeren, 'De rol van het OESO-Commentaar bij de uitleg van belastingverdragen en het Europese recht: trias politica onder toenemende druk?' in J.L.M. Gribnau (ed.), *Principieel belastingrecht, Liber Amicorum, Richard Happé* (Wolf Legal Publishers 2011) 95–108.

95 Concluded in Vienna, 23 May 1969.

96 See OECD Commentary (2010) to Article 5, para. 12, which paragraph has been further clarified in the OECD Discussion Draft of 12 October 2011: Interpretation and Application of Article 5 (Permanent Establishment) of the OECD Model Tax Convention, OECD, Paris, pp. 24-25.

97 See Article 5(2) CCCTB.

shorter time that there is no PE, despite the fact that conditions of the general PE definition may have been satisfied.[98]

The list of barred PEs under Article 5(3) CCCTB is identical to the list included in Article 5(4) OECD Model. Although the listed activities satisfy the conditions of the general PE definition or the project PE, they are deemed not to constitute a PE. The wording of the CCCTB provision has been tailored to the purposes of the CCCTB system. This means that no substantial differences can be identified if both provisions are compared. Looking again at the OECD Commentary, it can be argued that the following do not need to satisfy the requirement that the activity must have a preparatory or auxiliary character:

- use of facilities solely for the purpose of storage, display or delivery of goods or merchandise belonging to the taxpayer
- maintenance of a stock of goods or merchandise belonging to the taxpayer solely for the purpose of storage, display or delivery
- maintenance of a stock of goods or merchandise belonging to the taxpayer solely for the purpose of processing by another person, and
- maintenance of a fixed place of business solely for the purpose of purchasing goods or merchandise or of collecting information, for the taxpayer.

This requirement is included as a separate and independent requirement in Article 5(3)(e–f) CCCTB or, as the case may be, Article 5(4)(e–f) OECD Model. Where each of the activities is the only activity carried on at a fixed place of business, the place is deemed not to constitute a PE.[99]

The text of the agency PE provisions included in Article 5(4–5) CCCTB is also almost identical to the OECD Model provisions of Article 5(5–6). Again, the wording of the CCCTB provision has only been tailored to the purposes of the CCCTB system. If the two are compared, no substantial difference between the provisions can be identified.

---

[98] See OECD Commentary (2010) to Article 5, paras 16, 19 and 19.1, which paragraph has been further clarified in the OECD Discussion Draft of 12 October 2011: Interpretation and Application of Article 5 (Permanent Establishment) of the OECD Model Tax Convention, OECD, Paris, pp. 20-24.

[99] See OECD Commentary (2010) to Article 5, paras 21 and 23 which paragraphs have been further clarified in the OECD Discussion Draft of 12 October 2011: Interpretation and Application of Article 5 (Permanent Establishment) of the OECD Model Tax Convention, OECD, Paris, pp. 26–28.

Therefore, the same issues, which arise under the OECD Model provisions, can arise under the CCCTB.[100] One striking example is the discussion of whether a commissionaire structure can lead to a PE or not.[101]

The CCCTB PE provision ends, as does the OECD provision, with the rule that the mere control by or over a taxpayer does not create a PE.[102] The same is true in respect of the trade or business carried on by the subsidiary company that is managed by the parent company. Such an activity does not make the subsidiary company a PE of the parent company. The existence in one state of a PE of one company of a multinational group will not have any relevance as to whether another company of the group itself has a PE in that state.[103]

As indicated above, transparent entities have been addressed separately under the CCCTB system.[104] If an entity is treated as transparent in the Member State of its location, a taxpayer holding an interest in such an entity must include its share in the entity's income in its tax base. If an entity is not located in a Member State but in a third country, the question whether it is transparent must be determined according to the law of the taxpayer's Member State. If more than one group member holds an interest in the same entity located in a third country, a common agreement among the relevant Member States should clarify whether an entity is treated as transparent. If there is no agreement, the principal tax authority must decide. Taking the OECD Commentary into account as a benchmark, when an entity is treated as transparent, each partner will be considered to have a PE.[105] This means that the transparent entity's PE will be attributed to the individual partners and that they receive income from a PE. If this PE is situated in the EU and the partner is a non-resident company, the authors believe that partner satisfies the PE

---

[100] See, for example, OECD Discussion Draft of 12 October 2011: Interpretation and Application of Article 5 (Permanent Establishment) of the OECD Model Tax Convention, OECD, Paris, pp. 35–43.

[101] See, for example, Brian Arnold, 'Tax Treaty News' (2011) 65 *Bulletin for International Taxation* 7, 368–370.

[102] See Article 5(6) CCCTB and Article 5(7) OECD Model, respectively.

[103] See OECD Commentary (2010) to Article 5, para. 40 and 41.1.

[104] See Articles 84 and 85 CCCTB.

[105] See, for example, OECD Commentary (2010) to Article 5, para. 19.1, which paragraph has been further clarified in the OECD Discussion Draft of 12 October 2011: Interpretation and Application of Article 5 (Permanent Establishment) of the OECD Model Tax Convention, OECD, Paris, pp. 22–24.

conditions under the CCCTB system.[106] It will have to report the PE income proportionate to its participation in the transparent entity's profits and losses.[107]

Finally, the PE definition included in the CCCTB system may deviate from the PE definition under the actual DTCs concluded with third countries. As already mentioned, these DTCs remain valid as they are. The Directive only overrides DTCs concluded between Member States.[108] The differences in definition may lead to double taxation or double non-taxation, which does not contribute to a level playing field and is also inconsistent with the principle of international tax neutrality. Such a result could be avoided if, for such situations, the proposed definition were to be supplemented with a rule, which stipulates that for CCCTB purposes the PE definition of the DTC involved is to be adopted. This is the solution, which was included in the Netherlands Corporate Income Tax Act as from 1 January 2012, when the tax base exemption for foreign PEs was introduced.[109] For non-DTC situations, the proposed definition could remain in place. In the context of the tax base exemption in respect of non-DTC situations, the Netherlands has also included a PE definition, which to a large extent, is similar to the OECD definition.[110]

2.4.4 Attribution of Profit to the PE

2.4.4.1 Attribution of profits to the PE: How to identify PE profits in general?

A non-resident company that opts for the CCCTB system is subject to tax on all *income from an activity carried on through a PE* in a Member State.[111] The CCCTB system does not include any general rule on when income must be considered to be received from an activity carried on through a PE.[112] Articles 78 and 79 CCCTB only cover transactions between associated enterprises and, as will be indicated below, they

---

[106] For example Guglielmo Maisto, Chapter 3 in this book, section 3.3.2.3, seems to be hesitant as to whether a PE of transparent entity can be attributed to its partners.

[107] See Articles 84(1) and 89 CCCTB.

[108] See Article 8 CCCTB.

[109] See Article 15e(2)(a) *Wet op de vennootschapsbelasting 1969* (Corporate Income Tax Act 1969 (NL CITA)). See also, for example, Daniel Gutmann, Chapter 7 in this book, section 7.4.3.

[110] See Article 15f NL CITA.

[111] See Article 6(7) CCCTB.

[112] Article 93 CCCTB only provides for an allocation rule of assets to its economic owner, its legal owner, the group member that effectively uses the

might not even be effective in the context of the non-resident taxpayer and its EU-based PE. In any case, the CCCTB system does not provide a general rule for the allocation of income to a PE as, for example, Article 7(1–2) OECD Model does. Based on these provisions, the profits attributable to a PE:

> are the profits it might be expected to make, in particular in its dealings with other parts of the enterprise, if it were a separate and independent enterprise engaged in the same or similar activities under the same or similar conditions, taking into account the functions performed, assets used and risks assumed by the enterprise through the permanent establishment and through the other parts of the enterprise.

According to the OECD Commentary, the allocation rule of Article 7(2) has been based on the separate entity and arm's length principles.[113] This rule is a general rule and is not restricted to internal dealings between the various parts of an enterprise, such as internal dealings between head office and PE or between various PEs of the enterprise. The basic approach for the purposes of determining what are the profits that are attributable to a PE is the fiction that a PE is a separate enterprise and that such an enterprise is independent from the rest of the enterprise of which it is a part as well as from any other person. The second part of the fiction corresponds to the arm's length principle.[114] The attribution of profits to a PE will follow from the calculation of the profits or losses from all its activities, including transactions with independent enterprises, transactions with associated enterprises, and dealings with other parts of the enterprise. This analysis involves two steps:

- a functional analysis is undertaken;
- a factual analysis is undertaken.

Any transactions with associated enterprises attributed to a PE are priced in accordance with the guidance of the OECD Transfer Pricing Guidelines and these Guidelines are applied by analogy to dealings between the PE and the other parts of the enterprise of which it is a part.

According to the OECD, the functional and factual analysis will lead to:

---

asset, the lessor, or the lessee, as the case may be, in respect of the formula for apportionment as included in Article 86 CCCTB.

[113] See OECD Commentary (2010) to Article 7, para 3.

[114] See OECD Commentary (2010) to Article 7, paras 15–16.

- the attribution to the PE of the rights and obligations arising out of transactions between the enterprise of which the PE is a part and separate enterprises
- the identification of significant people functions relevant to the attribution of economic ownership of assets, and the attribution of economic ownership of assets to the PE
- the identification of significant people functions relevant to the assumption of risks and the attribution of risks to the PE
- the identification of other functions of the PE
- the recognition and determination of the nature of those dealings between the PE and other parts of the same enterprise that can appropriately be recognized, and
- the attribution of capital based on the assets and risks attributed to the PE.[115]

This means that assets and liabilities and profits which are effectively connected with the activities of a PE must be attributed to this PE.[116]

Whereas the CCCTB system does not include a general attribution rule as Article 7(1–2) OECD Model does, the words 'income from an activity carried on through a PE' in Article 6(7) CCCTB must be interpreted. The OECD provisions and its Commentary to it could be used as supplementary means to interpret these words. One of the benefits would be that the CCCTB interpretation and application and the DTC interpretation and application could be attuned to each other in order to avoid double taxation and double non-taxation. The authors believe that this approach is also consistent, at least to a certain extent, with EU law. In the context of the freedom of establishment, although the authors believe that the same will be true in respect of the free movement of capital, the CJ allows the requirement that an asset or liability must be managed and its operations must be directed and controlled by a PE in order to be protected by the freedom.[117] If an asset or liability is managed and its operations are directed and controlled by a PE, it is effectively connected

[115] See OECD Commentary (2010) to Article 7, paras 20–22.

[116] See OECD Commentary (2010) to Article 10, paras 31–32.2, Article 11, paras 24–25.2, Article 12, paras 20–21.2, Article 13, paras 27.1–27.2, Article 21, paras 5.1–6, Article 22, paras 3–3.2, and Article 24, para 49.

[117] See, for example, Case C-221/89 *Factortame II* [1991] ECR I-3905, paras 34–36. See also section 2.2 of this chapter and further, for example, Eric C.C.M. Kemmeren, *Principle of Origin in Tax Conventions, A Rethinking of Models*, Dissertation Tilburg University (Eric C.C.M. Kemmeren/Pijnenburg vormgevers·uitgevers, Dongen 2001) 177–181.

to that PE.[118] Therefore, the authors believe that in order to increase legal certainty, it is advisable to supplement the rule of Article 6(7) CCCTB with a general attribution rule based on the above analysis.[119]

Based on the above analysis the authors believe that it is also possible to properly attribute, for example, shares in company, debt claims and intangibles (such as patents) to a PE and, consequently, also the income derived from these assets: dividends, interest, and royalties. The authors also believe that based on these attribution rules, it is possible to attribute a PE to another PE if that PE is effectively connected with the latter PE. The authors do not see why the attribution of a PE should be treated differently from the attribution of any other asset or liability or a combination of assets and liabilities,[120] nor in particular why it should be treated differently from the attribution of shares in a company. Otherwise, a different treatment of legal forms would be the result and such a different treatment would seem to be inconsistent with EU law.[121] Subsequently, a non-resident taxpayer will be entitled to a tax base exemption or an ordinary tax credit, as the case may be, for profits from a subPE, proceeds from the disposal of a subPE, dividends and proceeds from the disposal of shares which are attributable to the EU-based PE of that non-resident.[122] Furthermore, it can invoke an ordinary tax credit in respect of interest, royalties or any other income when attributable to the EU-based PE.[123] Entitlement to the machinery of reduction of double

---

118 See further, for example, Eric C.C.M. Kemmeren, *Principle of Origin in Tax Conventions, A Rethinking of Models*, Dissertation Tilburg University (Eric C.C.M. Kemmeren/Pijnenburg vormgevers·uitgevers, Dongen 2001) 332–337.

119 The authors acknowledge that not all EU Member States are OECD member states: Bulgaria, Cyprus, Latvia, Lithuania, Malta, and Romania are not. Therefore, the non-OECD EU Member States may to a certain extent be reluctant to adopt rules based on OECD concepts. For example, it may be true that they have a preference for rules based on other concepts, such as Article 7 of the United Nations Model Double Tax Convention between Developed and Developing Countries (2011). However, the preference for basing rules on other concepts than OECD concepts does not change the authors' advice to supplement Article 6(7) CCCTB with a general attribution rule.

120 Dissenting, for example, H. Pijl, 'Non-discriminatie: objectvrijstelling voor buitenlands belastingplichtigen' (2012) 60 *Weekblad Fiscaal Recht* 62.

121 See, for example Case C-307/97 *Saint-Gobain* [1999] ECR I-6161 paras 42–43 and Case C-337/08 *X Holding* [2010] n.y.r. para 39.

122 See Arts 11(c–e), 72, 73, 74, and 75 CCCTB.

123 See Article 76 CCCTB. A full credit may be taken if a DTC between a Member State and a third country provides for such a credit. It should be noted that the credit will be calculated separately for each Member State or third country as well as for each type of income.

taxation is also consistent with EU case law and the ideas developed under the OECD Model.[124]

As already discussed, transparent entities have been addressed separately under the CCCTB system.[125] If an entity is treated as transparent in the Member State of its location, a taxpayer holding an interest in such an entity must include its share in the entity's income in its tax base. If this is income from an EU-based PE of a non-resident taxpayer, the partner must report its share in the PE profits as PE profits. If an entity is not located in a Member State but in a third country, the question of whether it is transparent must be determined according to the law of the taxpayer's Member State. If more than one group member holds an interest in the same entity located in a third country, a common agreement among the relevant Member States should provide the answer. However, if there is no agreement, the principal tax authority must decide. If the result is transparency, the partner has to report its proportionate share in the PE as PE profits.

As also indicated above, DTCs with third countries remain valid as they are.[126] The Directive only overrides DTCs concluded between Member States.[127] Most of the current DTCs with third countries include a provision similar to Article 7 OECD Model. However, as a result of the application of the formula of Articles 86 et seq. CCCTB, it may be true that more profits are attributed to a PE in an EU Member State than is allowed based on the arm's length principle laid down in actual DTC provisions with third countries which are similar to Article 7 (1–2) OECD Model.[128] If so, as a rule, the DTC attribution rule will prevail over the CCCTB formula.

---

124 See, for example Case C-307/97 *Saint-Gobain* [1999] ECR I-6161 and, as the case may be, OECD Commentaries (2010) to Article 24, paras 48–54 and 69–72. See further, for example, Eric C.C.M. Kemmeren and Hans-Peter Peeters, 'Avoidance Double Taxation and Its Interaction With European Triangular Arrangements' (2010) 19 *EC Tax Review* 1, 4–18.

125 See Articles 84 and 85 CCCTB.

126 See section 2.4.2.

127 See Article 8 CCCTB.

128 Here, the authors start from the assumption that the proposed CCCTB system will be amended in such a manner that the EU-based PE will also qualify as an individual group member. See section 2.4.1.3.

2.4.4.2 Adjustment of the EU-based PE income on the arm's length principle not possible?

A non-resident company that opts for the CCCTB system is subject to tax on all income from an activity carried on through a PE in a Member State.[129] A non-resident taxpayer is regarded as an associated enterprise to its PE in a Member State.[130] Although it is not explicitly so stated in the text of Article 78(1) CCCTB, the authors assume that the PE itself is also considered to be an associated enterprise to the non-resident taxpayer. Association is by nature a bilateral or multilateral and not unilateral concept. Therefore, it is hard to argue that the non-resident taxpayer is an associated enterprise to its PE, but the PE is not an associated enterprise to the non-resident taxpayer of which it is a part. Nevertheless, the authors feel that Article 78(1) CCCTB must be adjusted in order to clarify that both the non-resident taxpayer and its PE must be regarded as associated enterprises if the Commission wants to maintain this concept.

It is unclear why the CCCTB system deviates from the OECD concept for allocation of business profits laid down in Article 7 in conjunction with Article 5 OECD Model. On the one hand, the CCCTB system adopts the OECD PE definition, but, on the other hand, it does not adopt Article 7 OECD Model to attribute profits to such a PE. It only eats half of the OECD cake. For the attribution of income to a PE, it puts the PE completely on a par with an associated enterprise, like a subsidiary. This may have far-reaching consequences. For example, the OECD Commentary to Article 7 OECD Model may be completely irrelevant for the attribution of income to a PE, whereas the Commentary to Article 9 OECD Model and the Transfer Pricing Guidelines may be highly relevant as supplementary means for interpreting the income allocation rules to a PE.[131] In substance, the consequence may be that the fact that the PE is a part of the non-resident taxpayer must be ignored, but that the PE must be regarded as separate legal entity in relation to the other parts of the non-resident taxpayer. As result, it may be very hard to argue under the CCCTB that notional interest should not be taken into account, as a rule, in the relation between a PE and other parts of the enterprise of which the PE is a part.[132] This is basically the sound idea underlying Article

---

[129] See Article 6(7) CCCTB.

[130] See Article 78(1) CCCTB.

[131] See for the latest Transfer Pricing Guidelines: OECD Transfer Pricing Guidelines for Multinational Enterprises and Tax Administrations (OECD 2010).

[132] It should be noted that such an interest deduction may be limited if the interest is paid to associated enterprises resident for tax purposes in a low-tax

7(2) OECD Model and which is included in the OECD Commentary.[133] It could be argued that such interest should be taken into account because of the concept that puts the PE and the rest of the taxpayer on a par with associated enterprises. All tax arbitration structures which are available to associated enterprises and which are not available under Article 7 OECD Model would be imported in the CCCTB. The authors believe that this is undesirable, because profit allocation can easily be manipulated by the interest element. Therefore, the authors call upon the Commission to reconsider the starting point of classifying the non-resident taxpayer and its EU-based PE as associated enterprises. It would be better to link up with Article 7 OECD Model for the attribution of income to such a PE.

Assuming that the non-resident taxpayer and its PE are associated enterprises, the income attributed to such a PE must be done on the basis of the arm's length principle. If this is not done, the idea seems to be that an adjustment of the profits attributable to a PE in a Member State can be enforced based on Article 79 CCCTB. This provision reads as follows:

> Where *conditions* are made or imposed in relations between *associated enterprises* which *differ* from *those* that would be made between *independent enterprises*, then *any income* which would, *but for those conditions*, have accrued to *the taxpayer*, but, by reason of those conditions, has not so accrued, shall be *included* in the income of *that taxpayer* and taxed accordingly. [Emphasis added]

This provision seems to large extent to have been borrowed from Article 9 OECD Model. Nevertheless, there are differences. The wording of the CCCTB provision does not include a reference to 'commercial or financial relations', but covers any relation between associated enterprises. Therefore, in this respect, the scope of the CCCTB may be wider than that of Article 9 OECD. On the other hand, the OECD provision refers to 'one of the enterprises' and 'that enterprise', whereas the CCCTB refers to 'the taxpayer' or 'that taxpayer', as the case may be. Technically there seems to be a problem in respect of the adjustment of profits in the relation between a PE and the non-resident taxpayer. A PE

---

country outside the EU which does not exchange information with the Member State of the payer comparable to Directive 2011/16/EU. See Article 81(1) and (3) CCCTB.

133 See 2010 Commentaries on Article 7, paras 28–29; Commentaries on Article 7 (text until 22 July 2010), paras 28–29, and OECD, '2010 Report on the attribution of profits to permanent establishments' (OECD 2010) paras 114 and 152–158.

is not a taxpayer, but the non-resident taxpayer is.[134] Based on the text of Article 79 only the profits of a taxpayer can be adjusted. Given that the PE is not a taxpayer under the CCCTB system, it can be argued that based on the text of this provision it is not possible to adjust the profit attribution to a PE. The authors believe that this (potential) problem could be solved by replacing the words 'the taxpayer' and 'that taxpayer' by the words 'one of the associated enterprise' and 'that associated enterprise', respectively.

2.4.4.3 Transfer of assets towards a third country: Another (partial) loophole?

Based on Article 31 CCCTB, the transfer of a fixed asset by a non-resident taxpayer from its PE in a Member State to a third country is treated as a deemed disposal of that asset. Such a deemed disposal will not be triggered if the third country is an EEA Member State and an agreement on the exchange of information comparable to Directive 2011/16/EU is in place between that EEA Member State and the EU Member State in which the PE is situated. Considering Articles 78 and 79 CCCTB, the authors assume that the value to be taken into account must be based at the arm's length standard, i.e. the fair market value of the fixed asset must be included in the taxable base.[135]

The first striking element is that the final settlement provision (one could also refer to it as kind of exit tax) is restricted to fixed assets only. It seems that other assets and liabilities can be transferred from an EU-based PE to a third country without triggering taxation at that moment.[136]

Secondly, the final settlement tax will not be levied if information can be exchanged with an EEA Member State comparable to what has been laid down in Directive 2011/16/EU. In this context, a provision included in a DTC similar to Article 26 OECD Model will likely be sufficiently comparable; otherwise the rule would be completely ineffective. However, one may wonder whether a TIEA which only provides for exchange of information upon request is sufficiently comparable to the Directive. This Directive includes many more instruments, such as spontaneous and automatic exchange of information. Furthermore, in other provisions like Article 81(1) and (3), it is explicitly stipulated that an agreement on the

---

134 See Article 4(1) CCCTB.

135 See also, for example, Daniel Gutmann, Chapter 7 in this book, section 7.5.1, identifying lack of clarity as well.

136 See also, for example, Daniel Gutmann, Chapter 7 in this book, section 7.4.2.2.

exchange of information comparable to the exchange of information *on request* provided for in Directive 2011/16/EU is sufficient. One can read in this provision an argument that the information instrument threshold of Article 31 CCCTB is higher than of provisions like Article 81(1) and (3) CCCTB. On the other hand, it could be questioned whether it would be justified to refuse the exemption if the required information can be obtained upon request. It could be argued that such an instrument is sufficiently equivalent, because, with this instrument, the information required to apply and to check the exemption can be obtained without the necessity of using other instruments laid down in the Directive.[137] It is sufficient that it is possible to exchange information which enables Member States to effect a correct assessment of taxes.[138] Furthermore, the authors believe that this is not only true in relation to EEA Members, but also in respect of any third country with which sufficient instruments for the exchange of information have been agreed on through a DTC, a TIEA, or any other (multilateral) instrument, like the Multilateral Convention on Mutual Administrative Assistance in Tax Matters 2010.[139] Furthermore, excluding these non-EEA Member States does not contribute to international tax neutrality.

Thirdly, and more in general, one may wonder what the system of taxation is in respect of assets and liabilities other than fixed assets which are transferred to third countries and in respect of fixed assets which are transferred to EEA Member States with sufficient machinery for the exchange of information. In the context of the latter, it must be observed that the mere possibility of exchanging information does not create a taxable base upon transfer or later on, nor does it guarantee that at the end a tax due will be recovered. Therefore, granting an exemption merely on the basis of the possibility to exchange information on the transferred fixed asset is not an obvious choice.

The CCCTB system does not contain a general final settlement or an exit tax provision.[140] This leaves open the question of whether a loophole

---

[137] Compare, for example Case C-493/09 *Commission v Portugal* [2011] n.y.r. paras 48–50.

[138] See for example, Case C-451/05 *Elisa* [2007] ECR I-8251, para 29. See, in more detail, D.S. Smit, 'Freedom of investment between EU and non-EU Member States and its impact on corporate income tax systems within the European Union' (dissertation Tilburg 2011) 594–597.

[139] See also Case C-436/08 *Haribo Lakritzen Hans Riegel* [2011] n.y.r. paras 64–75.

[140] For example Article 49 CCCTB provides for a general rule for a taxpayer who leaves the system. Its assets and liabilities must be recognized at their value

exists or whether the CCCTB creates a taxable event upon actual realization, even when the assets and liabilities not covered by the taxation of Article 31 CCCTB are no longer part of the PE situated in the Member State. The question can be raised whether a DTC concluded between the Member State concerned and the third country involved allows such a deferred taxation if such a DTC is similar to the OECD Model, including provisions similar to Articles 7 and 13 OECD Model. It could be argued that after the transfer only the third country is allowed to tax the profits and capital gains realized. In such a case a loophole exists.

However, such a loophole could be avoided if the interpretation of the CCCTB and the DTC involved the reasoning of the German Federal Finance Court (*Bundesfinanzhof*) developed in its ruling of 28 October 2009, I R 99/08 could be applied. The Supreme Court ruled that it is possible both under German domestic tax law and under DTCs with rules similar to Articles 7 and 13 OECD Model to tax the unrealized capital gains which arise within the ambit of Germany's tax jurisdiction after the transfer at the time that they are actually realized. At the time these gains arose, the taxpayer had a PE in Germany, since his entire business was in Germany. As a result, the profits will be taxed upon realization in the same way as they are in the hands of resident taxpayers. The authors are very much in favour of this solution, because it is to a large extent in line with international tax neutrality, the principle of origin, and in any case with the residence-based compartmentalization,[141] and resident and non-resident taxpayers are taxed in the same way. As a result, a loophole

---

as calculated according to the rules of the CCCTB system, unless stated otherwise in the Directive. In substance, this provision stipulates that the taxpayer continues with same values outside the CCCTB system as used within the CCCTB system, in other words, no final settlement tax. See also, for example, J.A.R. van Eijsden, J.L. van de Streek, and S.A.W.J. Strik, *Common Consolidated Tax Base (CCCTB)* (Kluwer, Deventer 2011) 105. Similar approaches are found in other provisions. For example, Article 65 CCCTB provides that upon termination of a group, the consolidated tax base and any unrelieved losses of the group must be allocated to each group member in accordance with the formula applicable to the tax year of termination. Article 70(1) CCCTB provides that the transfer of a legal seat of a taxpayer which is a member of a group does not give rise to profits or losses for the purposes of determining the consolidated tax base.

[141] See for example, Kemmeren, 'The Netherlands: Pending Cases Filed by the Netherlands Courts: *The National Grid Indus* (C-371/10) and Feyenoord (C-498/10, X.) Cases' in Michael Lang, Pasquale Pistone, Josef Schuch, Claus Staringer, and Alfred Storck (eds), *ECJ – Recent Developments in Direct*

would be prevented and no restriction would exist and thus no inconsistency with EU law either.

However, it is questionable whether this is the system included in the CCCTB. Circumstantial evidence for the opposite can be found in, e.g., Articles 61 and 70 CCCTB. If, as a result of a business reorganization, a taxpayer no longer has a PE in the Member State in which it was resident on the date of its entry into the group, it is deemed to have a PE there for the purpose of applying the provisions of Article 61 CCCTB. In Article 70 CCCTB, a similar rule can be found. If a taxpayer no longer has a PE in the Member State from which assets were transferred in respect of a business reorganization, it is deemed to have a PE there for the purpose of applying the provisions of Article 70. Based on these provisions, it could be argued that, under the currently proposed CCCTB system, a tax claim in respect of a disappearing PE or disappearing assets and liabilities from a PE is lost; otherwise the provisions of Articles 61 and 70 CCCTB would be superfluous. The latter does not seem to be very likely.

Therefore, the authors believe that the proposed Directive should be supplemented with rules that establish the result of the approach of the German Federal Finance Court if the recovery of the tax can also be guaranteed through agreements with the third country involved, e.g. through a DTC which includes a provision similar to Article 27 OECD Model or through the Multilateral Convention on Mutual Administrative Assistance in Tax Matters 2010.[142] In this way, the CCCTB will also satisfy the requirements which the CJ has set in the *National Grid Indus* case in respect of exit taxes and other final settlement taxes, in which, by the way, the Court wrongly did not make a link with the levy of taxes, but with the payment of taxes.[143] In any case, based on this decision and

Taxation 2010 (Linde 2011) 171–174, which includes more in-depth suggestions as to how such a system could be made concretely operational.

[142] It should be noted that the CCCTB system does not include a rule which covers the situation that the non-resident taxpayer transfers assets and liabilities from another part of the non-resident taxpayer's enterprise to its EU-based PE. The authors believe that the CCCTB should also entail a provision for this situation stipulating that the PE book such assets and liabilities at fair market value at the moment of transfer (a step-up in basis). See also, for example, Daniel Gutmann, Chapter 7 in this book, section 7.4.1.

[143] See for a detailed discussion of this case, for example Tom O'Shea, 'Dutch Exit Tax Rules Challenged in National Grid Indus' (January 2012) *Tax Notes International* 201–205; Eric C.C.M. Kemmeren, 'The Netherlands: Infringement Procedure on Exit Taxes on Business (C-301/11)' in Michael Lang, Pasquale Pistone, Josef Schuch, Claus Staringer, and Alfred Storck (eds),

assuming that in these kinds of situations Article 63 TFEU can be invoked, which is still not clear (especially in the case of the transfer of single business assets),[144] the current provision should also be supplemented with an option to defer the payment of taxes due based on Article 31 CCCTB in respect of non-EEA Member States with which a sufficient machinery is available for (the exchange of information) in the context of recovery of taxes.[145]

Finally, the CCCTB system is silent on when a transfer takes place. The authors believe that a transfer is at hand if the asset is no longer effectively connected with the PE's business activities. This will not be the case if the asset is only temporarily used by another part of the non-resident taxpayer's enterprise than the EU-based PE and the asset is still managed and its operations are still directed and controlled by the PE. The asset remains effectively connected with the PE. However, if the asset is no longer managed and its operations no longer directed and controlled by the PE, but by another part of the non-taxpayer's enterprise, the asset has been transferred by the PE. This requirement is perfectly consistent with EU law.[146]

Therefore, the authors believe that the CCCTB should be supplemented with a definition of the term 'transfer' based on the above.

ECJ-Recent Developments in Direct Taxation 2011 (Linde 2012) 183–212; Daniel Gutmann, 'Liberté d'établissement et transfert de siège, A propos de CJUE, 29 November 2011, National Grid Indus' (2011) Feuillet Rapide Francis Lefebvre 9; Peter J. Wattel, 'Exit Taxation in the EU/EEA Before And After National Grid Indus' (January 2012) *Tax Notes International* 371–379 and Christiana HJI Panayi, 'National Grid Indus BV v Inspecteur van de Belastingdienst Rijnmond/kantoor Rotterdam: Exit taxes in the European Union revisited' (March 2012) *British Tax Review* 41–49.

[144] See, for example the pending Case C-35/11 *Test Claimants in the FII Group Litigation II*. The Netherlands Supreme Court left this question unanswered in the case where a Netherlands company moves its place of effective management to the Netherlands Antilles. The Court held that the exit tax applied was allowed under the grandfathering-clause of Article 64(1) TFEU, even if one were to assume that the free movement of capital could be relied on in the first place; HR 13 January 2012, 08/05322, *Vakstudie Nieuws* 2012/6.11.

[145] See also, for example, Daniel Gutmann, Chapter 7 in this book, section 7.3.

[146] See, for example, Case C-221/89 *Factortame II* [1991] ECR I-3905, paras 34–36. See further, for example, Eric C.C.M. Kemmeren, *Principle of Origin in Tax Conventions, A Rethinking of Models*, Dissertation Tilburg University (Eric C.C.M. Kemmeren/Pijnenburg vormgevers·uitgevers 2001) 177–181.

2.5 CONCLUSIONS AND RECOMMENDATIONS

It can be established that the idea of economic openness is the leading one under the CCCTB proposal, meaning that, as a general rule, the CCCTB regime should normally apply to first- and second-tier subsidiaries established in different Member States, irrespective of the fact that these subsidiaries are ultimately held by a non-EU parent. This is also in line with the benchmark of international tax neutrality. However, the fact that ultimate parent is in a non-EU Member State may, under certain circumstances, raise issues on the place of management of the first-tier subsidiary.

For clarity's sake, a specific anti-tax avoidance rule should be included in the CCCTB proposal aiming at combating tax avoidance schemes involving EU conduit companies held by non-EU parent companies. Based on the international tax neutrality benchmark, Member States should be allowed – or preferably even required – to levy withholding tax if the receiving EU conduit company qualifies as a fictitious establishment which does not carry on a genuine economic activity in the territory of its Member State of residence.

The current ban on interest deduction in Article 81 CCCTB has some weaknesses. In the authors' opinion, Article 81 CCCTB would be more effective if it were drafted as a general anti-tax avoidance clause, stating that interest deduction is denied if the principal aim of the loan arrangement was to reduce the CCC tax base. If the creditor is established in a 'suspect' third country, in particular a third country in which a generally low corporate income tax rate applies or which is not under any international obligation to exchange information with the Member State concerned, a presumption of abuse should apply. In addition, interest deduction should be denied if the creditor is established in a third country where a special tax regime applies for financing activities that would qualify as state aid under the Treaty provisions.

The CCCTB proposal rightly allows EU sister companies commonly held by a non-EU parent to benefit from the CCCTB regime, but arguably denies – wrongly – these benefits to an EU-resident company which holds a first-tier non-EU-subsidiary and a second-tier EU-subsidiary ('Papillon investment'). Although there is a risk that a loss of the second-tier subsidiary could be taken into account twice in such case (once directly through the consolidation and once through a devaluation of the shares in or loan receivable on the first-tier subsidiary) a categorical exclusion from the CCCTB regime would be disproportionate. The CCCTB regime should provide for a more proportionate case-by-case solution instead.

A non-resident company can only opt for the system in respect of income from an activity carried out through a PE maintained in a Member State. This means that the scope of the CCCTB system for non-resident taxpayers may be more limited than the scope of non-resident tax liability under a Member State's domestic corporate income tax law. Such a split in taxation is not desirable.

Article 6(3) CCCTB needs to be revised as follows:

- Determination of tax residence in a Member State should not be restricted under reference to registered office, place of incorporation, and place of effective management only. Instead, tax residence under the national laws of a Member State, irrespective of the criterion on which it is based, should constitute tax residence under the CCCTB regime, unless an agreement is in place between that Member State and a third country which allocates tax residence to that third country.
- The shipping residence rule could be supplemented with a rule that stipulates that if no home harbour is situated in one of the Member States and the operator does not have his residence in one of the Member States either, that a company will be deemed to be a non-resident.
- There is no good reason to exclude PEs of a qualifying third-country resident subsidiary from the group of a non-resident taxpayer.
- It must be possible to designate a PE as principal taxpayer in case the shares in a subsidiary are effectively connected with a PE of a parent company.
- The principal taxpayer rules must be supplemented in order to cover the situation in which a non-resident taxpayer holds shares in two or more qualifying subsidiaries which are residents in two or more Member States and, in addition to them, maintains one or more PEs in one or more Member States.

Each PE of a non-resident company should also be treated as an individual 'group member' in order to make sure that formula for apportionment can properly be applied.

The proposed Article 60 CCCTB seems to open the door to a flow of income from transactions – including intra-group interest and royalty payments – free from withholding taxes or any source taxation to large parts of the world. This cannot be the aim. Therefore, elimination of withholding taxes under this provision must be restricted. It seems to be necessary to supplement this restriction with a kind of branch profit tax. Most of the current DTCs with third countries will not allow such a branch profit tax. It will not be easy to effectively repair this potential loophole.

The CCCTB PE definition has been to a large extent inspired by the OECD Model. As a result, the same issues that arise under the OECD Model will also arise under the CCCTB. For the interpretation of this definition, the OECD Commentary is not decisive. It is only a supplementary means of interpretation. If a PE is situated in the EU and a partner is a non-resident company, that partner satisfies the PE conditions under the CCCTB system. The CCCTB PE definition may deviate from the PE definition under the actual DTCs concluded with third countries. The CCCTB PE definition must be supplemented with a rule which stipulates that for CCCTB purposes the PE definition of the DTC involved is to be adopted in case a DTC applies to the situation.

The CCCTB system does not include any general rule on when income must be considered to be received from an activity carried on through a PE. Whereas the words 'income from an activity carried on through a PE' in Article 6(7) CCCTB must be interpreted, Article 7(1–2) OECD Model and its Commentary to it could be used as supplementary means to interpret these words. It is advisable to supplement the rule of Article 6(7) CCCTB with a general attribution rule. It is possible to properly attribute, for example, shares in company, debt claims, and intangibles, such as patents, to a PE and, consequently, also the income derived from these assets: dividends, interest, and royalties. It is also possible to attribute a PE to another PE if that PE is effectively connected with the latter PE. Subsequently, the non-resident taxpayer can also invoke the machinery of reduction of double taxation. The application of the formula for apportionment may result in an attribution of more profits to a PE in a EU Member State than is allowed based on the arm's length principle laid down in actual DTC provisions with third countries. If so, as a rule, the DTC attribution rule will prevail over the CCCTB formula.

Article 78(1) CCCTB must be adjusted in order to clarify that both the non-resident taxpayer and its PE must be regarded as associated enterprises if the Commission wants to maintain this concept. For the attribution of income to a PE, the CCCTB system puts the PE completely on a par with an associated enterprise like a subsidiary. This may have far-reaching consequences. The OECD Commentary to Article 7 OECD Model may be completely irrelevant for the attribution of income to a PE, whereas the Commentary to Article 9 OECD Model and the Transfer

Pricing Guidelines may be highly relevant as a supplementary means for interpreting the income allocation rules to a PE. In substance, this may have as a consequence that it must be ignored that the PE is a part of the non-resident taxpayer, but that the PE must be regarded as separate legal entity in relation to the other parts of the non-resident taxpayer. As result, it may be very hard to argue under the CCCTB that notional interest should not be taken into account, as a rule, in the relation between a PE and other parts of the enterprise of which the PE is a part. The Commission must reconsider the starting point of classifying a non-resident taxpayer and its EU-based PE as associated enterprises. It may be better to link up with Article 7 OECD Model for the attribution of income to such a PE.

Assuming that the non-resident taxpayer and its PE are associated enterprises, the income attributed to such a PE must be done on the basis of the arm's length principle. The scope of Article 79 CCCTB may be wider than that of Article 9 OECD Model. On the other hand, it can be argued that it is not possible to adjust the profit attribution to a PE based on Article 79 CCCTB. This (potential) problem could be solved by replacing the words 'the taxpayer' and 'that taxpayer' by the words 'one of the associated enterprise' and 'that associated enterprise', respectively.

The CCCTB system does not contain a general final settlement or an exit tax provision. The final settlement provision of Article 31 CCCTB is restricted to fixed assets only. It seems to be that other assets and liabilities can be transferred from an EU-based PE to a third country without triggering taxation at that moment. The final settlement tax will not be levied if information can be exchanged with an EEA Member State comparable to what has been laid down in Directive 2011/16/EU. A provision included in a DTC similar to Article 26 OECD Model will likely be sufficiently comparable. The same is true for a TIEA which only provides for exchange of information upon request. Excluding these non-EEA Member States with sufficient instruments for the exchange of information is not justified.

The absence of a general final settlement or an exit tax provision leaves open the question of whether a loophole exists or whether the CCCTB creates a taxable event upon actual realization, even when the assets and liabilities not covered by the taxation of Article 31 CCCTB are no longer part of the PE situated in the Member State. To protect Member States' legitimate tax claims, the proposed Directive should be supplemented with rules that establish the taxation on the unrealized capital gains which have been arisen within the ambit of a Member State's tax jurisdiction after the transfer to a third country at the time that they are actually realized, if the recovery of that tax is guaranteed through agreements with the third country involved. In any case, Article 31 CCCTB must be supplemented with an option to defer the payment of taxes due in respect of non-EEA Member States with which a sufficient machinery available for (the exchange of information) in the context of recovery of taxes.

The CCCTB system should be supplemented with a definition of the term 'transfer'. An asset must be considered transferred if the asset is no longer managed and its operations no longer directed and controlled by the PE, but by another part of the non-taxpayer's enterprise.

Commentary

Theo Keijzer

INTRODUCTION

It is noticeable that the European Union as well as European leaders apparently try to make progress on the CCCTB dossier and manage to have it ready for political decision-making. This push can perhaps best be demonstrated by two quotes. The first quote relates to the Euro Plus Pact of March 2011:

> Developing a common corporate tax base could be a revenue neutral way forward to ensure consistency among national tax systems while respecting national tax strategies, and to contribute to fiscal sustainability and the competitiveness of European businesses. The Commission has presented a legislative proposal on a common consolidated corporate tax base.[147]

The second quotation is from a letter by both the German and French leaders to Mr Van Rompuy (translation by German/French Government from original French text):

> In line with the Euro Plus Pact, euro area Member's States should take all the necessary measures to improve competitiveness, foster employment, ensure stability of the euro area as a whole and deepen economic integration. In particular, further progress should be made on tax policy coordination to support fiscal consolidation and economic growth. Member states should commit to finalize the negotiation on the Commission's proposal on 'a common consolidated corporate tax base' before end 2012.[148]

---

[147] European Council, 20 April 2011, EUCO 10/1/11 REV 1, p. 20, see http://register.consilium.europa.eu/pdf/en/11/st00/st00010-re01.en11.pdf, accessed 18 September 2012.

[148] Letter by President of French Republic, Mr Sarkozy and the Chancellor of the German Federal Republic, Mrs Merkel to the President of the European Council, Mr Van Rompuy, dated 17 August 2011, see http://www.ambafrance-uk.org/French-and-German-leaders-defend, accessed 18 September 2012.

GENERAL OBSERVATIONS

The chapter by Kemmeren and Smit (hereafter 'the chapter' or 'the authors') provides a thorough analysis of topics and a vast array of situations that may arise when addressing the broad topic of EU non resident companies under CCCTB.

Although the chapter is extensive and well worth reading, it will be addressed that this does not mean that all statements can be agreed with.

The authors first develop a base line: international tax neutrality. They describe this as 'the *relation between taxes (burdens) and public goods (benefits)* should not be disturbed to the disadvantage of transnational investment.'[149] They continue that 'fair competition between foreign and domestic enterprises which carry on the same genuine economic activities under the same market conditions and using the same public goods in that state to the same extent is promoted.'[150]

Consequently, they reach the conclusion that source taxation should be included in the 'CCCT-base' and the base should exclude non-EU source taxation.[151] This in itself is already worth a full discussion. One of the angles left mainly untouched is the difficulty in delineating in-country and out-country sources. Moreover, a source-based CCCTB would clash when most tax systems in the developed world try to be residence based and work with some exemptions to reach a modicum of attraction for a country. Fortunately, the authors do not promote an absolute source approach, although in their chapter they frequently check provisions against their neutrality principle.

DETAILED OBSERVATIONS

The authors approach their brief for the chapter by outlining in an exhaustive manner two scenarios: the first scenario is 'EU-non-resident company invests in the EU through one or more EU subsidiaries' and the second scenario is 'EU-non-resident company invests in the EU through an EU branch'.[152] The following section is going to use the term sub or subs for subsidiary and permanent establishment ('PE') where the authors use the term 'branch'.

---

[149] See the chapter, section 5.
[150] See the chapter, section 5.
[151] See the chapter, section 5 et seq.
[152] See the chapter, section 1.

First Scenario: Investment through a Sub or Subs[153]

The authors raise the situation where a non-EU shareholder manages the EU sub such that they have a PE in the CCCTB area. The question is whether this allows the sub to be in the CCCTB framework. They rightly answer the question positively. However, the authors do not raise the impact of profit allocation as a result and the possible impact on tax neutrality. It would have been interesting to see more thoughts on this to see how the authors resolved the issue. When is management a true economic activity warranting a profit and where does the activity take place? These are difficult and complex issues that would probably require a separate chapter written by the authors. Some questions for research would be: what is management and especially in today's electronic era, what is an economic activity and how is it rewarded?

No doubt the authors must have enjoyed themselves with the various scenarios that can arise. They cover many such situations in their chapter. For example: they use an example of a foreign shareholder and EU sub in a country with withholding tax on dividend, interest and royalties.[154] Intra-CCCTB payments from one country and company to another are not subject to withholding tax. Where you interpose a company in a country without such withholding tax, the tax at source would be circumvented. The authors explore the question of how to stop this. They assume the draftsmen of the CCCTB are aware that anti-avoidance rules locally could stop such abuse but Article 60 CCCTB does not allow this in a treaty situation with a non-EU country. The authors argue that as a general principle the abuse of rights is not allowed but suggest including this in a separate article in the text of the CCCTB Directive as a specific anti-avoidance rule. If this is not the case, the CCCTB company would be better off than those companies outside CCCTB framework.

I am not in favour of GAARs (General Anti-Avoidance Rules) and SAARs (Specific Anti-Avoidance Rules), if only because they introduce complexity and the possibility of more planning to avoid tax. My preference and solution is for a mandatory enhanced relationship ('ER') for all those that opt for CCCTB. This not only has the benefit of reducing undesired use of provisions not intended but also is as transparent as possible for all parties concerned. Transparency in the relationship between taxpayer and Revenue authority is the best way forward. It reduces friction, uncertainty and should also result in less double

---

153 See the chapter, section 2.3.

154 See the chapter, section 2.3.1.2.2.

taxation, assuming the revenue authority consults with colleagues in other countries. This formal and informal consultation between various actors is key to a well-functioning transparency framework.

In section 2.3.1.3 of the chapter the authors describe another topic. Article 81 CCCTB deals with interest deduction. Interest is deductible where there is an exchange of information agreement. That's all; period. If not, one must meet various tests. The reason, according to the authors, lies in case law dealing with free capital movement and the extension to third countries. However, this condition is almost frivolous since most countries have a TIEA (Tax Information Exchange Agreement) even if with a low tax regime. Where interest is paid to a tax haven that does not tax the interest but has a TIEA, interest is deductible. The question is whether this is correct and reasonable. In order not to lose the main argumentation line in this commentary to the author's chapter, these issues will not be addressed any further.

The drafting of Article 81 CCCTB has probably suffered from the time lapse between the time of drafting and subsequent developments. Since the drafting, many hundreds of TIEAs have been concluded, including by low-tax countries. Hence, not having a TIEA can no longer be regarded as a relevant parameter or indicator of an abusive situation.

Again, the authors suggest combating this problem raised by converting Article 81 CCCTB to a GAAR where anyone is denied deduction when he tries to deduct interest when the principal aim of the loan is to reduce the CCCTB.

Several reasons against the usage of GAARs and SAARs have already been pointed out. The situation addressed with respect to interest deduction and Article 81 CCCTB does not change this view. ER is the solution where no proper textual and simple solution can be found to address the abuse envisaged.

The authors also address an interesting question mark in connection with the *Papillon* case.[155] This covers the following situation: an EU company holds a non-EU company which holds an EU company. The question is whether Article 55(1)(d) CCCTB allows a group to be formed between the two EU companies. Quite rightly the authors argue that it should be included. Any other conclusion would not have done justice to the *Papillon* case.

---

155 See this chapter, section 2.3.3; Case C-418/07 *Papillon* [2008] ECR I-8947.

Second Scenario: Investment through PE[156]

The authors address in the second scenario the subject to tax issue for foreign companies, in Article 6(7) CCCTB it reads 'subject to corporate tax under that system on all income from an activity carried on through a permanent establishment'. The authors cover a number of interesting topics and situations in this area. Rather than repeating and commenting, it is suggested to read section 2.4 in its entirety. An anomaly appears to exist with respect to Article 6(3) CCCTB, place of management. The authors describe the situation of the UK where place of management is not the relevant key but rather 'where the central management and control actually abides'.[157] Hence, a resident UK taxpayer must be seen as non-resident for CCCTB purposes. They urge the draftsmen in the EU Commission to amend Article 6(3) CCCTB.

The authors also urge that Article 4(7) CCCTB be amended such that any PE of a non-resident company is treated as an individual group member.[158] They reach this conclusion by investigating a situation where a foreign company has a PE in the EU and this PE has a foreign company as asset. The latter foreign company has a PE again in the EU. The latter PE is under Article 4(7) CCCTB not allowed to be grouped with the first PE. Quite rightly, the authors see this as incorrect, if only to avoid very complex and conflict prone profit attribution issues.

The authors also describe an interesting situation where withholding tax can be avoided, be it on royalty or interest.

> The question may arise as to the impact of these provisions if, for example an EU-based parent company pays a royalty to its third-country-resident qualifying subsidiary which itself maintains an EU-based PE, the EU-based parent and the EU-based PE form a group, and the intangible involved can*not* be attributed to the EU-based PE. [...] Can a withholding tax on the royalty payment from the EU parent to the non-EU subsidiary be avoided?[159]

Article 60 CCCTB prevents withholding tax between members of a group. Consequently, the payments to the foreign sub are not subject to withholding tax. The authors suggest restricting the elimination of withholding tax under Article 60 CCCTB. It is unclear whether this important principle should be amended; the commentator on the chapter written by Kemmeren and Smit is basically opposed to withholding taxes

---

156 See this chapter, section 2.4.
157 See this chapter, section 2.4.
158 See this chapter, last sentence section 2.4.1.3.
159 See this chapter, Figure 2.5 (Scenario 4).

as they are complex, administrative costly and frequently distort routine transactions and thus rather seek another solution or accept that a leak exists.

Then the authors turn to the definition of a PE and the attribution of profits to a PE.[160] They conclude that the reach of the CCCTB and OECD texts are the same; they imply to use the OECD wording as typically used in tax treaties:

> The differences in definition may lead to double taxation or double non-taxation, which does not contribute to a level playing field and is also inconsistent with the principle of international tax neutrality. Such a result could be avoided if, for such situations, the proposed definition were to be supplemented with a rule which stipulates that for CCCTB purposes the PE definition of the DTC involved is to be adopted.[161]

However, not all EU members are OECD member countries. These EU members have seen to display an allergy when it comes to making OECD principles an EU standard. Since the UN also develops its own guidelines, it is therefore suggested that the EU Commission, Taxud, looks at the analysis and try to eliminate the problems identified by the authors but without reference to the OECD.

Finally, the transfer of assets is addressed. The authors conclude, as does Gutmann,[162] that only fixed assets are addressed in Article 31 CCCTB.[163] The authors also conclude that consequently non-fixed assets should not trigger an exit tax. However, although the term 'transfer' is not defined, it is to be assumed that any value of a company leaving the company will be taxed. The basis for their conclusion seems to be uncertain. The authors conclude that a definition of transfer in the CCCTB should be added.[164]

CONCLUDING REMARKS

The authors' chapter and these comments thereon are part of a necessary journey to achieve an attractive, good, sensible and error-free CCCTB text. The chapter will certainly contribute to this process. An almost

---

[160] See the chapter, section 2.4.3.

[161] See the chapter, 35–36[Q18]; last paragraph of section 2.4.3.

[162] See Gutmann, Chapter 7 in this book, section 7.4.2.2.

[163] See the chapter, 41[Q18], first paragraph of section 2.4.4.3.

[164] See the chapter, 45[Q18], last paragraph of section 2.4.4.3.

error-free text may, however, be less of an issue if the EU were to follow the suggestion that ER must be made mandatory for all taxpayers in the CCCTB framework.

3. The meaning of 'resident taxpayer' and 'non-resident taxpayer' under the proposal for a Council Directive on a Common Consolidated Corporate Tax Base (CCCTB)

Guglielmo Maisto

3.1 INTRODUCTION

This chapter covers the meaning of 'resident taxpayer' and 'non-resident taxpayer' under the proposal for a Council Directive on a Common Consolidated Corporate Tax Base (CCCTB; hereinafter 'the Proposal') with a focus on the complex rules dealing with its personal scope.[1,2]

---

[1] Proposal for a Council Directive on a Common Consolidated Corporate Tax Base (CCCTB), COM(2011) 121/4. For an overview of the main aspects, see Christiana HJI Panayi, 'The Common Consolidated Corporate Tax Base and the UK Tax System' (2011) *The Institute for Fiscal Studies*, http://www.ifs.org.uk/publications/5961 (last accessed 13 August 2012). For some preliminary comments, see Michael Lang, 'The general anti-abuse rule of Art. 80 of the Draft Proposal for a Council Directive on a Common Consolidated Corporate Tax Base' (2011) 51 *European Taxation* 6, 223 et seq.; Marius Vascega and Servatius Van Thiel, 'The CCCTB Proposal: The next step towards corporate tax harmonization in the European Union?' (2011) 51 *European Taxation* 9/10, 374 et seq.; Luca Cerioni, 'The Commission's Proposal for a CCCTB Directive: Analysis and Comment' (September 2011) *Bulletin for International Taxation*, 515 et seq.; H.T.P.M. Van Den Hurk, 'The Common Consolidated Corporate Tax Base: A desirable alternative to a flat EU corporate income tax?' (2011) 4–5 *Bulletin for International Taxation*, 260 et seq.; Eric Kemmeren, 'CCCTB: Enhanced speed ahead for improvement' (2011) 20 *EC Tax Review*, 208 et seq.; Arjo van Eusden, 'The one-stop approach: A discussion of the administrative and procedural aspects of the CCCTB Draft Directive' (2011) 20 *EC Tax Review* 4, 217 et seq.; Notwithstanding the wide coverage of literature on the CCCTB in general, little attention has been paid so far to the personal scope of the Proposal. See Claus

An analysis of the subject matter reveals a lack of clarity about the relationship between domestic taxing rules of the Member States and the provisions laid down by the Proposal, particularly with regard to companies that are tax resident in a third State. This is so notwithstanding the provision laid down by Article 7 of the Proposal, which stipulates that 'national corporate tax arrangements' cease to apply where a company 'qualifies and opts' for the common system. There is no clear distinction between tax rules and rules regarding the determination of the taxable base especially for third-State residents.

Issues of interpretation also arise concerning the relationship between the provisions of the Proposal and tax treaties concluded by the Member States. Article 8 of the Proposal expressly provides that its rules override tax treaties concluded between Member States with the primary purpose of adopting definitions which are separate from those contained in double taxation agreements.[3] As to treaties concluded by the Member States with third States, the working papers relating to the Proposal[4] suggest an

Staringer, 'Requirements for forming a Group', in Michael Lang, Pasquale Pistone, Joseph Schuch and Claus Staringer (eds), *Common Consolidated Corporate Tax Base* (Linde 2008) 115 et seq. and, to a certain extent, Christiana HJI Panayi, 'The Common Consolidated Corporate Tax Base – Issues for Member States opting out and third countries' (2008) 48 *European Taxation* 3, 114 et seq. and Tom O'Shea, 'The Common Consolidated Corporate Tax Base (CCCTB) – Issues for Member States opting out and third countries: A Critique and some in-depth analysis' (2008) 48 *EC Tax Journal* 12, 1 et seq.

[2] Parliaments of the Member States have already expressed opinions on the Proposal, which, however, do not focus on the personal scope of the common system. See http://www.ipex.eu/IPEXLWEB/dossier/dossier.do?code=CNS&year=2011&number=0058 (last accessed 13 August 2012). See Philip Baker and Iloanna Mitroyanni, 'The CCCTB rules and tax treaties' in Michael Lang et al (eds), *Common consolidated corporate tax base* (Linde 2008) 637; see also Kristen Parillo, 'CCCTB could be adopted by subset of EU countries, Austrian academic says' (2011) *Tax Analysts*, where the author quotes the lecture given by Michael Lang at the 7th Annual International Tax Symposium hosted by the University of Florida Graduate Tax Program on 7 October 2011 in Gainesville, Florida.

[3] Under Art. 8 of the Proposal, '[T]he provisions of this Directive shall apply notwithstanding any provision to the contrary in any agreement concluded between Member States.'

[4] The main working papers addressing the personal scope of the Proposal are European Commission, Working Document 'International Aspects in the CCCTB' CCCTB\WP\019, 18 November 2005; European Commission, Working Document 'An Overview of the main issues that emerged at the first meeting of

alleged potential conflict between CCCTB rules and tax treaty provisions, and this assumption influenced the Commission's policy decision to apply the common system to companies that are residents and/or nationals of third countries. Indeed, it was found that an exclusion of third-State residents from the common system would have violated the non-discrimination provisions contained in several bilateral tax conventions concluded by Member States with third countries.[5,6]

---

the subgroup on International Aspects' CCCTB\WP\029, 2 March 2006; European Commission, Working Document, 'CCCTB: An Overview of the main issues that emerged at the second meeting of the subgroup on International Aspects (SG4)' CCCTB\WP\033, 24 May 2006; European Commission, Working Document 'An overview of the main issues that emerged at the third meeting of the subgroup on International aspects (SG 4)' CCCTB\WP\049, 23 November 2006; European Commission, Working Document 'The Territorial Scope of the CCCTB' CCCTB\WP\026, 17 February 2006 and European Commission, Working Document 'The Personal Scope of the CCCTB' CCCTB\WP\040, 26 July 2006.

[5] The current income tax directives may raise similar issues, for example, for parent companies that are resident in a Member State under the Parent-Subsidiary Directive or for companies resident of a Member State participating in one of the transactions covered by the Merger Directive, and which have a legal form available in a third State by virtue of their nationality in such State and which may be denied the common regime provided for by the relevant directive (see below at Section 3.2.2.). This could be viewed in the light of Art. 24(1) OECD Model. A similar issue might be said prima facie to apply to the Interest and Royalties Directive, which provides for its application to companies residing in Member States that are controlled by the same parent. The question could arise whether such parent is a resident of a third State for which it is unclear if the Directive applies. However, no issues of treaty discrimination would arise in such an instance as the alleged discrimination would not affect the taxation of the recipient associated company that is controlled by the third-State resident but rather exclusively the paying associated party which is applying the withholding tax on the interest or royalties.

[6] The reason for also including PEs of third-country companies within the scope of the Directive does not lie solely in the need to avoid a potential breach of the tax treaty obligations towards third countries under Art. 24(3) of OECD Model-based tax treaties (see European Commission, Working Document 'The Territorial Scope of the CCCTB' CCCTB\WP\026, 17 February 2006, para 36), but also in the recognition that '[a]ctivities carried out through a permanent establishment often represent an integral part of business conducted in the EU. [Excluding non-residents' income taxable within the CCCTB jurisdictions from the CCCTB] would also be very sensitive to the shifting of profit outside of the CCCTB and would require a system of prudent anti-avoidance rules' (see European Commission, Working Document 'The Territorial Scope of the CCCTB' CCCTB\WP\026, 17 February 2006, para 31).

The Proposal therefore makes the underlying assumption that the EU provisions should be capable of being accessed by third-country residents and nationals on the basis of double taxation agreements which contain a non-discrimination provision following Article 24 of the OECD Model Convention on the avoidance of double taxation of income and capital (the OECD Model).[7]

Bearing in mind these features of the Proposal, which will also be commented on in this chapter, the meaning can be examined of the expressions 'resident taxpayer' and 'non-resident taxpayer', which are rather intricate insofar as they both include references to other defined expressions or terms.[8] This chapter suggests revisions that may provide clarity and simplification while upholding the use of tax treaty definitions.

3.2 THE DEFINITION OF 'RESIDENT TAXPAYER'

The definition of resident taxpayer is laid down in Article 4(4) of the Proposal under which:

> 'resident taxpayer' means a *taxpayer* which is *resident for tax purposes in a Member State* according to Article 6(3) and (4). (Emphasis added)

The meaning of 'taxpayer' is defined by Article 4(1) of the Proposal as:

> a *company* which has opted to apply the system provided for by the Directive. (Emphasis added)

---

[7] The issue regarding the extension of EU tax rules to third-State treaty residents by virtue of the non-discrimination provisions laid down in tax treaties (which is dealt with in the conclusion of this chapter) is marginally covered in the literature by Alexander Rust, 'International tax neutrality and non-discrimination – A legal perspective', in Michael Lang et al. (eds), *Tax treaties: Building bridges between law and economics* (IBFD 2010), 633; with regard to access by third-State nationals to the same tax treatment granted by the other (EU) contracting states to nationals of other EU Member States. See also Jürgen Lüdicke, 'European Tax Law, quo vadis? – Comments by Prof. Jurgen Ludicke' (2008) *Bulletin for International Taxation*, 11. The issue is also addressed by the OECD public discussion draft, *Application and interpretation of Article 24 (non-discrimination)* of 3 May 2007, Annex, para. 3, 'Issues that require a more fundamental analysis of the issue of non-discrimination and taxation'.

[8] This chapter will not cover the scope of consolidation and the meaning of 'qualifying subsidiaries' laid down in Art. 54 of the Proposal.

On the meaning of 'company', Article 2(1) and (2) of the Proposal provides that the common system applies to:

> companies established under the laws of a Member State where both of the following conditions are met:
>
> (a) the company takes one of the forms listed in Annex I; and
> (b) the company is subject to one of the corporate taxes listed in Annex II or to a similar tax subsequently introduced. [Article 2(1)]

and

> companies established under the laws of a third country where both of the following conditions are met:
>
> (a) the company has a similar form to one of the forms listed in Annex I; and
> (b) the company is subject to one of the corporate taxes listed in Annex II. [Article 2(2)]

Lastly, under Article 6(3) of the Proposal, the meaning of 'resident for tax purposes in a Member State' is:

> a company that has its registered office, place of incorporation or place of effective management in a Member State and is not under the terms of an agreement concluded by that Member State with a third country, regarded as a tax resident in that third country.

The 'resident taxpayer' must therefore be (i) a 'company established under the laws of a Member State' or 'a company established under the laws of a third State' and (ii) a resident for tax purposes in a Member State. By reason of the several references included in each defined expression, the meaning of 'resident taxpayer' may be further fragmented and lead to the aggregation of these features: (i) an entity taking an eligible legal form either under Annex I or similar to those found in Annex I; (ii) subject to the corporate tax of a Member State; (iii) having its registered office, place of incorporation or place of effective management in a Member State; and (iv) not regarded as a resident of a third State under the double taxation agreement concluded with the Member State in which the registered office, place of incorporation or place of effective management is situated.[9]

---

[9] The definition of 'resident for tax purposes in a Member State' provided by Art. 6(3) refers to one treaty and one Member State only; however, 'Member

3.2.1 The Meaning of 'Company Established under the Laws of a Member State'

Article 2(1)(a) of the Proposal refers to companies '*established* under the laws of a Member State', the term 'established' being one that does not appear in the other income tax directives. The term has a non-tax legal meaning provided that any reference to tax terms in the Proposal is expressly mentioned and the Proposal adopts autonomous definitions.[10] Both the English version and the French version ('*constituées conformément à la legislation d'un Etat membre*') of the Proposal would suggest that this expression includes entities that are incorporated or governed by the company law of a Member State. Other linguistic versions of the Proposal suggest the same meaning.[11]

However, if the term 'established' is read in conjunction with Annex I, the conclusion could be drawn that it not only includes entities governed by the law of a Member State upon its creation, because the Annex also includes entities that are not necessarily governed by the law of a Member State (for example, Italy, which refers to private and public entities whose activity is wholly or principally commercial). Equally, 'established under the laws of' does not include 'tax residence', because 'tax residence' is an expression autonomously defined in the Proposal and a separate requirement stipulated in Article 6(3) regarding the definition of 'resident taxpayer' (in other words, a company having its registered seat, place of incorporation or place of effective management in a Member State). The requirement of the company being 'established' ranks prior to that of 'tax residence' stipulated in Article 6(3). It is

---

State' might be more than one if the company maintains two connecting factors in two Member States and the third connecting factor is a third State.

[10] The term 'established' is used in Art. 1 of the Convention on Mutual Recognition of Companies and Bodies Corporate (signed on 29 February 1968; *Bulletin of the European Communities,* Supplement No.2-1969, 7-16), which refers to 'companies under civil or commercial law, including cooperative societies, established in accordance with the law of a Contracting State which grants them the capacity of persons having rights and duties, and having their statutory registered office in the territories to which the present Convention applies ...'.

[11] The expression in the Spanish version is '*las sociedades* constituidas *con arreglo a la legislación de un Estado miembro*'; in the Portuguese version, '*sociedades* constituídas *nos termos da legislação de um Estado-Membro*'; in the Italian version, '*società* costituite *conformemente alle leggi di uno Stato membro*'; and in the German version, '*Gesellschaften, die nach dem Recht eines Mitgliedstaats* gegründet *wurden*'.

therefore possible that an entity is 'a company established under the laws of a Member State' pursuant to Article 2(1) but it is not a 'resident for tax purposes in a Member State' as it is a resident of a third State pursuant to Article 6(3) of the Proposal.[12]

Among the several interpretations which the term 'established' may suggest, in our opinion, the law of the State under which the company was created should take precedence and any inconsistency with the Annex may be explained by the inaccurate drafting of the provision.

Had the expression 'established under the laws of a Member State' been deleted, the provision would have achieved clarity with no prejudice to the intent of the Proposal.

3.2.1.1 The legal form requirement

3.2.1.1.1 The inconsistency between the expression 'eligible companies' and the legal forms listed in Annex I and the desirability of replacing 'companies by entities' Article 2(1) of the Proposal applies to 'companies' taking one of the forms listed in Annex I. The wording would suggest that the Annex exclusively includes entities having corporate legal forms (or in some States also partnerships) so that Member States would have the (limited) freedom to either include all corporate forms (including in some States partnerships as well) or to exclude some of them. By contrast, however, the Annex includes legal forms other than companies.[13]

---

12 On the meaning of 'constituted' in the definition of 'national' under tax treaties, see John Avery Jones and Jürgen Lüdicke, 'Art. 24(5) of the OECD Model in relation to intra-group transfers of assets and profits and losses' (2011) 3 *World Tax Journal* 2, 183, note 10, who take the view that the two terms ('established' and 'constituted') have the same meaning as that in the law under which the company derives its status.

13 For instance, with regard to France '*caisses d'épargne et de prévoyance*' and '*industrial and commercial public establishments and undertakings*' are included; with regard to Ireland 'bodies registered under the Industrial and Provident Societies' and 'trustee savings banks within the meaning of the Trustee Savings Banks Act, 1989' are included; with regard to Italy 'private and public entities whose activity is wholly or principally commercial' are included; with regard to Luxembourg '*association d'assurances mutuelles*', '*association d'épargne-pension*' and '*entreprise de nature commerciale, industrielle ou minière de l'État, des communes, des syndicats de communes, des établissements publics et des autres personnes morales de droit public*' are included; and with regard to Portugal 'public undertakings incorporated in accordance with Portuguese law' are included.

It is worth noting that the wording ('companies') used by the Proposal follows the income tax directives, which also make their provisions applicable to 'companies' having one of the forms listed in an Annex. In the income tax directives, too, Member States have included in the Annexes non-corporate legal forms as well so that there is a discrepancy between the wording used in the text of these directives and that used in the relevant Annexes insofar as they also include non-corporate legal forms.

The reference to 'companies' laid down by Article 2(1) of the Proposal is therefore not meant to exclude from the Annex legal forms other than companies.

It would be desirable to amend Article 2(1) and replace the term 'companies' with the term 'entities' both in the heading, which would then read 'eligible *entities*' rather than 'eligible companies', and in the text of paragraph 1, which would stipulate that 'the Directive shall apply to *entities* established under the law of a Member State when (a) the *entity* takes one of the forms listed in Annex I'.[14,15]

Ideally, the combination of this change with the prior suggestion to delete 'established' would rephrase Article 2(1) of the Proposal as 'the Directive shall apply to entities when (a) the entity takes one of the forms listed in Annex I'.[16]

3.2.1.1.2 On the desirability of listing legal forms in an Annex Article 2(1)(a) of the Proposal refers to companies taking 'one of the forms

[14] This is different from the meaning of 'company' under the OECD Model, which is defined as also expressly including non-incorporated entities. The Proposal simply employs the term 'company' without providing a proper definition to also include within such a term non-incorporated entities. Read in its context, the term 'company' must be attributed the special meaning of also denoting entities other than companies.

[15] This amendment proposal was included in the Proposal for a Council Directive amending Directive 90/435 of 23 July 1990 on the common system of taxation applicable in the case of parent companies and subsidiaries of different Member States and in the Proposal for a Council Directive amending Directive 90/434 of 23 July 1990 on the common system of taxation applicable to mergers, divisions, transfer of assets and exchanges of shares concerning companies of different Member States, COM(93) 293 final, 26 July 1993.

[16] The term 'entity' is used by the Proposal in Arts. 73 (switch-over clause), 81 (disallowance of interest deductions), 82 (controlled foreign companies), 83 (computation), 84 (rules for allocating the income of transparent entities to taxpayers holding an interest), 85 (rules for determining transparency in the case of third countries entities) and 89 (transparent entities).

listed in Annex I'. The use of a list was found preferable to a self-standing definition for reasons of legal certainty.[17]

The desirability of a strict list of legal entities for each Member State may be questioned, however. Legal entities introduced into the domestic legislation of Member States after the adoption of the Proposal would in a few instances fall outside the scope of the common system and require that the Annex be amended.[18] This is an issue which applies equally to the other income tax directives. There is, however, a specific feature of the Proposal that may influence the shaping of the legal form requirement. Indeed, the Proposal requires all the companies belonging to the group to be subject to the CCCTB. This condition (all-in clause) might be circumvented insofar as groups select a legal form that is not covered and may lead to consolidation of only some group entities.[19,20] The working group identified the risk of circumventing the all-in condition when it addressed the definition of residence and thus suggested the adoption of a common definition. The strict list of legal entities adopted for defining the eligible entities goes in the opposite direction and seems to be contradictory, since group entities could avoid the all-in condition through the legal form requirement.[21]

As a general policy statement, it would be desirable to eliminate the legal form requirement, which may be contrary to the principle of

---

[17] The list approach was supported by the Commission Services (see European Commission, Working Document, 'An overview of the main issues that emerged at the third meeting of the subgroup on group taxation (SG5 – 05 & 06 February 2007)' CCCTB\WP\053, 1 March 2007, para 18).

[18] This is true for Member States that have included in the list of eligible entities a closed number of legal forms or only corporate legal forms, such as Bulgaria, Czech Republic, Estonia, Greece, Spain, Ireland, Cyprus, Latvia, Lithuania, Hungary, Malta, Poland, Romania, Slovenia, Slovak Republic, Finland, Sweden and the United Kingdom.

[19] This issue was raised by the working group (see European Commission, Working Document 'The Personal Scope of the CCCTB' CCCTB\WP\040, 26 July 2006).

[20] The solution adopted by the Proposal is therefore inconsistent with the approach taken with regard to the definition of 'resident' for which it was decided to have a common definition in order to prevent a group entity from opting out through a change of residence from one Member State to another.

[21] The wish to avoid circumvention of the all-in condition in any event could have been satisfied through an anti-abuse provision stating that the abusive use of legal forms or change of residence would jeopardize the application of the CCCTB system to the group entities.

equality developed under EU law, the EU rules on freedom of establishment or the principle of equality as laid down in several constitutional provisions of the Member States.

In the first instance, the restriction to certain legal forms may be contrary to the principle of equality that may be found also in EU law. It was argued that the restriction to certain legal forms may be justified by the difficulty Member States have in characterizing some legal forms, especially those entities which are transparent for tax purposes, and by the progressive realization of the Single Market.[22] However, these arguments lay themselves open to the criticism that the harmful effect of the restriction is disproportionate to the extent that the list excludes several legal entities from the scope of the common regime. It may also be noted that the restriction is unnecessary as an increasing number of Member States over the years have removed the legal form requirement and included in the legal forms any entity that is a taxable person in the respective States. These Member States permit the application of the income tax directives (and also of the Proposal) to legal forms that will be introduced into the legal system of a Member State after the adoption of the directives. The principle of equality under EU law has always been applied to EU harmonized taxes[23] so that it might be difficult to apply this principle to taxes which remain within the exclusive competence of the Member States. The most recent case law of the ECJ, however, clarifies that legal forms should not be the basis for discrimination between tax regimes; hence, it might be argued that the restriction of the Annex to the income tax directives (and also to the Proposal) may be a restriction which violates the freedom of establishment of legal entities

---

[22] G.F. Boulogne and W.W. Geursen, 'Gaz de France: Dividends to companies not listed in the Parent-Subsidiary Directive are not exempt' (2010) 50 *European Taxation* 4, 135.

[23] Paul Craig and Grainne De Burca, *EU Law, Texts, Cases and Materials* (Oxford University Press 2007) 560 et seq.; Luisa Azzena, 'La costruzione del principio di eguaglianza nell'ordinamento comunitario' (2007) Diritto Pubblico comparato ed Europeo 1419 et seq.; Giuseppe Tesauro, *Diritto Comunitario* (Padova 2005) 116 et seq.; Takis Tridimas, *The general principles of EC law* (Oxford University Press 1999) 59 et seq.; Federico Ghera, 'Il principio di eguaglianza nel diritto comunitario e nel diritto interno' (1999) 5 *Giurisprudenza Costituzionale*, 3267 et seq.; Federico Donati, 'Principio fondamentale di eguaglianza e diritto comunitario' (1995) 7 *Giurisprudenza Costituzionale*, 1838 et seq. See also Case C-300/04, *M.G. Eman and O.B. Sevinger* [2006] I-8055, para 61; Case C-305/05, *Advocaten voor de Wereld VZW* [2007] I-5305, paras 45-46, Cases C-117/76 and C-16/77, *Albert Ruckdeschel & Co. and Hansa-Lagerhaus Ströh & Co. and Diamalt AG*, [1977] 1753, para 7.

established in accordance with the company law of a Member State. In the *Aberdeen* case,[24] the ECJ pointed out that company laws of the Member States have not been fully harmonized so that relying plainly on the difference of the legal form to assert a different tax regime is an unjustified restriction. An alternative regime may be justified if the different legal form is substantiated by another structure of the legal entity or its different functioning, which would have a bearing on the tax regime.[25]

With regard to the principle of equality under the domestic law of Member States, several national constitutions might find the restriction deprived of any reason and thus contrary to a fundamental principle of domestic law. For instance, I would not find it unreasonable to argue that the Annex violates Article 3 of the Italian Constitution insofar as it discriminates between two different foreign legal entities having similar features for the purposes of the application of the common system.

In conclusion, criticism may be expressed with regard to the listing approach, which is not eliminated by the comitology procedure laid down by Article 2 with regard to the delegated powers of the Commission to amend and revise Annexes I and II.

3.2.1.1.3 On the desirability of excluding entities subject to special accounting rules or special tax rules for the determination of income At first sight, the need to consolidate the economic results of several legal entities might suggest the exclusion, from the common system, of group entities that fail to meet the level of consistency required to permit the aggregation of profits into a common base.

For instance, the exclusion could have applied to entities that are subject to special accounting rules which are different from the accounting rules applicable to the other group entities so that the assessment or consolidation would be made more difficult to achieve and would equally

---

[24] Case C-303/07, *Aberdeen Property Fininvest Alpha Oy*. n.y.r.; For a comment of the decision, see A.C. Pato and P.G. Seize, 'EC law and investment funds: The *Aberdeen* case' (2009) 3 *EC Tax Review*, 114; Y. Robert, Séverine Lauratet, Pauline Tredaniel and Antoine Reillac,'Dividend withholding tax levied on investment fund: *Aberdeen* and its implications in France' (2009) 49 *European Taxation* 12, 606.

[25] Unfortunately, the Court of Justice missed the opportunity to clarify the issue in Case C-247/08, *Gaz de France*, n.y.r. perhaps since the question was posed only in terms of compatibility of domestic law with the Parent-Subsidiary Directive, and not in terms of compatibility of both domestic law and the Parent-Subsidiary Directive with primary EU law.

impair audits conducted by tax authorities.[26] This could be equally true for non-commercial entities that have no corporate form and conduct a business activity, and, as such, have to segregate the results of such business activity. However, no such exclusion seems to be justified as the Proposal does not rely on the accounting profit and, in itself, it considers the possibility to apply the common base to a segment only of the legal entity, in other words, the permanent establishment (PE) of a company residing in a third State when such PE is situated in a Member State.

Therefore, the scope of the Proposal does not suggest any reason to restrict the list of forms to be included in the Annex as compared to similar Annexes to the income tax directives. Yet attention was drawn to the possible exclusion of companies that are engaged in businesses which are subject to special rules on determination of income (for example, banking and insurance) reflecting specific industry requirements, but it was found desirable[27] not to exclude such companies and industries from the common system and, instead, provide special rules within the Proposal for the determination of income of companies engaged in special activities (for example, Article 30 regarding insurance companies or Articles 98–101 on the apportionment of the consolidated tax base). Similarly, entities that are subject to a comprehensive special set of rules for determining income would also be entitled to opt in, as the option for the CCCTB would make them subject to the common system (this is not the case, however, in those Member States which consolidate the aggregated income of each subsidiary as determined at the level of such subsidiary, so that income of the various group entities requires the application of the same rules for the determination of income in order to avoid arbitrage).[28]

---

[26] The ECJ has recognized the existence of the principle of the mutual recognition of financial statements and accounting rules of foreign entities (see Case C-250/95 *Futura Participations SA* [1997] I-2471, paras 30–32). This principle is not extended to relations with third countries where Directive 78/660/EEC is not applicable (see Case C-101/05 *Skatteverket* [2007] I-11531, para 62).

[27] European Commission, Working Document 'The Personal Scope of the CCCTB' CCCTB\WP\040, 26 July 2006.

[28] This is true in Italy for companies that are subject to the tonnage tax regime (Art. 155–161 of the Consolidated Tax Act).

3.2.1.1.4 The legal entities included in Annex I and the call for revisiting the list Annex I of the Proposal departs from the Annexes of the other income tax directives which are also not identical to one another.

In general, Member States have included in Annex I of the Proposal the same legal forms listed in the Annex to the Merger Directive. This is not the case, however, for Austria, which has followed the same list adopted in the Annex to the Parent-Subsidiary Directive, or for Portugal, Slovenia and the Slovak Republic, which have followed the list of entities included in the Interest and Royalties Directive.[29] Poland is the only Member State that adopted a list of entities which is different from any other list included in the Annexes to the other income tax directives.[30] Romania followed the same list of entities included in all other income tax directives, which exclude certain taxable persons for corporation tax

[29] Both of the lists of eligible entities under the Proposal and the Interest and Royalties Directive include all legal entities that could be formed under the Slovak Commercial Code to conduct a business activity in the Slovak Republic whose income is subject to company tax. As regards the Merger Directive, various legal issues exist (from the point of view of Slovak company law as well as Slovak tax law) concerning the application of the directive in practice to a *Verejná obchodná spoločnos* (partnership; in German: *offene Handelsgesellschaft*) or to a *Družstvo* (cooperative) and therefore these entities are not listed in the Annex to this directive.

[30] Indeed, the list includes two legal entities (*spółdzielnia* and *przedsiębiorstwo państwowe*) which are not mentioned in the Annexes to the other income tax directives. *Spółdzielnia* corresponds to 'cooperative entity' and such entities are governed by separate regulations; they have legal personality and are used mainly by individuals to construct and manage residential buildings and by farmers to manage collectively agricultural activity, and so on. *Przedsiębiorstwo państwowe* is a special type of legal entity owned totally by the State and usually engaged in some public activity (water, gas, electricity supply, transport, mining, and so on.) They are relicts from previous economic regimes. Both *spółdzielnia* and *przedsiebiortswo państwowe* are subject to general corporate income tax (like companies). To date, Poland has not been interested in including these entities in the list of entities covered by the directives for practical reasons as they do not pay dividends and they do not enter into cross-border financing or licensing arrangements; in addition, classic mergers and other types of restructuring activities are limited or excluded for these types of entities. In the case of the CCCTB, the situation is different: these entities are subject to corporate income tax under the same rules which apply to companies and they can hold shares in companies so that they can be subject to rules set forth in the Proposal.

purposes, such as limited partnerships, perhaps because of their limited use internationally.[31]

This being said, the Member States might consider reviewing critically the Annexes adopted for the income tax directives and improving them so as to remove inconsistencies. Indeed, the Annexes attached to the income tax directives are not identical and contain discrepancies that are not easily explained. On the one hand, the discrepancies regard the approach adopted by a Member State compared to other Member States in the same directive and, on the other hand, the approach adopted by a Member State in one directive in comparison with the approach taken by the same Member State in another income tax directive.[32]

The recent proposal for recasting the Interest and Royalties Directive confirms the lack of consistency insofar as it includes changes to the legal forms included in the Annex.[33]

That said, it would be desirable for Member States to adopt the more flexible approach similar to that adopted by Denmark, which includes

---

[31] Romanian company law includes five types of commercial companies or other legal entities: (i) *societate pe actiuni* (joint-stock company, which is similar to the Italian *società per azioni*); (ii) *societate in comandita pe actiuni* (partnership limited by shares, which is similar to the Italian *società in accomandita per azioni*); (iii) *societate cu raspundere limitata* (limited liability company, which is similar to the Italian *società a responsabilità limitata*); (iv) *societate in comandita simpla* (limited partnership, which is similar to the Italian *società in accomandita semplice*, but under the Romanian law has legal personality); and (v) *societate in nume colectiv* (general partnership which is similar to the Italian *società in nome collettivo*, but under Romanian law has legal personality). Of these five entities, the last two are not included in the Annex. Neither is there any clarification or guidance regarding the inclusion in the Annex of different types of company. A possible reason might be the fact that these two entities are not commonly used in practice (nor in cross-border activities), perhaps because of the unlimited liability of the partners (with the exception of limited partners in a limited partnership). The entities used most often in practice are the three mentioned in the Annex. With regard to entities from other countries included in the Annex (for example, the Italian *società cooperative*), Romania does not have comparable entities. There are some forms of partnerships/associations (for example, civil law partnership or joint ventures), but these do not have legal personality and in any event are transparent for tax purposes.

[32] For a critical review, see Guglielmo Maisto, 'The 2003 amendments to the EC Parent-Subsidiary Directive: What's next?' (2004) 4 *EC Tax Review*, 164 et seq.

[33] See Proposal for a Council directive on a common system of taxation applicable to interest and royalty payments made between associated companies of different Member States (recast) COM(2011) 714 final.

specific domestic corporate legal forms but also other companies whether or not incorporated in Denmark that are taxable persons under Danish corporate tax so as to avoid undue restrictions of access to the CCCTB, which would frustrate the scope of the directive.[34]

One may also look at inconsistencies by the same Member State in listing the eligible entities in the income tax directives.

Discrepancies by the same Member State in the various income tax directives are shown by the table annexed to this chapter. This also suggests the need for a review of the list of entities which is consistent with the lists adopted by the same Member States for the other income tax directives.

3.2.1.1.5 The desirability of a move from closed listing to illustrative listing Furthermore, it would be desirable to permit taxpayers having legal forms that are not listed to be entitled to the application of the common system, which should not be unreasonably withheld by the relevant Member State. Indeed, the reason for the Annex is to be found in the difficulty Member States have characterizing foreign entities for tax purposes so that the Annex would ensure that transparent entities are not included and cannot unduly enjoy the benefits of the common system. An entity which is not included in the Annex and which nevertheless is a taxable person (in other words, non-transparent for tax purposes) should thus not be denied access to the common regime. This amendment to the Proposal would make it consistent with the similar legal form requirement laid down by the Proposal for third-country eligible entities, for which the annexed list is meant to be non-exhaustive. The reasons for this discrepancy are found in the circumstance that Member States may among themselves establish the eligible legal forms insofar as they participated in the adoption of the directive, which is not the case for third countries, so that the legal forms for such latter countries as adopted by the Council might more likely be incomplete and require additional flexibility.

The resistance of Member States is somewhat confirmed by the scope of the comitology procedure laid down in Article 2(3) of the Proposal, which empowers the Commission to amend the Annexes to 'take account of the changes to the laws of the Member States concerning company forms.' The scope of the delegated powers is thus restricted to the acknowledgement of new legal forms, which limitation suggests the following comments. Firstly, the scope of the powers appears to be

---

[34] It would be desirable to apply the common rules to entities rather than companies which are taxable persons in the Member States.

consistent with the boundaries under which delegation can be exercised by the Council, namely 'to supplement or amend certain non-essential elements of the legislative act'.[35] Furthermore, the Commission is empowered to take account of the 'changes to legal forms', which literally excludes situations in which a transparent entity becomes opaque and therefore may come within the scope of the Proposal had such entity been excluded by a Member State by virtue of its transparency.

3.2.1.1.6 The eligibility of transparent entities A special issue concerns transparent entities that are excluded from the scope of income tax directives, the reason being that such directives have the primary aim of avoiding double taxation, which is not at stake when the entity is transparent for income tax purposes. There should be no reason to depart from this rule under the CCCTB to the extent that the income of such entities is attributable to shareholders that are eligible for the application of the common system. For this reason, the Proposal addresses the transparency issue under Article 84 exclusively when the transparent entity interests are held by a 'taxpayer', in other words, by either a 'resident taxpayer' or a 'non-resident taxpayer'.[36]

3.2.1.2 The subject-to-tax requirement

Article 2(1)(b) requires the company established under the law of a Member State to be 'subject to one of the corporate taxes listed in Annex II or to a similar tax subsequently introduced', and, as such, reflects the similar conditions laid down by the income tax directives. This may be explained by the fact that the Proposal deals only with the computation of the taxpayer (or group) taxable base, while it leaves Member States free to decide whether and at which rate resident companies (and local PEs) should be taxed, provided that such taxation does not conflict with other rules or principles of European law (for example, State aid rules, fundamental freedoms, or harmful tax competition). Thus, the fact that a company is exempt from tax under the domestic law of the relevant Member State does not by itself encroach on the effectiveness of the Proposal scheme. In this respect, it is worth noting that the Proposal does

---

[35] Art. 290(1) TFEU. See also the Communication from the Commission to the European Parliament and the Council, 'Implementation of Article 290 of the Treaty on the Functioning of the European Union' COM(2009) 673 final.

[36] For the application of transparency to entities located in a third State, see below at section 3.2.2.1.2 (The 'similarity' test) and at section 3.3.3 (The meaning of 'non-resident').

not contain the condition of the 'company not being exempt', which may be found in the income tax directives.

The income tax directives make reference to 'any other tax which may be substituted for any of the above taxes'.[37,38] Neither this nor the above-mentioned expression is comprehensive. Article 2(1)(b) of the Proposal does not specify whether the new tax is levied in addition to or in lieu of the tax listed in the Annex. This is a more precise wording than that used in the income tax directives, which refer only to taxes that are levied in substitution for the taxes covered by the directives and do not clearly require the tax to be similar (ambiguity may exist when a tax is replaced by another one but does not entirely meet the similarity test, such as the Italian local income tax that was replaced by the regional tax, which, however, does have a taxable base that is significantly different as it denies a deduction for labour cost and financial charges incurred by the taxpayer and equally excludes financial income and extraordinary items from the taxable base). The significance of the reference to new taxes, however, is softened by the EU Commission's right to amend Annex II so that no amendment of the Proposal is required. The failure by the Commission to amend Annex II does not prevent the common system from applying to taxes that are similar and which are introduced after the adoption of the Proposal.

Furthermore, Annex II includes the same taxes that are included in the other income tax directives. There is no exclusion of special regimes for determination of income such as companies that have opted for a tonnage tax regime whereby income is determined on the basis of the tonnage of vessels owned by the company. Domestic tax consolidation provisions generally exclude such companies from eligibility for consolidation to avoid inconsistencies between income of one group company being subject to ordinary rules of determination of income and another group entity being subject to different rules. Under the CCCTB, there is no such requirement as the option for the common system would make all group entities subject to the common rules for the determination of taxable income.

---

[37] For example, Art. 2(1)(c) of the Parent-Subsidiary Directive.

[38] The language used by the Proposal is also different from Art. 2 OECD Model, which refers to 'identical or similar taxes that are imposed after the date of signature of the Convention in addition to or in place of the existing taxes', which likewise raises criticism as it is difficult to conceive of new taxes that are 'identical' to existing taxes.

3.2.2 The Meaning of 'Company Established under the Laws of a Third Country'

3.2.2.1 The legal form

3.2.2.1.1 The desirability of a listing approach Article 2(2)(a) refers to companies that have a legal form 'similar' to one of the forms listed in Annex I.

The desirability of listing eligible entities of third countries is questionable. Indeed, the purpose and intent of the Annexes in the income tax directives and also under Article 2(1)(a) of the Proposal regarding the eligible entities of Member States is to be found in the wish to secure the application of the common system to entities that are taxable persons in the respective countries. Furthermore, it may be argued that in the income tax directives the Annex enabled Member States to limit the application of the common regime and control the loss of revenue deriving from it.

The first reason does not apply to the CCCTB in its relation to third countries. The wish to avoid the application of the common system to entities that are not taxable persons in the third country could have been secured by a condition of residence under a treaty to avoid double taxation concluded between the third country and the Member State in which the PE of the foreign non-EU company is established. As far as the loss of revenue is concerned, it is possible that the legal form requirement may be construed as the ability of the Member States and the EU Commission to exercise some discretion in applying the common system to non-EU countries, considering that certain Member States expressed concern about a possible loss of revenue deriving from the CCCTB.[39]

One may wonder if an unreasonable limitation of the application of the common regime to legal forms of a non-EU Member State can be contrary to the non-discrimination provision contained in the relevant treaty concluded between the third State and the Member State where the company is tax resident. Article 24(1) of the OECD Model prevents discrimination based on nationality, so that denying the CCCTB regime

---

[39] Note that in a recent Ernst & Young report for the Irish Department of Finance the conclusion is drawn that the CCCTB might shift revenue to Member States with higher corporate tax rates, with a detrimental effect for those Member States with lower corporate tax rates (for the report see http://www.ibec.ie/IBEC/Press/PressPublicationsdoclib3.nsf/vPages/Newsroom~ccctb-unlikely-to-make-europe-more-attractive-for-business-16-03-2011?OpenDocument, accessed 13 September 2012).

to legal forms existing in the third State which are similar to the legal forms of another contracting (EU Member) State might violate the treaty obligation. This could be the case if the company having a legal form of the third State and its effective place of management in a Member State was denied access to the common regime because of its failure to meet the legal form requirement.

The compatibility of the CCCTB with tax treaties concluded with third States was discussed during the drafting of the Proposal and the eligibility of third States seems to have influenced the inclusion of residents of third States but limited to their PEs in a Member State.[40]

It may be observed that EU law prevails over treaties concluded with third States after the establishment of the European Union. Consequently, a tax treaty provision would not permit a resident of a third State to have access to an EU regime which is reserved to EU residents. The denial of the EU regime would simply permit the third country to either terminate the treaty to the extent that such denial conflicts with the non-discrimination provision contained in the treaty.

The possible conflict between CCCTB and tax treaty non-discrimination rules suggests that a specific provision dealing with the relationship between the CCCTB and tax treaties with third countries should be introduced in the CCCTB directive.

3.2.2.1.2 The 'similarity' test The Proposal provides no guidance as to the test to be used to establish 'similarity' and empowers the Commission to adopt annually a list of third-country company forms that will be considered to meet the requirements laid down by Article 2(2)(a).

Firstly, it is worth noting that the similarity test should be conducted in respect of the entire list of entities included in the Annex and not confined to the list of the Member State in which the company meets the tax residence criterion laid down in Article 6(3). Only this conclusion would secure common application of the CCCTB to non-resident taxpayers, who should thus be eligible for the option regardless of the Member State in which they reside. One list of 'similar entities' that applies throughout all Member States would thereby be envisaged. There is indeed no other alternative than just one Annex for all the Member States. However, the similarity test will have to be conducted in relation to any and all the legal forms listed by all the Member States, which may raise interesting issues and lead to the conclusion that the criteria for

[40] See European Commission, Working Document 'The Territorial Scope of the CCCTB' CCCTB\WP\026, 17 February 2006.

conducting the similarity test are not entirely related to the legal characteristics of the entity. Indeed, Member States have included legal forms in the Annex having in mind the tax regime applicable to such entities. This is also true for Member States that have included in their list well-identified legal forms. For instance, the United Kingdom has included 'companies incorporated under UK law' as any such a corporation is a taxable person under UK corporation tax. It should therefore be concluded that the similarity should be satisfied to the extent that the legal form is subject *as such* to corporate tax in one Member State. It may be questioned whether there is an additional condition for similarity consisting in the non-transparency of the entity in the third State. For instance, an LLC owned by US-resident individuals that maintains its effective place of management in the United Kingdom should meet the test insofar as the legal form is similar to that of a company in the United Kingdom or in other Member States from a corporate law standpoint (limited liability, capital divided into shares, profit purpose, and so on). The circumstance that its income is taxed – in the third State – in the hands of the shareholders rather than the entity would not matter, as the entity is a taxable person in a Member State. The situation is different for a non-resident taxpayer that is transparent in the third State and is not a taxable person subject to comprehensive tax liability in a Member State but has a PE therein (in that case, the income would be taxed in the hands of the individuals in the third State, but the individuals would take the benefit of the CCCTB although it is not meant to apply to individuals).

As there may be only one Annex so that similarity will have to be the same for all Member States, it may be difficult to establish the criteria. Indeed, if one looks at certain States, only companies would be included, whereas for other countries the liability to company tax would be the relevant factor. However, it is worth noting that Article 3 refers to 'a list of third country company forms', which is considered to meet the requirements laid down by Article 2(2)(a).

The term 'company' is also used in Article 2(2)(a) and is not restricted to corporate forms or partnerships (as the Annex I indicates) so that the 'similarity' test cannot be based on the corporate/partnership versus non-incorporated/non-partnership legal form. The Commission may adopt a minimum standard approach and include entities which would be included in almost all Member States.

Similarity of the tax regime (transparency versus non-transparency) applies not only with reference to the Member State but also with reference to the third State. Indeed, a company which is subject to one of the corporate taxes levied by Member States is almost automatically similar.

The adoption of the list of similar entities must be done under the procedure laid down by Regulation No. 182/2011, which is thus different from the procedure laid down by Article 2(3) of the Proposal for the review of Annex I of the Proposal. It is indeed a non-legislative power exercised by the Commission which guarantees the uniform application of legislative acts.[41] The review of the conformity to rules which govern the delegation of powers by the Council presents features that are different from the delegation of powers regarding the revision of Annex I. Indeed, Annex I reflects the update of the legal forms and its scope is rather constrained; in contrast, the scope of the implementing powers laid down by Article 3 of the Proposal regards the creation of a list of entities so that is not only an update but also an amendment of the Proposal.[42] It should thus be examined whether the drawing up of the list remains within the prescribed boundaries of the implementing powers. This could be considered to be less evident for the reasons stated earlier, which show a variety of approaches as to the ways the list of entities could be drawn. However, the list of entities similar to the companies included in Annex I is not exclusive as entities not falling under that list of entities of a third State may still qualify as eligible companies. Thus, the role of the Commission has an executive function and not a legislative function.

Some final remarks have to be made in relation to entities of States that have special relations with the European Union. For instance, under Article 15 of the treaty concluded by the European Union with Switzerland, which applies the EU common regime on dividends, interest and royalties to Swiss parent and subsidiary companies, the legal forms included for Switzerland are the *Aktiengesellschaft*, the *Gesellschaft mit beschränkter Haftung* and the *Kommanditaktiengesellschaft*.

However, Swiss entities that may carry on an enterprise (see in bold text the forms included in the agreement between the European Community and the Swiss Confederation providing for measures equivalent to those laid down by Council Directive 2003/48/EC on taxation of savings income in the form of interest payments, concluded in Luxembourg on 27 October 2004) are:

---

[41] Art. 291(1) TFEU.

[42] Jurgita Samulenaite, *Delegation of powers in the EU before and after the treaty of Lisbon: Comitology in the CCCTB* (2010 Aarhus School of Business) 45.

- ***Aktiengesellschaft*** (*AG*): stock company – subject to corporate tax;
- ***Gesellschaft mit beschränkter Haftung*** (*GmbH*): limited liability company – subject to corporate tax;
- ***Kommanditaktiengesellschaft*** (*KAG*): stock company with unlimited shareholders – subject to corporate tax;
- *Genossenschaft*: cooperative company – subject to corporate tax;
- *Kollektivgesellschaft*: general partnership – *not* subject to corporate tax (transparent);
- *Kommanditgesellschaft*: limited partnership – *not* subject to corporate tax (transparent);
- *Unternehmensstiftung*: private foundation running an enterprise – subject to corporate tax;
- *Verein*: association with legal personality – subject to corporate tax; and
- public Institutions – subject to corporate tax.

With regard to companies established under the laws of Liechtenstein, Norway and Iceland, and having a legal form similar to the ones listed in the Annex, an unreasonable exclusion from the scope of the Proposal could lead to a breach of the freedom of establishment provided for in Article 31 et seq. of the EEA Agreement. A question might arise as to whether the absence of an exchange of information agreement between such countries and the relevant Member State (or a provision to that effect in a bilateral tax treaty), which is comparable to the exchange of information on request provided for in Directive 2011/16/EU, could make the exclusion of the above-mentioned companies from the scope of the Directive justified in the light of the need to combat tax avoidance and evasion. Article 3 of the Proposal requires similarity of the legal form and such similarity does not include exchange of information between tax authorities. Indeed, the list of entities included in Annex I does not make reference to the existence of exchange of information between tax authorities. One may argue that exchange of information is not mentioned in Annex I because information exchange between Member States relies on secondary EU legislation, so that absence of exchange of information might make the legal forms of third States not similar to the legal forms included in Annex I. However, where the companies established under the laws of EEA Member States are tax resident in a Member State, they are subject to the jurisdiction and fiscal controls of such Member State and information regarding these entities would be covered by the EU directive on exchange of information, so that exclusion would not appear necessary (non-proportional) in order to achieve the purpose of preventing tax avoidance and evasion. The situation might be different for a company of a third State being a 'non-resident taxpayer', which is dealt with in section 3.3 below.

3.2.2.2 The subject-to-tax requirement

Article 2(2)(b), like Article 2(1)(b), requires the company established under the law of a third State to 'be subject to one of the corporate taxes listed in Annex II or to a similar tax subsequently introduced'. For comments in this respect, refer to section 3.2.1.2 above.

3.2.3 The Meaning of 'Resident for Tax Purposes in a Member State'

3.2.3.1 The condition of the 'registered office, place of incorporation and place of effective management'

The meaning of 'resident for tax purposes in a Member State' differs from the meaning of 'resident' stipulated by the income tax directives insofar as it requires – unlike such directives – the entity to have 'its registered office, place of incorporation or place of effective management' in a Member State. This is the criterion used by Article 56 TFEU.

These are the main connecting criteria for 'tax residence' of companies in the Member States so that in most situations a company that is a tax resident of a Member State also meets in such State or in another Member State any of such three criteria. However, in some Member States, tax residence of a company is based on different connecting criteria. In Italy, for instance, a company may be resident for tax purposes if it maintains the place where its main and substantial activity is carried on ('main purpose') in the Italian territory. Consequently, a commercial entity having its place of incorporation, registered office and place of effective management in a third non-treaty State and being a resident of Italy by virtue of its main purpose, is a resident of Italy for tax purposes but it is outside the scope of the Proposal.[43]

The term 'place of incorporation' has a technical meaning in some domestic corporate legislation and this is also true to a lesser extent for the meaning of 'registered office'.[44]

---

[43] This is not the case in the income tax directives, which for Italy include private and public entities whose activity is 'wholly or principally commercial'.

[44] It is worth noting that as regards the legal forms, Annex I uses in addition to the term 'incorporated', the term 'constituted', which seems to include entities that are not incorporated but are subject to company tax, and also (for Ireland) the terms 'registered' or 'existing'.

Having said this, issues nevertheless arise as to why this condition was included in the meaning of residence and how the terms used therein should be interpreted.

The underlying reason for the condition may be found in the wish to coordinate the CCCTB system and tax treaties so that a tax resident for the purposes of the Directive is also considered a tax resident for the purposes of double taxation agreements by the States that apply the common system. Indeed, Article 4(1) of the OECD Model defines a 'resident' as a person who is liable to tax by virtue of its residence, domicile, place of management or any other criterion of a similar nature. The condition laid down by Article 6(3) of the Proposal secures the CCCTB-eligible entities to be resident for both the common system and the double taxation agreements that follow the OECD Model. The desirability to create consistency between the definition of residence for the CCCTB and the definition for treaty purposes is also shown by the fact that when dual residence in two Member States is at stake, the Proposal provides for a tiebreaker rule in Article 6(4) which is identical to the tiebreaker rule found in the OECD Model ('place of effective management'), and when dual residence in a Member State and in a third State is at stake, Article 6(3) permits the application of tiebreaker rules found in double taxation agreements. The latter conclusion seems to be confirmed by the circumstance that the Proposal simply makes reference to tax treaties in order to establish that a company which is a resident in a third country does not qualify as a resident for CCCTB purposes.[45] If the autonomous definition of residence is meant to coordinate the proposal and tax treaties, however, it is surprising that some of the adopted terms are not found in certain domestic tax legislation.

3.2.3.2 Dual residence in two different Member States

Article 6(3) of the Proposal provides that:

> [F]or the purposes of paragraphs 1 and 2, a company that has its registered office, place of incorporation or place of effective management in a Member

[45] See European Commission, Working Document 'An Overview of the main issues that emerged at the first meeting of the subgroup on International Aspects' CCCTB\WP\029, 2 March 2006, paras 16 and 17, which refer to the desirability of a common definition of 'residence' to avoid a company circumventing the CCCTB by simply moving to a Member State having a narrower definition of tax residence than another. The working paper does not mention a clear correlation between the CCCTB definition and Art. 4 OECD Model but refers to tax treaties as a tool to resolve dual residence situations and questions which definition should be used (place of effective management and/or other criteria).

> State and is not, under the terms of an agreement concluded by that Member State with a third country, regarded as tax resident in that third country shall be considered resident for tax purposes in that Member State.

Similarly to the income tax directives, the provision requires the company not to be a resident in a third State pursuant to a double taxation agreement concluded with such third State. However, treaty residence in the third State does not exclude application of the common system to the company which may opt as a non-resident company limited to the PE situated in a Member State.

The Proposal considers the situation in which the company is a resident in more than one Member State and provides in Article 6(4) that:

> 4. Where, under paragraph 3, a company is resident in more than one Member State, it shall be considered to be resident in the Member State in which it has its place of effective management.

This provision is not contained in the income tax directives, for which it is accepted that dual residence in two Member States does not rule out application of the common regime.[46] Therefore, a company may have the legal form of Member State A, be a resident of Member State B and be subject to tax in Member State C. This may be the case in which the company (i) is incorporated in State A, which does not regard incorporation as a tax residence criterion; (ii) maintains its legal seat in State B, which regards it as a tax resident according to domestic law; and (iii) is subject to tax solely in State C according to a treaty concluded between States B and C.

Dual residence in two Member States does not need to be resolved when income tax directives are at issue. For instance, dividends paid by a dual-resident subsidiary company to a parent company of another Member State have to be exempted from withholding tax pursuant to Article 5 of the Parent-Subsidiary Directive so that the obligation applies to both States of residence. Similarly, a parent company that is a resident of two different Member States is entitled to the relief laid down by Article 4 of

---

[46] See for example, Michele Gusmeroli, 'Triangular cases and the Interest and Royalties Directive: Untying the Gordian knot? – Part 1' (2005) 45 *European Taxation* 1, 2 et seq.; Michele Gusmeroli, 'Triangular cases and the Interest and Royalties Directive: Untying the Gordian knot? – Part 2' (2005) 45 *European Taxation* 2, 39 et seq.; Michele Gusmeroli, 'Triangular cases and the Interest and Royalties Directive: Untying the Gordian knot? – Part 3' (2005) 45 *European Taxation* 3, 86 et seq.

the directive, which is an obligation that applies to both Member States of which the parent company is a resident.

The Proposal requires resolving issues of dual residence and determining in which Member State the company is a resident for the purposes of application of the common system. Indeed, under Article 104, the option for the common consolidated tax base must be exercised in the State of residence of the parent company so that such State of residence must be identified for the common system to be applied.

Residence pursuant to Article 6(4) does not rely on double taxation agreements insofar as it attributes residence to the State in which the 'place of effective management' is situated regardless of the tiebreaker rule laid down by the treaty concluded between the two Member States. Pursuant to Article 8 of the Proposal, Article 6(4) in any case prevails over the applicable tax treaty between Member States. For instance, in several treaties concluded by Latvia, Lithuania and Estonia with other Member States, no tiebreaker rule is provided and the dual residence issue should be resolved by the competent authorities of the contracting States by mutual agreement: for CCCTB purposes this provision is irrelevant and the dual residence is to be resolved in the light of the place of effective management. Article 6(4) of the Proposal, moreover, also applies when no tax treaty exists between the two Member States. The meaning of 'place of effective management' should in any case be interpreted on the basis of the OECD Model.[47]

3.2.3.3 Dual residence in a Member State and in a third State

A different situation arises when the company has a legal form of a third State (for example, the United States) and is a tax resident of a Member State pursuant to domestic tax law of that Member State (for example, the United Kingdom).

The company is not a company of a Member State as its legal form is not included in Annex I, which for the United Kingdom covers companies incorporated therein.

The company may qualify as an eligible company of a third State (if its legal form is included in the list of legal forms of third States to be drawn up by the EU Commission pursuant to Article 3(1) of the Proposal or is similar to those found in Annex I). If the treaty between the Member

---

[47] See, however, European Commission, Working Document 'An Overview of the main issues that emerged at the first meeting of the subgroup on International Aspects' CCCTB\WP\029, 2 March 2006 that suggests an autonomous definition of 'place of effective management', which, however, was not included in the Proposal.

State and the third State provides for treaty residence in the Member State, the company would be a company resident in a Member State because it maintains its place of effective management in one Member State (Article 6(3) requires either place of incorporation or registered office or place of effective management to be in a Member State).

If, on the contrary, the company has a legal form that is not included in the list of legal forms to be drawn up by the EU Commission and is not similar to those found in Annex I, then the company would not be an eligible company. Thus, it would be excluded from eligible companies under the Proposal, irrespective of the fact that it is a resident of a Member State.

In practice, the Proposal permits a company that does not have the legal form of a Member State but is a resident thereof to enjoy the common system regardless of the inclusion in the legal forms laid down by Annex I, to the extent that its legal form is similar to the legal forms set out in that Annex.

The interpretative issue arises on the meaning of 'a company that has its registered office, place of incorporation or place of effective management in a Member State'. Does this refer to an eligible company? The reply is, yes, otherwise the common system would apply to companies other than eligible companies (in other words, companies that have a legal form which is neither included in Annex I nor is similar to those found in Annex I).

A similar reasoning could apply to Article 6(2) of the Proposal. If the tiebreaker rule provides for treaty residence in the third State, the company would not be eligible if the legal form is neither included in Annex I nor is similar to those found in Annex I.

It is worth noting that Article 6(3) requires the company not to be resident in a third State pursuant to a tax treaty concluded by such State with a Member State, which is slightly different from the similar condition laid down in the other income tax directives that require the company not to be 'outside the Community' pursuant to a tax treaty concluded with a third State.

3.3 THE DEFINITION OF 'NON-RESIDENT TAXPAYER'

3.3.1 In General

The definition of 'non-resident taxpayer' is laid down by Article 4(4) of the Proposal as 'a taxpayer who is not resident for tax purposes in a Member State according to Article 6(3) and (4).'

The 'non-resident taxpayer' must therefore be (i) a company established under the laws of a Member State or a third State and (ii) a resident for tax purposes in a third State. By reason of the several references included in each defined expression, the meaning of 'non-resident taxpayer' may be further fragmented and lead to the aggregation of these features: (i) an entity taking an eligible legal form either under Annex I (see 3.2.1.1. above) or similar to Annex I (see 3.2.2.1.); (ii) subject to one of the taxes listed in Annex II (see 3.2.1.2. and 3.2.2.2.); and (iii) not having its registered office, place of incorporation or place of effective management in a Member State, or having its registered office, place of incorporation or effective place of management in a Member State but being regarded as a resident of a third State pursuant to a tax treaty concluded by the third State with that Member State.

3.3.2 Peculiar Features of the Subject-To-Tax Requirement in Respect of Non-Resident Taxpayers

3.3.2.1 Subject to tax and comprehensive vs. limited taxation

It is worth noting that the Proposal does not contain the condition that the company be subject to tax 'by reason of his domicile, residence, place of management or any other criterion of a similar nature', which is found in the OECD Model. Therefore, it appears not to be necessary that the company is subject to tax as a tax resident (in other words, subject to the most comprehensive taxation under tax law).

The company should hence be considered to be subject to tax even when it is subject to limited taxation as a non-resident, but, in this latter case, considering the overall structure and purpose of the Proposal, the company should be subject to tax on its business income under domestic and tax treaty law, in other words, on income which can be attributed to a local PE thereof. In fact, there might be situations in which the third-State resident is subject to tax on income other than business income, such as income from immovable property situated in a Member State; this would not satisfy the condition laid down by the Proposal that should be construed as requiring the corporate tax to be applied to business income, in other words, to income derived through a PE. Therefore, if the third-State company does not have a PE under the domestic laws and applicable treaties, then such a company could not opt for the common system even if it maintains a PE under the Proposal. This approach to the term 'subject to tax' is the one most consistent with the personal scope of the CCCTB, as complemented by the definitions of residence and PE, which are also examined in the present chapter.

3.3.2.2 Subject to tax and permanent establishment

A non-resident taxpayer may opt for the common system limited to income from activities carried out through a PE in a Member State.

The definition of permanent establishment is provided by Article 5 of the Proposal, which confirms the policy of adopting autonomous definitions within the common system. However, this approach may raise issues of application of the common system. If the treaty between the third State and the Member State of the PE provides for a definition which is more restricted compared to the definition contained in Article 5 of the Proposal, then there would be no PE in a Member State pursuant to the tax treaty and there would be no business income to subject to the common system, as the bilateral treaty would prevent the business income from being subject to tax in the Member State. The third-country resident would be excluded from the common system as the 'subject to tax' requirement to be regarded as an eligible company would not be fulfilled. The subject-to-tax requirement should in fact be tested under the domestic laws of the Member State and supplemented by the applicable treaties concluded with the third State and not in the light of the definition of permanent establishment as defined by the Proposal. Indeed, the definition of permanent establishment laid down in Article 5 of the Proposal becomes applicable only after the option for the consolidation has been exercised and not at the prior time when the personal scope is established. This conclusion may be drawn on the basis of Article 7 of the Proposal, which states that when a company 'qualifies' and 'opts' for the system 'it shall cease to be subject to the national corporate tax arrangements in respect of all matters regulated by this directive unless otherwise stated.'

This conclusion is consistent with the circumstance that the Proposal sets out rules for the determination of income and does not affect the taxing rules which establish whether the entity is liable to tax (in other words, if the State's resident satisfies the territoriality rules under its domestic or treaty law).[48,49] The inability to opt for the common system would not raise the issue of the application of Article 24(3) of the OECD Model as there would be no PE of the third-State resident, which is a condition for the application of Article 24(3).

If, on the contrary, the definition of the bilateral treaty is broader than the definition of the Proposal, then the third-State resident would be subject to tax in the Member State by virtue of the treaty concluded with the Member State but would not be entitled to claim application of the common system if there is no PE pursuant to the Proposal. Nevertheless, there would be room to invoke Article 24(3) and claim the application of the CCCTB regime to the tax treaty PE.

In conclusion, the common system may apply solely if the company of the third State maintains a PE under both domestic (or treaty) law and under Article 5 of the Proposal.

3.3.2.3 Subject to tax and transparent entities

A special issue concerns the subject-to-tax requirement and transparent entities. As already mentioned above, Article 84 of the Proposal addresses the transparency issue by providing that a 'taxpayer' must include its share in the income of the entity in its tax base. The reference to 'taxpayer' seems to be intended to allow both a 'resident taxpayer' or a 'non-resident taxpayer' to apply the CCCTB in respect of its share in the income of the transparent entity.

The inclusion of non-resident taxpayers seems to be consistent with the possibility for non-resident taxpayers to apply the common system with regard to their PEs in Member States, since under the tax legislation of certain Member States, non-resident shareholders of local transparent entities are treated very similarly to non-residents having a local PE.

The Proposal, however, does not make it clear whether a Member State transparent entity owned by a non-resident could be regarded as a PE of the latter for the purposes of the Proposal, and allow the non-resident to qualify as 'subject to tax' in a Member State. The case is that of a non-resident which does not have a PE in any Member State but owns an interest in a Member State transparent entity: the non-resident would not

---

[48] This is different from the exemption of foreign income attributable to PEs of a resident taxpayer, which is a rule that has to do with the determination of income and not whether or not the entity is liable to tax.

[49] The relationship between domestic rules and the CCCTB rules also applies when there is no treaty between the company residing in the third State and the Member State in which it maintains a PE pursuant to Art. 5 of the Proposal, but not pursuant to the domestic law of the Member State.

qualify as 'subject to tax' in a Member State, unless the Member State transparent entity can be regarded as its own PE. This aspect deserves to be clarified under Article 84 of the Proposal.

3.3.3 The Meaning of 'Non-Resident'

The Proposal does not require the entity to be resident in a third State that has concluded a tax treaty with a Member State providing exchange of information, which is a requirement that is provided by tax consolidation rules of some Member States.[50] In such States, exchange of information is found to be necessary for the tax authorities to ascertain the proper application of the consolidation rules. It may be questioned in practice how non-resident taxpayers that are tax resident in non-treaty countries may cause problems of application or assessment of the common system. The Proposal, rather than denying the application of the common system to all companies which reside in third States not having treaties providing exchange of information with the Member State in which they maintain a PE, took the alternative of making some provisions of the Proposal regarding deductions or exemptions conditional upon the existence of exchange of information with the third State. For example, Article 31, under which 'the transfer of a fixed asset by a non-resident taxpayer from its PE in a Member State to a third country shall … be deemed to be a disposal of the asset' and that such provisions 'shall not apply where the third country is party to the European Economic Area Agreement and there is an agreement on the exchange of information between that third country and the Member State of the resident taxpayer or of the PE, comparable to Directive 2011/16/EU.' Article 81 also provides for similar restrictions for interest paid to entities located in a third State.

Nor does the Proposal require the entity to be subject to corporate tax in its State of residence, as taxation in a Member State is found to be sufficient to justify application of the common system. Tax transparency of the entity established under the law of a third country is prima facie immaterial, as the entity must be subject to one of the corporate taxes that apply in the Member States. However, it is possible – and desirable – that the transparency issue be dealt with under the 'similarity' test which the Commission will have to apply to determine which entities are

[50] Non-resident entities are sometimes admitted to domestic tax consolidation in certain Member States with respect to their local PEs, provided that a tax treaty exists between the non-resident entity State and the Member State. This is the case, for instance, of Italy, with respect to non-resident controlling entities.

'similar' to those listed in Annex I. If the test includes the tax regime so as to require non-transparency, then the Proposal prevents individuals of third countries from applying the common system, which is not intended since individuals resident in the Member States are denied access to the common system.[51]

3.4 CONCLUSIONS

The first fundamental principle laid down by the Proposal is the autonomy of its provisions from double taxation agreements concluded between Member States. This is shown not only by Article 7 of the Proposal, but also by the autonomous definitions of 'resident taxpayer' provided in Article 4(4) and 'permanent establishment' provided in Article 5. Furthermore, dual-residence situations between Member States are resolved on the basis of the 'place of effective management' criterion regardless of the tiebreaker rule laid down in the applicable tax treaty (although the function of the tax treaty is to allocate the taxing rights between the two States, which is different from the purpose of the tiebreaker rule under the CCCTB, which is to establish in which country the option has to be made for the application of the common system).

The reasons for this policy approach[52] have to do with the different wording of bilateral treaties and also with the observations and reservations that several Member States have included. Furthermore, reliance on double taxation agreements would make the CCCTB system to some extent dependent on tax treaties, which may be changed on a bilateral basis. On the contrary, the policy adopted by the drafters of the Proposal is to force bilateral treaties to be amended to adapt them to the common system.

The magnitude of these issues is limited and much less significant compared to the complexity of the rules dealing with the personal scope

---

[51] Art. 85 provides that the question whether or not 'an entity located in a third State' is transparent 'shall be determined according to the law of the Member State of the taxpayer. If at least two group members hold an interest in the same entity located in a third country, the treatment of the latter shall be determined by common agreement among the relevant Member States. If there is no agreement, the principal tax authority shall decide.' However, the provision refers to 'entities located' in a third State and does not apply to the determination of whether or not an entity meets the requirements laid down for a 'non-resident taxpayer'.

[52] See European Commission, Working Document 'International Aspects in the CCCTB' CCCTB\WP\019, 18 November 2005.

of the CCCTB. It would be more realistic to establish that the common system applies to any entity subject to corporate tax in a Member State.

The Proposal fails to address the relationship between taxing rules of the domestic laws of the Member States and the rules contained by the Proposal, and particularly with Article 5.

APPENDIX: COMPARISON OF THE PARENT-SUBSIDIARY, MERGER AND INTEREST AND ROYALTIES DIRECTIVES AND THE COUNCIL PROPOSAL FOR A DIRECTIVE ON CCCTB

Directive 90/435/EC **Parent-Subsidiary Directive***	**Directive 90/434/EC** **Merger Directive****	**Directive 2003/49/EC** **Interest and Royalties Directive**	**Proposal for a Council Directive on a Common Consolidated Corporate Tax Base (CCCTB) COM(2011) 121 final of 16 March 2011**
Annex **List of companies referred to in Article 2** **(a) companies incorporated under Council Regulation (EC) No 2157/2001 of 8 October 2001 on the Statute for a European company (SE) and Council Directive 2001/86/EC of 8 October 2001 supplementing the Statute for a European company with regard to the involvement of employees and cooperative societies incorporated under Council Regulation (EC) No 1435/2003 of 22 July 2003 on the Statute for a European Cooperative Society (SCE) and Council Directive 2003/72/EC of 22 July 2003 supplementing the Statute for a European**	**Annex** **List of companies referred to in Article 3** **(a) companies incorporated under Council Regulation (EC) No 2157/2001 of 8 October 2001 on the Statute for a European company (SE) and Council Directive 2001/86/EC of 8 October 2001 supplementing the Statute for a European company with regard to the involvement of employees, and cooperative societies incorporated under Council Regulation (EC) No 1435/2003 of 22 July 2003 on the Statute for a European Cooperative Society (SCE) and Council Directive 2003/72/EC of 22 July 2003 supplementing the Statute for a**	**Annex** List of companies covered by Article 3 of the Directive (a) Companies under Belgian law known as: 'naamloze vennootschap/société anonyme, commanditaire vennootschap op aandelen/ société en commandite par actions, besloten vennootschap met beperkte aansprakelijkheid/ société privée à responsibilité limitée' **and those public law bodies that operate under private law;** (aa) companies under Bulgarian law known as: 'събирателното дружество', 'командитното дружество', 'дружеството с ограничена отговорност', 'акционерното дружество',	**Annex I** **(a) The European company or Societas Europaea (SE), as established in Council Regulation (EC) No 2157/2001 of 8 October 2001 on the Statute for a European company (SE) and Council Directive 2001/86/EC of 8 October 2001 supplementing the Statute for a European company with regard to the involvement of employees,** **(b) The European Cooperative Society (SCE), as established in Council Regulation (EC) No 1435/2003 of 22 July 2003 on the European Cooperative Society (SCE) and Council Directive 2003/72/EC of 22 July 2003 supplementing the Statute for a European Cooperative Society**

Directive 90/435/EC Parent-Subsidiary Directive*	Directive 90/434/EC Merger Directive**	Directive 2003/49/EC Interest and Royalties Directive	Proposal for a Council Directive on a Common Consolidated Corporate Tax Base (CCCTB) COM(2011) 121 final of 16 March 2011
Cooperative Society with regard to the involvement of employees; (b) companies under Belgian law known as 'société anonyme'/ 'naamloze vennootschap', 'société en commandite par actions'/ 'commanditaire vennootschap op aandelen', 'société privée à responsibilité limitée'/'besloten vennootschap met beperkte aansprakelijkheid', **'société coopérative à responsibilité limitée'/'coöperatieve vennootschap met beperkte aansprakelijkheid', 'société coopérative à responsibilité illimitée'/'coöperatieve vennootschap met onbeperkte aansprakelijkheid', 'société en nom collectif'/'vennootschap onder firma', 'société en commandite simple'/'gewone commanditaire vennootschap', public undertakings which have adopted one of the abovementioned legal forms, and**	**European Cooperative Society with regard to the involvement of employees;** (b) companies under Belgian law known as 'société anonyme'/ 'naamloze vennootschap', 'société en commandite par actions'/ 'commanditaire vennootschap op aandelen', 'société privée à responsibilité limitée'/'besloten vennootschap met beperkte aansprakelijkheid',**'société coopérative à responsibilité limitée'/' coöperatieve vennootschap met beperkte aansprakelijkheid', 'société coopérative à responsibilité illimitée'/'coöperatieve vennootschap met onbeperkte aansprakelijkheid', 'société en nom collectif'/ 'vennootschap onder firma', 'société en commandite simple'/ 'gewone commanditaire vennootschap', public undertakings which have adopted one of the**	'командитното дружество с акции', 'кооперации', 'кооперативни съюзи', 'държавни предприятия' constituted under Bulgarian law and carrying on commercial activities; (p) companies under Czech law known as: 'akciová společnost', 'společnost s ručením omezeným', **'veřejná obchodní společnost', 'komanditní společnost', 'družstvo'**; (b) companies under Danish law known as: 'aktieselskab' and 'anpartsselskab'; (c) companies under German law known as: 'Aktiengesellschaft, Kommanditgesellschaft auf Aktien, Gesellschaft mit beschränkter Haftung' **and 'bergrechtliche Gewerkschaft'**; (q) companies under Estonian law known as: 'täisühing', 'usaldusühing', 'osaühing', 'aktsiaselts', 'tulundusühistu';	**with regard to the involvement of employees;** (c) companies under Belgian law known as 'société anonyme' /'naamloze vennootschap', 'société en commandite par actions'/ 'commanditaire vennootschap op aandelen', 'société privée à responsibilité limitée'/'besloten vennootschap met beperkte aansprakelijkheid', **'société coopérative à responsibilité limitée'/'coöperatieve vennootschap met beperkte aansprakelijkheid', 'société coopérative à responsibilité illimitée'/'coöperatieve vennootschap met onbeperkte aansprakelijkheid', 'société en nom collectif'/'vennootschap onder firma', 'société en commandite simple'/ 'gewone commanditaire vennootschap', public undertakings which have adopted one of the abovementioned legal forms, and**

other companies constituted under Belgian law subject to Belgian corporate tax and those public law bodies that operate under private law; (c) companies under Bulgarian law known as: 'събирателното дружество', 'командитното дружество', 'дружеството с ограничена отговорност', 'акционерното дружество', 'командитното дружество с акции', 'неперсонифицирано дружество', 'кооперации', 'кооперативни съюзи' 'държавни предприятия' constituted under Bulgarian law and carrying on commercial activities; (d) companies under Czech law known as: 'akciová společnost', 'společnost s ručením omezeným'; (e) companies under Danish law known as 'aktieselskab' and 'anpartsselskab'. **Other companies subject to tax under the Corporation Tax Act, insofar as their taxable income is calculated and taxed in accordance with the general tax legislation rules applicable to 'aktieselskaber';** (f) companies under German law known as 'Aktiengesellschaft', 'Kommanditgesellschaft auf	**abovementioned legal forms, and other companies constituted under Belgian law subject to the Belgian Corporate Tax;** (aa) companies under Bulgarian law known as: 'събирателното дружество', 'командитното дружество', 'дружеството с ограничена отговорност', 'акционерното дружество', 'командитното дружество с акции', 'кооперации', 'кооперативни съюзи', 'държавни предприятия' constituted under Bulgarian law and carrying on commercial activities; (c) companies under Czech law known as: 'akciová společnost', 'společnost s ručením omezeným'; (d) companies under Danish law known as 'aktieselskab' and 'anpartsselskab'. **Other companies subject to tax under the Corporation Tax Act, in so far as their taxable income is calculated and taxed in accordance with the general tax legislation rules applicable to 'aktieselskaber';** (e) companies under German law known as 'Aktiengesellschaft', 'Kommanditgesellschaft auf Aktien', 'Gesellschaft mit beschränkter Haftung',	(d) companies under Greek law known as: 'ανώνυμη εταιρία'; (e) companies under Spanish law known as: 'sociedad anónima, sociedad comanditaria por acciones, sociedad de responsabilidad limitada' and those public law bodies which operate under private law; (f) companies under French law known as: 'société anonyme, société en commandite par actions, société à responsibilité limitée' and industrial and commercial public establishments and undertakings; (g) companies in Irish law **known as public companies limited by shares or by guarantee, private companies limited by shares or by guarantee,** bodies registered under the Industrial and Provident Societies Acts **or** building societies registered under the Building Societies Acts; (h) companies under Italian law known as: 'società per azioni, società in accomandita per azioni, società a responsabilità limitata' and public and private entities **carrying on industrial and commercial activities**;	**other companies constituted under Belgian law subject to the Belgian Corporate Tax;** (d) companies under Bulgarian law known as: 'събирателното дружество', 'командитното дружество', 'дружеството с ограничена отговорност', 'акционерното дружество', 'командитното дружество с акции', 'кооперации','кооперативни съюзи', 'държавни предприятия' constituted under Bulgarian law and carrying on commercial activities; (e) companies under Czech law known as: 'akciová společnost', 'společnost s ručením omezeným', **'veřejná obchodní společnost', 'komanditní společnost', 'družstvo'**; (f) companies under Danish law known as 'aktieselskab' and 'anpartsselskab'. **Other companies subject to tax under the Corporation Tax Act, in so far as their taxable income is calculated and taxed in accordance with the general tax legislation rules applicable to 'aktieselskaber'**; (g) companies under German law known as 'Aktiengesellschaft', 'Kommanditgesellschaft auf

Directive 90/435/EC Parent-Subsidiary Directive*	Directive 90/434/EC Merger Directive**	Directive 2003/49/EC Interest and Royalties Directive	Proposal for a Council Directive on a Common Consolidated Corporate Tax Base (CCCTB) COM(2011) 121 final of 16 March 2011
Aktien', 'Gesellschaft mit beschränkter Haftung', **'Versicherungsverein auf Gegenseitigkeit', 'Erwerbs- und Wirtschaftsgenossenschaft', 'Betriebe gewerblicher Art von juristischen Personen des öffentlichen Rechts', and other companies constituted under German law subject to German corporate tax**; (g) companies under Estonian law known as: 'täisühing', 'usaldusühing', 'osaühing', 'aktsiaselts', 'tulundusühistu'; (h) companies under Greek law known as 'ανώνυμη εταιρεία', **'εταιρεία περιορισμένης ευθύνης (Ε.Π.Ε.)'and other companies constituted under Greek law subject to Greek corporate tax**; (i) companies under Spanish law known as: 'sociedad anónima', 'sociedad comanditaria por	**'Versicherungsverein auf Gegenseitigkeit', 'Erwerbs- und Wirtschaftsgenossenschaft', 'Betriebe gewerblicher Art von juristischen Personen des öffentlichen Rechts', and other companies constituted under German law subject to German corporate tax;** (f) companies under Estonian law known as: 'täisühing', 'usaldusühing', 'osaühing', 'aktsiaselts', 'tulundusühistu'; (g) companies under Greek law known as 'ανώνυμη εταιρεία', **'εταιρεία περιορ-ισμένης ευθύνης (Ε.Π.Ε.)'**; (h) companies under Spanish law known as 'sociedad anónima', 'sociedad comanditaria por acciones', 'sociedad de responsabilidad limitada', and those public law bodies which operate under private law;	(r) **companies under Cypriot law known as: companies in accordance with the Company's Law, Public Corporate Bodies as well as any other Body which is considered as a company in accordance with the Income tax Laws**; (s) companies under Latvian law known as: 'akciju sabiedrība', 'sabiedrība ar ierobežotu atbildību'; (t) companies incorporated under the law of Lithuania; (i) companies under Luxembourg law known as: 'société anonyme, société en commandite par actions and société à responsibilité limitée'; (u) companies under Hungarian law known as: 'közkereseti társaság', 'betéti társaság', 'közös vállalat', 'korlátolt felelősségű társaság',	Aktien', 'Gesellschaft mit beschränkter Haftung', **'Versicherungsverein auf Gegenseitigkeit', 'Erwerbs- und Wirtschaftsgenossenschaft', 'Betriebe gewerblicher Art von juristischen Personen des öffentlichen Rechts', and other companies constituted under German law subject to German corporate tax**; (h) companies under Estonian law known as: 'täisühing', 'usaldusühing', 'osaühing', 'aktsiaselts', 'tulundusühistu'; (i) companies under Greek law known as 'ανώνυμη εταιρεία', **'εταιρεία περιωρισμένης ευθύνης (Ε.Π.Ε.)'**; (j) companies under Spanish law known as 'sociedad anónima', 'sociedad comanditaria por acciones', 'sociedad de responsabilidad limitada', and those

acciones', 'sociedad de responsabilidad limitada', public law bodies which operate under private law. **Other entities constituted under Spanish law subject to Spanish corporate tax ('Impuesto sobre Sociedades');** (j) companies under French law known as ' société anonyme', 'société en commandite par actions', 'société à responsibilité limitée', **'sociétés par actions simplifiées', 'sociétés d'assurances mutuelles', 'caisses d'épargne et de prévoyance', 'sociétés civiles' which are automatically subject to corporation tax, 'coopératives', 'unions de coopératives',** industrial and commercial public establishments and undertakings, **and other companies constituted under French law subject to French corporate tax**; (k) the companies incorporated or existing under Irish law **known as public companies limited by shares or by guarantee, private companies limited by shares or by guarantee,** bodies registered under the Industrial and Provident Societies Act, **or** building societies incorporated under the Building Societies Acts **and trustee savings**	(i) companies under French law known as 'société anonyme', 'société en commandite par actions', 'société à responsibilité limitée', 'société **par actions simplifiées', 'sociétés d'assurances mutuelles', 'caisses d'épargne et de prévoyance', 'sociétés civiles' which are automatically subject to corporation tax, 'coopératives', 'unions de coopératives',** industrial and commercial public establishments and undertakings, **and other companies constituted under French law subject to the French Corporate Tax;** (j) companies incorporated or existing under Irish laws, bodies registered under the Industrial and Provident Societies Act, building societies incorporated under the Building Societies Acts **and trustee savings banks within the meaning of the Trustee Savings Banks Act, 1989**; (k) companies under Italian law known as 'società per azioni', 'società in accomandita per azioni', 'società a responsabilità limitata', **'società cooperative', 'società di mutua assicurazione',** and private and public entities whose activity is wholly or principally commercial;	'részvénytársaság', 'egyesülés', 'közhasznú társaság', 'szövetkezet'; (v) companies under Maltese law known as: 'Kumpaniji ta' Responsabilita Limitata', 'Soċjetajiet en commandite li l-kapital tagħhom maqsum f'azzjonijiet'; (j) companies under Dutch law known as: 'naamloze vennootschap' and 'besloten vennootschap met beperkte aansprakelijkheid'; (k) companies under Austrian law known as: 'Aktiengesellschaft' and 'Gesellschaft mit beschränkter Haftung'; (w) companies under Polish law known as: 'spółka akcyjna', 'spółka z ograniczoną odpowiedzialnością'; (l) commercial companies or civil law companies having a commercial form, cooperatives and public undertakings incorporated in accordance with Portuguese law; (w) companies under Romanian law known as: 'societăți pe acțiuni', 'societăți în comandită pe acțiuni', 'societăți cu răspundere limitată';	public law bodies which operate under private law; (k) companies under French law known as 'société anonyme', 'société en commandite par actions', 'société à responsibilité limitée', 'société **par actions simplifiées', 'sociétés d'assurances mutuelles', 'caisses d'épargne et de prévoyance', 'sociétés civiles' which are automatically subject to corporation tax, 'coopératives', 'unions de coopératives'**, industrial and commercial public establishments and undertakings, **and other companies constituted under French law subject to the French Corporate Tax**; (l) companies incorporated or existing under Irish laws, bodies registered under the Industrial and Provident Societies Act, building societies incorporated under the Building Societies Acts **and trustee savings banks within the meaning of the Trustee Savings Banks Act, 1989**; (m) companies under Italian law known as 'società per azioni', 'società in accomandita per azioni', 'società a responsabilità limitata', **'società cooperative', 'società di mutua assicurazione'**, and private

Directive 90/435/EC Parent-Subsidiary Directive*	Directive 90/434/EC Merger Directive**	Directive 2003/49/EC Interest and Royalties Directive	Proposal for a Council Directive on a Common Consolidated Corporate Tax Base (CCCTB) COM(2011) 121 final of 16 March 2011
banks within the meaning of the Trustee Savings Banks Act, 1989; (l) companies under Italian law known as 'società per azioni', 'società in accomandita per azioni', 'società a responsabilità limitata', **'società cooperative', 'società di mutua assicurazione',** and private and public entities **carrying on industrial and commercial activities** whose activity is wholly or principally commercial; (m) under Cypriot law: '*εταιρείες*' as defined in the Income Tax laws; (n) companies under Latvian law known as: 'akciju sabiedrība', 'sabiedrība ar ierobežotu atbildību'; (o) companies incorporated under the law of Lithuania; (p) companies under Luxembourg law known as 'société anonyme', 'société en commandite par actions', 'société à responsibilité limitée',	(l) under Cypriot law: 'εταιρείες' as defined in the Income Tax laws; (m) companies under Latvian law known as: 'akciju sabiedrība', 'sabiedrība ar ierobežotu atbildību'; (n) companies incorporated under the law of Lithuania; (o) companies under Luxembourg law known as 'société anonyme', 'société en commandite par actions', 'société à responsibilité limitée', **'société coopérative', 'société coopérative organisée comme une société anonyme', 'association d'assurances mutuelles', 'association d'épargne-pension', 'entreprise de nature commerciale, industrielle ou minière de l'État, des communes, des syndicats de communes, des établissements publics et des autres personnes morales de droit public', and other companies**	(z) companies under Slovenian law known as: 'delniška družba', **'komanditna delniška družba'**, 'komanditna družba', 'družba z omejeno odgovornostjo', **'družba z neomejeno odgovornostjo'**; (y) companies under Slovak law known as: 'akciová spoločnos', 'spoločnosť s ručením obmedzeným', 'komanditná spoločnos', **'verejná obchodná spoločnos', 'družstvo'**. (m) companies under Finnish law known as: 'osakeyhtiö/ aktiebolag, osuuskunta/ andelslag, säästöpankki/ sparbank' and 'vakuutusyhtiö/ försäkringsbolag'; (n) companies under Swedish law known as: 'aktiebolag' and 'försäkringsaktiebolag';	and public entities whose activity is wholly or principally commercial; (n) under Cypriot law: 'εταιρείες' as defined in the Income Tax laws; (o) companies under Latvian law known as: 'akciju sabiedrība', 'sabiedrība ar ierobežotu atbildību'; (p) companies incorporated under the law of Lithuania; (q) companies under Luxembourg law known as ' société anonyme', 'société en commandite par actions', 'société à responsibilité limitée', **'société coopérative', 'société coopérative organisée comme une société anonyme', 'association d'assurances mutuelles', 'association d'épargne-pension', 'entreprise de nature commerciale, industrielle ou minière de l'Etat, des communes, des syndicats de communes, des établissements publics et des autres personnes**

'société coopérative', 'société coopérative organisée comme une société anonyme', 'association d'assurances mutuelles', 'association d'épargne-pension', 'entreprise de nature commerciale, industrielle ou minière de l'Etat, des communes, des syndicats de communes, des établissements publics et des autres personnes morales de droit public', and other companies constituted under Luxembourg law subject to Luxembourg corporate tax; (q) companies under Hungarian law known as: 'közkereseti társaság', 'betéti társaság', 'közös vállalat', 'korlátolt felelősségű társaság', 'részvénytársaság', 'egyesülés', 'szövetkezet'; (r) companies under Maltese law known as: 'Kumpaniji ta' Responsabilita' Limitata', 'Soċjetajiet en commandite li l-kapital tagħhom maqsum f'azzjonijiet'; (s) companies under Dutch law known as 'naamloze vennnootschap', 'besloten	**constituted under Luxembourg law subject to the Luxembourg Corporate Tax**; (p) companies under Hungarian law known as: 'közkereseti társaság', 'betéti társaság', 'közös vállalat', 'korlátolt felelősségű társaság', 'részvénytársaság', 'egyesülés', 'közhasznú társaság', 'szövetkezet'; (q) companies under Maltese law known as: 'Kumpaniji ta' Responsabilita Limitata', 'Soċjetajiet en commandite li l-kapital tagħhom maqsum f'azzjonijiet'; (r) companies under Dutch law known as 'naamloze vennootschap', 'besloten vennootschap met beperkte aansprakelijkheid', **'Open commanditaire vennootschap', 'Coöperatie', 'onderlinge waarborgmaatschappij', 'Fonds voor gemene rekening', 'vereniging op coöperatieve grondslag' and 'vereniging welke op onderlinge grondslag als verzekeraar of kredietinstelling optreedt', and other companies constituted under Dutch law**	(o) companies incorporated under the law of the United Kingdom.	**morales de droit public', and other companies constituted under Luxembourg law subject to the Luxembourg Corporate Tax**; (r) companies under Hungarian law known as: ' közkereseti társaság', 'betéti társaság', 'közös vállalat', 'korlátolt felelősségű társaság', 'részvénytársaság', 'egyesülés', 'közhasznú társaság', 'szövetkezet'; (s) companies under Maltese law known as: 'Kumpaniji ta' Responsabilita Limitata', 'Soċjetajiet en commandite li l-kapital tagħhom maqsum f'azzjonijiet'; (t) companies under Dutch law known as 'naamloze vennootschap', 'besloten vennootschap met beperkte aansprakelijkheid', **'Open commanditaire vennootschap', 'Coöperatie', 'onderlinge waarborgmaatschappij', 'Fonds voor gemene rekening', 'vereniging op coöperatieve grondslag' and 'vereniging welke op onderlinge grondslag als verzekeraar of kredietinstelling optreedt', and other companies**

Directive 90/435/EC Parent-Subsidiary Directive*	Directive 90/434/EC Merger Directive**	Directive 2003/49/EC Interest and Royalties Directive	Proposal for a Council Directive on a Common Consolidated Corporate Tax Base (CCCTB) COM(2011) 121 final of 16 March 2011
vennootschap met beperkte aansprakelijkheid', **'Open commanditaire vennootschap', 'Coöperatie', 'onderlinge waarborgmaatschappij', 'Fonds voor gemene rekening', 'vereniging op coöperatieve grondslag', 'vereniging welke op onderlinge grondslag als verzekeraar of kredietinstelling optreedt', and other companies constituted under Dutch law subject to Dutch corporate tax**; (t) companies under Austrian law known as 'Aktiengesellschaft', 'Gesellschaft mit beschränkter Haftung', 'Versicherungsvereine auf Gegenseitigkeit', **'Erwerbs- und Wirtschaftsgenossenschaften', 'Betriebe gewerblicher Art von Körperschaften des öffentlichen Rechts', 'Sparkassen', and other**	**subject to the Dutch Corporate Tax**; (s) companies under Austrian law known as 'Aktiengesellschaft', 'Gesellschaft mit beschränkter Haftung', **'Erwerbs- und Wirtschaftsgenossenschaften';** (t) companies under Polish law known as: 'spółka akcyjna', 'spółka z ograniczoną odpowiedzialnością'; (u) commercial companies or civil law companies having a commercial form **as well as other legal persons carrying on commercial or industrial activities, which are** incorporated **under** Portuguese law; (ab) companies under Romanian law known as: 'societăți pe acțiuni', 'societăți în comandită pe acțiuni', 'societăți cu răspundere limitată'; (v) companies under Slovenian law known as: 'delniška družba',		**constituted under Dutch law subject to the Dutch Corporate Tax**; (u) companies under Austrian law known as 'Aktiengesellschaft', 'Gesellschaft mit beschränkter Haftung', 'Versicherungsvereine auf Gegenseitigkeit', **'Erwerbs und Wirtschaftsgenossenschaften', 'Betriebe gewerblicher Art von Körperschaften des öffentlichen Rechts', 'Sparkassen', and other companies constituted under Austrian law subject to Austrian corporate tax**; (v) companies under Polish law known as: 'spółka akcyjna', 'spółka z ograniczoną odpowiedzialnością', **'spółdzielnia', 'przedsiębiorstwo państwowe'**; (w) commercial companies or civil law companies having a commercial

companies constituted under Austrian law subject to Austrian corporate tax; (u) companies under Polish law known as: 'spółka akcyjna', 'spółka z ograniczoną odpowiedzialnością'; (v) commercial companies or civil law companies having a commercial form **and** cooperatives and public undertakings incorporated in accordance with Portuguese law; (w) companies under Romanian law known as: 'societăţi pe acţiuni', 'societăţi în comandită pe acţiuni', 'societăţi cu răspundere limitată'; (x) companies under Slovenian law known as: 'delniška družba', 'komanditna družba', 'družba z omejeno odgovornostjo'; (y) companies under Slovak law known as: 'akciová spoločnosť', 'spoločnosť s ručením obmedzeným', 'komanditná spoločnosť; (z) companies under Finnish law known as 'osakeyhtiö'/'aktiebolag', 'osuuskunta'/'andelslag', 'säästöpankki'/'vsparbank' and 'vakuutusyhtiö'/'försäkringsbolag'; (aa) companies under Swedish law known as 'aktiebolag', **'bankaktiebolag'**, 'försäkringsaktiebolag',	'komanditna družba', 'družba z omejeno odgovornostjo'; (w) companies under Slovak law known as: 'akciová spoločnosť', 'spoločnosť s ručením obmedzeným', 'komanditná spoločnosť . (x) companies under Finnish law known as 'osakeyhtiö'/'aktiebolag', 'osuuskunta'/'andelslag', 'säästöpankki'/'sparbank' and 'vakuutusyhtiö'/'försäkringsbolag'; (y) companies under Swedish law known as 'aktiebolag', 'försäkringsaktiebolag', **'ekonomiska föreningar', 'sparbanker', 'ömsesidiga försäkringsbolag'**; (z) companies incorporated under the law of the United Kingdom.		form, cooperatives and public undertakings incorporated in accordance with Portuguese law; (x) companies under Romanian law known as: 'societăţi pe acţiuni', 'societăţi în comandită pe acţiuni', 'societăţi cu răspundere limitată'; (y) companies under Slovenian law known as: 'delniška družba', **'komanditna delniška družba'**, 'komanditna družba', 'družba z omejeno odgovornostjo', **'družba z neomejeno odgovornostjo';** (z) companies under Slovak law known as: 'akciová spoločnosť', 'spoločnosť s ručením obmedzeným', 'komanditná spoločnosť, **'verejná obchodná spoločnosť', 'družstvo'**; (aa) companies under Finnish law known as 'osakeyhtiö'/'aktiebolag', 'osuuskunta'/'andelslag', 'säästöpankki'/'sparbank' and 'vakuutusyhtiö'/'försäkringsbolag'; (bb) companies under Swedish law known as 'aktiebolag', 'försäkringsaktiebolag', **'ekonomiska föreningar', 'sparbanker', 'ömsesidiga försäkringsbolag'**; (cc) companies incorporated under the law of the United Kingdom.

Directive 90/435/EC **Parent-Subsidiary Directive***	**Directive 90/434/EC** **Merger Directive****	**Directive 2003/49/EC** **Interest and Royalties Directive**	**Proposal for a Council Directive on a Common Consolidated Corporate Tax Base (CCCTB) COM(2011) 121 final of 16 March 2011**
'ekonomiska föreningar', 'sparbanker', 'ömsesidiga försäkringsbolag'; (ab) companies incorporated under the law of the United Kingdom.			

Notes: * Unlike the list found in this chapter, the current list of companies that is relevant for the purposes of the parent-subsidiary regime is that found in Council Directive 2011/96/EU of 30 November 2011 on the common system of taxation applicable in the case of parent companies and subsidiaries of different Member States (recast). However, the list found in the Directive 90/435/EC is reported here to better highlight differences with other directives.
** Unlike the list found in this chapter, the current list of companies that is relevant for the purposes of the merger directive is that found in Council Directive 2009/133/EC of 19 October 2009 on the common system of taxation applicable to mergers, divisions, partial divisions, transfers of assets and exchanges of shares concerning companies of different Member States and to the transfer of the registered office of an SE or SCE between Member States (codified version). However, the list found in the Directive 90/434/EC is reported here to better highlight differences with other directives.

4. Withholding taxation

Joachim Englisch

4.1 INTRODUCTION

Under an EU Common Corporate Tax regime, withholding taxes need to be addressed in three different scenarios affecting companies or groups that have opted for such a tax regime.[1] First, regarding deduction of tax at source on the occasion of intra-group transactions: the levy of withholding taxes would be in conflict with the consolidation of such intra-group transactions, to be effected through their elimination for the purposes of calculating the taxable base, as provided for in Article 59 of the Commission's proposal for a CCCTB Directive.[2] Second, income from investments made by group members may be subject to withholding taxes in a Member State or in a third country. As regards Member States, it is necessary to decide whether the fundamental concept of revenue-sharing by way of formulary apportionment, which is one of the cornerstones of the draft CCCTB Directive,[3] is compatible with the simultaneous levy of withholding taxes based on the notion of "source country entitlement". Moreover, and in particular vis-à-vis withholding taxes imposed by third countries, the sharing formula might have to be applied to the revenue cost of the credit method, in so far as the latter is chosen to avoid international double taxation of group companies. Finally, withholding taxes also raise certain questions in the inverse situation of dealings between CCCTB group members and other (external) entities: Should outbound dividend, interest, and other payments

[1] The Commission has proposed introducing a Common Consolidated Corporate Tax Base (CCCTB) on an optional basis, see the explanatory memorandum to the Commission Proposal for a Council Directive on a Common Consolidated Corporate Tax Base (CCCTB), COM(2011) 121/4, 16 March 2011, p. 5.

[2] In the following, all articles without further specification refer to the draft CCCTB Directive proposed by the Commission in March 2011 (see footnote 1).

[3] See Articles 86 to 102 of the draft CCCTB Directive.

made by the group be subject to a uniform withholding tax as established by a common system for all Member States? And should the withholding tax revenue be integrated into the revenue-sharing mechanism under formulary apportionment?

1. The second issue (of withholding taxes that affect the group as a recipient of inbound payments) has been excluded from the scope of this chapter. However, related topics will be addressed to the extent that they become relevant in the context of the other two aspects of withholding taxes under a CCCTB.
2. As regards the imposition of withholding taxes on intra-group transactions, Article 60 provides that there shall be no deduction of tax at source:

   > No withholding taxes or other source taxation shall be charged on transactions between members of a group.

   Even though this provision is perfectly in line with the rationale of group consolidation for tax purposes, it gives rise to some points of debate in the margins of the concept of "source taxation". Moreover, the temporal aspect of the prohibition of withholding taxes, as well as related administrative issues, are not as yet entirely clear. The chapter will discuss these topics in its second section.
3. As far as the levy of withholding taxes on payments effected by group members to other entities is concerned, the proposed directive's provisions are rather fragmentary: there is an obvious lack of harmonization regarding structures and rates of national withholding taxes levied by Member States on such outbound payments. Instead, the draft CCCTB Directive provides that the revenue raised through withholding taxes on certain categories of payments (interest and royalties) shall be shared among all the Member States in which the group is established. To that effect, Article 77 specifies:

   > Interest and royalties paid by a taxpayer to a recipient outside the group may be subject to a withholding tax in the Member State of the taxpayer according to the applicable rules of national law and any applicable double tax convention. The withholding tax shall be shared among the Member States according to the formula applicable in the tax year in which the tax is charged pursuant to Articles 86 to 102.

The provision of Article 77 is in certain conflict with the overall objective of the Commission's proposal to reduce compliance costs for business and administrative costs for tax authorities. In particular, it gives rise to considerable interpretative difficulties, as will be discussed in depth below in the third section of this chapter. It is also respectfully submitted that the arguments which have been brought forward by the Commission for the application of formulary apportionment also to the proceeds of certain types of withholding taxes on outbound payments made by CCCTB group members are scarcely convincing. And if one were to accept them as valid, the substantive scope of Article 77 would be inconsistent, as will also be demonstrated in the third section of this chapter. Besides these issues, I will also briefly discuss the relationship between the fundamental freedoms (see Article 26 TFEU) and the existing corporate tax directives, on the one hand, and Article 77, on the other hand.

4.2 NO WITHHOLDING TAXES ON INTRA-GROUP TRANSACTIONS

4.2.1 Substantive Scope of Article 60

It has already been mentioned that Article 60 requires the abolition of "withholding taxes or other source taxation" on transactions between members of a CCCTB group. The wording of the provision is rather broad. One could therefore wonder whether all kinds of taxes levied on occasion of, or as a consequence of such transactions are prohibited in the source country, in other words, in the Member State where the paying group member is resident or established. This could affect transaction taxes levied in that source country, such as, for example, a real estate transfer tax, capital duties, an eventual future financial transaction tax, or even value added tax. Moreover, in some Member States – for instance, in Germany – municipal business or trade taxes are still charged besides corporate tax. As rather archaic territorial taxes, they will sometimes also be levied on certain payments (for example, interest or royalties) with sufficient nexus to the relevant tax jurisdiction, by taking those payments into account for the purpose of calculating the taxable base. This could also be understood as some form of taxation "at source" of those payments, which might be inadmissible under Article 60 if the payment is related to an intra-group transaction.

However, if interpreted contextually, the concept of "source taxation" prohibited under Article 60 must be understood to refer only to corporate tax arrangements within the meaning of Annex II of the draft directive. As can be inferred from Article 6 (6) and (7) and Article 7, read together with Article 2 (1) (b), the scope of the draft CCCTB Directive is, in principle, limited to the levy of the corporate taxes mentioned in Annex II and related withholding taxes. Moreover, it is also evident from Article 14 (1) (d) and (j), read together with Annex III, that profit-based municipal business or trade taxes must be distinguished from "corporate taxes". Pursuant to Article 7, only the latter would be governed by the rules of the CCCTB Directive instead of the national corporate tax systems, once an option for the CCCTB system becomes available and is exercised by a qualifying group of companies. Since harmonization does not extend to other taxes such as the ones listed in Annex III, they cannot be affected by the prohibition of "source taxation" provided for in Article 60.[4]

This contextual argument is furthermore supported by a purposive construction based on the rationale of Article 60. As can be inferred from the insertion of this provision into Chapter IX of the draft CCCTB Directive, the abolition of withholding taxes or other source taxation is conceived as a corollary (in other words, a flanking measure) to the concept of a *consolidated* tax base. The effect of consolidation under the common tax regime may not be undermined by national taxes levied on intra-group transactions. The scope of Article 60 therefore should not extend any further than the scope of the other rules on consolidation, which is defined in Article 57: consolidation concerns the "tax bases" of the members of a CCCTB group, as can furthermore be concluded from Article 4 (11). These tax bases are calculated according to the rules of the proposed draft directive for the purposes of corporate taxation only, as stated in Article 6 (6, 7) and Article 7, in recitals 4, 5 and 8 to the preamble, as well as in the explanatory memorandum to the draft directive. Other taxes such as transaction taxes or municipal trade or business taxes are not covered by the CCCTB option to consolidate, and therefore are also unaffected by Article 60.

Therefore, the scope of Article 60 is essentially limited to the following forms of taxation: first, withholding taxes that have sufficient nexus to corporate taxes within the meaning of Annex II. Such nexus can be affirmed if the withholding tax is either creditable against the respective corporate tax in a scenario not covered by the CCCTB, or if the levy of the withholding tax excludes an additional levy of corporate tax that would normally be due (final withholding tax on corporate income). Second, "other source taxation" in the form of corporate tax within the meaning of Annex II levied by assessment.

---

[4] For a similar reasoning within the framework of the Merger Directive 90/434/EEC, see Case C-352/08, *Modehuis Zwijnenburg* [2010] ECR I-4303, paras 49 et seq.

4.2.2 Timing and Administrative Aspects

4.2.2.1 Relevant period: Group membership

By virtue of Article 60, Member States must refrain from levying withholding taxes on transactions between "members of a group". This implies that Member States may require tax deductions until the moment that group membership within the meaning of the directive enters into effect, and that Member States may also reinstate their system of withholding taxation once at least one of the two taxpayers involved in the transaction has ceased to be a group member. As will be discussed in the following, some administrative aspects of this temporal dimension of Article 60 still need to be clarified.

According to Article 4 (7), the term "group member" means any taxpayer belonging to the same group, as defined in Articles 54 and 55. These provisions establish certain minimum thresholds of corporate control and economic integration, based on the three criteria of voting rights, ownership rights, and entitlement to profits; they furthermore specify the necessary territorial nexus to the EU internal market. Pursuant to Article 58 (1), a taxpayer becomes a member of a group on the date when the aforementioned thresholds are reached. The draft CCCTB directive does not provide for an equally explicit rule regarding the criteria and temporal dimension of a termination of group membership. Article 58 (1) merely states that "the thresholds of Article 54 must be met throughout the tax year". As explained in recital 16 to the preamble, this phrase must be understood to imply that a company leaves the group "immediately" when the relevant thresholds are no longer met. The preparatory materials also support such an interpretation of Article 58 (1).[5] As a consequence, the prohibition of withholding taxes on intra-group transactions laid down in Article 60 does not apply any more from that moment on, notwithstanding the continued application of the CCCTB system as a whole to the leaving group member(s), as required by Article 105 (3).

Pursuant to Article 56, group membership of a taxpayer is furthermore terminated with immediate effect if the taxpayer is liquidated or is the subject of a declaration of insolvency. Under these conditions, too, Article 60 no longer applies. Moreover, Article 58 (2) creates a special rule according to which group membership is annulled *retroactively*, for

[5] See European Commission, Workshop, "CCCTB: Transactions and Dealings between the Group and Entities Outside the Group" CCCTB/RD/003, 1 September 2010, p. 4, point 10.

the purpose of the chapter on group consolidation, if the participation and control thresholds established in Article 54 have not been maintained for at least nine consecutive months since the date on which the taxpayer initially joined the group.[6] An eventual abstention from the levy of withholding taxes during the period of "preliminary" group membership, in compliance with Article 60, would then *ex post facto* turn out to have been a disproportionate interference with the tax sovereignty of the respective Member State, since it was ultimately not required as a flanking measure to group consolidation under the CCCTB consolidation regime.

Against this background, it is respectfully submitted that the Commission's proposal fails to address some related practical and administrative issues. First, it would seem reasonable to give Member States an opportunity to verify the relevant criteria of group membership, as defined in Article 54, before an eventual domestic requirement of deduction of withholding taxes at source is dispensed. If the competent authority verifies that the criteria had indeed been fulfilled, but meanwhile deduction of tax at source has already been carried out, a repayment of the withholding tax levied contrary to Article 60 would still be sufficient in order to accomplish the objective of group consolidation underlying that provision. The temporal drain of liquidity could be compensated by a standard interest payment. On the other hand, if no such safeguard of the financial interests of Member States is provided for, and the criteria for group membership and the ensuing exemption from the withholding tax obligation have in reality not been fulfilled, a Member State may find it hard or impossible to subsequently enforce the corresponding tax liability. It is therefore suggested to complement Article 60 with procedural elements such as the possibility for Member States to issue and require an official certificate or attestation of entitlement to a withholding tax exemption, and additional rules on repayment and interest compensation. The provisions of Article 1 paras 11 to 13, 15, and 16 of the Interest and Royalties Directive[7] and of Article 107 (1)[8] could serve as a model in this regard.

---

[6] See, to this effect, also the deliberations of European Commission, Workshop, "CCCTB: Transactions and Dealings between the Group and Entities Outside the Group" CCCTB/RD/003, 1 September 2010, p. 4, point 10.

[7] Council Directive 2003/49/EC on a common system of taxation applicable to interest and royalty payments made between associated companies of different Member States [2003] OJ L 157/49.

[8] Article 107 (1) of the draft CCCTB Directive provides a procedure for the control of the fulfillment of the criteria of Articles 54 and 55 with respect to the

Along the same lines, a notification obligation regarding the termination of group membership of (at least) one of the (former) group members engaged in a contractual relationship involving payment obligations, in analogy to the one laid down in Article 1 (14) Interest and Royalties Directive, should also be included in Article 60 of the CCCTB Directive. In the context of Article 60 it seems an adequate precaution to require the principal taxpayer (see Article 4 (6)) to immediately inform the paying company or permanent establishment, and possibly also the competent authority of the source State, that the withholding tax exemption for intra-group payments no longer applies. While it can be expected that the paying as well as the receiving entity will be aware of this fact in most instances, this need not necessarily be the case, especially since the ownership right and profit entitlement thresholds of Article 54 (2) (b) may also be fulfilled indirectly through interests held in intermediate subsidiaries.

Finally, the possibility of a retroactive repeal of group membership until the completion of the first nine months of its existence should be reflected in an option for Member States to require a provisional deduction of withholding taxes on intra-group payments made by or to the new group member during that period. Should the criteria set forth in Article 54 then have been maintained for more than nine months, the provisional withholding tax would have to be repaid to the group member that has received the corresponding payment.

4.2.2.2 Transactions rather than payments as temporal connecting factor

It should be pointed out that timing mismatches between the prohibition of withholding taxes under Article 60, on the one hand, and national rules on the arising of the obligation to deduct tax at source, on the other hand, are likely to occur. According to its wording, Article 60 applies to "transactions" between group members, rather than to the corresponding payments. The provision thereby aligns with the rules on consolidation, which provide for the elimination of "transactions directly carried out between members of a group" from the common consolidated tax base (Article 59), rather than for an elimination of intra-group payments. These parallels must be assumed to be intentional rather than coincidental, because the abolition of withholding taxes laid down in Article 60 has been conceived as an essential flanking measure to group consolidation,

original members of a presumed group that are covered by the notice to opt for the CCCTB regime.

as has already been explained above. Therefore, the temporal scope of application of both regimes should be identical.

In the context of the rules on consolidation, Article 59 (2) lays down that "for the purpose of determining whether there is an intra-group transaction, both parties to the transaction must be group members at the time that the transaction is effected and the associated revenues and expenses fall to be recognized." This temporal condition makes reference to the CCCTB rules on the accrual of revenues and the incurrence of deductible expenses. Revenues and expenses will therefore be consolidated only when they result from transactions between companies that were group members at the point of time specified in Articles 18 and 19. Pursuant to these provisions, it is relevant at which time the right to receive the payments and the corresponding obligation to make them has arisen, and the amount of payment due can be quantified with reasonable accuracy. Article 18 explicitly states that the time of the actual payment is irrelevant in this context. For the reasons given above, the same temporal conditions will have to apply in the context of Article 60. It is therefore incumbent on Member States to refrain from levying withholding taxes only with respect to transactions carried out directly between companies that were group members at the time when the obligation to make the payment subject to withholding tax has arisen and could be quantified with reasonable accuracy.

However, national rules on the levy of withholding taxes will frequently require the paying entity to carry out the tax deduction at the time when the *payment is effected*. Therefore, the point of time that is relevant for the determination of whether the paying company is exempt from this obligation pursuant to Article 60 will frequently not coincide with the time at which the obligation to deduct would usually arise. The paying company will often have to make a *retrospective* analysis as to whether the payment at issue has its legal justification in a transaction that falls within the temporal scope of Article 60. Not every payment that is made from a CCCTB group member to another group member will benefit from Article 60, and not every payment that is effected after (at least) one of the contracting parties has left the group will necessarily be outside the temporal scope of that provision. Mismatches may occur "at the margins" of group membership.

Since the department of the paying company that is responsible for the tax deduction at source may not always be immediately aware of all relevant facts in this context, this creates the danger of under-taxation or over-taxation. For that reason, too, it would be desirable to authorize Member States to require provisional withholding taxes during an initial period of group membership and/or make the withholding tax exemption dependent upon an official certificate (which would be issued with a certain time lag), while at the same time, the directive should also establish repayment and interest payment obligations in the case of a deduction of tax at source contrary to Article 60.

4.3 WITHHOLDING TAXES ON PAYMENTS MADE TO ENTITIES OUTSIDE THE GROUP

4.3.1 Relevance of Article 77: First Sentence

As has already been mentioned above, the Commission does not attempt to harmonize the structure or rates of withholding taxes through its proposal for a draft CCCTB Directive.

At first glance, Article 77 could be understood as requiring the abolition of national withholding taxes on payments from a CCCTB taxpayer to another entity except for withholding taxes on interest and royalties. This could be inferred by way of an *a contrario* reasoning to the explicit admission that "interest and royalties paid by a taxpayer to a recipient outside the group may be subject to a withholding tax in the Member State of the taxpayer": if express authorization is granted to Member States to continue the levy of such withholding taxes, could this not imply a tacit prohibition of taxation at source of other types of payments?

But as evidenced by recital 18 to the draft directive's preamble, Article 77 does not intend to limit Member State's sovereign power to impose withholding taxes on any kind of payments. The preamble presupposes the continued existence of withholding taxes on dividends, even though the latter are not mentioned in Article 77. The preparatory materials also reveal the merely declaratory character of the introductory phrase of this provision: According to point 18 of the Commission's 2007 working paper on the CCCTB project,[9] "withholding taxes and other source taxation on payments made by a taxpayer to a non-taxpayer, whether EU resident or not, would continue to be governed by domestic and tax treaty arrangements." Member States would therefore not be required, by virtue of Article 77, to alter their system of withholding taxes.

One could therefore wonder whether the first sentence of Article 77 is not redundant altogether and should better be abandoned in the final

[9] European Commission, "CCCTB: possible elements of a technical outline", 26 July 2007, CCCTB/WP057\doc\en, p. 7.

version of the proposed directive. However, it does have some clarifying effect if read together with the second sentence of Article 77:[10] according to this provision, which will be discussed in detail below, the revenue generated by withholding taxes on interest and royalties will be shared among Member States according to the general rules of CCCTB formulary apportionment. Against this background, it is not self-evident that Member States still have discretion as to the extent to which they impose such withholding taxes. Therefore, the first sentence of Article 77 may be regarded as useful to affirm the unfettered sovereignty of Member States in this regard. However, it is respectfully suggested that it would then be clearer to have the statement that is currently to be found in sentence 2 of Article 77 precede the one of sentence one. The provision should thus be formulated as follows:

> Withholding taxes on interest and royalties paid by a taxpayer to a recipient outside the group which are levied in the Member State of the taxpayer shall be shared among the Member States according to the formula applicable in the tax year in which the tax is charged pursuant to Articles 86 to 102. The eventual levy of such withholding taxes continues to be governed by the applicable rules of national law and any applicable double tax convention.

4.3.2 No Common Withholding Tax Regime

The first sentence of Article 77 furthermore clarifies that withholding taxes on interest and royalties shall be levied "according to the applicable rules of national law and any applicable double tax convention." This implies an abstention, on the part of the Commission, from harmonization of national withholding taxes even to the extent that the revenue ensuing from their imposition is to be shared among all Member States that benefit from formulary apportionment (by virtue of the second sentence of Article 77). It is moreover emphasized that the directive does not affect existing tax treaties or the sovereign power of Member States to negotiate future international agreements relating to withholding taxes on interest and royalties. This is consistent with the overall concept of the proposed CCCTB regime: domestic or DTC rules on withholding taxes levied on occasion of *outbound* payments to non-members of a CCCTB group do not interfere with the concept of a common consolidated tax base for the group itself. Since there is no conflict with the directive's

---

[10] The author owes this insight to a comment made by E. Kemmeren in the panel discussion, which is gratefully acknowledged.

objective, the latter should not affect the remaining sovereignty of Member States to set the legal framework for withholding taxes.

Notwithstanding the above observations, the question remains whether it would not be preferable for a future CCCTB directive to also establish a common system of withholding taxes on outbound payments made by a CCCTB taxpayer to another entity. The Commission itself has voiced concerns that a lack of common arrangements could result in distortions in patterns of investment within the internal market.[11] Indeed, it is likely that jurisdictions which impose only low or even no withholding taxes – either by virtue of their domestic legislation or because of their tax treaty obligations – would become more attractive locations for holding companies, for group financing companies, or for intermediate royalty holding companies within a group of companies that has opted for the CCCTB regime: Affiliated companies or investors who are outside the scope of CCCTB consolidation of intra-group transactions, and therefore do not benefit from the corresponding abolition of all withholding taxes on intra-group payments, could choose such jurisdictions in order to route their dividend, interest, or royalty income to their country of residence without (significant) withholding tax burdens. This is particularly relevant for offshore companies or other third-country investors.

However, the ensuing distortions in the allocation of resources within the internal market are not uniquely related to the features of the CCCTB proposal. They already arise under current company tax planning schemes and other forms of international tax arbitrage, when taxpayers allocate investments, capital or IP to EU jurisdictions with beneficial domestic withholding tax regimes or to Member States that have concluded tax treaties providing for super-reduced withholding tax rates. Frequently, taxpayers also avail themselves of opportunities for tax treaty shopping or directive shopping in that context;[12] in particular, the rules

---

[11] See European Commission, "CCCTB: possible elements of a technical outline", 26 July 2007, CCCTB/WP057\doc\en, point 18; see also Marc Burgeois and Eric Von Frenckell, "Relation to Taxpayers outside the Group" in Michael Lang et al. (eds), *Common Consolidated Corporate Tax Base* (Linde 2008) 195, 206; Malcolm Gammie and Christiana HJI Panayi, "Inbound Investment and Thin Capitalization" in Michael Lang et al. (eds), *Common Consolidated Corporate Tax Base* (Linde 2008) 821, 834 (in footnote 56).

[12] See Luc de Broe, *International Tax Planning and Prevention of Abuse* (IBFD 2008) 5 et seq.

on the abolition of withholding taxes laid down in Article 5 Parent-Subsidiary Directive[13] and in Article 1 (1) Interest and Royalties Directive play an important role for many international group structures. Consequently, a common EU policy on withholding taxes, which would necessarily have to be accompanied by some form of agreement or understanding on a common tax treaty policy vis-à-vis third countries, should not be pursued within the framework of the CCCTB project, even if it furthermore facilitates tax arbitrage of the aforementioned kind.

Instead, this Herculean task should be dealt with on a separate and more comprehensive basis, especially since its integration into the CCCTB project would certainly exacerbate political agreement on the proposal for a CCCTB Directive put forward by the Commission. Inserting a second paragraph in Article 77 should be contemplated, though, which would lay down an express obligation for Member States to enact anti-jurisdiction-shopping legislation with respect to the withholding taxes on interest and royalty payments. While such an obligation can also be inferred from the general Union law principle that abuse of rights is prohibited, as established in the settled case law of the ECJ,[14] it would be in the interest of legal certainty to specify the scope of such an obligation and the relevant criteria in an explicit provision of secondary law. To allow for more flexibility, the Commission could be authorized to adopt implementing provisions (Article 291 TFEU) or even delegated acts (Article 290 TFEU) that elaborate further on the type of schemes that should be considered abusive in this context; Article 11 (2) of the

[13] Council Directive 90/435/EEC on the common system of taxation applicable in the case of parent companies and subsidiaries of different Member States [1990] OJ L 225.

[14] See, for instance, Case C-321/05, *Kofoed* [2007] ECR I-5795, para 38; Cases C-80/11 and C-142/11, *Mahagében and Dávid*, paras 41–42; for a good overview and further references, see also Opinion of Advocate General Poiares Maduro, Case C-255/02, *Halifax* [2006] ECR I-1609, points 62 et seq.; Luc de Broe, *International Tax Planning and Prevention of Abuse* (IBFD 2008) 755 et seq. (non-tax cases) and 800 et seq. (tax-related cases); Rita de la Feria, *Prohibition of abuse of (Community) law: The creation of a new general principle of EC law through tax* (2007) 45 and the conference volume edited by Rita de la Feria and Stefan Vogenauer, *Prohibition of Abuse of Law: A New General Principle of EU Law?*, (Hart Publishing 2011); for a critical assessment, see Englisch, *Curbing "Abusive" International Tax Planning under EU Law* (2012).

proposal for a directive on a common system of financial transaction tax[15] could serve as a model in this regard.

Besides, common rules for withholding taxes levied on payments made from a CCCTB taxpayer to another (non-consolidated) entity are also not essential with a view towards the rules of formulary apportionment that form an integral part of the Commission's proposal (see Articles 86 to 102). As regards the possible distortions in the patterns of investment that can be expected as a consequence of the present array of different national and tax treaty rules on withholding taxes, they should not have a significant impact on the allocation of the taxable base to individual Member States. Royalties or other intangible assets that are conveyed to a CCCTB group, and whose placement within the group might be influenced by withholding tax considerations, are not normally a relevant factor for formulary apportionment (see Article 93). The same applies for shareholdings in subsidiaries held by a CCCTB parent company that has been established in a typical holding jurisdiction with low or no withholding tax rates on dividends and/or interest payments. Equity or loan capital provided to a group financing company also does not, in itself, influence the apportionment of the common consolidated base. Finally, the number of staff employed in the context of the aforementioned activities can be expected to be relatively moderate and should usually not have a significant effect on the labour factor of the apportionment formula (as specified in Article 90).

Admittedly, it seems odd that the national withholding tax policy and tax treaty policy of each Member State should influence the amount of (withholding) tax revenue that accrues to all Member States, by virtue of an analogous application of formulary apportionment as provided for in Article 77. It should be noted, though, that under the current proposal this would only affect withholding taxes on interest and royalties. In particular, the proposed Article 77 does not extend the revenue-sharing obligation to withholding taxes on dividends. Moreover, this effect merely shows that the entire concept of apportionment of tax revenue collected through withholding taxes on outbound payments is highly questionable, as will be discussed below at section 4.3.4.

---

[15] Proposal for a Council Directive on a common system of financial transactions and amending Directive 2008/7/EC, COM(2011) 594 final.

4.3.3 No Exemption from other Union Law Requirements regarding Withholding Taxes

The first sentence of Article 77 would clearly not dispense Member States from their primary Union law obligations laid down in the founding treaties. This observation is a direct consequence of the quasi-constitutional rank of primary law, which cannot be overridden or suspended by legal acts of the very Union institutions that are bound by it.[16] If the wording of a piece of secondary EU legislation so permits, it should therefore not be interpreted so as to interfere with primary law requirements, since it would otherwise be null and void.[17] The referral to "the applicable rules of national law or any applicable DTC" regarding the levy of withholding taxes in Article 77 of the draft CCCTB Directive can be interpreted as a mere confirmation that *this particular directive* does not interfere with the sovereign power of Member States to set the legal framework for their respective withholding taxes, *without prejudice* to other Union law restraints. This is indeed suggested by the reference only to "applicable" norms of domestic or tax treaty law. The provision must therefore not be construed to grant Member States "carte blanche" to deviate also from superior Union law requirements.

Domestic or tax treaty rules on withholding taxes on interest and royalty payments therefore would still have to respect the fundamental freedoms listed in Article 26 TFEU, unless their infringement could be justified by overriding reasons in the public interest. Hence, Member States could not have recourse to Article 77 in order to shield discriminatory or restrictive withholding tax regimes from scrutiny as to their compatibility with the freedom of establishment (Article 49 TFEU), the freedom to provide services (Article 56 TFEU), or the guarantee of free

---

[16] See Koenraad Lenaerts and Piet Van Nuffel, *European Union Law* (3rd edn, Thomson, Sweet & Maxwell 2011) paras 22–002 et seq.; Paul Craig and Gráinne de Burca, *EU Law* (5th edn Oxford University Press 2011), 109; Damien Chalmers, Gareth T Davies and Giorgio Monti, *European Union Law* (2nd edn Cambridge University Press 2010) 100; L. Steiner and J. Woods, *EU Law* (10th edn Oxford University Press 2009) 51 et seq.

[17] Case C-305/05 *Ordre des barreaux francophones et germanophone* [2007] ECR I-5305, para 28; see also Karol P.E. Lasok and Timothy Millett, *Judicial Control in the EU* (Richmond Law & Tax 2004) para. 688; Koenraad Lenaerts and Piet Van Nuffel, *European Union Law* (3rd edn, Thomson, Sweet & Maxwell 2011) para 21-061; Damien Chalmers, Gareth T. Davies and Giorgio Monti, *European Union Law* (2nd edn Cambridge University Press 2010) 158 et seq.; Paul Craig and Gráinne de Burca, *EU Law* (5th edn Oxford University Press 2011), 109 et seq.

movement of capital (Article 63 TFEU).[18] In particular, Member States would still have to adhere to the relevant case law of the ECJ, especially the *Scorpio* ruling[19] and subsequent Court decisions on withholding taxes.[20]

Arguably, Article 77 would also not pre-empt the application of other secondary EU legislation that limits the discretion of Member States with respect to the imposition of withholding taxes on interest and royalty payments. In particular, the interdiction of withholding taxes on cross-border payments between associated companies, laid down in Article 1 (1) Interest and Royalties Directive, would still hold valid in an intra-Union context.[21] Neither the preparatory materials nor the explanatory memorandum or the preamble to the draft CCCTB Directive contain any indication to the contrary. This could have been expected, though, had the Commission really intended a partial carve-out of Article 1 (1) Interest and Royalties Directive, since such an exception would jeopardize the objective of that directive.

As can be inferred from the preamble to the Interest and Royalties Directive, it seeks to ensure that interest and royalty payments between associated companies of different Member States are subject to tax only once, by abolishing source country taxation. This objective is not made obsolete by Article 77, because the latter provision does not provide for an alternative approach towards avoiding international double taxation. By contrast, the continued application of Article 1 (1) Interest and Royalties Directive will not impair the CCCTB project in general, or the apportionment of withholding taxes under the second sentence of Article 77 in particular, because the latter provision does not establish a conflicting minimum tax deduction at source; the revenue-sharing obligation presupposes rather than commands the levy of a withholding tax. A purposive construction of Article 77 should therefore leave room for the continued application of Article 1 (1) Interest and Royalties Directive.

---

18 See Case C-168/01, *Bosal Holding* [2003] ECR I-9409, para 26.

19 See Case C-290/04, *Scorpio Konzertproduktionen* [2006] ECR I-9461.

20 See, in particular, Case C-345/04, *Centro Equestre da Lezíria Grande* [2007] I-1425; Case C-379/05, *Amurta* [2007] ECR I-9569; Case C-303/07, *Aberdeen Property Fininvest Alpha* [2009] ECR I-5145; Case C-540/07, *Commission v Italy* [2009] ECR I-10983; Case C-284/09, *Commission v Germany*, n.y.r.; see also Simader, "Withholding taxes and the effectiveness of fiscal supervision and tax collection" [2010] 2 *Bulletin for International Taxation* 115.

21 Likewise Malcolm Gammie and Christiana HJI Panayi, "Inbound Investment and Thin Capitalization" in Michael Lang et al. (eds), *Common Consolidated Corporate Tax Base* (Linde 2008) 821, 834 et seq.

However, for the sake of legal certainty it would be desirable that in the final version of the CCCTB Directive, Article 77 or at least the preamble would explicitly address the relationship with other acts of secondary legislation.

4.3.4 (Ir)rationality of applying the Revenue Sharing Formula to certain Withholding Taxes

It follows from the above that the most relevant specification of Article 77 is to be found in its second sentence; it consists in the application of formulary apportionment, as envisaged in Articles 86 to 102, to the revenue from withholding taxes on interest and royalties as well. The source State where the paying group member is located would thus be obliged to share the corresponding tax revenue with all other Member States in which the group member is established. By contrast, withholding taxes on other categories of payments or income would exclusively accrue to the treasury of the collecting Member State and would not be shared across the group. The reasoning underlying this disparate allocation of tax revenue can be found in recital 18 to the preamble of the draft CCCTB Directive:

> When withholding taxes are charged on interest and royalty payments made by taxpayers, the proceeds of such taxes should be shared according to the formula of that tax year. When withholding taxes are charged on dividends distributed by taxpayers, the proceeds of such taxes should not be shared since, contrary to interest and royalties, dividends have not led to a previous deduction borne by all group companies.

The same arguments had already been put forward in a slightly more elaborate and cautious wording in the materials for the 2010 CCCTB workshop in Brussels:[22]

> The rationale behind this difference in treatment lies with the fact that interest and royalty payments are generally tax deductible at source and it should thus be assumed that the relevant cost will have already been shared among the group members. This is not the case for dividends, which are after-tax payments and have normally led to no shared deduction of costs. It seems therefore reasonable that dividends do not lead to any similar sharing of the revenues from withholding tax.

---

[22] Workshop on the Common Consolidated Corporate Tax Base, 1 September 2010: Transactions and dealings between the group and entities outside the group, Room Document, CCCTB\RD\003\doc\en.

It should be noted, though, that this view was initially disputed in the CCCTB working subgroup on international issues.[23] And it is indeed highly questionable whether it is really "reasonable", in the light of the logic inherent to the allocation effects of a common corporate tax base, to extend formulary apportionment to withholding taxes levied on payments that qualify as deductible expenses of a CCCTB taxpayer.

Since the assessment of income as a taxable base is based on corporate *profits*, rather than on corporate creation of gross value, it is a consistent feature of the CCCTB that interest and royalty payments are, in principle, deductible. The deduction of such cost factors diminishes the taxable income of the entire group under the proposed CCCTB regime and thus reduces each Member State's potential revenue share, because the CCCTB provides for a common consolidated taxable base for *group* income, to be allocated among Member States. By contrast, withholding taxes are traditionally conceived not as taxes on the income of the paying entity – a group member – but rather as taxes on the income of the recipient of the respective payment – an *entity outside the group*. The latter is the taxable person, whereas the former is legally supposed to act only as a "tax collector at source",[24] notwithstanding the fact that the real tax incidence will depend on price elasticity in the relevant market. This legal concept is normally also reflected in the normative framework for withholding taxes: It is the *payee* rather than the payer who may claim a reduction or refund of withholding taxes, or a foreign tax credit, under a DTC or based on unilateral measures intended to avoid international double taxation. Likewise, in a purely domestic setting a withholding tax will usually be credited (unless it is final) against the tax liability of the income *recipient* in his annual tax assessment.

Against this background, I cannot see why it would be reasonable to compensate a Member State for a pro-rata reduction of the group's tax base under the CCCTB regime by way of a partial entitlement to a tax on the income of another taxpayer. The shrinking of the taxable base is a direct consequence of the deductibility of certain expenditure, which in itself is also perfectly consistent with the concept of direct taxation of corporate income, and does not call into question the fairness of the allocation mechanism in a tax system where the harmonized base is a

---

[23] Malcolm Gammie and Christiana HJI Panayi, "Inbound Investment and Thin Capitalization" in Michael Lang et al. (eds), *Common Consolidated Corporate Tax Base* (Linde 2008) 821, 834.

[24] This is also the understanding of the ECJ in the context of the withholding tax concept of the Parent-Subsidiary Directive; see Case C-284/06 *Burda* [2008] ECR I-4571, para 52.

common consolidated one for the entire group and for all Member States in which this group is resident or established. By contrast, the levy of a withholding tax on the corresponding payments is a manifestation of the still unfettered tax sovereignty of each Member State, which has been deliberately placed outside the scope of the harmonized system. The exercise of that remaining tax sovereignty does not in any way have an impact on the common consolidated tax base, which remains the same irrespective of whether and at which rate a withholding tax is levied. Therefore, any revenue that results from such a withholding tax imposed at the discretion of each Member State should not have to be shared with other Member States. There is nothing that the latter States should have to be compensated for.

Furthermore, the reasoning of the Commission also seems incoherent in the light of the allocation of taxing rights under the Interest and Royalties Directive. Pursuant to Article 1 (1) Interest and Royalties Directive, interest or royalty payments arising in a Member State shall be exempt from any taxes imposed on those payments in that State, in so far as the Directive applies. Even though the respective Member State will, as a general rule, permit the paying company to treat the payments as deductible expenses for corporate tax purposes, the Directive does not allow that Member State to levy a withholding tax on the corresponding interest or royalties income in the hands of its recipient. While such an approach is debatable, it has been championed by the Commission, and it is therefore inconsistent to link the deductibility of such payments to an entitlement to withholding tax revenues under the proposal for a draft CCCTB Directive. Admittedly, there are other examples in international tax law where a link between the deduction of payments, on the one hand, and an entitlement to tax the corresponding income of the recipient of the payments, on the other hand, has indeed been established; most notably in DTC provisions inspired by Article 15 (2) subparagraphs (b) and (c) OECD MC.[25] But it is obvious that in the context discussed here, consistency with the Interest and Royalties Directive is far more relevant than consistency with the recommendations of a different international organization concerning a different kind of income.

It is acknowledged that at least with respect to interest payments, a different perspective could seemingly be adopted, which is unrelated to the official explanation of a link between deduction of payments and their taxation at the hands of the recipient, though: one could argue that according to the logic inherent to taxing consolidated group income, all

---

[25] See the OECD Model Commentary on Article 15, para 6.2.

Member States where group members are located have contributed to the generation of the interest income (in other words, the return on loan capital) that is received by the entity outside the group. Therefore, all of those Member States should also have a share in the revenue that accrues from withholding taxes on interest payments. However, there are two objections to this position. First, the logic of group taxation ends where group membership ends. If withholding taxes are correctly characterized as taxes on the income of the recipient, rather than taxes on the income of the paying entity, it seems more adequate to adopt the perspective of the payee. From his point of view, it is only the legal entity that received the loan, rather than the group as a whole, which has generated the income that is subject to withholding taxation. Second, the exclusion of withholding taxes on dividend income from the revenue-sharing mechanism cannot be reconciled with such a position. Since these withholding taxes, too, are levied on a return of capital that has been generated by the group as a whole – if one were to adopt the group perspective – the ensuing revenue should also be shared, notwithstanding the fact that a first layer of taxation is already realized at group level.

Finally, the proposed tax revenue-sharing does not respect the *nexus* between the remaining *tax sovereignty*, on the one hand, *and budgetary sovereignty*, on the other hand, in areas of taxation that have not as yet been comprehensively harmonized, such as is the case with respect to the withholding taxes dealt with in Article 77. It makes sense to leave Member States the freedom to decide whether to levy a withholding tax and if so, at which rate, only if the fiscal consequences of this decision will be exclusively borne by that Member State. This is required by the principles of political responsibility and accountability. The revenue-sharing undermines the foundations of these principles and will set an incentive for a "race to the bottom" with respect to withholding tax rates on interest and royalty payments. Taking into account secondary effects (promotion of *domestic* employment and a corresponding rise in payroll taxes that need not be shared, promotion of the *domestic* financial sector, and so on), it would in many cases be more attractive for Member States to lower their withholding taxes so as to become an attractive holding location, financial hub or IP jurisdiction, instead of collecting relatively high withholding taxes that must be shared, anyway. Therefore, the proposed treatment of withholding taxes on dividends – no revenue-sharing – should be the model for all kinds of withholding taxes.[26]

---

[26] This view is seemingly not shared by Marc Burgeois and Eric Von Frenckell, "Relation to Taxpayers outside the Group" in Michael Lang et al.

It should be noted that the revenue allocation provision of Article 77 would indeed make more sense in the inverse scenario of inbound payments *received by a group member*: If a Member State levies a withholding tax on income that forms part of the common consolidated tax base, it should have to share the revenue based on the same formula that also governs the partition of the tax base. This should be required regardless of the category of income (interest, royalties, dividends, or other income) and also regardless of whether the payer is subject to the CCCTB regime or not. At present, Article 76 provides that the revenue cost of a foreign tax credit for withholding taxes levied on non-exempt group income "shall be shared among the members of a group according to the formula applicable … pursuant to Articles 86 to 102". This applies also when it is another Member State that has imposed the creditable withholding tax. It is not comprehensible why the same conclusion has not also been drawn for the proceeds of the withholding tax itself. The current state of affairs leads to a situation where a Member State is allowed to tax group income for its own fiscal benefit at the expense of all other Member States. This tends to favour capital-importing Member States and is in open contradiction to the concept of a CCCTB where the allocation of taxable income depends on formulary apportionment rather than on the traditional notion of source country entitlement.

(eds), *Common Consolidated Corporate Tax Base* (Linde 2008) 195, 206, who see a distinct justification for the exclusion of withholding taxes on dividend payments from the revenue apportionment obligation: they reason that withholding taxes on non-deductible dividend payments can be considered to be a peculiar form of corporate tax levied upon the distribution of corporate profits, and thus have the same economic effect as an increase of the corporate tax rate applicable for distributed profits. Since Member States are still free, under the CCCTB proposal of the Commission, to set their national corporate tax rate to be applied on their portion in the common consolidated tax base, they should also retain full control over the corporate tax rate – including the withholding tax rate – on dividends and should be exclusively entitled to the corresponding tax revenue. It is respectfully submitted that this reasoning is not entirely convincing, because the amount of profit distributions subject to a dividend withholding tax may well be different from the respective Member State's share in the common tax base. If the dividend withholding tax were to be conceived as an extension of the corporate tax liability of the distributing company, the underlying concept of source country entitlement would thus interfere with the CCCTB concept of corporate taxation based on formulary apportionment.

4.3.5 Inconsistencies of the Special Regime for Interest and Royalties

Even if one accepts the premise of the Commission pursuant to which the deductibility of interest and royalty payments under the CCCTB regime should be matched by a sharing of related withholding tax revenues, it is respectfully submitted that several inconsistencies remain under the current proposal.

4.3.5.1 Apportionment of withholding tax also in case of certain non-deductible payments

First, Article 77 does not provide for an exception from the revenue-sharing obligation in situations where the relevant payments are not deductible. While deductibility of interest and royalty payments as business expenses is the general rule under Article 12,[27] this rule is not without certain qualifications. In particular, Article 81 contains a specific thin capitalization rule for interest paid to an associated enterprise resident in a third country. Albeit the scope of application of this thin cap rule is rather narrow,[28] it should not be ignored in the context of Article 77 that interest payments caught by this special anti-abuse rule[29] will not be deductible. It is furthermore conceivable that the same consequence could arise under the general anti-abuse clause of Article 80 (1).[30] Since the tax treatment of interest payments would thus be assimilated, at least with respect to their non-deductibility, to the taxation of dividend payments, it would be consistent with the Commission's aforementioned reasoning to extend those parallels in their treatment also to the apportionment of withholding taxes: In so far as these are levied on such interest payments, the revenue should remain exclusively with the source country, just as in the case of dividends.

---

[27] As regards interest payments in particular, Article 12 of the draft CCCTB Directive specifies that deductible expenses include "costs incurred in raising equity or debt for the purposes of the business." See also Malcolm Gammie and Christiana HJI Panayi, "Inbound Investment and Thin Capitalization" in Michael Lang et al. (eds), *Common Consolidated Corporate Tax Base* (Linde 2008) 821, 838.

[28] This is due to the conditions for application laid down in Article 81 (1) and to the escape clause of Article 81 (3).

[29] The conception as a special anti-abuse rule can be inferred from the heading of Chapter XIV, of which Article 81 forms an integral part.

[30] Pursuant to Article 80 (1) of the draft CCCTB Directive, "artificial transactions carried out for the sole purpose of avoiding taxation shall be ignored for the purposes of calculating the tax base."

The same applies for both interest and royalty payments, in so far as they would not result in a reduction of the common tax base due to a transfer pricing adjustment as specified in Article 79. Finally, such a situation could also arise under the provision of Article 15, pursuant to which:

> benefits granted to a shareholder who is an individual, his spouse, lineal ascendant or descendant or associated enterprises, holding a direct or indirect participation in the control, capital or management of the taxpayer, as referred to in Article 78, shall not be treated as deductible expenses to the extent that such benefits would not be granted to an independent third party.

Admittedly, the instances of non-deductibility of interest or royalty payments referred to in the above paragraphs would often be identified by the competent tax authorities only years after the payment has been effected, in the course of a tax audit; and they would frequently be subject to dispute or even litigation between authorities and the taxpayer. If the reassessment of those payments were to also have to imply a reallocation of the corresponding withholding tax revenue, as argued above, this could add an element of administrative complexity to the revenue-sharing mechanism under the Commission's CCCTB proposal. It would have to be decided – preferably by way of an implementing regulation within the meaning of Article 291 (2) TFEU (see also Article 131 of the draft directive) – when and how to accomplish the recision of the initial revenue apportionment: upon reassessment or only when the latter becomes final, by way of netting with current revenue-sharing obligations of that Member State or through separate payments, and so on.

It could therefore seemingly be argued that the present Commission proposal's indifference, for the purposes of Article 77, between deductible and non-deductible interest and royalty payments could be justified as a simplification measure, because it avoids the administrative costs associated with subsequent adjustments. However, in the author's view, such a reasoning would ultimately not be convincing, since the same type of administrative problems would arise under the present proposal in the case of a subsequent (full or partial) refund of the original withholding tax to the recipient of the interest or royalty payments, or in the case of a recharacterization of such payments in dividend payments in the wake of an audit examining hybrid financial instruments. Both scenarios can also involve difficult legal assessments and, consequently, lengthy disputes and litigation with the taxpayer, but this has not motivated the Commission to abandon its revenue-sharing proposal under Article 77. It would therefore be inconsistent to defend a different position regarding the implications that a reassessment of the deductibility of interest and royalty payments should have in the context of that provision. Instead, a *de minimis* rule along the lines of Article 114 (7) should be adopted.

Finally, it is worth mentioning that the present concept of Article 77 does not alter the fiscal incentive for the competent tax authorities – in particular, for the principal tax authority as defined in Article 4 (22) – to apply the provisions of Article 15 and Articles 79–81 rigorously. It would always be beneficial for all Member States involved to determine the non-deductibility of interest or royalty payments under any of those anti-abuse provisions, because this would increase the common tax base while not affecting the apportionment of corresponding withholding taxes. By contrast, such a finding could be fiscally detrimental if the withholding tax would then accrue exclusively to the Member State that has levied it, as would be the consequence of what is advocated here: Other Member States, possibly including the Member State of the principal taxpayer within the meaning of Article 4 (6), might end up with a smaller portion of tax revenue if their corporate tax rate is lower than the rate of the withholding tax that has been imposed on the interest or royalty payments. Since the apportionment formula is identical for both, the common consolidated tax base and the withholding tax revenue covered by Article 77, the positive revenue effects of an increase in the tax base would then be over-compensated by the negative effects of no longer sharing the withholding tax revenue. In a similar vein, both effects would neutralize each other if the relevant tax rates are identical.

Should such a scenario materialize in the Member State where the principal taxpayer is resident or established, it is conceivable that the principal tax authority (cf. Articles 4 (22), 122 (1)) would not be inclined to initiate an audit with a view towards reassessing interest and royalty payments. And even if such payments were to be scrutinized in an audit with a view towards Article 15 or Articles 79–81, the principal tax authority might not feel compelled to issue an amended assessment (cf. Article 114) but instead prefer an interpretation that excludes the disputed payment from the scope of the aforementioned anti-avoidance provisions. However, in the author's view, this possibility does not call into question the above criticism of the present conception of Article 77. First, the relevant withholding tax rate would only exceptionally be higher than the corporate tax rate of the Member State where the principal taxpayer is resident or established, or the corporate tax rate of other Member States that are entitled to a portion of the common tax base. Second, the Commission's proposal contains sufficient "checks and balances" to limit the discretion of the principal tax authority vis-à-vis the interest of other

Member States and their competent authorities (see Articles 114 (6), 122 (1), and 123 (1)). After all, similar conflicts could also arise in other situations, for example, regarding the assessment of payments made in the context of hybrid financial instruments.

Besides, the set of problems discussed above is an additional argument for the primary position favoured in this chapter: They could all be avoided if the revenue-sharing of withholding taxes on outbound payments was abandoned altogether, as suggested by the inherent logic underlying formulary apportionment under the CCCTB proposal.

4.3.5.2 Apportionment only of withholding taxes on interest and royalties

It is furthermore respectfully submitted that the situations analysed in the preceding section are not the only ones with respect to which the nexus that has been established by the Commission between the deductibility of payments and the apportionment of the corresponding withholding tax is not sufficiently reflected in Article 77. Whereas its scope is too broad in the case of non-deductible interest and royalty payments, the provision is also formulated too narrowly in another aspect.

This is seen in the fact that there are some jurisdictions within the EU that levy a withholding tax also on other payments that would constitute deductible expenses under the CCCTB rules, such as for example, payments that can be characterized as rental income or income from consultancy services in the hands of their recipient. According to the logic underlying Article 77, those withholding taxes should also be allocated among all Member States that are entitled to a share in the common consolidated tax base. However, the substantive scope of the apportionment obligation laid down in the aforementioned provision is limited to interest and royalty payments. Since it is not apparent that an inclusion of other types of deductible payments subject to a withholding tax would have impaired legal certainty or entailed any other disadvantages, the failure to do so must be characterized as another deficiency of the norm.

One could also wonder whether it is reasonable to restrict the scope of the revenue-sharing obligation of Article 77 to tax revenue that has been raised through the imposition of withholding taxes. In many instances, a withholding tax on interest or royalty income will not be final, especially if the recipient is resident or established in the Member State that collects the withholding tax. Instead, it has the character of a provisional charge that will eventually be credited against the final tax liability as determined in a tax assessment.[31] The final tax liability may then be higher or lower than the amount of withholding tax. In rare instances, a Member State may also refrain altogether from levying a withholding tax but nevertheless impose some tax burden by way of tax assessment.

At first sight, it would seem consistent to apportion this final tax burden, rather than the preliminary withholding tax burden, among all Member States that are entitled to a portion of the common consolidated tax base, if one were to accept the rationale underlying Article 77 (*quod non*) according to which a reduction in the tax base of the CCCTB taxpayer should be compensated by a sharing of the charge levied on the corresponding outbound payments. Since the latter constitutes a tax burden that is legally imposed on and supposedly borne by the recipient of the payment, one could argue that where applicable, it should be the final tax burden relating to those payments, as determined through a tax assessment of the recipient entity, instead of a merely provisional withholding tax that ought to be shared across Member States. The same would have to apply *a fortiori* if no withholding tax was levied prior to a tax assessment. Such a proposition would seemingly also be supported by the provision of Article 1 (1) Interest and Royalties Directive that establishes a ban on source country taxation by expressly referring to "any taxes imposed on [interest and royalty] payments in that State, whether by deduction at source or by assessment …". The provision thus underlines the equivalence of both methods of taxation for the concept of source country taxation of interest and royalty payments.

However, on closer inspection it should be acknowledged that the coverage only of withholding taxes in the specific context of Article 77 can be defended on several grounds: first, interest and royalty payments will usually not be assessed separately in an income tax assessment of their recipient, but as an integral element of the latter's aggregate income. The proportion of the final tax burden that corresponds to those payments might therefore be influenced by other factors such as losses from unrelated activities or lump-sum deductions. Hence, there would no longer be a strict correlation between the tax revenue generated by the

[31] M. Vogel, "Comment on the Proposal for a Council Directive on a Common Consolidated Corporate Tax Base ("CCCTB")" (2011) *Highlights Insights on European Taxation* 53, even seems to argue that only provisional withholding taxes are caught by Article 77, whereas final withholding taxes are forbidden, and explains this position with the concept of a "withholding" tax. However, neither the wording of Article 77 nor the notion of "withholding tax" support this position.

interest and royalty payments and their tax-relieving effect under the CCCTB regime, as required by the inherent logic of Article 77. Second, an extension of the revenue-sharing obligation to final tax burdens would significantly complicate the necessary clearing mechanism. The calculation of the pro-rata tax burden corresponding to the relevant payments is less obvious than the determination of the withholding tax burden, its collection is less certain, and it is furthermore prone to subsequent amendments. Against this background, the situation is also clearly different from a prohibition of source country taxation, as laid down in Article 1 (1) Interest and Royalties Directive, where the problems discussed above do not arise.

4.3.6 Compliance and Administrative Issues

4.3.6.1 Characterization of payments as interest or royalties

The revenue-sharing obligation of Article 77 raises the difficult issue of defining the legal notion of interest and royalties, to be distinguished from payments with a different legal justification, and from dividend payments in particular. In the context of Article 77, both concepts obviously need to be interpreted as autonomous concepts of Union law so as to ensure an unambiguous scope of the entitlement of other Member States to the withholding tax revenue collected by the source State. The theoretical alternative of a recourse to the domestic tax systems of the Member States, or to the tax treaties concluded by them, would entail the danger of qualification conflicts, and the draft directive does not provide for any priority rules to resolve them. Moreover, such a referral to national concepts – in particular, the domestic definitions of the respective source country – or to those of international agreements or models would be inadequate: Only an autonomous Union law interpretation can accomplish a matching demarcation of the concepts of interest and royalties, on the one hand, and profit distributions, on the other hand, for the purposes of both the withholding tax apportionment rules of Article 77 and the rules on the deductibility or non-deductibility of payments under the draft CCCTB Directive. More specifically, the notion of non-deductible "profit distributions" in Article 14 (1) (a) must not overlap with the notions of "interest" and "royalties" in Article 77, considering that the rationale of the latter provision consists in establishing a revenue-sharing obligation only when the respective payments constitute deductible expenses (as interest or royalties) under the CCCTB regime.

In the current proposal of the Commission, the notion of "interest and royalties" is not substantiated any further in Article 77. Admittedly, it seems reasonable to assume that the definition of "interest" in Article 81 (2)[32] for the purposes of the draft directive's thin capitalization regime is also relevant in the context of Article 77;[33] identical expressions within a single legal act should normally also be interpreted congruently, unless this would clearly lead to inadequate results. But it would nevertheless be preferable to include that definition in the list of Article 4 so as to avoid disputes as to whether it is really a general one to be applied throughout the directive. It would also seem advisable to elaborate on the criteria for the characterization of hybrid financial instruments in an implementing directive or regulation. Moreover, for the sake of legal certainty the concept of "royalties", too, should be specified in the draft directive; Article 2 (b) Interest and Royalties Directive could serve as a model in this regard. The attainment of a greater degree of legal certainty through detailed rules of secondary or tertiary Union law is even more important in the light of the obvious reluctance of the European judiciary to adjudicate questions related to tax allocation among Member States, even in harmonized areas of taxation.[34]

It should be noted that the autonomous interpretation of the notion of "interest and royalties" that is advocated in this chapter would only be binding upon Member States for the purposes of the withholding tax apportionment required by Article 77, in other words, at the level of international *tax revenue allocation*. It would not affect the international *allocation of taxing rights* under tax treaty rules, or the domestic system of withholding taxes, since these aspects still fall under the unfettered tax sovereignty of the Member States and would not be harmonized by the CCCTB Directive, as demonstrated above at 4.3.1. The substantive scope of national or DTC provisions concerning the levy of withholding taxes on "interest" or "royalties" would thus still have to be determined by the methods of interpretation that are relevant in the respective legal context, regardless of their understanding within the legal framework of Article 77.

---

32 Pursuant to Article 81 (2), "the term 'interest' means income from debt-claims of every kind, whether or not secured by mortgage and whether or not carrying a right to participate in the debtor's profits, and in particular, income from securities and income from bonds or debentures, including premiums and prizes attaching to such securities, bonds or debentures. Penalty charges for late payment shall not be regarded as interest."

33 Likewise M. Vogel, "Comment on the Proposal for a Council Directive on a Common Consolidated Corporate Tax Base ("CCCTB")" (2011) *Highlights Insights on European Taxation* Year 4, No 6, 53.

34 See, for example, Case C-277/09, *RBS Deutschland Holdings*, n.y.r.

As a consequence, not all the tax revenue collected by way of withholding taxes on "interest" or "royalties" within the meaning of domestic or tax treaty rules would necessarily have to be shared with other Member States where CCCTB group members are resident or established. The apportionment rule of Article 77 would apply only in so far as those concepts of non-harmonized national and international tax law concur with the Union law concepts of Article 77. In a similar vein, withholding taxes on payments that are characterized as "dividend" income or as another kind of income of the receiving company for the purposes of establishing the duty to deduct taxes at source under domestic law, or under the allocation rules of a tax treaty, must nevertheless be shared with other Member States if the payments qualify as "interest or royalties" within the meaning of Article 77.

Under the current conception of the draft directive, eventual disputes among Member States regarding the interpretation of the notion of "interest and royalties" under Article 77, which can be expected to arise, in particular, in the aforementioned cases of definitional mismatches, would have to be decided by the ECJ: the issue would have to be brought before the Court by way of an action for an alleged infringement of an obligation under the EU Treaties, as regulated in Article 259 TFEU, if the source State refuses to share its withholding tax revenue based on a disputed characterization of the underlying payments. This could strain the resources of the ECJ through manifold proceedings, while leaving Member States in a limbo for many years in cases with significant budgetary implications. It is therefore suggested that the draft directive should be amended to provide for a mandatory dispute settlement mechanism in the context of Article 77; an action before the ECJ should only be admitted where no agreement can be brokered.

4.3.6.2 Clearing mechanism

Unlike the original concept of formulary apportionment enshrined in Articles 86 to 102, Article 77 is not concerned with the apportionment of the (common consolidated) tax base, but rather with the apportionment of tax revenue. This requires an international revenue-clearing mechanism, which is not as yet provided for by the draft CCCTB Directive, though. This legislative gap still needs to be closed.

An issue that could add significant administrative complexity to the clearing procedure and that should be addressed in this context is the eventual need for subsequent adjustments when the recipient company is entitled to a withholding tax refund.[35] It is suggested here that a refund should have an impact on the amount of withholding tax revenue that is subject to apportionment under Article 77 only to the extent that it can be claimed because the deduction of tax at source was carried out contrary to the domestic or tax treaty rules on withholding taxes. By contrast, a refund that is based on the preliminary character of a withholding tax, and that is claimed after the final tax assessment, should not be taken into account, in line with the confinement of the revenue sharing obligation of Article 77 to tax revenue that originates from a deduction at source (see above at section 4.3.5.2).

[35] See also Malcolm Gammie and Christiana HJI Panayi, "Inbound Investment and Thin Capitalization" in Michael Lang et al. (eds), *Common Consolidated Corporate Tax Base* (Linde 2008) 821, 834.

Commentary

Dennis Weber and Jan van de Streek

INTRODUCTION

Withholding tax issues are rather fragmentarily dealt with in the proposed CCCTB Directive. The issues are made more difficult by the consolidation element of the CCCTB Directive and relationship with tax treaties between Member States and third countries, which is not provided for in the directive. It is therefore understandable that the chapter Joachim Englisch prepared is limited to some selections.[36] His chapter mainly focuses on the prohibition on charging withholding tax on intra-group transactions (Article 60 of the draft CCCTB Directive) as well as on the so-called shared revenue of the withholding tax imposed by the Member States on certain outbound payments (Article 77 of the draft CCCTB Directive). He takes a critical look at both the technical side of these provisions and at the policy choices underlying these provisions.

Given the available space, it is not possible to respond to each part of Englisch's comprehensive chapter. A selection had therefore to be made. Because the authors of this commentary assume that the technical imperfections identified by Englisch will have been removed in the final directive, the opportunity is used to react to two of Englisch's striking opinions of a European political nature. His first opinion is that the harmonization process is rightly limited to corporate tax and does not also cover withholding taxes imposed by Member States. His second opinion elaborates on this, and comes down to the fact, given the sovereignty the Member States have to levy a withholding tax, in any case, Member States should not be obliged to share withholding tax revenue.

These two statements shall be discussed in the following, given the expected race to the bottom under the CCCTB Directive in respect of withholding taxes levied by Member States and third countries, and the

[36] Joachim Englisch, this chapter.

desirable tax treaty politics between Europe and third countries following the entry into force of the CCCTB Directive.

INBOUND AND OUTBOUND CAPITAL FLOWS OF A SINGLE COMPANY

Inbound Payments

First, a look is taken at the position of a single company that has opted for the CCCTB system. Even without the consolidation element, numerous complex questions arise. Where a single company receives dividends, interest and royalties from a third country (inbound payments), the question arises whether these payments must be included in its taxable profit. The answer is affirmative in principle because the common tax base is not territorially limited. Under the CCCTB so-called "world-income" is taxed. This is expressly stated in Article 6(6) CCCTB. Under this provision, a company resident in a Member State which opts for the system is subject to corporate tax under that system on all income derived from any source, whether inside or outside its Member State of residence.

Unlike interest or royalties received from a third-country resident, dividends received from third-country residents are in principle exempt. The CCCTB proposal provides for a very generous participation exemption (see Article 11(c) CCCTB).[37] For instance there is no minimum participation requirement or minimum holding period. Since dividends received are exempted, the CCCTB does not provide for a credit for any withholding tax imposed by a third country on those dividends. Credit relief is, however, available for withholding tax levied on interest and royalties by a third country. This credit is laid down in Article 76 CCCTB and applies regardless of any tax treaty concluded by Member States. The relationship between the credit of Article 76 CCCTB and tax treaties is discussed below.

An *ordinary credit* is unilaterally granted under the CCCTB system for non-EU sourced interest and royalties to avoid double taxation. The credit is limited to the usual two limits. The first limit is the withholding tax actually charged by a third country. The second limit is the corporate tax attributable to the interest or royalty payments received by the single

[37] An exception to this is the "switch over" clause of Article 73 CCCTB, which is not discussed here.

company. The last limit allows for a fixed deduction of expenses related to interest or royalty income and the collection of such income (net credit). Such expenses are deemed to be 2 per cent of the income, unless the taxpayer demonstrates that the expenses are lower. The authors of this commentary think that the fixed deduction of 2 per cent is rather generous for taxpayers, especially in a situation in which the asset generating passive income (such as a debt-claim or intellectual property) is financed by a loan.[38] Finance charges quite often exceed 2 per cent.

The credit must be calculated for each type of income (interest/royalties) and per country. Any unrelieved withholding taxes cannot be carried forward to future years.[39] Finally a no-refund provision is included in the CCCTB Directive. A credit for withholding tax charged by a third state can never exceed the corporate tax payable by a single company (no-refund provision).[40]

Outbound Payments

Payments made by a single company to recipients situated in third countries (outbound payments) may be subject to withholding tax imposed by the Member State of which the single company is a resident. It is important to note that Member States keep their sovereignty to levy a withholding tax. Any withholding tax imposed by a Member State on interest, royalty or dividend payments made by a single company is therefore outside the scope of the CCCTB system. The levy of withholding tax must of course be in accordance with the applicable tax treaty and must for that matter also be in line with the freedoms laid down in the Treaty on the Functioning of the European Union.

Relationship with Tax Treaties with Third Countries

Now that the CCCTB system provides for a credit for any withholding tax charged on interest and royalties (Article 76 CCCTB) by third

---

[38] See also Jacques Malherbe and Daniel Garabedian, "Common Consolidated Corporate Tax Base (CCCTB) International issues credit method for portfolio dividends, interest and royalties" in Michael Lang et al. (eds), *Common consolidated corporate tax base* (Linde 2008) 705.

[39] A carry forward for outstanding credits is missing: see *Transactions and dealings between the group and entities outside the group* (Room Document of 1 September 2010), para. 12.

[40] Remarkably, this does not apply to withholding tax charged by Member States to the CCCTB company.

countries, the question arises as to how this credit relates to a tax treaty concluded between a Member State and a third country. Article 76(5) CCCTB only states that the no-refund provision does not apply if a tax treaty between the Member State of which the single company is a resident and a third country provides otherwise. Nothing is said about any other deviations between the credit of Article 76 CCCTB and relief under tax treaties. For example, what is right if a tax treaty between a Member State and a third country provides for a *full credit* or *tax sparing* credit?

The European Commission addressed the relationship between tax treaties with third countries and the CCCTB Directive in the working documents. The following is noted in these documents:

> In conformity with the principle of supremacy of EU law, the common rules will generally take precedence over rights and obligations arising from (bilateral or multilateral) agreements between Member States. A different treatment is envisaged for agreements between Member States and third countries concluded before the Directive enter into force. To the extent that they may incorporate right and obligations which are not in line with the Directive, those agreements will not be effected.[41]

What this comes down to is that any tax treaties with third countries that were concluded before the CCCTB Directive enters into force remain applicable.[42] The order of priority between the CCCTB Directive and tax treaties concluded between Member States and third countries as indicated by the European Commission corresponds with the priority between the treaties and international agreements between Member States and third countries provided for by Article 351 TFEU. In practice, this means that tax treaties concluded with third countries which pre-date the CCCTB will apply in any case if such a tax treaty provides for a more generous relief than an ordinary credit.[43]

It is pointed out that it seems as if the CCCTB rules may be "overruled" by a tax treaty with a third country temporarily only, as the Member States must take all steps necessary to resolve conflicts.[44] The question is, for that matter, whether the Union has exclusive competence

---

[41] *Transactions and dealings between the group and entities outside the group* (Room Document of 1 September 2010), para. 3.

[42] For existing treaties the *pacta sunt servanda* principle of international law is therefore observed.

[43] Cf. *Transactions and dealings between the group and entities outside the group* (Room Document of 1 September 2010), para 12.

[44] By analogy with Article 351 TFEU.

to conclude new tax treaties with third countries following the entry into force of the CCCTB Directive.[45] Are individual Member States disqualified? The question seems to be answered affirmatively in respect of relief for any withholding tax imposed on CCCTB companies as it is clear that tax treaties affect the CCCTB double tax credit or alter its scope.[46] This effect is sufficient to transfer competence to the Union.

DIVIDENDS, INTEREST AND ROYALTIES RECEIVED FROM THIRD COUNTRIES BY A CONSOLIDATED GROUP (INBOUND PAYMENTS)

Shared Credit in respect of Withholding Tax on Interest and Royalties

Where a consolidated group receives interest or royalties from a third country, the CCCTB Directive provided for a "shared credit" (Article 76(2) CCCTB). The credit for any withholding tax charged by a third country is, just as the interest and royalties, apportioned on the basis of the sharing mechanism. The shared credit on the basis of a simple example is going to be illustrated.[47] In this example, tax treaties are ignored for now.

Example:

Companies MS 1 and MS 2 opt for the CCCTB and form a consolidated group. The companies are situated in Member State 1 and 2, respectively. Company MS 2 receives a royalty of 100 from a third country from which 15 per cent tax is withheld at source by this third country. Based on the apportionment formula, the consolidated tax base is divided 50-50 between company MS 1 and company MS 2. The tax rate in Member State 1 is 10 per cent and 20 per cent in Member State 2. What credit must be provided for by each Member State?

Member State 1 must give a credit of 5, as the first limit is 7.5 (15 × 50 per cent share) and the second limit is 5 (100 × 50 per cent share × 10 per cent tax rate).

Member State 2 must give a credit of 7.5, as the first limit is 7.5 (15 × 50 per cent share) and the second limit is 10 (100 × 50 per cent share × 20 per cent tax rate). In this example, no relief is available for an amount of 2.5 of the withholding tax paid.[48]

---

45 See O.C.R. Marres, *CCCTB and tax treaties* (forthcoming) para 2.
46 See Article 3(2) TFEU.
47 The expenses to be allocated to the portfolio income are ignored.
48 As mentioned above, there is no carry forward of credits.

The question arises as to how the shared credit of Article 76(2) CCCTB relates to tax treaties Member States have concluded with third countries. Assume in the above example that Member State 2 has concluded a tax treaty with a third country on the basis of which a third country must reduce its withholding tax to zero.[49] How will this third country respond? It can be imagined that the third country will be reluctant to reduce the withholding tax on the royalty payment to zero because of the so-called "piggyback" effect.[50] Through consolidation and apportioning, half of the royalty is taxed in Member State 1 with which Member State the third country has not concluded a tax treaty. There is therefore a possibility that the introduction of the CCCTB Directive will be a reason for third countries to limit treaty benefits.[51]

A challenging issue arises if Member State 2 in the above example grants a tax sparing credit of 15 per cent under the treaty with the third country (existing at the time of entry into force of the CCCTB Directive). Although the third country does not withhold any tax at source in this scenario, Member State 2 still grants a credit of 7.5. What will Member State 1 do? It is suspected that, although obligations under existing tax treaties continue to apply, this does not go so far that Member State 1 must also provide for a tax sparing credit.

Treaty Shopping Invitation

Now that the CCCTB system invites consolidated groups to treaty shop more extensively, one wonders what the international political attitude of third countries is going to be. Already treaty shopping is an existing problem[52] and will increase under the CCCTB. A consolidated group will try to channel dividends, interest and royalties from third countries to the

---

[49] Notwithstanding consolidation and apportionment, it is assumed that company MS 2 qualifies as a treaty resident (Article 4 OECD Model Convention) and can moreover be deemed to be the beneficial owner of such royalties (Article 12(3) OECD Model Convention).

[50] See also Maikel Evers, "De CCCTB en haar grenzen, Enkele internationale aspecten van een communautaire belastinggrondslag" ("The CCCTB and its limits; Some international aspects of a common tax base") (2008), Maandblad Belastingbeschouwingen, pp. 427–437.

[51] O.C.R. Marres also arrives at that conclusion in *CCCTB and tax treaties* (forthcoming) section 4.

[52] See for a recent overview of the issues Luc de Broe, Nathalie Goyette, Philippe Martin, Roy Rohatgi, Stef van Weeghel and Phil West, "Tax treaties and tax avoidance: application of anti-avoidance provisions" (July 2011), *Bulletin for International Taxation* 375–389.

group via the most favourable tax treaty with a third country. A consolidated group naturally always seeks to minimize the withholding tax burden on interest, royalties and even more so on dividends. As has been shown, withholding taxes on interest and royalties cannot always be fully credited (*shared ordinary credit*). As far as dividends are concerned, the CCCTB Directive does not even provide for a credit for withholding taxes.

To minimize the withholding tax burden, the income-generating asset (for example a shareholding, debt-claim or intellectual property right) must be held by the group member situated in the Member State that has concluded the most favourable tax treaty with the third country. If this is not (already) the case, the debt-claim or intellectual property right may be transferred to such group member via a tax-free intra-group transaction (Article 59 CCCTB).[53] The transfer of a shareholding is automatically tax free due to the participation exemption (see Article 11(d) CCCTB). A tax-free cross-border reallocation of assets within a group of companies to minimize withholding taxes is usually not possible under the Member States' current tax systems. Often there are (huge) hidden reserves in royalty-generating assets that become subject to tax if these assets are transferred within a group. As a result, these assets are often locked-in in a Member State. Moreover, it is currently not always possible to reshuffle shareholdings free of tax within a group due to a limited participation exemption.

Following a tax-free reallocation of an income-generating asset within a group, the income received can in its turn be rechanneled within the group also free of tax. Such rechanneling is not subject to corporate tax (Article 59 CCCTB) or withholding tax (Article 60 CCCTB).[54] Such exempted re-channelling is often not possible under the current tax systems of the Member States. In the case of a back-to-back construction quite often a "spread" must be reported as taxable income and, despite the Parent-Subsidiary Directive and the Interest and Royalties Directive, withholding taxes may be imposed.

Tax planning opportunities with the objective of circumventing withholding taxes levied by third countries do not seem to have significant

[53] Alternatively, the place of effective management could be transferred to a Member State that has concluded the most favourable tax treaty with a third country. A transfer of the place of effective management within a consolidated group is not a taxable event.

[54] Even in the case of a back-to-back construction no spread has to be reported as taxable income under the CCCTB system.

consequences for the corporate tax liability of the group. The apportionment formula of Article 86 CCCTB is more or less unaffected. The reallocation of shareholdings, debt-claims and intellectual property rights has no effect on the asset factor as it includes fixed tangible assets only (Article 86(1) CCCTB).[55] Dividends, interest and royalties are furthermore not included in the asset factor (Article 95(2) CCCTB). The allocation or reallocation of a shareholding, debt-claim or intellectual property right will have a negligible effect on the labour factor.[56]

DIVIDENDS, INTEREST AND ROYALTIES PAID BY A CONSOLIDATED GROUP TO RECIPIENTS IN THIRD COUNTRIES (OUTBOUND PAYMENTS)

Shared Revenue of Withholding Tax on Interest and Royalties

As mentioned above, the CCCTB proposal does not entail harmonization of withholding tax levied by the Member States. The CCCTB proposal does contain what the commentators call an "anti-frustration provision" for the situation in which a consolidated group pays interest and/or royalties to recipients outside of the group. The term "anti-frustration provision" is explained below. This provision applies in principle to any interest or royalty payment to a recipient outside of the group, but due to the nature of the topic, the focus shall be on payments to recipients in third countries.

The provision that is referred to is Article 77 of the CCCTB Directive. Based on this provision, withholding tax levied by a Member State on an interest or royalty payment to a recipient outside of the consolidated group must be shared with the group's other Member States. The withholding tax is divided according to the formula applicable in the tax year in which the withholding tax is charged pursuant to Articles 86 to 102 of the CCCTB Directive. This gives rise to the question as to what is the ratio of this provision. Para. 18 of the preamble to the CCCTB Directive states the following:

> When withholding taxes are charged on interest and royalty payments made by taxpayers, the proceeds of such taxes should be shared according to the

[55] In addition, the anti-abuse provision guarding against "base shifting" cannot be applied (Article 70 CCCTB), as the asset factor is not substantially changed.

[56] Managing these assets usually is not very labour intensive.

formula of that tax year. When withholding taxes are charged on dividends distributed by taxpayers, the proceeds of such taxes should not be shared since, contrary to interest and royalties, dividends have not led to a previous deduction borne by all group companies.

This explanation shows the anti-frustration nature of the provision. The provision intends to take away any uneasy feelings caused by a deduction of interest and royalty payments from the consolidated profit. This tax deduction is borne by the entire group's Member States in accordance with their share in the consolidated profit. To compensate this tax deduction, the European Commission is of the opinion that it is reasonable to divide the withholding tax levied by a Member State on this outbound interest or royalty. Unlike Englisch, the commentators believe that Article 77 of the draft CCCTB Directive is appropriate.[57] It is a policy choice that seems to be justified on grounds of reasonableness.[58] The fact that withholding taxes are not harmonized under the proposed CCCTB Directive does not affect Member States' decision to share withholding tax revenue. That the withholding tax to be divided does not relate to group income, and is therefore also not charged at the expense of the group (but at the expense of the recipient in a third country)[59] is irrelevant for the justification of this policy choice in our view. Such policy choices are made more often in international or domestic tax law. See, for example, Article 15 of the OECD Model Convention relating to the allocation of income from employment. Based on this provision, taxation at source of income from short-term employment is avoided to the extent that the employment income is not allowed as a deductible expense in the source state.[60]

To ensure that shared withholding tax revenue does not affect a Member State's sovereign right to levy withholding taxes, the first sentence of Article 77 of the CCCTB provides that interest and royalties paid by a taxpayer to a recipient outside of the group may be subject to

[57] Joachim Englisch, this chapter, section 4.3.4.

[58] Also Jacques Malherbe and Daniel Garabedian, "Common Consolidated Corporate Tax Base (CCCTB) International issues credit method for portfolio dividends, interest and royalties" in Michael Lang et al. (eds), *Common consolidated corporate tax base* (Linde 2008) 705; Philip Baker and Iloanna Mitroyanni, "The CCCTB rules and tax treaties" in Michael Lang et al. (eds), *Common consolidated corporate tax base* (Linde 2008) 627 et seq seem to share this opinion.

[59] Only the interest or royalty-paying group member is required to withhold tax.

[60] See Article 15(2a) and (2b) of the OECD Model Convention.

a withholding tax in the Member State of the taxpayer according national law and any applicable double tax treaty. It seems that the reference to double tax treaties specifically seeks to ensure that Article 3(2) TFEU is not applicable. Based on this provision, the Union has exclusive competence to conclude international agreements in so far as its conclusion may affect common rules or alter their scope. Despite the fact that the withholding tax on outbound interest and royalties is shared, the Member States do have the right to individually conclude tax treaties with third countries relating to withholding tax. Unlike Englisch, the commentators find Article 77, first sentence, CCCTB a welcome clarification that the shared revenue does not affect a Member State's competence.[61] It would therefore be preferable that Article 77, first sentence, CCCTB is not deleted in the final directive.

Rat Race to the Bottom

The question arises as to whether following the entry into force of the CCCTB Directive there will be some withholding tax income left to be shared between the Member States. Like Englisch, a rat race to the bottom in respect of withholding tax on outbound interest and royalties charged by the Member States is feared.[62] The same applies, in our opinion, to withholding tax charged by the Member States on outbound dividends (which for that matter do not have to be shared with other Member States). What would drive such a rat race?

Firstly, the mandatory sharing with other Member States of any withholding tax imposed on outbound interest and royalties is not exactly an incentive to preserve the levy of withholding tax.[63] The CCCTB proposal fails to provide details on any clearing system for the allocation of withholding tax. In the commentators' view, a Member State should in any case be allowed to cover its administrative costs for charging and collecting withholding tax by means of a "first share". Only if there is a surplus should the shared revenue of Article 77 of the CCCTB come into play.

Secondly, it seems obvious that taxpayers will seek to minimize the European withholding tax burden on outbound dividends, interest and royalties. In order to achieve this, passive income must leave the consolidated group via the Member State with the lowest withholding tax

---

[61] Joachim Englisch, this chapter, section 4.3.1.

[62] Joachim Englisch, this chapter, section 4.3.4.

[63] See also S.R. Pancham, "CCCTB en bronbelastingen" ("CCCTB and withholding taxes") (2011), *Weekblad voor Fiscaal Recht*, para. 3.2.3.

burden. A low withholding tax burden in a Member State can be the result of its national law (for example, no withholding tax), or of any tax treaties this Member State has concluded with third countries (reduction of the withholding tax rate, even to nil). This form of tax planning is an existing problem under the Parent-Subsidiary Directive and the Interest and Royalties Directive that is expected to increase under the CCCTB Directive. Dividends, interest and royalties can flow untaxed towards a recipient in a third country as a result of the elimination of results on intra-group transactions (Article 59 CCCTB) and the ban on withholding tax on such transactions (Article 60 CCCTB). This should be clarified by giving a simple example.[64]

Example:

Assume that a consolidated group plans to borrow money from a group financing company established in a third country. Group company 1, located in MS 1, needs the money. If group company 1 were to borrow the money directly from the group financing company, MS 1 deducts 10 per cent withholding tax from the interest paid to the group financing company. There is no tax treaty between MS 1 and a third country. MS 2 has concluded a tax treaty, however, with the third country in which the group financing company is established on the basis of which the MS 2 is not allowed to charge withholding tax on interest. It is therefore attractive for the group to borrow money from the group financing company via the group company situated in MS 2. Group company 2, borrowing from the finance company based in a non-EU country, can subsequently lend the money intra-group to group company 1 tax free.

If the group in this example does not have a company in Member State 2, the group can establish a conduit company specifically for this objective. This example illustrates that the consolidation element, in conjunction with the ban on the imposition of withholding tax on intra-group transactions, is an open invitation to use the most favourable convention. Unlike the treaty shopping described above, this form of treaty shopping adversely affects the treasuries of the Member States. For the groups themselves, treaty shopping with the objective of minimizing the European withholding tax burden, has hardly any consequences for their corporate income tax burden. As it is, the apportionment formula factors are not substantially affected (see also above).

[64] See for another example in respect of outbound dividends the article of Eric Kemmeren and Daniël Smit, Chapter 2 in this book, section 2.3.1.2.2.

CONCLUSIONS

The CCCTB project addresses the European corporate tax base harmonization. Withholding tax issues are, however, closely related to this. This applies both to withholding taxes on inbound and outbound payments. The withholding tax issues put the relations with third countries on edge. As a consequence of the consolidation element of the CCCTB Directive, consolidated groups can minimize withholding taxes on inbound payments imposed by third countries as well as withholding taxes on outbound payments levied by European Member States. It seems likely that a double rat race to the bottom will break out, with budgetary consequences for the Member States and third countries.

In the commentators' view, the harmonization of withholding tax levied by the Member States on outbound payments made by groups is worth considering. Perhaps even a minimum rate can be agreed. Such a harmonized European withholding tax system in Europe fits together harmoniously with Europe's possible exclusive competence to conclude tax treaties with third countries in respect of withholding tax levied by third countries following the entry into force of the CCCTB Directive. A harmonized withholding tax system would then constitute a comfortable negotiation base to reduce the withholding taxes levied by third countries or even bring it down to zero.

5. CCCTB and fiscally transparent entities: A third countries' perspective

Yariv Brauner

5.1 INTRODUCTION

The CCCTB project is moving away from an unstable situation: being on the cusp between tax competition and cooperation and coordination of tax policies, the frontline in the battle between proponents of tax competition and of harmonization. Therefore, despite being a purely European creature, the CCCTB carries with it an importance far beyond Europe and European tax policy. At its core, it takes a position in support of political transparency, fairness and humility, representing a daring and novel tax policy initiative that focuses on the people, the constituency. Of course, peripherally, it also has political implications, primarily within Europe.

The general goal of CCCTB is to ameliorate, if not eliminate, undesirable tax competition and waste that are based on differences in tax rules rather than directly in tax rates. These differences often result in over or under-taxation due to, for instance, qualification conflicts that are difficult to solve and often are not – even when modern tax treaties apply. Unfortunately, these differences are also mostly not a consequence of intellectual or ideological differences between tax systems. Rather, it is more often that history, arbitrariness and incongruous political circumstances led to their existence.

Yet, more specifically, the CCCTB "aims to tackle some major fiscal impediments to growth in the Single Market,"[1] such as over and under-taxation (often referred to as "double taxation" or "double non-taxation"), and the costs of compliance and administration of taxes in

[1] Proposal for a Council Directive on a Common Consolidated Corporate Tax Base (CCCTB) COM(2011) 121/4.

Europe. Here again, the tension between competition and harmonization is apparent. On the one hand, this is a proposal for a "common" tax base, yet on the other hand it is careful to assert that "The common approach proposed would ensure consistency in the national tax systems but would not harmonize tax rates."[2]

The treatment of transparent entities under the current proposal serves as a typical illustration of these tensions. The proposal takes a stand and provides a general rule, and one that does not simply replicate a universal norm. Yet at the same time the proposal ignores, or refrains from falling into the trap of difficult cases (the proper articulation depends on one's point of view), to which it could not provide an acceptable rule. The general rule is, on the one hand, a balanced rule, supporting European unity and at the same time pro-European residence states, yet on the other hand it is minimal in scope and conservative, careful in its assertion of harmonization power.

It seems that the Commission was particularly cautious in this area, where, although some common norms have developed in some international fora (as discussed below in this chapter), there is an apparent and significant difference in the interests of different countries and an inherent lack of an acceptable theoretical underpinning. This is particularly due to the artificiality of the separate corporate personality legal fiction. It obviously still frustrates many countries that face the challenge of the surge of use of business and investment done by and through multiple arrangements that are not simply incorporated, some of which represent packages of contractual obligations that do not have parallels within their jurisdiction.

All these tensions multiply in the context of our discussion today. Third countries are naturally important for the EU, involving almost half of European-related business and investment.[3] Such third countries naturally struggle with the same classification problem that European countries face regarding transparent entities, and some of them partner with the EU or some European countries in other important fora for international tax policymaking, such as the OECD. Thus, norms must promote not only European interests that are complex enough to figure out themselves due to the diversity and competition within the Union, but also accommodate very significant and equally complex relationships between the Union (and single European countries) and third countries.

---

2 Ibid.

3 Eurostat website2010, http://epp.eurostat.ec.europa.eu/cache/ITY_OFFPUB/KS-SF-12-003/EN/KS-SF-12-003-EN.PDF, accessed 10 January 2012.

European developments are similarly significant to the third countries themselves, since they are either major trade partners of the EU, or are indirectly affected by the power of the EU over international norms.

Written by a third country scholar, this chapter focuses on the technical challenges of the subject of this chapter that are posed to all involved. The chapter begins with an exposition of the issues; it continues with a discussion of the efforts of the United States to deal with the challenge of transparent and hybrid entities, followed by the OECD discourse, and some examples from other countries. In conclusion, the actual proposal is analysed against the background of prior treatment by others. Finally, this chapter takes a critical position, yet it does so with much interest in and support of the CCCTB project and its contribution to international tax discourse and the international tax regime.

5.2 THE PROPOSED DIRECTIVE

5.2.1 In General

The proposed directive includes an elective harmonized consolidated corporate tax regime. The regime is based on corporate consolidation and apportionment of a (single) consolidated tax base between jurisdictions[4] based on a formula that comprises three equally weighted factors: labour (payroll and number of employees, each item counting for half), assets and sales. Administratively, each group is able to deal with only one tax authority – that of its parent's state of residence.

Consolidation is allowed for companies and PEs, based on participation (over 75 per cent of equity or rights to profits) and control (more than 50 per cent of voting rights).[5] In addition, the proposal acknowledges a concept of associated enterprises (generally based on a 20 per cent participation threshold) outside the consolidated group that is brought into the regime in cases "Where conditions are made or imposed in relations between associated enterprises which differ from those that would be made between independent enterprises."[6] Interestingly, this

---

[4] Technically the apportionment is oddly enough done among the consolidating (incorporated) entities and their eligible PEs, and not among the tax jurisdictions involved.

[5] Proposal for a Council Directive on a Common Consolidated Corporate Tax Base (CCCTB) COM(2011) 121/4, supra note 1, 13. There is also a nine-month minimum requirement for group membership.

[6] Ibid.

anti-abuse rule brings into the regime normal transfer pricing, and presumably arm's length analysis through the back door.[7]

The sensitivity of the project dictated understandable conservatism. One of the most conservative aspects of the proposal is the extreme adherence to the legal fiction of separate corporate personality. In fact, the proposal goes even beyond the mere adherence to the fiction, a vice common to essentially all tax systems – it simply confines itself in a very anachronistic world where only corporations, PEs and individuals exist as acceptable "players."[8] Indeed, thinking carefully about the treatment of other players, such as transparent and hybrid entities, makes life much more difficult. No country, let alone multi-country arrangements, has done a very good job dealing with this challenge. This chapter attempts to answer the question of whether this reduced scope is appropriate or desirable.

The chapter takes a perspective that is at first wider than the mere European perspective: first, because this book focuses on the third countries' perspective on the CCCTB within the European project; second, because much more work has been done in the context of tax treaties on the treatment of transparent entities than in Europe alone, while at the same time there is much synergy between developments in tax treaties and in European taxation; finally, because it seems to be the case that the OECD's approach has significantly influenced the CCCTB. The chapter makes some separate comments on this influence in the last part.

5.2.2 Transparent Entities

The proposed directive includes chapter XV that is devoted to transparent entities. Article 84 of the proposal reads:

> Article 84: Rules for allocating the income of transparent entities to taxpayers holding an interest
>
> 1. Where an entity is treated as transparent in the Member State of its location, a taxpayer holding an interest in the entity shall include its share in the income of the entity in its tax base. For the purpose of this calculation, the income shall be computed under the rules of this Directive.
> 2. Transactions between a taxpayer and the entity shall be disregarded in proportion to the taxpayer's share of the entity. Accordingly, the income of the taxpayer derived from such transactions shall be considered to be a proportion

---

[7] Ibid., Arts. 78–79.
[8] Ibid., Arts. 54–55.

> of the amount which would be agreed between independent enterprises calculated on an arm's length basis which corresponds to the third party ownership of the entity.
> 3. The taxpayer shall be entitled to relief for double taxation in accordance with Article 76(1),(2),(3) and (5).

This very minimal reference to transparent entities leaves many questions unanswered. It presents a seemingly simple position: the law of the state in which the transparent entity is located prevails for the purposes of characterizing such an entity. As a derivative of a transparency determination, rights' holders in such entities are treated transparently as well, in other words, as if they earned the income directly. The provision also clarifies their eligibility to double tax relief with respect to such income.

This seemingly straightforward approach represents a departure from the dominant, if not consensus, approach that looks to the state of residence of the taxpayers (the rights' holders) rather than the state of the transparent entity.[9] Moreover, the discourse to date involved the choice between the state of the source of income and the state of residence of the taxpayers.[10] The choice of the proposal is therefore unique. An obvious query may be raised with respect to circumstances where the transparent entities are located in third countries, in other words, outside the EU. The proposal explicitly refers to these circumstances in Article 85, which reads:

> Article 85: Rules for determining transparency in the case of third country entities
>
> Where an entity is located in a third country, the question whether or not it is transparent shall be determined according to the law of the Member State of the taxpayer. If at least two group members hold an interest in the same entity located in a third country, the treatment of the latter shall be determined by common agreement among the relevant Member States. If there is no agreement, the principal tax authority shall decide.

In the case of a transparent entity located in a third country the rule therefore reverts to the more or less universally accepted rule mentioned above.

What is the difference? Why diverge from the international norm in cases of transparent entities located in Member States? Beyond the incoherence it creates odd incentives, since a decision that a transparent

---

[9] OECD, The Application of the OECD Model Tax Convention to Partnerships (OECD, Issues in International Taxation), No. 6, 1999.

[10] Ibid.

entity is located inside or outside the EU also means that the laws of different Member States prevail, potentially leading to intra-EU competition that seems *prima facie* undesirable. I suppose that the purpose of Article 85 is to prevent a case where the rules of a third country would control the classification of an entity. Yet, beyond perhaps a fear that non-EU law may change with no EU control, the logic of this is unclear. Moreover, the fear of legal manipulation "at the expense" of the EU seems very remote, and it is misguided since the primary effect of this choice of law is intended to be on the division of the tax base among European countries and not between Member States and third countries, leaving essentially nothing for a third country to gain even if it wished and was able to manipulate its own laws for this purpose. The cost of the legal duality, however, may be significant since it creates incentives to restructure and potentially EU internal competition over jurisdiction.

In both situations, technically, one must first identify where the (suspected) transparent entity is located, although the proposal does not provide guidance how to do that. Location of entities is, as already mentioned, an unusual indicator in international taxation. Is it the place of incorporation? The place of effective management? Location of the productive assets? It is very possible that there may be multiple locations for unincorporated entities. The proposal includes a tie-breaking rule for corporate residence in Article 6(4) that follows the OECD norm of place of effective management, yet it does not refer to location, only to residence, and hence cannot be used for our purposes.

A question was raised about a case where the state of residence treats an entity as transparent, and therefore requires inclusion of income, and relieves double taxation, yet the state of the entity's location or other involved jurisdictions do not treat it as transparent. Article 84 does not mention such cases, but only cases where the state of location treats an entity as transparent.

Further questions arise about the calculation of income items under the rules of the proposal. Article 84 requires income inclusion according to the directive. Yet it is possible that the income is fully or partly calculated not under the directive. The transparent entity, if indeed treated as transparent, is not eligible for consolidation as such.

The next chapter (XVI) of the proposal, discussing the operative rules for (the formulary) apportionment of the CCCTB, includes only this reference to transparent entities, in Article 89, which reads:

Article 89: Transparent entities

Where a taxpayer holds an interest in a transparent entity, the factors used in calculating its apportioned share shall include the sales, payroll and assets of the transparent entity, in proportion to the taxpayer's participation in its profits and losses.

The key issue of double tax relief is also referred to very generally, providing for it in Article 84(3) with no elaboration. Immediate questions are whether relief is required only with regard to taxation by the state of location or also for the taxation of the transparent entity's income anywhere else.

Further, the reference is to Article 76, skipping Article 76(4), in other words, expenses are not allowed when calculating the FTC limitation. This must mean that the proposal refers only to withholding taxes, but this is not explicitly mentioned.

This question is particularly challenging in the case of a transparent entity located in a third country. Such a country has no comity with the EU, and this provision may create incentives that are difficult for Union Member States to stomach.

Additionally, the process set out in Article 85 seems lengthy and burdensome, not in line with the spirit of the proposal in general. Nonetheless, this discomfort reminds one of the wisdom of not adopting the international norm generally.

Another challenge is the switch-over clause of Article 73, which generally requires a switch-over from an exemption to a tax credit in certain cases – generally of low taxation of the relevant income.

The problem is that if such entities are treated as not transparent by the state of residence and as transparent in the state of location they are not taxed and hence automatically loses the exemption regardless of the actual effective tax rate suffered by the taxpayers. They get a limited FTC, but that may not be sufficient and, of course, is different from exemption.

5.2.3 The Challenge

After reading this proposal one can begin to think about the issues at stake. The first and most direct set of issues raised by transparent or hybrid entities relates to their classification. Taken most simplistically, an entity may be transparent or not, which in a world where only corporations and individual taxpayers exist, means that they are either treated similarly to corporations, in other words, taxed separately by a separate corporate tax regime, or are not considered a taxpayer, but rather as conduits through which investments of individuals and other corporations are conducted. Even this simple picture presents serious challenges to tax law, since, even in the most basic of cross-border scenarios, with one country of residence (of the partners in a partnership, for example) and one country of source, in which the transparent entity (partnership) is legally organized, actually located, and its income arises. This is because the countries of source and residence may not agree on the classification of this entity. Yet, even if they agree on the classification, they may have different rules for allocating the tax items of the partnership, different source rules, and so on. Who should then decide: the country that ultimately taxes the investors, is likely to have the most complete and comprehensive information and which ensures the elimination of double taxation – the residence country – or the country of source that actually allowed the entity to exist: it is organized under its laws, and in this example is also the country where the income was generated and that has the natural first bite at the income. A more realistic picture will, of course, include at least one more jurisdiction, if the country of the partnership and the country of source would be separated. This would lead to a triple dilemma. A triple dilemma is more complex not only because of the multiplicity of options and interests involved but also because the current international tax regime is essentially bilateral and deals rather poorly with situations involving more than two countries.

A complete review of the challenges that transparent entities pose to international taxation is interesting, yet well beyond the scope of this chapter. It will only mention that the picture above is indeed simplistic since the decision about transparency of an entity does not necessarily mean ignoring it – it may be subject to various obligations, it may be taxed as a special taxpayer regardless of a general transparency rule, and it may be considered a resident of its country of organization, for example, even if it is not treated exactly like a corporation. Also, entities are truly different from one country to another, and the rules that apply to them are different, so a classification as "X" (say "partnership") in one country does necessarily mean exactly the same thing in another.

Finally, transparent entities present challenges beyond simple conflicts of classification. For example, many source rules rely on residence, which is a strange yet very common concept for transparent entities. This may lead to situations where income clearly arises in one country, colloquially speaking, yet its source is considered to be in another. Another example is the treatment of ownership ratios that are very commonly used in international taxation. It is clear sometimes that transparent entities make decisions at the entity level, and hence may assert their power, which is what these ratios try to track, at that level.

Yet, if they are considered transparent, the owners that may have nothing to do with the power asserted through these decisions may be considered as if they actually had made them. This is a challenge because one may either calculate the ratio at the partners' level or the partnership level and it may be problematic to do it one way for one purpose and another for another. Yet most partnership taxation regimes actually do exactly this: mix some aggregate and entity approaches, thinking that any "pure" approach would be too unrealistic and either oppressive or too exposed to abuse.

Once this challenge turns up in the cross-border context, however, the discussion goes beyond what is theoretically correct or fairest or cheapest to enforce, since national interests are involved. The European project, being a novel exercise of an unprecedented multinational arrangement, is under pressure to consider all this, the interests of its Member States and the interests of the single market, and maybe even the interests of the Commission as a political institution inside the Union. Once third parties are involved, however, there are even more considerations: certain third countries are very important trade partners of the Union, there are certain internal obligations that involve trade with third countries – most notably the free movement of capital, the EU or EU key members also partner with third countries in fora such as the OECD. It is not difficult to see the multiplicity of interests involved and the potential for clashes.

The proposal chose to focus solely on the classification issue (qualification conflict), and only on the simple scenario where the sole concern is a potentially transparent entity located in a third state. In that case the (European) residence state rules alone or together with other co-residence Member States. Note that this does not solve the conflict if there is one between the state of the transparent entity and either the state of source or the state of residence, if there is one. It merely attempts to solve the conflict, if it exists, between the EU Member States involved, and really only for the purposes of the apportioning of the income under the CCCTB regime. Later parts will elaborate further on this and make an evaluation; however, first, the chapter turns to the experience in the United States, the OECD and some other states in order both to evaluate the decisions reflected in the proposal, the scope of potential problems in comparison to the scope of the rules provided for in the proposal, and to further understand the challenges that await the project. It discusses, next, the United States as the first jurisdiction to seriously confront the issue of transparent entities, which has been struggling with that issue ever since.

5.3 THE THIRD COUNTRIES' PERSPECTIVE

5.3.1 United States

The United States has acquired much experience in dealing with the challenges that transparent entities have been presenting to international tax law in the last few decades. In 1997, after a long, generally unsuccessful battle to impose its standards on questions of entity classification, the United States adopted a primarily elective regime for the classification of business entities, both domestic and foreign, colloquially termed "check-the-box."[11]

As is well known in the international tax community by now, with respect to foreign entities this regime treats the primary forms of incorporating large, often publicly traded entities as corporations with separate legal (and taxpaying) personality, on the basis of a closed list published in the regulations. Forms that do not appear in the list are essentially free to elect treatment as transparent or not for US tax purposes. Absent an election, a default rule assigns classification according to the limited liability status of the entity owners. Roughly at the same time, many US states introduced new forms of doing business, generally called limited liability companies (LLC), that allow limited liability to all investors, yet are treated as transparent for tax purposes (absent an election to the opposite under the above-mentioned regime).

These two events presented tempting opportunities to taxpayers in both the inbound and outbound contexts. The US decision to employ a norm that was not universally used, let alone an elective norm, for domestic law purposes immediately resulted in inflation in the use of what are often called hybrid entities. It is common in the United States to call entities that are treated as transparent for US purposes, yet not for foreign purposes, "hybrid" entities. Similarly, entities that are treated as transparent for foreign law purposes, yet not for US purposes, are often called "reverse-hybrids." These hybrid entities[12] may simply arise from (or exist because of) qualification conflicts, yet they may also be part of tax planning based on a "check-the-box" election. Note that one consequence of making "check-the-box" elective is that even entities that would clearly be classified in a single manner under the laws of all countries could "become" hybrids by an election.

---

11 Treasury Regulation §301.7701-3.

12 When used generally, the term "hybrid entities" includes "reverse hybrids."

Against this background, the 1996 US Model Income Tax Treaty introduced the term "fiscally transparent" and generally followed the regular conservative principles of international taxation. Article 3(1)(c) of the US Model, through the "enterprise" definition, took an aggregate approach, providing that a resident of a treaty partner would be considered to be directly earning income when such income is earned through an entity that is physically transparent under the laws of the state of residence. Article 4(1)(d) provides that income earned by an entity that was fiscally transparent by one of the treaty partners would be treated as earned by a resident of a treaty partner if such treaty partner views such income as income of a resident.

The key issue was the definition of a fiscally transparent entity, where the test that has been developed is whether the owners of the entity were required to consider the income as earned directly by them or not. Note that this is a residence-country-focused approach, dependent on the legal status in such country even when there is no actual taxation by a specific residence country for whatever reasons.

Note that there is also a preliminary stage where one must determine that income is indeed earned "through" a transparent entity. Regular anti-abuse and other domestic rules normally apply in order to make this determination.

Presented with these legal opportunities, taxpayers began to extensively use hybrid entities, and most notably, a scheme based on the United States-Canada tax treaty was devised to minimize taxation of US operations of Canadian companies. These companies established US LLCs that were fiscally transparent in the United States, but not so under Canadian law. Consequently, payments made, say interest, often by true United States subsidiaries (the operating corporations in the United States) to the LLCs were considered in the United States as if paid directly to the Canadian parent. Such interest was therefore eligible for treaty benefits (10 per cent withholding tax for interest), yet in Canada it was ignored as payments between two US corporations (subsidiary and LLC). Furthermore, when the LLC distributed the earnings to the Canadian parent, such a distribution was often exempt in Canada, leading to an overall very advantageous effective tax rate of only 10 per cent.

In response, the Treasury Department issued proposed and temporary regulations in 1997, finalized in 2000, pursuant to IRC §894. These regulations limit the availability of US treaty benefits for income earned by fiscally transparent entities (whether they are considered as such by US law or the laws of its relevant treaty partner) to income considered to be derived by a resident of the US treaty partner.

A similar tax planning scheme, now using a US limited liability partnership (LLP) that was considered fiscally transparent by Canada, for example, yet elected to be treated as a corporation for US tax purposes, resulted in similar tax savings. The LLP now earns dividends from its US operating subsidiaries, and pays interest to the Canadian parent. The dividends are not taxable in the United States and are often exempt in Canada, and the interest payments do not exist for Canadian purposes, yet enjoy the benefits of the tax treaty between the United States and Canada, resulting, again, in an overall effective tax rate of only 10 per cent.

Again, in response, the Treasury Department wrote regulations under IRC §894, first in 2000, to be amended later in 2002. These regulations took a somewhat different approach, re-characterizing the interest paid by the LLP to the Canadian parent as dividends, disallowing the interest deduction to the LLP, yet allowing it treaty benefits as applied to dividends (even when the rate is lower than the rate for interest).

Actual treaty practice generally followed the US Model, yet has not been identical to it. The first treaty to adopt transparent-entity provisions similar to the ones in the US Model was the 1996 treaty between the United States and Luxembourg. Since then, similar provisions were included in the 2001 treaty with the United Kingdom and the 2004 Protocol with the Netherlands.

The 2003 treaty with Japan included a more detailed reference to the issue of transparent entities, in a way expanding the treatment provided for by the IRC §894 regulations to all applicable taxes (not only withholding taxes). Article 4(6) provides specific examples, including an interesting example under which a Japanese (wholly) owned US LLC earns US source income. The LLC is treated as a non-transparent entity under Japanese law and hence the income is not eligible for treaty benefits even though the United States views the LLC as a transparent entity and does not tax it on a worldwide basis. Again, the primacy of the residence country classification prevails.

Interestingly, for the purposes of this chapter, a 2005 competent authority agreement with Mexico limited the application of these rules, when the circumstances include a transparent entity of a third country, to situations where the third country concluded a comprehensive exchange of information agreement with Mexico.

Another interesting aspect is the effect of the saving clause contained in Article 1(4) of the US Model. The Treasury Technical Explanation asserts that the fiscally transparent entities provision is not an exception to the saving clause, and hence the United States may tax, for example, a US LLC that has elected to check-the-box even if it is wholly owned by residents of a treaty partner, and such treaty partner classifies the LLC as a transparent (look-through) entity. This result goes against the general premise that the laws of the state of residence prevail.

In conclusion, the United States has been the most proactive country in recent decades in its attempt to regulate the tax treatment of business entities. Yet, perhaps due to mistakes, perhaps due to the normal politics involved in any course of legislative and regulatory action, the US regime serves more as an example of the complexity and difficulties of taxing transparent entities than as a successful model for dealing with the issue. Much of the blame must be laid at the feet of the highly criticized check-the-box regime that has doubtlessly been the main fuel in the recent surge of use of hybrid entities due to its strict electivity. Another somewhat unique feature of the US tax system that has made things worse is the lack of a GAAR and the resort to specific, multiple anti-abuse rules, as demonstrated above in this context, that often follow slightly or more than slightly divergent philosophies and approaches, and hence are difficult to coordinate and certainly do not present a coherent policy.[13] Nonetheless, as demonstrated in the next section, much of the challenge is the inherent complexity of the matter: the legal ability to use arrangements that operate as united and coherent economic units while operating in a legal world that generally operates according to the separate corporate personality fiction, not accepting economic reality or legal nuances, in other words, anything other than simple corporations, despite their ubiquity.

5.3.2 The OECD

5.3.2.1 The OECD Partnership Report

In 1999, after a long process of consultation and discussion, the OECD published what has since become a focal point in the discourse of international taxation on unincorporated business entities.[14] The report, known as the "Partnership Report," took a position quite similar to that of US law, generally requiring source countries to follow the classification of residence countries in cases of income earned through partnerships. This requirement is, however, limited to cases where there is actual taxation by the residence countries of the same income with respect to

---

[13] Conversely, one may argue that this approach is practically more effective since it can achieve a better protection of principles, if only second best, in comparison to a GAAR that would reflect a lower common denominator.

[14] OECD, The Application of the OECD Model Tax Convention to Partnerships (OECD, Issues in International Taxation), No. 6, 1999.

which treaty benefits are claimed. The actual guidance in the report is not as clear as this statement, as the report refrained from making it, and rather used a set of examples that provide a pragmatic rather than a single principled normative solution.

Despite the direct reference and application to partnerships, the report actually discusses the wider issue of the treatment of unincorporated business arrangements under the current international tax regime, albeit not comprehensively.

The report states that most countries (OECD members) generally follow, for tax purposes, the legal status of business entities as determined pursuant to domestic private law. It uses as an example, and a benchmark, a system that recognizes only individuals, corporations and partnerships for tax purposes.[15] The report adds that problems arise not only from the different classification of entities, but also from the different treatment of similarly classified entities. To resolve these conflicts, the report chose, first, to clarify that partnerships may be classified as persons for tax treaty purposes, although such classification does not necessarily make them resident in a tax treaty partner (state). They may be resident if they are "liable to tax" in such a state, and this may be the case if they are not treated transparently under domestic tax law. Yet, when they are treated as transparent entities, it is the partners rather than the partnership that are liable to tax in their respective countries of residence and hence they, and not the partnership, are eligible for tax treaty benefits, if available. Finally, the report clarified that a state of residence must grant double taxation relief, under Article 23, based on the qualification under the law of the state of source, even in cases of qualification conflicts. Yet it is not required to grant such relief in cases of conflicts resulting from differences of interpretation or application of different provisions of tax treaties. The report ends with an interesting list of relevant entities in OECD member countries and their important characteristics that demonstrates the diversity and wealth of legal structures even within the relatively homogenous community of rich countries.

The report received ample attention in subsequent scholarship, yet one notable conceptual critique is Michael Lang's critique of the report.[16] Lang's critique begins with a conceptual complaint about the framework of the report. He accurately argues that this framework and the basic

---

[15] Unsurprisingly, this is the position of US federal income tax.

[16] Michael Lang, *The Application of the OECD Model Tax Convention to Partnerships: A Critical Analysis of the Report Prepared by the OECD Committee on Fiscal Affairs* (LindeVerlag Wien, 2000).

assumptions made by the writers of the report led to its conclusions, although the framework and assumptions are at best questionable. In particular, the emphasis on resorting to domestic law under Article 3(2), and the quasi-legislative role of the commentary, led to the primacy of a focus on the aggregate approach and on the resolution of conflicts rather than on reconciliation and dissolution of such conflicts. Avoidance of double taxation (or non-taxation) is not necessarily the only thing that a treaty does or is even its sole focus. Lang does not have a quarrel with the clarification that partnerships are persons under tax treaty law, but rather with the unprincipled approach the report took. He counters with his view of the OECD examples to demonstrate this. This excellent exposition is just one example of the fact that the OECD has only begun to scratch the surface in its regulation of the taxation of transparent entities, and of the inadequacy of its unprincipled approach in the area. Since the Commission has generally followed the lead of the OECD on the matter, similar criticism awaits it.

5.3.2.2 Treaty practice of other countries

Many countries have faced difficulties dealing with the laws of the United States pertaining to hybrid entities. Even Canada, after signing a new treaty containing a solution to some of the issues, continues to litigate against some of the most common tax planning schemes using these structures.[17] Other countries had to negotiate treaties or competent authority agreements to ensure relief of double taxation in cases involving transparent entities.[18] An immediate question in our context is whether the European Union will now need to sign some sort of an agreement with the United States, or whether the agreements of the United States with the Member States are sufficient even though they are not identical.

---

[17] Kristen A. Parillo, "Canada Will Litigate Questions on Treatment of U.S. LLCs Under Fifth Protocol, Canadian Official Says" (September 2010) *Tax Notes International* 187–1 (28 September 2010).

[18] See, for example, new treaty with Belgium (effective 1 January 2008), the 2006 Protocol with Germany (effective 1 January 2008), and the 2006 Competent Authorities Agreement with Spain (Announcement 2006-21, 2006-14 IRB 703).

5.4 ANALYSIS

5.4.1 Classification Issues

The complexity and difficulty of regulating the taxation of transparent entities is obvious at this point. This section attempts to isolate the most important aspects of the particular issue in front of us: third-country perspectives on the treatment of transparent entities under the recent Commission proposed CCCTB directive. One key issue must be understood from the outset: the scope of the proposal, and as a derivative the scope of our main focus here, is quite limited: how to treat income in the generation of which transparent entities were involved in constructing a consolidated corporate tax base for corporate groups that elect to do so under the proposal. This chapter does not directly examine the actual taxation or non-taxation of transparent entities, although the proposal will have some effects on their effective taxation, through inclusion (or not) in such groups and through the effect of double tax relief rules.

Regardless of scope, the most basic question regards the classification of the transparent entities in the simple case of income earned by a transparent entity that is owned by an EU company, say the group's parent for the sake of simplicity. If a tax treaty applies, there will normally not be a conflict of qualification, since the proposal grants the EU country primacy in the classification, and so do most tax treaties. If the EU residence country classifies it as transparent, then it should include the income in the consolidated tax base and the third country would normally accept this under a tax treaty and impose its capped source taxation that will be credited (or exempt) to the taxpayer by the country of residence. In this preliminary stage it should be noted that three potential issues arise: first, as already mentioned, attaching a transparent entity to its "location" is problematic and unsatisfactory, especially when it represents a deviation from international tax practice with no explanation. Second, the proposal does not say what to do when the country of the transparent entity is a third country (it is to be assumed that the "location" of the entity is clear). In that case, even a tax treaty may not reverse the conflict if it were a two-country situation only. Nevertheless, planning opportunities still exist, as demonstrated by the United States' response to reverse hybrids. This situation is further complicated in a three-country situation, however, where the country of source and the country of residence both classify an entity as transparent, yet the country of location does not. Note that classification as transparent or non-transparent does not necessarily change the end result –

inclusion in the tax base and corresponding relief of double taxation – but it presents a potential for different treatment. This is also the third issue: there really are several options for inclusion of income in the tax base: direct income of the parent company, of course, income of a qualifying subsidiary, income from a permanent establishment (PE), and income assigned through allocation based on a transaction with an associated enterprise. The two less solid points of connection are, first, the inclusion of income from a PE, since it is possible to have a transparent entity without a PE, even if less common. There is no good reason for inclusion of PE income separately. Second, the tribute to OECD orthodoxy and the arm's length standard is merely awkward and difficult to understand, and if one believes that an anti-abuse rule of this specific kind is required then why include a 20 per cent threshold? It is merely confusing and unnecessary.

A related conceptual question is whether these results are justified and beneficial to Europe. The different rules of Articles 84 and 85 provide more control to the countries of residence, and particularly to the residence of the parent company when it owns the structure through transparent entities in third countries. It is not clear why this is a good rule, beyond the mere pretence of keeping the power over characterization within Europe. The real problem here is not for the third countries that continue to tax in their own ways, but rather for the less powerful and less risk-taking European jurisdictions. This difference in rules may encourage internal competition for jurisdiction within Europe that is based on law, not economics and hence is likely to be wasteful, and, more likely, will result in inefficient restructuring that is difficult to justify. A simple anti-abuse rule or clarification would have been better here.

The slightly more complicated situation of a three-country transaction has already been mentioned. Again, in the simplest of situations there should be no conflicts, since the country of residence determines classification when the country of location classifies an entity as transparent. Now, if the country of source classifies an entity as transparent too, there is little potential for difficulty, but this is not necessarily the case if the country of residence and/or the country of location classify the entity as non-transparent. In that case a tax treaty normally grants the country of location (if also a country of residence) the right to classify and the treaty between the country of residence and country of source does not apply. This may result in, for example, a withholding tax rate difference. It is hard to see the reason for this; however, one has to say, that it is not really the proposal but generally the weakness of tax treaties dealing with tax treaties that causes these issues.

The issues mentioned above may not seem very significant, yet they create pressure on and opportunities for third countries. Some additional clarifications could go a long way toward eliminating some of these frictions.

A second set of issues relates not to the classification conflict directly, but rather to its derivative implications, such as characterization and source determinations. Conflicts of characterization are not, of course, unique to the proposal, since current tax treaties generally avoid them, yet they may be more acute in this context because the main focus of the proposal is on the tax base, and characterization issues are at the bottom – at the basis of the tax base – and conflicts here are extremely difficult to solve. Even if interpretation leads to the primacy of the country of residence of the parent company, which sounds logical, and even if tax treaties can be reconciled with the consolidated base, there will certainly be conflicts with different classifications of third countries. Some of the conflicts may be relieved by what seems to be a strong mandate to the country of residence to relieve double taxation, if interpreted that way. Source rules follow characterization, of course, so characterization conflicts may result in source distortions, and double taxation (or even under-taxation). Moreover, many of the source rules in the current international tax regime are simply based on the country of residence. In this context, even when sometimes, for taxation purposes (in other words, inclusion in the base) it would not matter whether a third-country entity is classified as transparent or not, it would matter for source purposes, and hence for relief of double taxation purposes, despite the wide scope of the relief of double taxation mandate. All this holds, assuming that characterization and source are the same for both inclusion and double tax relief purposes. A related issue is the scope of double tax relief in cases where third countries impose withholding taxes on payments by transparent entities. This issue may be resolved by a tax treaty, but not necessarily so. Similarly, third countries such as the United States may employ anti-abuse rules that will affect the scope of taxation in the European Union. The legitimacy of these rules may become an issue in cases of conflicts between the European Union and third countries. This may be a remote issue and it has not been particularly problematic under tax treaties, yet some of the US treaty overrides have been more problematic. The question now becomes the extent to which is it left to the Member States to deal with this or whether it is now an issue at the EU level.

Other issues go beyond classification and have presented problems in the United States: first, the calculation of ownership shares in and through transparent and particularly hybrid entities. This was important for special tax rates for dividends, application of anti-deferral regimes and more. Second, branch taxes may present problems if not considered to be identical to withholding taxes. Finally, being a consolidation regime, the proposal does not say anything about structures when the transparent entity is the real parent and headquarters of the group. This presents tax planning opportunities that may be beyond the scope of the actual proposal, yet it might have been useful to articulate the EU approach to this closely related issue.

Finally, a more technical European issue is the default rule in Article 85 in cases where there are multiple states of residence. The proposal says that the tax authorities of the principal country will break the tie, yet it is possible that such a country is not among the jurisdictions at stake. In this case, the solution is awkward and may encourage unnecessary internal competition for jurisdiction within Europe.

5.4.2 Income Apportionment Issues

Article 89 requires apportionment of income based on the proportional holding of the taxpayer in the transparent entity and calculation at that entity's level. The rules are not entirely clear, yet two issues arise.

First, in partnerships, when the income allocation is not simply proportional, distortions may consequently arise. For example, it is possible that one partner will be allocated the income from certain assets, yet not from others, while for CCCTB purposes it seems to be the case that apportionment is proportional. This opens up opportunities for tax planning and even some traps for the unwary, especially since the assets part does not include intangibles. Moreover, allocation rules in partnerships are likely to be more divergent than others. The recent OECD initiative on allocation of profits to PEs would make things even more complex when the practical effect of a hybrid or transparent entity results in a PE in the third country, at least from the perspective of the EU residence country. There would now be normal treaty rules following the arm's length principle, and CCCTB rules that are formulary and all this in the context of usually divergent allocation regimes for partnerships.

Second, there may be different relationships between income and factors of production in third countries in comparison to the EU Member States, so it is possible that a disproportionately high value of assets, sales and employees, for example, in a third country would give rise to relatively little income, yet still be apportioned to the transparent entity in the third country. This is not necessarily an issue unique to transparent entities, but rather an issue in any formulary apportionment, yet it is more complex due to the unique allocation issues involving transparent entities and the increased difficulties of attribution to them.

One should note also that the formulary apportionment in the proposal is of the consolidated tax base among the group members rather than among the countries. Such a regime does not capture the complete benefits that formulary apportionment can provide since it preserves residence influence and legal status beyond economically significant presence. Alternatively, if one views the formulary apportionment regime, as I do, as beneficial due to its transparency rather than covert arbitrariness, such a result is not fully achieved under the proposal since the primary element of countries splitting the tax base regardless of legal status being in complete control of taxpayers and their lawyers is not met.

5.5 CONCLUSION

This book provides a unique opportunity to examine one of the most interesting phenomena on the current international tax agenda. This opportunity is particularly unique due to the existence of an actual proposed directive "on the table." Some of the fundamental critiques of the proposal directly affect the subject of this chapter, the taxation of transparent entities, which may be viewed by some, and apparently also by the Commission as secondary.[19]

Nevertheless, the Commission has taken a very clear stand in favour of a "pragmatic" approach that mirrors the OECD's approach to the issue. The most obvious price of this approach is that it does not follow, and alas does not even pretend to follow, any clear principles. This price is not merely academic, since it results in lack of clarity and legal certainty, but, even worse, it sends a confused policy message. In truth, it is not difficult to see even from this preliminary discussion that the Commission has not seriously thought of the interests of the EU Member States when it came up with this proposal. In many ways, it does not even seriously address anti-abuse concerns that are particularly relevant in the context of our discussion of third countries. As briefly demonstrated above, it is often the case that third countries are left with an advantage, either directly or via incentives for internal competition (for jurisdiction) among Member States due to the proposal. It seems that the primary

---

[19] This conclusion is based merely on the brevity of reference to the issue in the Proposal for a Council Directive on a Common Consolidated Corporate Tax Base (CCCTB) COM(2011) 121/4.

focus of the proposal in our context was to find a system that would seem administratively "workable" for the tax authorities of the Member States, and one that would fit into the OECD approach (which, alas, is not necessarily based on the same interests as those of Europe).

On the positive side, most practical cases are well covered by the proposal and it seems unlikely that its treatment will result in controversial consequences in such cases. Obviously, the pragmatic success of the proposal, if adopted, will depend on extensive guidance that will need to be given in much more detail and with better attention to policy choices and the potential responses of third countries.

The more general issue of the relationship between the CCCTB and tax treaties should be as critical here as in any other of the areas discussed in this book. Recent experience, especially that of the United States with respect to application of tax treaties to LLCs, has shown that unless the framework is changed, extensive renegotiations are needed for even a basic hope of coordination of qualification conflicts. Note that the reluctance of the Commission to adopt a true formulary regime, divorced from the arm's length principle and the legal personality of non-parent enterprises will necessitate the solution to all of the same problems under the CCCTB.

In conclusion, the Commission has taken a courageous step forward in presenting this proposal, yet Europe will probably be better served if some of the choices made were even more progressive. In the context of transparent entities, the Commission has barely taken a firm stand. This chapter has attempted to demonstrate the perils in taking such a passive approach to the issue. It has further attempted to raise some of the most important issues that a serious approach may need to tackle, as well as to suggest some manners of confronting such issues. As transparent entities are increasingly used in international tax planning, and particularly in the more sophisticated schemes, it is safe to say that this is just the beginning of the discussion and hopefully it will be of use to future analyses.

Commentary

Christian Kaeser

INTRODUCTION

When designing new rules it is always wise to broaden the perspective and analyse how others approached the same issues and which problems their solutions encountered. Brauner went down this road, starting with what is likely the most prominent example of a tax system handling transparent entities, the US "check-the-box" rules, to then explore the OECD Partnership Report, closing with a brief remark about problems of many countries when dealing with the US practice. The latter leads Brauner to the question of whether the EU Member States will have to enter into some sort of agreement or new treaties with the US to resolve any potential conflicts regarding "hybrid" entities. The material compiled by Brauner is helpful in the overall discussion of how to handle the classification of an entity as fiscally transparent or non-transparent. It is no surprise that the comparison could not bring to light anything reasonable when it comes to the question of apportionment of taxable profit of a group between different jurisdictions. This is because this question is one specific to the CCCTB, being a common corporate tax base and system for all Member States rather than a single unilateral approach as that of the US and other states. It cannot be compared to the traditional approach of allocating the right to tax specific income of one person to one or the other country partner to a double tax treaty (DTT).

SPECIFIC QUESTIONS

Why is a Regulation such as Article 84 Regarding European Transparent Entities Necessary?

The profit and loss of a European resident transparent entity will be included in the CCCTB and therefore be apportioned between the group companies. Income of a non-transparent European entity will only be included in the CCCTB when the specific requirements of the CCCTB are met (in other words, minimum participation). In case those requirements are not fulfilled the income of the latter entity will only be relevant for the CCCTB once it is distributed up to a parent company being part of a CCCTB tax group. It is therefore decisive to determine whether a legal entity resident in one of the Member States is fiscally transparent or not.

Does the Primacy of the Country of "Location" Make Sense in this Context?

A thought regarding the referral to the classification in the country of location of the transparent entity: with the possibility of more than one interest holder from different Member States it is quite clear that the rules cannot refer to the classification of the Member State of residence of the interest holder because this might lead to a different classification of one and the same entity; a conflict between the Member States of the interest holders which would have to be resolved at some level. Nevertheless, a different classification still remains even within the EU where one of the partners in a transparent entity includes his profit share in this partnership according to CCCTB rules whilst the partner is not opting for the CCCTB scheme. It is obvious that the apportionment to the country of residence and location as per the CCCTB factors will deviate from the profit share of the very partner under the partnership agreement. But even so no double or under-taxation should be created because the apportionment is tied to the taxpayer's participation in the profits and losses of the transparent entity.

Is "Location" a Reasonable Term to Circumscribe the Specific Problem at Hand?

No, it is not but it reflects the problems in international tax practice when dealing with transparent entities. The term "residence" is linked to the resident being subject to tax in the country of his residence. As the transparent entity is not subject to tax in "its" country when treated as transparent, the EU was apparently looking for an alternative wording. It is worth noting that "location" is not used by the OECD MC – neither in the context of Articles 3 or 4 nor in that of Article 6 (where "situated" is used to describe the necessary link of immovable property to the source country). The Commentary uses the term e.g. in the context of Articles 5 and 8 to describe a certain geographical place in one of the contracting states.

How does Article 89 tie in with Article 84?

If the profit and loss of a transparent entity resident in one of the Member States belong to a shareholder who in turn participates in a CCCTB tax group, the question arises how this profit and loss participation should be treated within the apportionment mechanism of the CCCTB. Different answers to this question seem possible depending on whether a DTA allows the country of residence of the shareholder to tax his above-mentioned participation or if this right does only belong to the country of residence of the transparent entity. For example, the CCCTB could only recognize those participations which are taxable under a DTA in the hands of the shareholder in his country of residence and apportion them using the normal parameters (in other words, without a view to the transparent entity itself). Or the CCCTB would recognize each and every participation regardless of any existing DTAs between the countries involved. The CCCTB rules take the latter approach. Hence, it is self-explanatory that the rules need to include the transparent entity itself in the apportionment mechanism. This rule is found in Article 89. It does not deviate from the basic apportionment rule for CCCTB purposes. Because of its binding nature for all Member States no conflict should arise from this mechanism between the Member States.

Why is a Regulation such as Article 85 regarding Third-Country Transparent Entities Necessary?

The profit and loss of a third country transparent entity will be included in the CCCTB and therefore be apportioned between the group companies. Income of a non-transparent third country entity will not be included in the CCCTB because the CCCTB only allows the inclusion of legal entities resident in one of the Member States. The income of a non-transparent third-country legal entity will only be relevant for the CCCTB once it is distributed up to a parent company being part of a CCCTB tax group. It is therefore paramount to determine whether a third-country legal entity is fiscally transparent or not.

How does Article 89 fit in with Article 85?

With regard to third countries one would have expected that within the CCCTB only the profit and loss can be included and apportioned for which a right to tax at least of one of the Member States exists. But Article 89 takes the same approach as for transparent entities resident in one of the Member States. This creates an inherent conflict because within Article 84 the system operates in an environment where the rules are binding for all countries (=Member States) involved. This is not the case under Article 85 as the third countries do not participate in the CCCTB system and are therefore legally not touched by it. In terms of the consequences one has to distinguish:

- If the Member State of residence of the shareholder has the right to tax the shareholders participation in profits and losses of a transparent third-country entity because either the transparent entity does not create a PE or the income does not belong to a PE in the third-country, the apportionment approach might lead to "white income": the third country will not claim any right to tax the apportioned income whilst the income apportioned to the third country will not be taxed in any of the Member States of the respective CCCTB tax group.
- If the Member State of residence of the shareholder has the right to tax the shareholder's participation in profits and losses of a transparent third-country entity because no treaty between this country and Member State of residence of the shareholder exists or such a treaty exists but the credit method is applied for business income from a PE, a risk of an unrelieved double taxation will remain. This is the case because the third country will rightfully claim its right to tax the income under the DTA or according to its local law whilst it might be difficult to credit this tax against the tax of the residence of the shareholder.
- If there is no right to tax the shareholder's participation in profits and losses of a transparent third-country entity because the treaty contains the exemption method, the apportionment according to Article 89 will breach the obligation of the respective Member States under the DTA.

It can be seen that the effects of Article 89 for third-country transparent entities are somewhat problematic. The reason for this might be found in the basic struggle to classify and handle transparent entities in an international context. This raises a couple of very specific questions for which Brauner's work on the US and OECD approaches is helpful.

First, a Systematic Issue: Why are or should Legal Entities be Fiscally Transparent?

For a system trying to design a consolidated tax base it should have been a starting exercise to analyse the reasoning for any consolidation of profits and losses between different legal entities. If it comes to transparent entities the obvious first thought would be to tie the fiscal transparency to the legal transparency of the entity, especially regarding the personal liability of the shareholders for any losses of the entity. It would lead too far to explore this road any further but might be a key to understanding and resolving many of the problems attached to "hybrid" entities.

With this basic Thought in Mind, is the Classification Battle a Battle that Can be Won?

As always the answer depends on the specific circumstances. In a common binding system the classification system can be solved by various alternative measures. The system could deny the existence of fiscally transparent entities, it could give common binding criteria to determine whether an entity is fiscally transparent or not, it could refer to the local classification of either the partners/interest holders in the respective entity or the residence or "location" of the entity or decide to go for an elective system like the US check-the-box rules. Because of the binding character in a common system such as the CCCTB a conflict between various jurisdictions would be solved by each of these methods. With no common system the answer is different: a classification conflict – in the absence of common classification rules – can only be avoided or, as the case may be, resolved if one of the countries involved gives up its classification and follows that of the other country. Article 85 does not take this approach because it gives the Member States of the partner in a third-country transparent entity the power to classify the entity as transparent or non-transparent according to its local tax regime. The CCCTB approach will therefore not avoid or resolve any classification conflicts relating to third-country transparent entities.

How about an Elective Classification System as an Alternative?

The US check-the-box rules could act as a role model for a system in which the taxpayer elects the status of a legal entity as fiscally transparent or non-transparent. Besides problems with legal entities having more than one shareholder (would the shareholders have to agree about the characterization or could each of them elect the status individually or should the legal entity elect its status itself?) such an election would, at least from a German perspective, encounter serious problems regarding the basic principles of taxation such as "equality of taxation" and "legality of taxation". In its purest form it would in a way conflict with the CCCTB itself because the taxpayer could decide whether to follow the standard rules for including a legal entity in its CCCTB or opt for transparency. The examples given by Brauner about US/Canadian tax schemes using hybrid entities illustrate the core issue: A national classification system will always create qualification conflicts as long as this system does not solely reflect the classification of the other state, in other words, is linked to the other system. With the CCCTB a multinational approach binding the Member States will automatically solve this issue within the EU – but not towards third countries. This gives rise to planning opportunities.

Planning opportunities arise in particular in more complex environments. In the following example a Member State Parent Co (e.g. a German AG) holds 100 per cent interest in a US LLC. The LLC is structured under BMF Reg. dated 19 March 2004 as transparent but did not check-the-box for US purposes and therefore will be regarded as non-transparent in the US. From a CCCTB perspective the interest expense will be taken into account when calculating the Member State parent's European group profit – regardless of whether a PE is created by US LLC's activities or not. At the same time the interest expense will be treated in the US as tax deductible and can be used to offset other income. The structure works when US LLC acts as the parent of a US consolidated tax group.

How about the Approach taken in Article 85: Country of Residence of the Shareholder/Partner in a (Transparent) Third Country Entity Determines the Transparency of the Latter?

The absence of a common characterization opens the door for multiple planning opportunities. When the inclusion of income from a third country entity is not desirable from a CCCTB perspective the interest in this entity can be held via a Member State subsidiary of the Member State parent company resident in a country that does not characterize the third-country entity as transparent – if the inclusion is desirable, the interest could be held via a subsidiary in a Member State with opposite classification rules.

6. Deductibility of gifts to charitable bodies in third countries

Roman Seer

6.1 RELEVANT PROVISIONS IN THE PROPOSAL FOR A CCCTB DIRECTIVE

The following provisions of the proposal for a Council Directive on a Common Consolidated Corporate Tax Base (hereafter: of the proposed CCCTB Directive) are relevant to the topic of this chapter:

- Article 12: Deductible expenses

  Deductible expenses shall include all costs of sales and expenses net of deductible value added tax incurred by the taxpayer with a view of obtaining or securing income, including costs of research and development and costs incurred in raising equity or debt for the purposes of the business.

  Deductible expenses shall also include gifts to charitable bodies as defined in Article 16 which are established in a Member State or in a third country which applies an agreement on the exchange of information on request comparable to provisions of Directive 2011/16/EU. The maximum deductible expense for monetary gifts or donations to charitable bodies shall be 0,5% of revenues in the tax year.

- Article 14: Non-deductible expenses

  1. The following expenses shall be treated as non-deductible:
     (a) profit distributions
     (h) monetary gifts and donations other than those made to charitable bodies as defined in Article 16;

- Article 16: Charitable bodies

  A body shall qualify as charitable where the following conditions are met:

  (a) it has legal personality and is a recognized charity under the law of the State in which it is established;

(b) its sole or main purpose and activity is one of public benefit; an educational, social, medical, cultural, scientific, philanthropic, religious, environmental or sportive purpose shall be considered to be of public benefit provided that it is of general interest;
(c) its assets are irrevocably dedicated to the furtherance of its purpose;
(d) it is subject to requirements for the disclosure of information regarding its accounts and its activities;
(e) it is not a political party as defined by the Member State in which it is established.

6.2 CHARACTER OF CHARITABLE CONTRIBUTIONS IN AN INCOME TAX SYSTEM

Article 10 of the proposed CCCTB Directive follows the *net income principle* to measure the taxable profit of the company group. The tax base shall be calculated as revenues less deductible expenses; profit means an excess of revenues over deductible expenses (Article 4 (9) of the proposed CCCTB Directive). Not every company expense is deductible, only those expenses which are made to obtain or secure income. Like income taxation in general, the proposed CCCTB Directive distinguishes between the phase of *income realization* and the phase of *income spending*. The spending of realized income is fundamentally irrelevant for the tax base which has to reflect the ability to pay tax. Thus, the taxable profit is independent of its distribution (see Article 14 (1) (a) of the proposed CCCTB Directive). Even charitable contributions are an act of profit spending, not an act of the phase of profit realization. Charitable gifts are not related to business activities. Only if the donations are part of a sponsoring campaign, especially to improve the image of the company, can they be treated as expense intended to obtain or secure income. In this case the expenses are fully deductible to measure the realized profit properly.

In contrast, the German Federal Tax Court has characterized charitable donations as *business expenses*.[1] In the court's view, a company as a legal entity has no "private sphere"[2] with the consequence that all company

[1] Bundesfinanzhof (Federal Tax Court) [1981], Bundessteuerblatt Part II [1982], I R 149/77 [177]; Federal Tax Court [1987], Bundessteuerblatt Part II [1988], I R 126/85 [220].

[2] See Federal Tax Court [1996], Decisions of the Federal Tax Court (BFHE) volume 182 [1997], I R 54/95, [123]; Federal Tax Court [2007], Bundessteuerblatt Part II [2007], I R 32/06, [961].

expenses are first of all business expenses. Then the tax legislator may decide whether business expenses such as charitable gifts are non-deductible or deductible to a limited extent. This case law is not very convincing. Notwithstanding the quality of a company as a legal business entity it is very possible to distinguish between operating and non-operating expenses. To support charitable bodies by donation is a voluntary decision of the board or/and the shareholders of the company. Especially in personally run companies which are steered by family shareholders, non-business related motives will be dominant in the decision to make gifts to a charitable body.

With regard to Article 12 sentence 2 of the proposed CCCTB Directive the dogmatic distinction as to whether a charity donation is an act of income realization or income spending seems to be – prima facie – a solely theoretical question. However, the answer is relevant for the justification of the deduction of gifts and its limitation or exclusion. If charitable gifts are fundamentally business expenses of the company, tax legislators have to justify limitations or even exclusions of the deductibility as exceptions to the general net principle (as a principle to coherently realize the tax purpose). If charitable gifts are an act of income spending, a legislative decision not to allow deduction of the expenses from the tax base matches with the general net principle and needs no further argumentation. From this point of view, conversely, the deduction of charitable contributions has to be justified as a tax benefit or incentive (social purpose clause) and as an exception from the general net principle.

6.3 JUSTIFICATION OF THE LIMITED DEDUCTION OF CHARITABLE CONTRIBUTIONS

From my point of view charitable contributions are fundamentally acts of *income spending*, not business expenses. Therefore, tax legislators do not have to recognize them in determining how the taxable income is to be computed. However, it is part of legislative discretion to subsidize charitable bodies by deducting expenses of charitable gifts from the taxable income of the donor. The common justification for granting tax reliefs in favour of non-profit organizations is the idea that these organizations relieve the states from their governmental (especially social) responsibilities and tasks.[3] A supplementary argument is that tax

[3] Ineke A. Koele, *International Taxation of Philanthropy* (1st edn, IBFD 2007); T. von Hippel and W. Rainer Walz "General Report" 75, Beltrame

reliefs for philanthropic organizations foster the altruistic activities of citizens in a pluralistic civil society.[4] The principle of subsidiarity mandates to leave these organizations financial means without taxes. From the point of view of the subsidiarity theory charitable contributions have the character of a tax surrogate (*tax surrogate theory*).[5] A tax relief for a tax surrogate should be consistently allocated as a *tax credit* on the level of the tax, not on the level of the tax base. However, if the tax rate is not progressive, but proportional – like almost all of the corporate tax rates – this structural mistake does not run the risk of creating inequality. The states never get a full relief from their public (social) tasks via substitution by charitable bodies. Therefore, it makes sense to *limit the tax relief* in two ways:

- Deductions from the tax base only partially grant a "tax credit" subject to the corporate tax rate (*relative limitation*);
- The deductible sum of all charitable contributions is limited to a certain percentage of the taxable income of the fiscal year (*absolute limitation*).

Both instruments together prevent taxpayers from having a real option between tax and charitable contributions. The state revenue is not jeopardized by shifting too much tax revenue into non-profit organizations. It remains the decision of the state how much or how few financial means are kept in this third sector.

6.4 DEDUCTIBILITY OF CHARITABLE CONTRIBUTIONS UNDER EU CASE LAW

The tax surrogate theory is focused on the national state budget. Therefore, it is not surprising that most national tax codes have allowed

"France" 285, Lindencrona "Sweden" 421 f., Koller "Switzerland" 445, Taboada, "Spain" 485, Colombo "USA" 573 in W. Rainer Walz, Ludwig von Auer and Thomas von Hippel (eds), *Spenden- und Gemeinnützigkeitsrecht in Europa* (1st edn, Mohr Siebeck Tübingen 2007); Roman Seer, "Gemeinwohlzwecke und steuerliche Entlastung" in *Deutsche Steuerjuristische Gesellschaft (DStJG)* (volume 26, Verlag Dr. Otto Schmidt Cologne 2003) 11, 21.

[4] Beltrame "France" in W. Rainer Walz, Ludwig von Auer and Thomas von Hippel (eds), *Spenden- und Gemeinnützigkeitsrecht in Europa* (1st edn, Mohr Siebeck Tübingen 2007).

[5] Stephan Geserich, *Das Spendenrecht* in DStJG (volume 26, Verlag Dr. Otto Schmidt Cologne 2003) 245, 248.

the deduction only of such charitable contributions that have been made to foundations which are established within the state.[6] However, in a globalized world, charitable activities are not locally or nationally restricted. Large foundations are parts of worldwide networks and spend their financial means and manpower in third countries all over Africa, Asia and Latin America to improve infrastructures and fight poverty. These activities are even in the interest of national states. The multitude of activities of non-governmental organizations (NGO) replaces development aid by the states. National tax incentives for charity foundations which are engaged in development activities abroad can also be justified by the tax surrogate theory.

Since the ground-breaking decisions of the European Court of Justice (ECJ) in the *Walter Stauffer*[7] and *Hein Persche*[8] cases, a solely domestic ("landlocked"[9]) approach violates Article 63 Treaty on the Functioning of the European Union (TFEU). The *Stauffer* decision dealt with an inbound case about the tax-exempt status of a philanthropic Italian organization that owns and rents out German-situated real property. The ECJ saw a *restriction of the freedom of capital movement* in the former German limitation of the tax exemption on foundations subject to unlimited tax liability which are established in Germany. The Court decided that no overriding requirements in the general interest were found that justified the unequal treatment of the Stauffer organization. The Court pointed out that the *effectiveness of fiscal supervision* may constitute such an overriding requirement of general public interest. Therefore, the national Member State is authorized to apply measures enabling it to ascertain in a clear and precise manner whether the foundation meets the conditions imposed by national law in order to be entitled to the exemption and to monitor its effective management, for example, by requiring the submission of annual accounts and an activity report.[10]

For this chapter the core relevant decision is the later *Persche* decision which dealt with the deductibility of a charitable contribution to a charity

---

6 T. van Hippel and W. Rainer Walz "General Report" in W. Rainer Walz, Ludwig von Auer and Thomas von Hippel (eds), *Spenden- und Gemeinnützigkeitsrecht in Europa* (1st edn, Mohr Siebeck Tübingen 2007) 163.

7 *Centro di Musicologia Walter Stauffer v Finanzamt München für Körperschaften* [2006] ECR I-8203 Case C-386/04.

8 *Hein Persche v Finanzamt Lüdenscheid* [2009] ECR I-359 Case C-318/07.

9 This term is used by Ineke A. Koele, "How will international philanthropy be freed from landlocked tax barriers?" [2010] 50 *European Taxation* 9, 409.

10 *Centro di Musicologia Walter Stauffer v Finanzamt München für Körperschaften* [2006] ECR I-8203 Case C 386/04.

foundation located abroad (outbound case). With regard to this constellation the ECJ went on to see a restriction of the free movement of capital and payments (Article 63 TFEU) if the deductibility is limited to domestic organizations because the willingness of the taxpayer to make cross-border gifts will be reduced by this disadvantageous tax provision. Furthermore, the ECJ kept its *distance from the national tax surrogate theory* and the arguments of the German, Spanish, Irish and UK governments that the domestic charitable foundations are fulfilling charitable responsibilities which would otherwise be the duty of the Member State.[11] From the European point of view, this justification of a national distinction is only a question of budgetary compensation (because of a lower need for financial means for public services) that leads *solely to tax revenue aspects* which are not accepted in settled case law as a relevant public interest to justify a discrimination or restriction of fundamental freedoms.[12] If the EU Member States keep the deductibility of gifts to charitable bodies in their income and corporate tax codes, they have to give up their landlocked approach and have to enlarge the tax benefits for gifts granted to equivalent foreign charitable bodies. Since Article 63 TFEU protects not only capital movement between EU Member States but also between EU Member States and third countries, the national tax benefits must also include gifts to equivalent charitable bodies established in third countries.

However, the ECJ realized again – in line with the *Stauffer* decision – the need to safeguard the effectiveness of fiscal supervision. The Member States are authorized to require the taxpayer to *provide such proof* as the Member State may consider necessary in order to determine whether the conditions for deducting expenses provided for in the national legislation at issue have been met.[13] Unlike the inbound *Stauffer* case, the taxpayer donating in an outbound situation has to provide evidence of the *sphere of a third person* (the foreign charitable body). The donor may not have all the information necessary for the tax authorities to verify whether that body satisfies the conditions required by the national legislation for the grant of tax advantages, particularly those relating to the manner in which the funds paid are managed. Nevertheless, in the *Persche* decision the ECJ held that it is usually possible for a donor to obtain from that

11 *Hein Persche v Finanzamt Lüdenscheid* [2009] ECR I-359 Case C-318/07 [44–46].

12 *Hein Persche v Finanzamt Lüdenscheid* [2009] ECR I-359 Case C-318/07, [para 46].

13 *Hein Persche v Finanzamt Lüdenscheid* [2009] ECR I-359 Case C-318/07, [para 54].

body documents confirming the amount and nature of the gift made, identifying the objectives pursued by the body and certifying the propriety of the management of the gifts which were made to it during previous years.[14] The *burden of proof* for the fulfilment of the national legal requirements of the quality of the recipient charitable body is borne by the donating taxpayer. Even the existence of Council Directive 77/799/EEC[15] does not change this burden-of-proof allocation. The ECJ held in the *Persche* decision that the directive does not require the donor's Member State to take recourse to the mechanism of mutual assistance under that directive each time that the information provided by that donor is not sufficient to determine whether the recipient body fulfils the conditions laid down by the national legislation for the grant of tax advantages. Each Member State has to assess the specific cases in which information concerning transactions by taxable persons in its territory is lacking and to decide whether those cases justify submitting a request for information to another Member State.[16]

The aforementioned case law has been continued by the ECJ in two further decisions: In a Belgian inheritance tax case (*Missionswerk Heukelbach e.V.*) the ECJ again rejected the national tax surrogate theory as a justification for a strongly reduced inheritance tax rate exclusively in favour of charitable bodies established in Belgium (Wallonië). A Member State may require a sufficiently close link between the bodies which that Member State recognizes as pursuing some of its social purposes and the activities pursued by those bodies. But the Member State cannot grant such advantages only to bodies which are established in its territory and whose activities are capable of relieving that State of its responsibilities.[17] Once again, the ECJ has characterized the relief of national state social services as a pure budgetary, fiscal argument which is not capable of justifying any restriction or discrimination.[18] As a result, the German charitable body "Missionswerk Heukelbach e.V.", receiving a legacy

---

14 *Hein Persche v Finanzamt Lüdenscheid* [2009] ECR I-359 Case C-318/07 [57].

15 Council Directive (EEC) 77/799 concerning mutual assistance by the competent authorities of the Member States in the field of direct taxation (EC Mutual Assistance Directive) [1977] OJ L 336, 15.

16 *Hein Persche v Finanzamt Lüdenscheid* [2009] ECR I-359 Case C-318/07 [64, 65].

17 *Missionswerk Werner Heukelbach eV v État belge* [2011] Case C-25/10 ECJ [30].

18 *Missionswerk Werner Heukelbach eV v État belge* [2011] Case C-25/10 ECJ [31].

from a Belgian testator, had to be treated like a Belgian charitable body that as legatee pays only a reduced inheritance tax.

The *Persche* decision has been finally confirmed by the ECJ in the *EU Commission versus Austria* case.[19] Under Article 258 TFEU the EU Commission has filed an action for failure to fulfil obligations by allowing the deduction of gifts to research and teaching institutions from the taxable income only if these institutions are established in Austria. The ECJ held that the Member States are in general free to define the objectives in the public interest that they wish to promote by granting tax advantages to private or public bodies. But they have to exercise this discretion in accordance with EU law. While a Member State may lawfully reserve the grant of tax advantages to bodies pursuing certain objectives in the public interest, it may not – however – reserve the benefit of those advantages solely to bodies established in its territory.[20] Once again, the ECJ rejects the argument of a national tax surrogate as a solely budgetary, fiscal interest that cannot justify any discrimination or restriction of the free movement of capital.

6.5 CONSEQUENCES FOR THE DESIGN OF ARTICLES 12, 14 AND 16 OF THE PROPOSED CCCTB DIRECTIVE

As a result of the case law of the ECJ and the infringement procedure activities of the EU Commission initiated in parallel, several EU Member States have been forced to resolve elements of their landlocked legislation referring to cross-border charity contributions.[21] Two extreme positions are possible: the *most liberal approach* is realized in the Netherlands, which had removed all landlocked elements of its legislation by 1 January 2008.[22] Gifts to foreign charities are fully deductible for Netherlands-resident individuals and corporate donors. However, this new tax benefit is only applicable if the foreign charity is established within the EU or in a country with which the Netherlands has concluded a tax treaty with an appropriate exchange of information clause (such as Article 26 OECD Model 2005). The foreign charity can register by a

---

19 *European Commission v Republic of Austria* [2011] Case C-10/10.

20 *European Commission v Republic of Austria* [2011] Case C-10/10, [33].

21 Koele, footnote 3, 413, mentions Belgium, Bulgaria, Czech Republic, Denmark, France, Germany, Greece, Latvia, Luxembourg, the Netherlands and Slovenia.

22 Ibid.

self-assessment declaration to get a formalized tax-exempt status. For this purpose the foreign charity has to declare itself to be compatible with a list of key requirements. It will get an automatic response about the desired status.[23] An example of the *opposite position* is the tax legislation of Hungary. Hungary has abolished the tax incentives for charity contributions entirely and by means of this harsh legislation prevents any conflict with Article 63 TFEU.[24] The example of Hungary shows the risk of rejection of the national tax surrogate theory. National states only feel responsible for the social welfare in their own territory. Therefore, they are only willing to grant tax benefits for charitable contributions that are linked to their country. *The broader the scope of the recipient foreign charitable bodies the less will be the willingness of the national state to keep tax benefits for charity gifts in general.* This context may trigger a very restrictive national tax policy which does not care about philanthropic activities of the society and throws the baby out with the bath water. Other Member States are steering middle-ground courses. For instance, Germany has enlarged the scope of deductible charitable contributions even for EU and EEA Member States up to 20 per cent of their taxable net market income of the tax year. As a further requirement for recipient foreign charitable bodies Sec. 10b para. 1 sentences 3–5 German Income Tax Code 2010 provide that the foreign state has to give assistance by information exchanges according to Directive 77/799/EEC[25] and for the recovery of claims according to Directive 2008/55/EC.[26] Charitable bodies established in third countries could still not be beneficiary recipients of deductible gifts. However, this general restriction may violate Article 63 TFEU which protects also the free capital movement from a Member State to a third country external to the EU.

Against this background Articles 12, 14 and 16 of the proposed CCCTB Directive can be characterized as a *compromise*. As an EU common project no possibility exists to distinguish between EU Member States and the location where the charitable body has been established. In light of the aforementioned case law of the ECJ, tackling restrictions of capital movements, a general exclusion of charitable bodies situated in third countries is not an option either. Thus, Article 12 sentence 2 of the

---

23 Koele, footnote 3, 413.

24 Ibid, 414.

25 Council Directive (EEC) 77/799 concerning mutual assistance by the competent authorities of the Member States in the field of direct taxation (EC Mutual Assistance Directive) [1977] OJ L 336, 15.

26 Council Directive (EC) 2008/55 on mutual assistance for the recovery of claims (EC Recovery of Claims Directive) [2008], OJ L 150, 28.

proposed CCCTB Directive enlarges the deductible expenses for gifts donated to charitable bodies established in third countries. The downside of this far-reaching approach is seen in the limitation of Article 12 sentence 3 of the proposed CCCTB Directive to a *maximum deduction of only 0.5 per cent of the taxable income* of the fiscal year. This ceiling is far below the limits of national tax codes we are used to within the EU.[27] Ceilings of 5 per cent (e.g. Belgium for corporate donors), 10 per cent (e.g. Czech Republic, Italy, the Netherlands, Spain), 15 per cent (e.g. Denmark), 20 per cent (e.g. Germany, France) or even without any limit (e.g. the United Kingdom) of the taxable income are known. The proposed CCCTB Directive clearly shows the effect of an increase of the deductibility of worldwide charitable contributions. To safeguard the national budgets the legislators will reduce the maximum deductible amounts. A significant reduction of the maximum of tax deduction is not in line with the subsidiarity principle and its idea of civil (free) societies in which citizens pursue philanthropic purposes by themselves instead of paying taxes and hoping that the state will manage it. This relativizes the aim of the EU law of doing away with "landlocked tax barriers".[28] In my opinion, the tax surrogate theory still makes sense. *The further the distance between the Member State's society and the foreign charitable body and its purpose, the less the responsibility of the Member State to grant a tax benefit for contributions to this charitable body.* This points out the necessity to distinguish between EU-charitable bodies and charitable bodies established in third countries on the level and intensity of fiscal supervision.

Article 12 sentence 2 of the proposed CCCTB Directive tries to ensure – in line with the case law of the ECJ – the effectiveness of *fiscal supervision* as an important public interest. Therefore the provision sets a *certain benchmark* for the mutual assistance of tax authorities. The minimum standard is laid down in the new Council Directive 2011/16/EU to the extent that it deals with information exchange upon request.[29] The standard is a "major" information clause such as Article 26 OECD Model 2005 or an equivalent Tax Information Exchange Agreement (TIEA) like Article 5 OECD TIEA Model 2002 (see further below under section 6.6). The information exchange agreement is necessary as it means to ensure the fulfilment of the preconditions of Article 16 of the

[27] Hippel and Walz, footnote 3, 159 f.

[28] Ineke A. Koele, "How will international philanthropy be freed from landlocked tax barriers?" [2010] 50 *European Taxation* 9.

[29] Council Directive (EU) 2011/16 on administrative cooperation in the field of taxation (EU Cooperation Directive) [2011], OJ L 64,1.

proposed CCCTB Directive by the recipient body. As a starting point Article 16 (a) of the proposed CCCTB Directive fundamentally accepts the *charitable status* that has been given by the third home state of establishments under its law. The only further requirement is that the charitable body has to be a legal entity with a legal personality. Additionally, Article 16 (b) of the proposed CCCTB Directive defines the term "charitable" very broadly and includes nearly every philanthropic purpose such as religious, environmental or sportive purposes. However, Article 16 (b) of the proposed CCCTB Directive keeps two restrictions: The sole or at least main purpose and activity of the organization has to be one of *public benefit* (general clause). But every purpose mentioned further in Article 16 (b) Proposed CCCTB Directive has to be considered to be of public benefit if a general interest exists. It is quite unclear what this means and what the right perspective is for determining the *general interest*. Is it the general interest of the EU or the interest of the state of establishment? Who is authorized to characterize the nature of the interest?

To make it clearer I would like to introduce an example: a EU taxpayer (a company that has opted for the CCCTB) donates money to a religious (Islamic) body in a Middle East state. The competent EU Member State's principal tax authority (see Article 4 para. 22 of the proposed CCCTB Directive) suspects that the religious body is using the money to finance a campaign to enact the sharia as the official civil and criminal law and to infringe the civil human rights of women. Let us assume that a tax treaty between the EU Member State and the Middle East state exists with a "major" information clause like Article 26 OECD Model 2005. Let us further assume that a poll gives some evidence that the majority of the Middle East state's population is in favour of the introduction of the sharia and a diminished role of women.

From my point of view, the public interest has to be defined on the *basis of EU standards of human rights* and the *separation of state and religion*. Therefore, the competent tax authority has to examine whether the religious activities of the recipient body are in line with fundamental EU rights and values.

Article 16 (c) of the proposed CCCTB Directive requires that the assets of the recipient body are irrevocably dedicated to the furtherance of its purpose. Even this requirement is not as clear as it – prima facie – looks. Does this provision cover organizations that are only collecting gifts to pass them on to other charitable bodies? What purpose is relevant for the decision about the deductibility of the gifts: the purpose of collecting money or the indirectly pursued purpose of the final recipient of the gifts? If the latter is relevant (which is what I would like to propose), how this final recipient body has applied the given funds has to be examined.

Article 16 (d) of the proposed CCCTB Directive requires further the *disclosure* by the charitable body *of the information* regarding its accounts and its activities. The provision leaves open whether the charitable body has to be subject to the disclosure requirements under the national law of the state of establishment or whether it is even possible that the recipient charitable body complies with this requirement voluntarily. In other words: Does this provision assume the applicability of the subject-to-disclosure requirements in other laws or does the EU provision create the disclosure requirement by itself? I think the deduction of the charitable gift cannot depend on the national law of the recipient charitable body if that body fully complies with the EU provision.

6.6 NECESSITY OF AN APPROPRIATE INFORMATION EXCHANGE STANDARD

If Article 63 TFEU compels broadening the scope of the national tax benefits of charitable contributions (like the deduction from the tax base) on a global level, the need for a sufficient control over the international flow of grants becomes vital. When cross-border charitable contributions can flow without measures to effectively control the ultimate destination and use of the funds being considered, this can easily lead to an *abuse of the charitable status*.[30] The first step is to control the *equivalence* of the foreign charitable body (see above section 6.5). This cannot only be a normative equivalency test[31] but must rather be also an equivalency test regarding the practical pursuit of the charitable purpose. The tax-driven mission to safeguard the realization of the philanthropic purpose here meets the on-going fight against money laundering and terrorism financing. Therefore, the tax authorities should be encouraged to share information in the fight against terrorism.[32] Even the OECD has already signalled this problem in its "Report on Abuse of Charities for Money-laundering and Tax Evasion".[33] The report states that tax evasion and tax fraud through the abuse of charities is a serious and increasing risk in

---

30 The view taken by Ineke A. Koele is very clear (footnote 9), 415.

31 Koele, footnote 28, 416.

32 Ibid, 417.

33 *OECD Report*, "Report on Abuse of Charities for Money-laundering and Tax Evasion" (24 February 2009) http://www.oecd.org/dataoecd/30/20/42232037.pdf, accessed 23 July 2012.

many countries although its impact is variable. The OECD recommends several measures to combat the abuse of the charitable status. The *exchange of information* in general plays an important role as well at the information exchange between tax authorities, law enforcement agencies and others in particular.[34] The EU Commission has realized the necessity of a working information exchange system even in the context of the implementation of a CCCTB system. Regarding *cross-border donations within the EU* the competent tax authority can use the means of Council Directive 2011/16/EU on administrative cooperation in the field of taxation.[35] Chapter II Sec. I of the Directive deals with the exchange of information on request:

Article 5 – Procedure

At the request of the requesting authority, the requested authority shall communicate to the requesting authority any information referred to in Article 1 (1) that it has in its possession or that it obtains as a result of administrative enquiries.

Article 6 – Administrative enquiries

1. The requested authority shall arrange for the carrying out of any administrative enquiries necessary to obtain the information referred to in Article 5.
2. The request referred to in Article 5 may contain a reasoned request for a specific administrative enquiry. If the requested authority takes the view that no administrative enquiry is necessary, it shall immediately inform the requesting authority of the reasons thereof.
3. In order to obtain the requested information or to conduct the administrative enquiry requested, the requested authority shall follow the same procedures as it would when acting on its own initiative or at the request of another authority in its own Member State.

Article 7 – Time limits

1. The requested authority shall provide the information referred to in Article 5 as quickly as possible, and no later than six months from the date of receipt of the request. However, where the requested authority is

---

[34] *OECD Report* (footnote 33), listed additional recommendations: Maintenance of a central registry of all suspicious activities to identify and analyse trends; Maintenance of reliable information of the real level of threat, vulnerability and compliance; Implementation of cross-functional teams; implementation of an automated cross-check system; identification and development of relevant data sources; input of "abuse of charities" indicator on suspicious files.

[35] Council Directive (EU) 2011/16 on administrative cooperation in the field of taxation (EU Cooperation Directive) [2011], OJ L 64,1.

already in possession of that information, the information shall be transmitted within two months of that date.

2. In certain special cases, time limits other than those provided for in paragraph 1 may be agreed upon between the requested and the requesting authorities.
3. The requested authority shall confirm immediately and in any event no later than seven working days from receipt, if possible by electronic means, receipt of a request to the requesting authority.
4. Within one month of receipt of the request, the requested authority shall notify the requesting authority of any deficiencies in the request and of the need for any additional background information. In such a case, the time limits provided for in paragraph 1 shall start the day after the requested authority has received the additional information needed.
5. Where the requested authority is unable to respond to the request by the relevant time limit, it shall inform the requesting authority immediately and in any event within three months of the receipt of the request, of the reasons for its failure to do so, and the date by which it considers it might be able to respond.
6. Where the requested authority is not in possession of the requested information and is unable to respond to the request for information or refuses to do so on the grounds provided for in Article 17, it shall inform the requesting authority of the reasons thereof immediately and in any event within one month of receipt of the request.

The conditions governing administrative cooperation are crucial for the quality of the mutual assistance between sovereign states. Article 18 of Directive 2011/16/EU has abolished the bank secrecy from fiscal year 2011 on:

Article 18 – Obligations

1. If information is requested by a Member State in accordance with this Directive, the requested Member State shall use its measures aimed at gathering information to obtain the requested information, even though that Member State may not need such information for its own tax purposes. That obligation is without prejudice to paragraphs 2, 3 and 4 of Article 17, the invocation of which shall in no case be construed as permitting a requested Member State to decline to supply information solely because it has no domestic interest in such information.
2. In no case shall Article 17 (2) and (4) be construed as permitting a requested authority of a Member State to decline to supply information solely because this information is held by a bank, other financial institution, nominee or person acting in an agency or a fiduciary capacity or because it relates to ownership interests in a person.
3. … .

In order to control sufficiently *outbound (external) donations to charitable bodies outside the EU* Article 12 sentence 2 of the proposed CCCTB Directive adapts the EU standard. Gifts to a charitable body established in a third country are only deductible if this country applies an agreement on the exchange of information on request which is comparable to the provisions of Directive 2011/16/EU. If the third country did not conclude such an agreement, the gifts are not deductible. Article 12 sentence 2 CCCTB does not leave any room for a further examination whether the recipient body is a charitable body that individually fulfils the requirements of Article 16 of the proposed CCCTB Directive. The context of Article 12 and Article 16 of the proposed CCCTB Directive offers the following system:

1. Tier: *Abstract requirements* of an existing information exchange agreement and its equivalence to Council Directive 2011/16/EU;
2. Tier: *Concrete requirements* of the quality of the recipient body as a charitable body in the sense of Article 16 of the proposed CCCTB Directive including its factual activities.

Article 12 sentence 2 of the proposed CCCTB Directive has omitted to define the signatory parties to the information exchange agreement. The function of the first-tier precondition is to make an examination of the concrete requirements of the charitable body (second tier) possible in the first place. Taking this into account Article 12 sentence 2 of the proposed CCCTB Directive cannot mean that the third country has simply concluded information exchange agreements with some countries. The right party to the agreement must instead be the *Member State of the principal tax authority* (Article 4 para 22 of the proposed CCCTB Directive), which is competent to examine the deductibility of the gifts to charitable bodies.

Another question is the equivalence of the information agreement. The wording will rarely be exactly the same as the provisions of Council Directive 2011/16/EU. "Comparable" means *essentially similar*. In this sense information exchange clauses which follow Article 26 OECD Model 2005 or Article 5 OECD TIEA Model 2002 are in general similar. The comparison fails if the clause provides only information in tax-treaty conflict cases (the "minor" information clause). This narrow application field is insufficient. Another omission would be if the third country is not obliged to use all its measures which are allowed under its national law to get the requested information. Moreover, the clause is only essentially comparable if it rejects the bank secrecy for purposes of the information exchange as do Article 26 para. 5 OECD Model 2005 or Article 5 para. 4 OECD MA TIEA 2002.

Finally, Article 12 sentence 2 of the proposed CCCTB Directive does not require only a "concluded" information exchange agreement, but furthermore that this agreement of information exchange on request being applied. This means that a signed paper is not sufficient enough. The information agreement has to actually be applied in practice. The benchmark of good practice of an exchange agreement is illustrated by Articles 6 and 7 Council Directive 2011/16/EU cited above. If the tax authority of the third country does not answer requests properly or answers only with a significant time gap in comparison to the standard of Article 7 or if the tax authority of the third country does not use its own lawful means to get the requested information, the concluded information exchange agreement is not being used in practice and is not being applied by the third country. However, if the third country has concluded an information exchange agreement or a "major" information exchange clause as part of a tax treaty, a presumption exists that its tax authority applies these provisions. Therefore, the principal tax authority has to give evidence about its negative experiences with the tax authorities in mutual assistance matters.

6.7 BURDEN OF PROOF UNDER EU CASE LAW

The taxpayer fundamentally bears the burden of proof for the deductibility of the gifts donated to a charitable body. The ECJ has clarified this even in the light of Article 63 TFEU in the *Persche* case:[36] Member States are authorized to require the taxpayer to *provide such proof* as the Member State may consider necessary in order to determine whether the conditions for deducting expenses provided for in the national legislation at issue have been met. Even the existence of a Council directive on administrative cooperation such as Directive 2011/16/EU will not change this burden-of-proof allocation.[37] The ECJ has stated that Council Directive 77/799/EEC does not require the donor's Member State to have recourse to the mechanism of mutual assistance under that directive each

---

36 *Hein Persche v Finanzamt Lüdenscheid* [2009] ECR I-359 Case C-318/07 [54].

37 *Hein Persche v Finanzamt Lüdenscheid* [2009] ECR I-359 Case C-318/07 [57].

time that the information provided by that donor is not sufficient.[38] For tax authorities it is very difficult to effectively oversee the operations of a foreign body, especially in third countries.[39] Therefore, the taxpayer has to bear *a fortiori* the burden of proof for outbound gifts to bodies in third countries.

On the other hand, we have to take into account that the taxpayer has to provide evidence about circumstances in the *sphere of a third person* (the foreign charitable body). In a number of cases it will be nearly impossible for the taxpayer to get detailed information from (and about) the recipient charitable body established in a third country. As a part of the settled case law the ECJ points out the *proportionality principle* in the sense that even any justified restriction of the freedom of capital movement on the grounds of the public interest generally not go beyond what is necessary to attain the objective of the legislation in question.[40] Under this rule, the burden of proof of the taxpayer cannot remain independent of his/her power to get the relevant information, on the one hand, and the power of the tax authority to examine the case by ex officio using the means of information exchange on request (such as Council Directive 2011/16/EU) on the other hand. The proportionality principle calls for sub-principles to balance out the individual freedom of capital movement (Article 63 TFEU) and the public interest in fiscal supervision and the prevention of abuse of a charitable status. An appropriate principle in the law of evidence is the *sphere theory*.[41] The taxpayer has to bring the facts which *are located in his/her sphere* or are obtainable for him/her with reasonable efforts. Beyond this level the tax authority is obliged subsidiarily to use with reasonable efforts ex officio its means to examine the facts including the use of a request for information exchange. If the taxpayer brings all the facts grounded in his/her sphere, the tax authority has to use complementarily all means grounded in its sphere to clarify the relevant facts. Between both measures there is an interdependence which influences the burden of proof. However, this

---

38 *Hein Persche v Finanzamt Lüdenscheid* [2009] ECR I-359 Case C-318/07 [64].

39 Koele, footnote 31, 417.

40 *Centro di Musicologia Walter Stauffer v Finanzamt München für Körperschaften* [2006] ECR I-8203 Case C-386/04 [32]; *Hein Persche v Finanzamt Lüdenscheid* [2009] ECR I-359 Case C-318/07 [41]; *European Commission v Republic of Austria* [2011] Case C-10/10 [29].

41 In the German tax procedure law accepted in the meantime, see Roman Seer in K. Tipke and H.W. Kruse (eds), *Abgabenordnung/Finanzgerichtsordnung* (General Tax Code/Tax Court Code, November 2011), Sec 96FGO para 90 ff.

flexible evidence rule has to give an answer to what happens if, despite all reasonable efforts, neither the taxpayer nor the competent tax authority are able to verify the charitable status and the concrete application of the donated funds. To decide this final case we need a fixed burden-of-proof rule as a *last resort*. The answer is again given by the sphere theory: The taxpayer has to finally bear the burden of proof because he has donated the gift voluntarily to a foreign body and is applying for a tax deduction for his/her benefit. Thus, the taxpayer has to take the final procedural risk.

With this result, the burden of proof system can be viewed as a further precautionary instrument against the abuse of charities. It forces the taxpayer to be careful about the choice of unknown and non-transparent charitable bodies. The recipient charitable body has to immediately be prepared to supply the donor with appropriate information and records about their activities and the application of the donated funds. Articles 12, 14 and 16 of the proposed CCCTB Directive contain the following *evidence steps* by balancing out the individual and public interest under the sphere theory:

1. Business expenses of the company are deductible without limitation (Article 12 sentence 1 of the proposed CCCTB Directive): the character of sponsoring has to be explained by the taxpayer, who bears the burden of proof.
2. A gift to a charitable body is deductible subject to limitations (Article 12 sentence 1 of the proposed CCCTB Directive): the taxpayer has to supply evidence about the character of the recipient body in the sense of Article 16 (a)–(e) of the proposed CCCTB Directive by furnishing the tax authority with its statute, a certificate about its legal personality and charitable status in its home state of establishment and an activity report, including a financial statement of the application of the donated funds.
3. If the non-EU state where the charitable body is established has not concluded an information exchange agreement (or clause) with the EU Member State of the principal tax authority, this competent EU tax authority has to deny the deduction without further examination. If the non-EU state has concluded an information exchange agreement (or clause), but the competent tax authority of the non-EU state does not apply it, the principal tax authority has to deny the deduction of the gifts as well. However, the principal tax authority has to supply the evidence for the non-application of the information exchange agreement (or clause) by the foreign tax authority and bears the burden of proof at this point.

4. Apart from that, the principal tax authority has to verify the documents and statements of the taxpayer. If the principal tax authority is still in doubt about whether the preconditions of Article 16 of the proposed CCCTB Directive have been fulfilled, it has to address a request to the taxpayer to give further information about questions specified by the tax authority. If the request is unspecified, the tax authority has to bear the burden of proof because it can be assumed that it has already received the necessary information.
5. If the taxpayer is unable to give further information outside his/her sphere and even with reasonable efforts he/she is unable to get the requested information from the charitable body, the principal tax authority has to request the competent tax authority in the state of establishment of the charitable body for certain information (use of the information exchange agreement or clause).
6. If the foreign tax authority is not able or not willing to give the requested information in a proper manner, the facts remain unproven. As a last resort the taxpayer has to bear the burden of proof with the consequence of non-deductibility of the gifts.

6.8 SUMMARY

1. Charitable contributions are in general not related to business activities and are acts of profit spending, not of profit realization. The deduction of charitable contributions from the taxable income has to be justified as a tax benefit or tax incentive (social purpose clause) and as an exception to the general net principle.
2. A common justification for the deduction of charitable contributions from taxable income is that the recipient charitable body relieves the state of their governmental (especially social) responsibilities. From this point of view, which fits the idea of subsidiarity, charitable contributions have the character of a tax surrogate.
3. In its settled case law the ECJ has rejected the idea of a national tax surrogate as a justification for the limitation of tax benefits to domestic charitable bodies. The ECJ characterizes such national legislative acts as discrimination or restrictions which violate the freedom of capital movement (Article 63 TFEU). In the eyes of the ECJ the relief of national state social services is a solely budgetary (fiscal) argument which is not capable of justifying any restriction or discrimination in general.

4. Since Article 63 protects not only the capital movement between EU Member States but also between EU Member States and third countries, the tax benefits must also include gifts to charitable bodies established in third countries. This consequence follows the proposed CCCTB Directive by enlarging the scope of deductible gifts by third-country privileged recipients.
5. But the rejection of the national tax surrogate theory leads to reduction of the philanthropic tax benefits in general: the broader the scope of recipient foreign charitable bodies the less the willingness of the national states to keep up tax benefits for charity gifts. Therefore, the proposed CCCTB Directive limits the ceiling of the deduction as a compromise to only 0.5 per cent of the taxable income in the fiscal year. This ceiling is far below the common ceilings of the national tax codes of most EU Member States.
6. Notwithstanding, case law of the ECJ mentioned under section 6.3, the tax surrogate theory is still sensible: The further the distance between the Member State's society and the foreign charitable bodies and their purpose the less the responsibility of the Member State to grant tax benefits for contributions to this charitable body. This correlation leads to a distinction between EU charitable bodies and charitable bodies established in third countries at least on the level of fiscal supervision.
7. When cross-border charitable contributions can flow without effectively controlling the ultimate destination and use of the funds, this can trigger an abuse of the charitable status. In line with the case law of the ECJ fiscal supervision is an important public interest. Therefore, Articles 12 and 16 of the proposed CCCTB Directive recommend controlling the equivalence of the charitable bodies established in a third country not only on the basis of written statutes, but also on the grounds of their factual activities. Their sole or at least main purpose and activity has to be one of public interest in the sense of EU standards of human rights, democracy and the separation of state and religion. Furthermore, the equivalence test requires a disclosure of the information regarding the accounts and activities of the charitable body.
8. As the main element of fiscal supervision Article 12 sentence 2 of the proposed CCCTB Directive requires the existence of a structurally guaranteed information exchange by the third country where the charitable body is established. The provision sets the new Council Directive 2011/16/EU as a benchmark. On the abstract (normative) level the third country has to conclude an information exchange agreement with the EU Member State of the principal tax

authority which is essentially similar to Article 26 OECD Model 2005 or Article 5 OECD TIEA Model 2002. This minimum standard will not be met only by "minor" information clauses or "major" information clauses which keep the bank secrecy as an obstacle to the supply of information. On the level of concrete application of the information exchange provisions the information exchange policy of the third state must tie in with the good practice which is illustrated in Articles 6 and 7 Council Directive 2010/16/EU.

9. ECJ case law accepts that the taxpayer bears the burden of proof for the deductibility of gifts donated to charitable bodies in general. For the tax authorities it is very difficult to effectively oversee the operations of a foreign body, especially one located in a third country. Therefore, the taxpayer has to bear *a fortiori* the burden of proof for outbound gifts to bodies in third countries. However, under the proportionality principle the burden of proof has to be balanced out between the individual freedom of capital movement (Article 63 TFEU) and the public interest in fiscal supervision. An appropriate principle to achieve this is the sphere theory: The taxpayer has to present the facts which are located in his/her sphere or are obtainable for him/her with reasonable efforts. Beyond this level, the tax authority is obliged subsidiarily to use its means to examine the facts ex officio with reasonable efforts, including the use of a request on information exchange.
10. According to these findings, a burden of proof system can be seen as a further precautionary instrument against the abuse of charities. Combined with the sphere theory, Articles 12, 14 and 16 of the proposed CCCTB Directive provide six evidentiary steps by balancing out the individual and public interest. They are listed above under section 6.7.

Commentary

Mitchell A. Kane

Professor Seer has provided in his chapter a thorough examination of the question of deductibility of gifts to charitable bodies in third countries under the proposed Council directive regarding a common consolidated corporate tax base. There are two features of the proposed directive's treatment of this issue which are particularly worthy of note. First, donations to charitable bodies in third countries are deductible essentially on the same terms as donations to charitable bodies in Member States, at least where certain informational requirements are met. This commentary will refer to this feature as the "parity" provision. Second, donations to charitable bodies (in both Member States and third countries) are deductible only up to 0.5 per cent of revenues for a taxable year. This commentary will refer to this feature as the "cap" provision. Interestingly, this cap appears to be substantially lower than analogous caps under the national laws of various Member States. For example, some countries, such as the United Kingdom, apply no cap at all. German law likewise presents a notable contrast to the proposed directive. Specifically, Germany applies a cap under a sort of split-rule, according to which the cap on deductibility is set at the higher of 20 per cent of net income or 0.4 per cent of gross revenues plus payroll. Presumably the German reference to a gross base, in addition to a net base, is meant to allow space for deductibility of fixed contributions in years where a company has low net income, or even a loss. Germany also allows a carry-forward of any disallowed deductions under the cap.[42] By contrast, the cap under the proposed directive refers only to a revenue base and has no carry-forward provision.[43] The likely consequence of this is that in medium to high profit years the proposed directive could very likely set the cap at a rate well below that under the national law of Member States

[42] Körperschaftsteuergesetz, § 9(1) Nr. 2.

[43] I thank Erik Röder for calling my attention to these distinctions between German law and the approach under the proposed directive.

such as Germany that permit calculation of a cap on a net basis at relatively higher rates.

In light of the basic parity approach under the proposed directive, it would be unwise to analyse the issue of donations to third-country charitable bodies in isolation. Rather, a full understanding of the proposed directive's treatment of the third-country case is best developed within the scope of an analysis that considers the broader issue of donations to charitable bodies formed in any state outside that of the transferor, whether a Member State or a third country. This is precisely the tack that Professor Seer has followed in his chapter, which places the analysis of donations to charitable bodies in third countries within the context of a general discussion of the following issues: the overall character of charitable donations as business expenses or not; the justification for deductibility of charitable donations to the extent they are not business expenses; and the ECJ jurisprudence on the deductibility of charitable donations to organizations in other countries.

Professor Seer reaches the following conclusions on these three matters. First, he finds that charitable donations are generally not to be considered business expenses. Second, he takes the deduction of charitable donations to be justified in certain cases, notwithstanding the fact that they are not business expenses, on the grounds of a tax surrogate theory. That is, to the extent that the charitable body performs functions which relieve the sovereign of its obligations, then such donations function as tax surrogates and ought to be removed from the tax base. To the extent the body does not relieve the sovereign of its obligations, then the above-stated justification fails and the donation should not be deductible.[44] Given the rationale underlying the tax surrogate theory, it is not surprising that national legislation has tended to afford deductions only in

---

[44] Professor Seer notes an alternate possibility, which is that the donation be deductible in order to encourage the altruistic activity of citizens, regardless of relieving the sovereign of obligations. See Roman Seer, "Deductibility of Gifts to Charitable Bodies in Third Countries". Others have explored further ways in which one might seek to justify a charitable deduction. For example, the charitable deduction may empower minorities that are otherwise under-represented in the political process or may offer incentives for private actors to monitor non-profits. See David Schizer, "Subsidizing Charitable Contributions, Incentives, Information and the Private Pursuit of Public Goals", (2009) 62 *International Tax Law Review* 221. In this commentary I will focus on the surrogate theory, however, both because it forms a crucial part of Professor Seer's analysis and because it would seem to form a part of the justification for the deduction, regardless of the merits of these alternate possibilities.

the case of donations to bodies internal to the state.[45] In other words, although sovereigns sometimes undertake obligations that are to be fulfilled in third countries, this is the exception rather than the rule. At the very least, it is to be expected that a donation to a third-country charitable body will relieve the sovereign of fewer obligations than a donation to a like organization in the home country. Third, the ECJ jurisprudence on these matters, chiefly the *Hein Persche* case, has required that to the extent a Member State allows deductibility of charitable donations at all, it must do so in a non-discriminatory way that does not impede the free movement of capital under Article 63 TFEU.[46] Thus, Member States must allow deductibility for transfers to internal bodies and bodies organized in another Member State on equal terms. The basis for this decision is that limiting deductibility to internal bodies serves only a revenue preservation function and as such cannot justify an incursion on the fundamental freedoms. Professor Seer finds an inevitable tension here. The tax surrogate theory survives as the best justification for charitable donation deductions, notwithstanding the ECJ's jurisprudence. Thus, the theory that undergirds the national legislation in the first place is at odds with the result under ECJ decisions that such national legislation be applied in a non-discriminatory fashion.

Based on these conclusions Professor Seer suggests that the approach to charitable donations under the proposed directive should best be understood as a "compromise". The first feature mentioned above, parity, is to be understood as flowing from the ECJ jurisprudence. Because the *Persche* case is based on Article 63 TFEU, which also applies in the case of capital movements to third countries, it follows that the principle articulated therein likewise applies to donations to organizations in third countries. But the second feature mentioned above, the cap (at a level lower than many national provisions), is to be understood as a concession to the implications of the tax surrogate theory. That is, unlimited deductibility or fairly high caps on deductibility under national law, as applied to donations to foreign bodies, cannot be justified under a tax surrogate theory. Moreover, for amounts that are deductible (that is, amounts under the cap) it becomes particularly important that the Member State be able to confirm that the foreign body is directing the funds to beneficial uses. At the very least, a deduction ought not to

---

45 The other chief way in which national legislation could seek to limit deductibility to cases in which there is a meaningful relief of the sovereign's obligation is through the substantive standards governing what constitutes a "charitable" body in the first place.

46 *Hein Persche v Finanzamt Lüdenscheid* [2009] ECR I-359 Case C-318/07.

follow in cases where the funds are put to uses that represent interests adverse to the Member State, as would be the case, for example, with funding of terrorist activities. Deductibility in such a case would indeed represent a true perversion of the tax surrogate theory. This is the basic function of the proposed directive's insistence on meaningful information exchange with third countries as a pre-requisite to deductibility (under Article 12) and specification of what counts as a "charitable body" (under Article 16). Under Professor Seer's "compromise" explanation of the proposed directive's treatment of charitable donations, the bulk of the interpretive and pragmatic questions would arise regarding the issues of whether an exchange of information agreement is sufficient and in the interpretation of the term "charitable body". These issues are accordingly developed in detail in the latter half of his chapter.

Professor Seer's reading of the proposed directive's treatment of this issue is highly plausible. For purposes of this comment, though, a couple of alternate possibilities are suggested. It is intended to focus on two particular issues. The first relates to the issue whether donations to charitable bodies can be considered to be business expenses. It is suggested that this issue raises the prospect of additional interpretive complexities under the proposed directive, in addition to the issues related to information exchange and the proper scope of the term "charitable body". The second issue relates to Professor Seer's depiction of the 0.5 per cent cap as a compromise provision which takes account of the ECJ jurisprudence, while also paying heed to the tax surrogate theory. This analysis is going to be built upon below, placing it more fully within the context of the operation of the CCCTB, considering especially the fiscal impact of deductibility under the proposal's allocation formula and the nature of reciprocal incentives regarding cross-border contributions to charitable bodies. The suggestion will be that once the broader operation of the CCCTB under the proposed directive is considered, the case for a cap on deductibility regarding donations to charitable bodies in Member States and the case for a cap with respect to third countries stands on quite different grounds. It is by no means clear, even under a tax surrogate theory, that the cap should be set the same in the two cases. This analysis thus calls into question both the parity and cap features of the proposed directive on this matter.

CONTRIBUTIONS AS BUSINESS EXPENSES: A PROBLEM OF INTERPRETATION

Professor Seer takes a strong position that charitable donations made by firms not be considered business expenses. This underlies the basic chain of argument leading to his "compromise" interpretation of the proposed directive. That is, because the expenses are not business expenses, their deductibility must be independently justified. The best justification is the tax surrogate theory, which runs into trouble in the case of cross-border transfers, notwithstanding the ECJ stance on the matter.

It is suggested, however, that one should consider the consequences that follow from an acknowledgment that at least some transfers from firms to charitable bodies appropriately constitute deductible business expenses. Surely one can come up with extreme cases where this claim is compelling. For example if one considers a Member State firm that enters into business in a third country for the very first time. The management of the firm has no personal connection or history with the jurisdiction. It is supposed that the firm undertakes some environmentally sensitive operation, such as construction of a factory on land adjacent to a protected habitat. Simultaneously the firm makes contributions to a local environmental non-profit organization, heavily publicizing the contribution. It is difficult to see how this is much different than straightforward deductible expenses in the category of advertising.[47] It is ultimately an empirical question what proportion of transfers to charitable bodies are of this type and what proportion are better characterized as essentially personal charitable contributions of firm managers. Even so, once the category of business expense contributions is admitted at all, a difficult interpretive quandary under the proposed directive is going to be faced. Specifically, to the extent contributions are of this type, are they subject to the cap or not? The relevant provisions here appear in Articles 12 and 14 of the proposed directive:

---

47 The author does not read Professor Seer's chapter as rejecting this sort of characterization. For example, he specifically states, "Only if the donations are part of a sponsoring campaign, especially to improve the image of the company, can they be treated as expense intended to obtain or secure income." Having acknowledged this possibility, though, the chapter does not further analyse potential interpretive ambiguities under Articles 12 and 14 of the proposed directive.

Article 12 – Deductible Expenses

Deductible expenses shall include all costs of sales and expenses net of deductible value added tax incurred by the taxpayer with a view of obtaining or securing income, including costs of research and development and costs incurred in raising equity or debt for the purposes of the business.

Deductible expenses shall also include gifts to charitable bodies as defined in Art. 16 which are established in a Member State or in a third country which applies an agreement on the exchange of information on request comparable to provisions of Directive 2011/16/EU. The maximum deductible expense for monetary gifts or donations to charitable bodies shall be 0,5% of revenues in the tax year.

Article 14 – Non-deductible expenses

The following expenses shall be treated as non-deductible:...

(h) monetary gifts and donations other than those made to charitable bodies as defined in Article 16; ...

There are two plausible interpretations. First, transfers to charitable bodies that can be independently characterized as business expenses could be deductible without limit under the first paragraph of Article 12. Second, transfers to charitable bodies could be deductible only up to the cap under the second paragraph of Article 12, regardless of their character as independent business expenses. This issue is not easily resolvable based on the existing text. The text could be read to favour the second interpretation, as the last sentence of the second paragraph seems to apply the cap in unqualified terms to any "monetary gifts or donations to charitable bodies". Alternatively, one could read that sentence to be inapplicable, either on the grounds that it qualifies only the first sentence of the second paragraph of Article 12 or that the relevant transfers here are neither "monetary gifts" nor "donations" based on their character as business expenses. Article 14(h) does not resolve this one way or the other. That provision applies an absolute disallowance of a deduction in cases where the recipient of a transfer fails to constitute a "charitable body". In all cases where the transferee *does* satisfy the Article 16 requirements, the above ambiguity remains.

In terms of justification, it would seem that the better answer here is that such transfers should be deductible without limit, as they do not present the issues that would justify a cap in the first place (namely, inapplicability of a tax surrogate theory). Cutting in the other direction, though, is an administrative concern. If it is difficult for administrators to distinguish the two types of charitable contribution, as I predict it would be, then this provides a sound reason for applying the cap across the board. Indeed, although a extreme case was presented in the text above, it is believed that the business expense issue is in fact pervasive across a range of transfers. Even if the primary purpose of a charitable donation is to further the donative interests of firm managers, it might be possible in many cases for the firm to suggest the donation *also* improved its reputation and was taken at least in part "with a view of obtaining or securing income". If so, then under the first interpretation offered above this would lead to the conclusion that a single transfer should be split, with some portion deductible without limit and some other portion subject to the cap. This raises administrative challenges that may best be avoided, pointing in the direction of an across-the-board cap as under the second interpretation.

PARITY AND THE CAP: A PROBLEM OF JUSTIFICATION

This comment began with the observation that the two noteworthy features of the proposed directive's approach to charitable donations are (i) parity of treatment for donations to organizations in Member States and third countries and (ii) the relatively low overall cap on deductibility of such contributions as compared to domestic law. In the following, the justification for these features shall be elaborated. Professor Seer's "compromise" interpretation of the proposed directive is one way of approaching this justificatory issue. As I understand this interpretation, parity arises on the basis of the existing ECJ jurisprudence and the cap is understood to satisfy in part the fact that sizable deductions are not warranted where the tax surrogate theory does not really apply. Although the word "compromise" connotes something of a second-best solution, I would suggest initially that Professor Seer's interpretation could be extended on its own terms to justify both of these two features as flowing from a tax surrogate theory of charitable deductions.

First, a parity result would follow from the fact that under the tax surrogate theory a deduction should be denied full stop whenever the funds are ultimately used on matters that would not have plausibly been funded by the sovereign contemplating a deduction. From this standpoint it would seem that Member States and third countries stand largely in the same position. Sovereigns generally do not raise taxes and then pay for services from their central budget where those services arise within the geographic scope of foreign states, regardless whether the foreign state is part of a common economic union or not. At one point, Professor Seer raises a different possibility, stating: "The further the distance between the Member State's society and the foreign charitable body and its purpose, the less the responsibility of the Member State to grant a tax benefit for contributions to this charitable body."[48] This language possibly suggests some type of continuity analysis, wherein the tax surrogate theory applies best within a single country, then second best in Member States, and worst of all in third countries. But Professor Seer does not really develop that line of argument, stating in the next sentence: "This points out the necessity to distinguish between EU-charitable bodies and charitable bodies established in third countries on the level and intensity of fiscal supervision."[49] In other words, the chief disparity between Member States and third countries is about information and supervision. The task there is to ensure that the body in receipt of a donation is in fact doing something in the public interest broadly construed. That task is *not* to ensure, though, that the charitable body is actually spending funds on an activity that the sovereign granting the deduction would have otherwise funded.

Second, the cap result could be justified on the grounds that countries do sometimes fund services in foreign territories. Even though this is the exception rather than the rule, it does happen. But because it is relatively rare, the amount should be low. This point reflects the basic qualm of Professor Seer with the ECJ jurisprudence. The extension of existing national caps to the foreign situation would seem too generous under the tax surrogate theory and the proposed directive corrects the matter.[50]

Although these points would seem to provide a basic justification for the parity and cap aspects of Article 12 of the proposed directive, they do not seem to take full account of the operation of the CCCTB more generally. To see how this would play out, it will be useful to consider both the fiscal impacts and donors' incentives for transfers to Member State charitable organizations and third-country charitable organizations under current law versus the case contemplated under the proposed directive.

---

48 See Seer, footnote 44, p. 13.

49 Ibid, p. 13.

50 Note, of course, that there are limits to how much a directive governing corporate taxation can resolve an issue that also relates to the individual sphere. Even with a cap in place, as under the proposed directive, a firm could make a taxable distribution of profit to an individual shareholder, who in turn makes a donation to a foreign charitable body. That sort of donation would simply be analysed under national law and existing ECJ jurisprudence. It would very likely, then, be deductible on more favourable terms than under the proposed directive.

One should consider the contributions from a Member State company to a charitable body in another Member State first. Under existing jurisprudence where a company in Member State A makes a contribution to a charitable organization in Member State B, Member State A must grant deductibility on the same terms as would be permitted for a wholly domestic transfer. For the sake of analysis, suppose that Member State A does permit deductibility up to some cap. Two important consequences follow. First, the fiscal cost of granting the deduction would be borne wholly by Member State A. As discussed above, this is generally inconsistent with the tax surrogate theory of charitable contributions. Second, the operation of ECJ jurisprudence here ensures that on transfers from a Member State B company to a Member State A charitable body deductibility is *also* required from the Member State B tax base to the extent that such deduction would follow for an internal transfer. This second aspect cuts against, perhaps substantially, the possible tension between ECJ jurisprudence and the tax surrogate theory. In other words, the ECJ jurisprudence requires deductibility for transfers inconsistent with the tax surrogate theory but it does so on a *reciprocal* basis. It is true that we get inducement of transfers from Member State A firms to Member State B charitable bodies, even though the former may not be relieved of any governmental obligation by virtue of the transfer. But there is also inducement of financial flows in the opposite direction, from Member State B firms to Member State A charitable bodies. It should be noted, however, that under current arrangements these counterbalancing incentives are unlikely to be of equal magnitude. Most relevantly, the marginal rates in Member State A and Member State B may well be different, leading to different value for the deduction. Additionally, Member State A and Member State B may apply different caps. Thus, to the extent that firms hit the relevant cap, the incentivizing deduction is no longer available. The fact that this may kick in at different levels can be expected to differentially incentivize charitable contributions. This will especially be the case where a jurisdiction simply disallows, as is permissible under ECJ jurisprudence, all charitable contribution deductions (applying, effectively, a cap of zero).

Matters look importantly different in a CCCTB world. If one considers the two points of fiscal impact and reciprocal incentives mentioned above: first, under the CCCTB it would no longer be the case that the fiscal cost of the deduction would be borne entirely by the Member State where the company is organized. Rather, the fiscal impact of this would be determined under the allocation formula (except in the case of a purely domestic company that opts for the CCCTB). Second, there would no longer be as substantial an issue of *differential* incentives as under current law. Regarding divergences in different national level caps on deductibility this follows from the fact that the proposed directive would apply the unified cap of 0.5 per cent for all companies. Regarding divergences in marginal rates this follows from the fact that fiscal impact is no longer determined by the marginal rate of the transferor's jurisdiction. If Member State A and Member State B from above are compared hypothetically, different marginal rates across A and B need not differentially incentivize charitable contributions into those two jurisdictions because, again, the fiscal impact is determined under the CCCTB allocation formula. Marginal rates would continue to differ across Member States, of course, but this would not systematically bias cross-border charitable donations as under the status quo. At this point, a return to the hypothetical of Member State A and Member State B shall be made. It is assumed that these two states have different marginal rates. Under the CCCTB, the magnitude of the incentive for a charitable donation from Member State A firm to Member State B charitable body and the magnitude of the incentive for a donation running in the opposite direction would become more and more equal as the allocation factors for the two firms became more and more equal. At the extreme, where the allocation factors are identical, the donations would be equally incentivized, notwithstanding the differential marginal rates across Member State A and Member State B (or, for that matter, differential marginal rates across the rest of the European Union).

The bottom line with Member State to Member State transfers is that there is a compelling reason to have a harmonized approach to the deductibility of payments originating from different Member State firms. This would seem to increase the chance of reciprocal transfers, as compared to the incentives under current law. However, identifying a compelling reason why such harmonization should be achieved through a cap (and especially a low cap relative to national law) is more difficult. After all, one could also achieve a harmonized approach with *no* cap. Essentially, under the operation of the CCCTB the failure of the tax surrogate theory is not nearly as relevant as under current law. Thus, the argument produced above – that a *low* cap partially reinstates a tax surrogate theory under current ECJ jurisprudence which is hostile to it – applies with much less force. A *low* cap here seems to stand in need of further justification.

The analysis of transfers from Member State firms to third-country charitable bodies looks rather different. Under existing law, the fiscal impact of a deduction is borne entirely by the Member State granting the deduction. Unlike the Member State-Member State case, however, there is *no* legal mechanism to push in the direction of reciprocal flows. The third country is not governed by the ECJ jurisprudence and thus need not offer deductibility on payments from its firms to Member State charitable bodies at all. Indeed, in many cases deductibility will be denied in such circumstances. Under the CCCTB, the fiscal impact of granting the deduction will now be shared across Member States according to the formula. Bolstering the tax surrogate theory here would require offsetting incentives for charitable contributions from the third country to the Member States. But there is no such mechanism for this because the third country is not within the scope of the CCCTB or ECJ jurisprudence. Here a low cap seems perfectly justified under the basic argument set out above. This is a case where the tax surrogate theory breaks down. One might even suggest, on these grounds, that the cap should be set at zero with respect to third countries. The two immediate objections to this, however, are that it may seem too far out of line with ECJ jurisprudence and that reciprocal incentives are in fact likely greater than zero to the extent that the third country permits deductibility on transfers to internal organizations which then go on to deploy funds in Member States.

CONCLUSION

This commentary raised two specific issues that would seem to warrant further discussion and investigation. First, as an interpretive matter the proposed directive is indeterminate regarding the proper application of the cap on deductibility of contributions to charitable bodies where such transfers arguably constitute independent business expenses. Second, as a justificatory matter the application of a uniform low cap on deductibility in the case of both donations to Member States and third countries is problematic. The approach of the proposed directive can be understood as a compromise between the ECJ jurisprudence on the issue and the continuing vitality of the tax surrogate theory. The difficulty, however, is that under the operation of the CCCTB generally, the tax surrogate theory would seem to hold greater continuing validity for transfers to Member State charitable bodies than to third-state charitable bodies. This would point in the direction of different approaches to the cap, but for the fact that this collides with the ECJ's interpretation of Article 63 TFEU. If parity is demanded by that jurisprudence but the caps should in principle be set at different levels under the basic theory underlying the national provisions, the difficult question that remains is the best absolute level at which to set a uniform cap.

7. Transfer of assets to third countries

Daniel Gutmann

7.1 RELEVANCE OF THE TOPIC

The transfer of assets between a head office (HO) to and from a permanent establishment (PE) of the same company is a standard practice of business life. From a "traditional" income tax perspective, such a transfer triggers numerous questions: how this transfer should be dealt with from a transfer pricing perspective; how it affects the allocation of profits to the PE; to what extent and under which conditions (including timing conditions) such a transfer should be considered to be a sale and, consequently, a taxable capital gain.

The latter issue is probably the most sensitive one, as it goes without saying that the state where the asset was originally located may well lose its taxing right on future capital gains on said assets. It may therefore be tempted to exercise its taxing power immediately upon the transfer, which is also a good way to deter companies from relocating their high-value intangibles in low-tax countries.

Comparative law shows a great diversity in the way countries treat transfers of assets to/from HO to PE.[1] This is probably why the OECD Model does not directly deal with all these issues. Only the Commentary do so, by stating that exit taxation is not incompatible as such with the Model. The Commentary on Article 7 provides that:

> there may be a realization of a taxable profit when an asset, whether or not trading stock, forming part of the business property of a PE situated within a State's territory is transferred to a PE or the HO of the same enterprise situated in another State. Article 7 allows the former State to tax profits deemed to arise in connection with such a transfer (para. 21).

Along the same line, the Commentary on Article 13 provides that:

---

[1] IFA, The attribution of profits to permanent establishments, Cahiers de droit fiscal international, Vol. 91b, subject II, 2006.

> in some States the transfer of an asset from a PE situated in the territory of such State to a PE or the HO of the same enterprise situated in another State is assimilated to an alienation of property. The Article does not prevent these States from taxing profits of gains deemed to arise in connection with such a transfer, provided, however, that such taxation is in accordance with Article 7 (para. 10).

Under the system of the CCCTB, the internal transfer of assets raises both classical and new issues. Classically, the geographical move of the assets triggers problems relating to the allocation of profits to the PE and transfer pricing.

There is however more at stake:

- first of all, where an asset is transferred outside the "CCCTB area" (which is here defined as the perimeter of the entities which fall within the scope of the CCCTB), such a transfer entails a potential risk of circumvention of the apportionment formula which, as is known, takes assets into account together with sales and labour. Internal transfers of assets may therefore harm the interests of the country where the assets were located before the transfer. It should be observed, though, that such an abuse of the apportionment formula is not specific to transfers of assets to third countries and may well exist in the case of transfer of assets within the CCCTB area;
- secondly, internal transfers of assets may have the effect of excluding income generated by these assets from the consolidated tax base. It is therefore not only the country of origin whose interests are harmed; more generally, all the CCCTB countries where the group is established lose tax revenue because of this transfer of assets. This collective loss of revenue is specifically entailed by transfer of assets to HO or PE situated in third countries.

This accumulation of both an individual and a collective harmful effect of internal transfers of assets probably explains why Article 31 of the EC Proposal of 16 March 2011 for a Common Consolidated Corporate Tax Base (hereafter "the Proposal") prevents internal transfers of assets by establishing an exit tax provision which is worded in the following way:

> 1. The transfer of a fixed asset by a resident taxpayer to its permanent establishment in a third country shall be deemed to be a disposal of the asset for the purpose of calculating the tax base of a resident taxpayer in relation to the tax year of the transfer. The transfer of a fixed asset by a

non resident taxpayer from its permanent establishment in a Member State to a third country shall also be deemed to be a disposal of the asset.

2. Paragraph 1 shall not apply where the third country is party to the European Economic Area Agreement and there is an agreement on the exchange of information between that third country and the Member State of the resident taxpayer or of the permanent establishment, comparable to Directive 2011/16/EU.

This rather strong reaction against transfers of assets to a third country raises a number of interesting questions which I will try to assess in this chapter:

- is exit taxation really necessary?
- which third countries should be excluded from the exit tax?
- which transfers are concerned by the exit tax?
- how is the transfer of asset taxed?

7.2 IS EXIT TAXATION REALLY NECESSARY?

The mechanism of an exit tax consists in exercising a taxing right where it appears that a transfer (either of residence of a person or of the location of an asset) will end up depriving the state of origin from its taxing right in the future. The rationale for taxing the transfer of assets to a third country should therefore be the assumption that said transfer will necessarily entail a loss of revenue for the country of origin and for the CCCTB countries where the group is established.

However, this assumption is not always correct. As the Swedish reporter showed in his contribution to the IFA volume on attribution of profits to PEs,[2] a state which provides for worldwide taxation of resident companies does not lose its taxing right where an asset is transferred to a PE in a third country, where (i) there is no double tax treaty in force between the state of the HO and the state of the PE, or (ii) there is a double tax treaty providing for an imputation system. The situation is different, of course, where a different method applies to eliminate double taxation or where an asset is transferred from a PE in the source country to the HO in another country.

What is the situation under the Proposal? According to Article 6.6 of the Proposal, "a company resident in a Member State which opts for the system provided for by this Directive shall be subject to corporate tax

---

[2] K. von Uthmann, Cahiers de droit fiscal international (see note 1) 617.

under that system on all income derived from any source, whether inside or outside its Member State of residence". However, Article 11, (e) of the Proposal provides for the exemption of income of PEs situated in third countries. At first sight, the mechanism of exit taxation is therefore fully justified insofar as assets transferred outside the "CCCTB area" are no longer taxable in the CCCTB area.

A second look nevertheless leads to a more complex approach. Indeed, in some situations, the exemption method provided for by Article 11, (e) is set aside in order to protect the consolidated tax base. A "switch-over" mechanism indeed applies where the foreign PE is situated in a country where it is the subject to a substantially lower level of taxation.[3] In these cases, the CCCTB area is "extended" to third countries, with the result that the revenue risks associated with these assets are not logically comparable to the risks which exist where the asset is outside the scope of the CCCTB system. One may therefore wonder whether the Proposal is consistent with itself where it establishes a systematic principle of exit taxation while it is not always necessary to go that far. We will see in section 7.5 hereunder that this might prove to have an effect on the compatibility of the Proposal with the freedom of capital movement.

Another layer of complexity stems from the fact that the switch-over clause must be combined with existing or future double tax treaties concluded with third countries. Whether the switch-over clause will actually apply where it conflicts with tax treaties is still unclear at this stage. It must indeed be observed that the Room Document established by the European Commission on "transactions and dealings between the group and entities outside the group" provides that:

> agreements between Member States and third countries concluded before the CCCTB enters into force shall not be affected by conflicting common rules, in other words, existing DTCs with third countries will take precedence over any conflicting CCCTB rules. For example, if switch over from exemption to credit is not foreseen under a DTC with a third country (because double taxation is relieved by exemption), then this "CCCTB" rule will not be applied in the context of that DTC. Member States would be expected to undertake the necessary steps to generally align their existing international agreements with the Directive to remove these differences.[4]

---

[3] Proposal for a Council Directive on a Common Consolidated Corporate Tax Base (CCCTB) COM(2011) 121/4. Art. 73.

[4] European Commission, Working Document "Room Document of 1 September 2010", CCCTB\RD\003\doc\en, para. 9.

If this way of treating conflicts between tax treaties and the CCCTB Directive is eventually adopted, then a fairly tricky situation may arise: while some internal transfers will effectively entail a loss of the state of origin's taxing right (where the applicable tax treaty will provide for exemption), some other internal transfers will not (where the CCCTB approach prevails as a consequence of the adaptation of the treaty with the third country).

7.3 WHICH THIRD COUNTRIES SHOULD BE EXCLUDED FROM THE EXIT TAX?

A third country is a country which is not a Member State. This holds true even in the likely event that some Member States decide not to join the CCCTB approach and only enhanced cooperation takes place for the purpose of implementing the CCCTB. It is worth mentioning, therefore, that Article 31 is absolutely silent regarding the potentially realistic situation where an internal transfer of assets takes place in favour of a PE/HO situated in a Member State which is not implementing the CCCTB. This should certainly be corrected at a later stage.

This being said, one must recall that Article 31 provides for a distinction between several categories of third country: (i) those which are a party to the European Economic Area Agreement and with which there is an agreement on the exchange of information, comparable to Directive 2011/16/EU and (ii) all other third countries.

Why is that so? The answer is to be found in the implicit assumption that the transfer of assets to a PE in a third country must be examined from the sole perspective of the freedom of establishment. This approach seems to be a reversal of the earlier point of view of the Commission. The Commission did indeed state in 2006 that an immediate collection of tax at the moment of transfer of such assets constitutes a restriction on the free movement of capital unless there is a lack of cooperation between the country of origin and the country where the asset is located after the transfer.[5]

However, from a theoretical perspective, it is not all obvious why an internal transfer of assets should necessarily be considered a mere attribute of the freedom of establishment. Besides, even if we assume that

[5] European Commission, Working Paper "Communication to the Council, the European Parliament and the European Economic and Social Committee, Exit taxation and the need for co-ordination of Member States' tax policies", COM (2006) 825 final, para. 5.

internal transfer of assets should fall within the scope of the freedom of establishment, it remains that the EU could perfectly decide to provide for a tax deferral on assets transferred to third countries with which tax treaties exist and allow the country of origin to maintain its taxing right.

Against this background, Article 31.2 of the Proposal should, in my view, be corrected in two ways:

- there is no reason why the transfer of assets to countries which are *not* a party to the EEA should give rise to exit tax if a mutual assistance procedure comparable to that organized by European Directives exists. If one accepts that Article 64 TFEU is relevant, it must apply with all third countries beyond the EEA. This conclusion is supported by the case law of the European Court of Justice.[6]
- on the other hand, the Proposal could reinforce the difference between cooperative third countries and non-cooperative third countries by requiring the first ones, not only to exchange information as under Directive 2011/16/EU, but also to provide assistance in the field of recovery of claims.

To make this latter suggestion clear, it is essential to say that it relies on an implicit assumption regarding the combination between para. 1 and para. 2 of Article 31: if the proper interpretation of the current version of Article 31 is that exit taxation takes place immediately for transfers of assets to non-cooperative third countries, while a deferral (but not a full exemption of hidden reserves at the date of the transfer[7]) is granted for transfers of assets to cooperative third countries, then it would be justified for the state of origin to subject this deferral to the condition that the other country not only provides information regarding the life of this asset (in particular, whether it has been sold or transferred to yet another country) but also assistance regarding the recovery of the claim. If no such assistance is required, then the rights of the country of origin could not be properly protected after the transfer.

---

6 Haribo Lakritzen Hans Riegel BetriebsgmbH, C-436/08 and Österreichische Salinen AG, C-437/08.

7 Should Art. 31.2 be interpreted as granting a final exemption of the transfer, it would certainly be peculiar to subject such an exemption to the existence of exchange of information, as B. Wiman rightly points out ("Business reorganizations within the group", in D. Weber (ed.) (2012), *CCCTB: Selected Issues*, Conference held in Amsterdam, 10–11 June 2011.

7.4 WHICH TRANSFER IS CONCERNED?

7.4.1 An Outbound Transfer

Article 31 of the Proposal deals with outbound transfers only. It establishes an exit tax where the asset is transferred from (i) a HO in a CCCTB country to a PE in a third country, or (ii) from a PE in a CCCTB country to any entity (either a HO or any other company) in a third country. Article 31 is silent on the reverse hypothesis of an inbound transfer from (i) a HO in a third country to a PE in a CCCTB country or (ii) a PE in a third country to a HO or another PE in a CCCTB country. This may probably be explained by the fact that an inbound transfer does not trigger any revenue risk for the states. Another explanation seems to be that including an inbound taxation rule in the CCCTB Directive providing for a step-up would create a distortion in countries which do not normally provide for such a step-up in their domestic legislation.[8] It is, however, too bad that the Proposal does not take this opportunity to provide for a clear rule governing the way assets should be valued in this circumstance.

7.4.2 A Transfer of a Fixed Asset

7.4.2.1 A "transfer"

The concept of "transfer" is not defined in the Proposal. The triggering event for exit taxation therefore remains unclear.

Most probably, the concept of transfer refers to a change in the attribution of economic ownership. This statement is justified by the idea, which is explicit in Article 93 of the Proposal, that an asset should in principle be included in the asset factor of its economic owner. More clarity would, however, be welcome, notwithstanding the fact that the Proposal, in accordance with Article 290 TFEU, already grants the Commission the power to lay down rules on the definition of legal and economic ownership in relation to leased assets.

Along the same lines, one would expect the Proposal to provide some clarity on the duration element of the concept of "transfer". Must a transfer necessarily be final? Would a temporary transfer qualify as a "transfer"? According to which criteria should one distinguish between

---

[8] Whether this explanation is fully convincing may be discussed, as this distortion may be eliminated by Member States through a reform of their domestic rule on inbound transfers.

final and temporary transfers? Answers to these questions would be essential, as the concept of "economic owner" does not in itself shed light on these issues.[9]

7.4.2.2 "Fixed asset"

It is easy to see that Article 31 is not applicable in the case of transfer of inventory. In the light of comparative law, such an exclusion is all but self-evident, as many countries do not distinguish between transfers of inventory and fixed assets to foreign permanent establishments. So why has inventory been excluded?

At first sight, a simple answer consists in saying that only fixed assets are included in the "asset factor" of Article 92 for the purpose of allocating the tax base between the entities of the group. In other words, the transfer of inventory outside the CCCTB area has no effect on the apportionment formula. Whether CCCTB states may still levy exit tax on transfers of inventory to third countries consequently seems to remain a matter both for the domestic legislation and the tax treaty to solve.

This explanation is, however, unsatisfactory because in other cases, the exit tax applies even though the apportionment formula is not affected. Indeed, according to Article 4 (14) of the Proposal, the category of fixed assets includes tangible, *intangible* and *financial* assets. On the other hand, Article 92 of the Proposal includes in the "asset factor" only "fixed *tangible* assets". By comparing these two provisions, it is clear that Article 31 ends up levying an exit tax on transfers of intangible fixed assets, while such transfers do not affect the apportionment formula.

I do not think that the Proposal goes wrong in this respect. As pointed out in the introduction, the purpose of an exit tax in the Proposal is not only to fight the abuse of the apportionment formula. It is also to protect the taxable base of the group as a whole and the collective revenue of CCCTB countries. In the light of this goal, and considering the very high value of intangibles in the contemporary economy, it is perfectly logical to apply an exit tax to intangibles even though their transfer does not affect the formula.

Coming back to inventory, and against this background, the Proposal's exclusion might be attributable to practical reasons rather than theoretical or political ones: control over inventory is harder than over fixed assets; the amounts at stake are often inferior than those involved of transfer of fixed (tangible or intangible) assets.

---

[9] Proposal for a Council Directive on a Common Consolidated Corporate Tax Base (CCCTB) COM(2011) 121/4. Art. 4 (20).

7.4.3 "A" Fixed Asset

It is worth mentioning that Article 31 applies even though only one asset is transferred to a PE or a HO situated in a third country. In the CCCTB system, a tax effect is therefore given to the transfer of an individual asset to a third country, while no tax effect is given to the transfer of an individual asset to another CCCTB country. This stems from Article 70 of the Proposal which establishes an anti-abuse rule where "substantially all the assets of a taxpayer are transferred and the asset factor is substantially changed".

The system is internally consistent. While Article 70 is designed to fight the circumvention of the asset factor (which takes place only where the asset factor is substantially changed), Article 31 aims at limiting revenue losses which are attributable to the transfer of assets outside the CCCTB area. There is no need to amend Article 31 in this respect.

7.4.4 Transfers to/from a "Permanent Establishment"

Article 31 of the Proposal applies to transfers to/from a "PE". The concept of PE is defined in Article 5 in a way which corresponds almost entirely to that of the OECD Model. Consequently, there is a very low risk of seeing a different concept of PE in a tax treaty following the OECD Model concluded with a third country. It is unclear, though, whether the concept of PE enshrined in Article 5 applies for the sole purpose of implementing the CCCTB rules between CCCTB states with respect to PEs located in the CCCTB area (or outside the CCCTB area, where no tax treaty exists with the third country), or whether CCCTB states are also supposed to apply this definition of PE where an asset is transferred to a "PE" located outside the CCCTB area in a tax treaty country.

Let it be clear that a systematic implementation of the definition of PE of Article 5 regarding transfers of assets to PEs located in third countries would lead to very problematic results because of the divergence between the treaty definition of PE and the Proposal's definition. This risk may not be fully excluded: even OECD countries do not always copy and paste the OECD Model; besides, the third country may not be an OECD country and may therefore have concluded a tax treaty providing for a different concept of PE. In practice, the risk of divergence between the two definitions of PE is probably higher in a situation where an asset is transferred to a non-OECD third country with which a tax treaty exists and contains a definition of PE which is broader than that of the Proposal and of the OECD Model. In this situation, the third country will consider that the asset has been transferred to a PE on its territory and will tax the asset accordingly, while the Proposal will not see any PE in a third country and will accordingly abstain from implementing the exit tax of Article 31 – with a risk of double taxation being left if the asset is deemed to be both connected to a third-country PE (because of the tax treaty) and to the HO in the CCCTB country (because of the stricter definition of PE in the Proposal). Conversely, one can imagine an opposite situation where the tax treaty provides for an even stricter definition of PE than the Proposal: in that case, the asset will be considered as not being transferred to the third country according to the applicable DTC but as being transferred according to the Proposal, thereby triggering exit taxation!

This kind of conflict between the PE concepts in tax treaties and in the Proposal should not exist. The best way to prevent it is simply to make clear in the future CCCTB Directive that, for the purpose of implementing Article 31 to transfers to/from HO to/from PEs, the concept of PE provided by the tax treaty should prevail over the concept of PE in the Proposal. Only where no tax treaty is applicable with the third country should the PE concept of the Proposal apply.

7.5 HOW IS THE TRANSFER OF ASSET TAXED?

According to Article 31 of the Proposal, the transfer of asset "shall be deemed to be a disposal of the asset for the purpose of calculating the tax base in relation to the tax year of the transfer". This sentence is far from self-explanatory. It does not provide for any clear solution regarding the tax base and the timing of taxation.

7.5.1 What is the Tax Base?

The concept of deemed disposal leaves open the debate whether the disposal is deemed to take place at market value, accounting value or any other value. The drafters of Article 31 probably thought that the obvious interpretation of the provision led to the conclusion that the fair market value should be taken into account in order to compute a capital gain equal to the difference between the fair market value and the book value. However, considering the existence of diverging approaches in comparative law, why was an explicit provision not inserted in this respect?

7.5.2 Timing Issues

As far as timing issues related to taxation are concerned, many possible systems may exist in tax law: the hidden reserves may be taxed either at the moment of the transfer or later. Where a deferral is granted, it may take two alternative forms: either no gain is actually recognized at the moment of the transfer, or a gain is recognized but the payment of the tax is deferred until the moment the asset is actually alienated (and the tax base might even be revised at that moment).

It is a pity that Article 31 does not provide for a clear tax regime in this respect. Certainly, the concept of "deemed disposal" implies that a gain is supposed to take place at the moment of the transfer. Besides, the deemed disposal exists for the purpose of calculating the tax base "in relation to the tax year of the transfer". One may see in the combination of these observations a strong presumption in favour of immediate taxation.

In my view, however, the wording of Article 31 is not crystal clear. One might also understand it as meaning that a gain should be recognized for the purpose of calculating the taxable income of the year of the transfer, but the mere fact that a gain is recognized does not automatically mean that it should be taxed immediately. If Article 31 were a provision belonging to a purely domestic tax system, there would be little doubt that the hidden reserves should be taxed immediately. But since Article 31 is enshrined in a draft Directive, one might also infer from its ambiguity that the CCCTB states are left free to decide whether they want to tax the hidden reserve immediately or to provide for a deferral of taxation. The current wording of Article 31 is therefore unsatisfactory in this respect.

It is clear, indeed, that harmonization is absolutely necessary in the field of timing of exit taxation, otherwise law shopping inside the CCCTB area might well develop for the purpose of enjoying tax deferrals. In practice, the risk would be that companies would organize tax-free internal transfers of assets within the CCCTB area which would be combined with further transfers outside the CCCTB area.

So what is the most appropriate solution to timing issues, if any? In my view, account should be taken of the recent case law of the European Court of Justice, and particularly of the *National Grid Indus* case.[10] Although this case was about a transfer of place of effective management, not about a transfer of assets, we have already pointed out that the

---

[10] National Grid Indus, C-371/10.

main lessons to be drawn from the case law in the first matter are also relevant for cases involving transfer of assets. It is also necessary to recall that no difference should result from the fact that the *National Grid Indus* case related to freedom of establishment rather than to freedom of capital movement.

This being said, the correct reasoning seems to be the following:

- an exit tax on a transfer of assets to/from a PE/HO situated in a third country is a restriction to the freedom of capital movement because it puts at disadvantage an internal transfer of asset which would not give rise to any taxation if it took place within the same Member State;[11]
- in light of the *National Grid Indus* case, taxation of the hidden reserves on such transfers of assets may be justified by the objective of ensuring a balanced allocation of taxing powers between the CCCTB countries, taken collectively, and the third country:[12] indeed, the ECJ would probably agree that the transfer of an asset of a company which is a member of a CCCTB group to a third country cannot mean that the CCCTB countries have to abandon their right to tax a capital gain which arose within the ambit of their powers of taxation before the transfer.[13]

Let it be observed, at this stage, that where the CCCTB countries do not lose their taxing power after the transfer of the asset,[14] no such justification may be accepted.

However, the proportionality principle definitely seems to prevent such taxation from taking place automatically at the moment of the transfer. Indeed, immediate taxation goes far beyond what is necessary to ensure the preservation of the taxing power of the CCCTB countries where the country of origin may obtain mutual assistance from the third country in the field of exchange of information and recovery of tax claims. In such a situation, the recovery of tax when the capital gain is actually realized

---

[11] One might wonder here whether the correct comparison should not rather be made with an internal transfer of assets within the CCCTB area. The conclusion is the same anyway.

[12] One might wonder whether the ECJ would accept extending the concept of "balanced allocation of taxing powers between Member States" and accept as a justification the "balanced allocation of taxing powers between CCCTB States and third countries". I do not see why it should refuse to do so.

[13] See by analogy the wording of the *National Grid Indus* case, para. 46.

[14] See above, section 7.2.

is a less restrictive measure than the immediate recovery of the tax debt upon the transfer of the asset. The guidelines provided by the *National Grid Indus* case in this respect should therefore be used in order to partially rewrite Article 31 of the Proposal.

7.6 CONCLUSION

The main conclusions which are reached after analysing the current version of Article 31 of the Proposal are the following:

- the wording of Article 31.1 should be clarified by saying that the "deemed disposal" concept leads to immediate taxation, as a matter of principle;
- a paragraph 2 should be added after Article 31.1 in order to define both the concept of "transfer" and the taxable base; it should also clarify that, under Article 31, the PE concept is to be interpreted by reference to the tax treaty concluded between the country of origin and the country where the asset has been transferred;
- the current Article 31.2 (Article 31.3 after modification) should provide that Article 31.1 does not apply where the asset transferred to a third country remains taxable in the CCCTB area;
- a new Article 31.4 should offer the possibility of a tax deferral regarding assets transferred to any third country with which a tax treaty is in force and provides for exchange of information and assistance in the recovery of tax claims under conditions similar to European directives.

More generally, the study of Article 31 shows that one of the greatest challenges of the CCCTB is to define properly the relationship between the CCCTB area and third countries. The fact that exit taxation is designed to protect the collective interest of CCCTB countries makes it more and more difficult to think about the relationship with third countries in terms of country-to-country relationships. How we will apply freedom of capital movement will also have to change in the future: instead of comparing purely domestic situations with international ones, we will have to get accustomed to comparisons between "intra-CCCTB area" situations and "CCCTB area/rest of the world" situations. The CCCTB, in other words, will force us to develop completely new intellectual structures.

8. The limits to interest deductibility: An ad hoc anti-abuse rule in the proposal for a CCCTB Directive

Pasquale Pistone

8.1 INTRODUCTION

The proposal for a CCCTB Directive (hereinafter: the CCCTB Directive)[1] marks an important step in the evolution of the short history of European Union secondary law on tax matters, for being the first normative text including a supranational definition of abuse and a GAAR supplemented by two ad hoc anti-abuse clauses, or SAARs.[2] Unlike all other directives, the goal here is not to merely allow EU Member States to apply their anti-abuse clauses, or to counter abuse solely within the specific boundaries of ad hoc provisions, but rather to provide a comprehensive framework within which the benefits of secondary Union law apply to genuine transactions only. This is an important development that will prevent some shortcomings at the interpretative level concerning the boundaries of tolerance of abusive practices[3] and secure a level playing field within the European Union.

---

1 This chapter takes into account the amendments contained in the resolution of 19 April 2012 with which the European Parliament approved the proposal for a CCCTB Directive drafted by the European Commission.

2 An additional clause with an equivalent effect to a SAAR may be found in Article 79 of the proposal for a CCCTB Directive. However, the author does not regard such a clause as an anti-abuse clause in strict European law terms, since its function is rather to ensure that transfer pricing between associated enterprises complies with the proper allocation of taxing powers between States. Insofar as actual evidence of abuse is not required for the purpose of applying Article 79, from the perspective of European Union law this clause should therefore not be included within the boundaries of abuse.

3 The author wishes to refer to case law of the ECJ concerning the anti-abuse provision contained in the Merger Directive. The fact that the clause

The chapter mainly focuses on the wording, scope and effects of one of the ad hoc anti-abuse clauses contained in the proposed CCCTB Directive, in other words, Article 81, and its impact on relations with third countries, with a view to detecting the potentially critical points that may arise in the interpretation and application of such a provision. However, some additional remarks are needed for the same purpose in respect of two other provisions included in Chapter XIV (Anti-abuse Rules), namely Article 80 (General anti-abuse rule) and the other SAAR, in other words, Article 82 (Controlled foreign companies).[4] This is particularly important in order to understand the influence of the legal context on the interpretation and application of Article 81.

Although Article 81 CCCTB Directive does not contain any reference to "abuse", "abusive practices", or any of their synonyms contained in Article 80 CCCTB Directive, such as for instance "artificial transactions", its essence is intrinsically related to the function of countering abusive practices and not just because it is contained in the chapter on anti-abuse rules. This conclusion is also confirmed by the fact that the preliminary part of the CCCTB Directive specifies that "the system should include a general anti-abuse rule, supplemented by measures designed to curb specific types of abusive practices", adding an explicit mention to the limitation:

> on the deductibility of interest paid to associated enterprises resident for tax purposes in a low-tax country outside the Union which does not exchange information with the Member State of the payer based on an agreement comparable to Council Directive 2011/16/EU concerning mutual assistance by the competent authorities of the Member States in the field of direct taxation.

---

was designed to allow – rather than to oblige – EU Member States to counter abusive practices led the ECJ (see 5.7.2007, case C-321/05, *Kofoed*, paras. 40–41 and 20.5.2010, case C-352/08, *Zwijnenburg*, paras. 49–54) to take the wrong conclusion that the lack of direct effect of such a clause could in fact allow EU Member States to apply the Directive in the presence of abusive practices as well. As the Merger Directive is secondary law, this in fact runs against the settled case law of the ECJ concerning EU primary law, according to which no one is allowed to invoke European law in respect of abusive (and fraudulent) practices (14.12.2000, case C-110/99, *Emsland-Stärke*, para. 51).

[4] The analysis of this clause is the object of a separate chapter (see Panayi, C., *CFC Rules within the CCCTB*, Chapter 9) and for this reason the author will limit his remarks on Article 82 CCCTB Directive to the extent that is required to understand the implications of the specific reference to such a provision contained in Article 81.3.a CCCTB Directive and draw some parallels between the two articles as to the respective conditions for application.

Furthermore, the anti-abuse function of Article 81 is clearly also apparent if one looks at its scope, rationale and wording. The provision applies to interest payments made by a CCCTB enterprise to an associate enterprise resident in a low-tax third country not exchanging information on cross-border income. This shows that it aims at countering deductions of mainly tax-driven interest payments with third countries. These elements find several confirmations in the wording of the provision, which will be analysed throughout this chapter.

However, compliance with the conditions set in Article 81 CCCTB Directive does not automatically bring the deduction of interest payments into a safe haven, since the existence of a general anti-abuse clause in Article 80 does not exclude the fact that the deduction of an interest payment may still be denied as a consequence of the application of the latter provision. This will be the case when the analysis of factual elements indicates that such a payment is in fact an artificial transaction carried out for the purpose of avoiding taxation following the interpretation of the expression "artificial transaction" that the European Court of Justice (ECJ) will give on the basis of its case law on abusive practices.

Amendment 28 by the European Parliament to the original draft of the proposed CCCTB Directive slightly changed the wording of Article 80, in the author's view without altering much in substance. In particular, the expressions "for the sole purpose of avoiding taxation" were replaced by "mainly for the purpose of avoiding taxation". The rapporteur indicated that this was done with a view to excluding the relevance of the intention and allowing the clause to apply on the basis of the facts only, thus making it more effective.[5]

The author, however, believes that a real need for such a change did not in fact exist, since settled case law of the ECJ regards all transactions or series of transactions that may not be justified on grounds other than avoiding taxation, as lacking a valid substance and thus by their own nature liable of constituting abusive practices. Accordingly, to the extent that the "main" and "sole purpose" is to be interpreted synonymously in this context, a textual reference as well to the main purpose in Article 80

---

[5] See Amendment 15 on Recital 20 of the draft CCCTB Directive. This amendment also indicates, as a policy suggestion, that "Member States should not be prevented from introducing and coordinating additional measures among each other in order to reduce the negative effects of low-tax countries outside the Union, which do not exchange necessary tax information". The latter specification seems rather obvious, considering that almost the whole world is currently deeply engaged in a war at tax evasion in the framework of global fiscal transparency.

would in fact be substantially equivalent to the one initially proposed. This is possibly one of the arguments to prove that the desire for a greater effectiveness of the approach to abusive practices will not necessarily be the consequence of this change, but rather result from a broader context, mainly centred on the case law of the ECJ.

Furthermore, besides the goal officially pursued by the rapporteur with this change and the importance of taking into account *travaux préparatoires*, the author submits that the outcome of the law-making process should be then left to the sole judicial body competent interpret to European Union law, in other words, the ECJ, which will extract the meaning of each provision and expression in a way that corresponds with its actual wording and in conformity within the legal system. Accordingly, any time that the law-makers achieve results that in fact are not in accordance with the technically correct interpretation, the ECJ will simply have to ignore them. In this specific case, characterizing the purpose mainly on the basis of the adverb instead of the adjective simply does not imply any repercussion on the intention. Besides, case law of the ECJ on abusive practice is already sufficiently clear in taking into account not intention as such, but rather as it is reflected in the actual facts.[6]

This chapter will now focus on the analysis of Article 81 CCCTB Directive in its function as the ad hoc anti-abuse clause included in the Directive, first putting the emphasis on the scope and wording of its three paragraphs and then taking into account the problems that can arise in relations with the applicable national, international and supranational law in tax matters.

Although the entire content of this chapter focuses on issues involving the relations between the European Union and its Member States, on the one hand, and third countries, on the other hand, the author will not carry out a general analysis of such problems and will only address those specific issues as they involve the interpretation and application of Article 81 of the proposed CCCTB Directive.

---

[6] ECJ, 21.2.2006, case C-255/02, *Halifax*, paras 74–75.

8.2 THE SCOPE: PAYMENTS TO ASSOCIATED ENTERPRISES RESIDENT IN THIRD COUNTRIES

Article 81 CCCTB Directive sets the subjective and objective conditions for disallowing the deductions of interest payments between associated enterprises that are residents of third countries.

Interest payments with non-associated enterprises are kept outside the scope of Article 81. The definition of associated enterprises is contained in Article 78 CCCTB Directive. Article 9 OECD MC seems to represent the main source of inspiration for the definition of Article 78 CCCTB Directive. However, the actual wording of the latter provision is in various respects broader and more specific than that of the former one. In some cases the difference is the outcome of the different legal context;[7] in other cases it is possibly the consequence of the goal to bring more certainty to the definition of associated enterprises.[8]

Accordingly, interest payments with associated enterprises not located in third countries are not covered by Article 81 CCCTB Directive. This may be regarded as the logical consequence of the fact that within a CCCTB system there should be no issue of tax-driven deductions of interest. In the absence of a definition of "third country" in Article 4 CCCTB Directive, this conclusion is of course based on the assumption that only associated enterprises within the EU can be consolidated within the CCCTB regime and that therefore third countries are non-EU Member States. However, this may not be true to the extent that the CCCTB Directive will be approved on the basis of the enhanced

[7] See, for instance, the reference to "taxpayers not in the same group", contained in the second paragraph of Article 78.1 CCCTB Directive, or the references to the situations involving permanent establishments and third countries, included in the third paragraph of Article 78.1 CCCTB Directive. In theory, this may also be the case in which, according to Article 78.2.c CCCTB Directive, a *de facto* participation in the management is deemed to exist. However, the wording of such a clause would perhaps cover situations in which the same result would necessarily be reached also on the basis of a more general clause, such as the basic rule contained in Article 78 CCCTB Directive and Article 9.1 OECD MC.

[8] This generally applies to the thresholds contained in Article 78.2 CCCTB Directive and concerning the 20 per cent holding of voting rights and capital, the de facto participation in the management and the fact that an individual, his spouse and ascendants or descendants must be treated as a single person.

cooperation mechanism,[9] giving rise to some important discrepancies within the European Union.

The relevance of third countries in the CCCTB Directive is different from that which third countries have under any other directive in tax matters. While for directives removing tax obstacles within the internal market any third-country element is potentially able to prevent their application, this proposed directive specifically regulates its application in the presence of elements involving third countries. Insofar as a group of companies opts for having its overall profit in the European Union taxed under the CCCTB rules, the levying of corporation tax falls under the competence of the European Union through a kind of optional *EU acquis* that so far has never been seen in direct tax matters.

This certainly implies a different outcome from the tax regime that would otherwise apply and may have some repercussions in relations with third countries whose analysis falls beyond the scope of this chapter. On the one hand, EU Member States are required to ensure consistency between this optional regime within the internal market and the exercise of their taxing powers in relations with third countries, which must not harm the rights and obligations based on the clauses contained within the CCCTB Directive. On the other hand, any different treatment within the European Union due to the very existence of the directive may not give rise to an issue of discrimination in relation to third countries, as this is an immediate consequence of the stronger tax integration within the European Union, which is not comparable to the integration in relations with non-EU Member States.

For the purposes of this chapter the author points out that the need to exercise taxing powers in consistency with the CCCTB regime implies that Member States are deprived of the substance of their competence whenever the application of such a regime is at stake. This means, for instance, that the existence of abuse should be determined on the basis of the definition contained in Article 80 (as interpreted by the ECJ in combination with the prohibition of abuse in European Union law), rather than on the basis of any existing national provision or equivalent judicial technique. Likewise, Article 81 implies that Member States are not free to determine whether or not they should disallow the deduction of interest payments under the CCCTB regime in relations with third countries, but are obliged to do so when the conditions of Article 81 are met.

---

[9] This scenario was concretely envisaged by the European Parliament's legislative resolution, on which see the new recital 4a, introduced by the amendment 6 to the original draft for a CCCTB directive.

However, three critical issues may possibly arise in relations with third countries as to the application of Article 81.

First, the CCCTB Directive would in fact create a potential – at least procedural – issue in situations involving associated enterprises situated in EEA countries. Interestingly, Article 81 does not contain a carve-out for such countries of the type that is instead contained in Article 82.2 CCCTB Directive in respect of the application of CFC legislation in the presence of an agreement on exchange of information. Accordingly, one may wonder about the reason for such a discrepancy between two SAARs that are in fact targeted at countering two types of abusive practice and possibly raise a similar issue from the perspective of the potential abusive implications arising from the establishment of an associated enterprise (Article 81 CCCTB Directive) and a controlled foreign company in an EEA State. A possible answer to such a discrepancy between the two provisions could be that the carve-out based on exchange of information is in fact otherwise possible under Article 81 CCCTB Directive, taking into account the specific clause of Article 81.1. However, for at least two reasons the author believes that the discrepancy may still give rise to some difficulties in the application. Article 81.1 makes the deduction of interest subject to additional conditions than the presence of an agreement on exchange of information. Furthermore, considering the combined effect of Article 81.3.a and 82.2 CCCTB Directive, one could consider setting up an associated enterprise in an EEA country and thus having an easier access to the deduction of interest than that to which it would otherwise be entitled on the sole basis of Article 81 CCCTB Directive. At present, only Iceland and Norway fulfil the conditions indicated in Article 82.2 CCCTB Directive, but the author likewise believes that good drafting should limit the need for normative changes beforehand, in particular in situations, such as the issue of secondary European Union law, where this is particularly difficult. The critical issue could then be taken further and leads one to consider why a carve-out has only been included in respect of EEA countries and not with third countries that have concluded a European international agreement with the European Union that is in essence an equivalent source of rights and obligations for the non-EU Contracting State. However, considering that for the purpose of this chapter the relevance of Article 82.2 CCCTB is only indirect, the author will not further enquire into the issue and will accept that there has been a policy decision of the European Commission to limit the proportionality of the reaction to abusive practices in cases on which a European court (in other words, the ECJ or the EFTA Court) can have exclusive interpretative jurisdiction.

A second critical point concerning the geographical scope of the limitation contained in Article 81 CCCTB Directive arises as to the payments made to the overseas countries and territories (OCTs). The recent evolution of case law of the ECJ in tax matters[10] has now set some clearer conditions for determining when and to what extent such tax jurisdictions should be regarded as equivalent to third countries. Such criteria will certainly become relevant insofar as no specific clause or additional document is issued in this respect. Since this may create some additional tax biases, the author would therefore recommend including such a document in the final text of the CCCTB Directive.

A third potentially critical issue may arise insofar as the proposal for a CCCTB Directive will not be introduced in all EU Member States, but rather only in a more limited number of countries in compliance with the enhanced cooperation procedure. Since this procedure is in fact only possible when evidence of the failure to achieve unanimity on the proposal is given, this critical point can only arise to the extent that the current proposal is rejected by some EU Member States. However, since the national parliaments of some Member States have already expressed their unwillingness to support the proposal for a CCCTB Directive under the principle of subsidiarity, there are already some concrete signs that the EU Council may fail to achieve the required unanimity for approving it. Consequently, also taking into account the specific references to this scenario included in the legislative resolution of 19 April 2012 by the European Parliament,[11] the author finds it useful to further elaborate on this. From the moment at which the replacement of the old with the new EU directive on exchange of information is completed, the obligation for non-CCCTB countries of the European Union will certainly put them in a

---

[10] In particular, see ECJ, 5.5.2011, case C-384/09, *Prunus*. However, on 23.12.2011 new cases (cases C-24/21, *X BV* and C-27/12, *TBG Limited*) were referred on direct tax matters from the Netherlands to the ECJ on issues concerning overseas countries and territories. This time, the preliminary questions referred in the framework of this case specifically concern the right to apply secondary EU law on direct tax matters. See further on them in *Smit*, The Netherlands: pending cases *X BV*, C-24/12 and *TBG Limited*, C-27/12: discriminatory taxation of outbound dividends, the Netherlands overseas countries & territories and the free movement of capital, in Lang, Pistone, Schuch, Staringer and Storck (eds), *ECJ – Recent Developments in Direct Taxation 2012* (2013), 165 et seq.

[11] In particular, if unanimous consensus cannot be reached, the legislative resolution by the European Parliament has concretely included amendments to the proposed CCCTB Directive that will allow for its approval under the enhanced cooperation mechanism.

different situation than that of non-CCCTB countries that are not EU Member States. From the perspective of European Union law, this conclusion is unlikely to be challenged, especially insofar as one considers the following two points in the current case law from the ECJ. On the one hand, it has set up a presumption of effectiveness in exchange of information within the European Union, whereby, on the other hand, it allows the effectiveness of fiscal supervision to constitute a valid and proportionate ground for justifying discriminatory tax treatment even in the presence of evidence disclosed by the taxpayer, except when the confirmation of the factual pattern can be gathered through an exchange of information clause contained in a tax treaty with a non-EU Member State.

Accordingly, in the event of a CCCTB Directive to be introduced by means of the enhanced cooperation procedure under Article 116 TFEU, payments to an associated enterprise resident in a non-CCCTB country of the European Union may not be disallowed under the SAAR currently contained in Article 81 (nor may the final text include an extension of this clause to cover such situations), since this would otherwise run in conflict with general European Union law as it is currently interpreted by the ECJ. Nevertheless, the author believes that this should not represent a major problem, especially if one considers that Article 80 of the proposed CCCTB Directive would still apply to such situations and make it possible to counter abusive practices under a common notion of abuse that is to be interpreted and applied by the ECJ throughout the European Union.

After having clarified the geographical scope of Article 81, the focus should now be shifted on the interpretation of the conditions that are included in Article 81.1 and 81.3 CCCTB Directive, in the presence and absence of tax treaties on exchange of information with third countries.

8.3 APPLICATION IN THE PRESENCE OF AN AGREEMENT ON EXCHANGE OF INFORMATION (ARTICLE 81.1)

The wording of Article 81.1 CCCTB Directive sets two conditions in the negative form for the purpose of allowing the deduction of interest between associated enterprises in relations with third countries.

8.3.1 The First Condition

The first condition requires that exchange of information is possible with the third country of residence of the associated enterprise on similar conditions to the ones that apply within the European Union under Directive 2011/16/EU.

The second condition is based on two alternatives, according to which profits of the third-country associated enterprise are either taxed at a statutory rate that is not lower than 40 per cent of the average one recorded within the EU (Article 81.1.a), or not otherwise subject to a special tax regime that would make it liable to a substantially lower level of taxation than that of the general regime. Both groups of conditions require some specific legal analysis in order to ascertain the potential critical issues that can arise from their interpretation and application in the relations with third countries.

The wording of the first condition requires the existence of an agreement that is comparable, in other words, equivalent, to Directive 2011/16/EU. This rule has two corollaries.

First, no other legal instruments of international law, or other means, exist for the EU tax authorities to obtain information that is needed in respect of the payment of interest to an associated enterprise resident in a third country. This means that unilateral declarations of non-EU Member States concerning the willingness to exchange information would only be relevant for such a purpose insofar as, under the conditions set by Article 31.2.b of the Vienna Convention on the Law of Treaties, they could be regarded as being in connexion with the conclusion of the treaty and accepted by the other parties as an instrument related to the treaty. This conclusion does not prevent an actual obligation for the non-EU Contracting State from otherwise arising and being regarded as falling within the notion of agreement for the purposes of Article 81.1 CCCTB Directive. Accordingly, there is no doubt that non-EU countries that have ratified the OECD-Council of Europe multilateral convention on mutual assistance would in principle be eligible to be included among the ones having an agreement that is comparable to the EU Directive on exchange of information, thus meeting the first condition that is required for avoiding the application of Article 81 CCCTB Directive. Similar conclusions could be reached to the extent that some form of automatic exchange of information is introduced in relations with non-EU countries.

Second, nothing other than the existence of such agreement is required for the purpose of meeting the first condition set by Article 81.1. This can give rise to some complicated situations from various perspectives. The author finds it useful to mention and analyse at least two here.

Insofar as an agreement with a third country indeed exists and meets the standards of the EU Directive for exchange of information upon request, such a clause is (usually) formulated in a way that it creates rights and obligations for the two Contracting States to exchange that information that is required to the EU Contracting State (if, as is normally the case, it is included in a bilateral treaty). Due to this wording of the condition in Article 81.1, no further evidence should be required by the associated enterprises to claim the entitlement to the first (of the two) condition(s) upon which the right to claim deduction of interest is based in such a provision.

Therefore, if the two Contracting States have such an agreement and the non-EU Member State is in fact unwilling to exchange the information that is required by its EU contracting counterpart, this outcome should be irrelevant from the perspective of the first condition included in Article 81.1. In other words, such a condition is drafted in such a way that the taxpayer may not be asked to bear the consequences of the failure to exchange information between the two Contracting States.

Accordingly, it should make no difference whether such failure is due to an improper request by the EU Contracting State, an improper interpretation by the non-EU requested State (for instance, of critical issues such as the prohibition of fishing expeditions and the different interpretations of the concept of subsidiarity in the request for information by the EU requesting State) or a mere (temporary or permanent) lack of effectiveness in the mechanism set by the agreement. However, the author is not overly concerned about possible loopholes arising in this context, since the application of the GAAR contained in Article 80 CCCTB Directive on the basis of the settled case law of the ECJ and the need to secure an effective fiscal control should prevent European Union law from applying to possible abusive deductions of interest payments to non-EU associated enterprises.[12]

A more critical issue arises in the author's view (and here is the second of the two points mentioned above) as to the possibility of sharing information among tax authorities of EU Member States that one of them has received from a third country on the basis of a bilateral tax treaty.

From a purely tax treaty perspective, the wording of Article 26.2, and, in particular, of its reference to "information obtained … shall be disclosed only to persons or authorities … concerned with the assessment or collection …" and "use the information only for such purposes" is generally interpreted as prohibiting the flow of information to States

---

[12] However, this does not automatically imply that the same threshold for disallowing the interest payment would be maintained as under Article 81 CCCTB Directive.

other than the contracting ones.[13] The 2005 amendment to the Commentary on Article 26 OECD has confirmed this interpretation and included it in para. 12.2, according to which "the information received by a Contracting State may not be disclosed to a third country unless there is an express provision in the bilateral treaty between the Contracting States allowing such disclosure".

Although the CCCTB mechanism follows a formula and is essentially implemented by what is known as the principal authority, which then takes care of liaising with those of all other Member States involved, issues concerning the deduction of interest payments with third countries could raise the need to let the information flow within the European Union between the principal authority and that of the authority of the other EU Member State from which the payment is being made.[14] Therefore, a latent conflict could arise between the scope of tax treaties with third countries and a limit in the effective use of information that is required for the purpose of effectively countering abusive deductions of interest payments in such a context.

A similar situation would instead not occur within the European Union, where information freely flows on a multilateral basis among its Member States. A solution to such a problem at the interpretative level would still be possible under Directive 77/799/EEC, since that directive contained no specific prohibition in this respect. Accordingly, the need to interpret European Union law in compliance with its supremacy over national law (including tax treaties not grandfathered by Article 351.1 TFEU) could have justified the need for an EU Member State to share such information with other EU Member States when the conditions for spontaneous exchange of Article 4.1 were met. However, this possibility is now specifically precluded by the wording of Article 24.2 Directive 2011/16/EU, thus opening up a potential problem in the application of the first condition set by Article 81.1 CCCTB Directive and the possibility for EU Member States to dispose over comparable information in relations with third countries to that which is available under the EU Directive within the internal market. Problems would not arise often (or rather would not be insurmountable) in cases where the bilateral tax

[13] Theoretically, the wording of Article 26.2, after the 2012 Update to the OECD MC, could be compatible with the possibility of giving consent to the forwarding of the information to a non-Contracting State, but this does not seem to be the reason for amending the provision and therefore this possibility should be seen as rather remote in practice.

[14] This is not the case when the payment of interest is made by a resident of the country of the principal tax authority.

treaty network of the third country involves all relevant CCCTB countries,[15] but rather in situations where such a network is incomplete.

8.3.2 The Second Condition

The second condition applies in two alternative forms. The interpretation and application of either alternative is rather complex, also taking into account the fact that they are included in a text drafted in the negative form, in other words, which indicates the situation in which the disallowance may not apply.

The wording of Article 81.1.a) sets out conditions for the disallowance of the deduction based on three main elements: i) the levying of a tax on profits, ii) under general statutory corporate tax rate, iii) at a rate that is below 40 per cent of the average statutory corporate tax rate applicable in the Member States.[16]

Although one would be inclined to interpret the notion of profits in the light of the definition contained in Article 4.9 CCCTB Directive,[17] the context seems to otherwise require, since it links the very idea of a 'tax on profits' to the existence of a corporation tax in the third country. Accordingly, the issue arises as to whether a tax on profits can exist in a given case despite the existence of an actual corporation tax. A positive answer to this question is difficult without possible back-up from the ECJ, though not impossible. For such purposes one may recall the interpretation given by the ECJ to the notion of taxes levied on profits under the Parent-Subsidiary Directive, which was deemed to include taxes other than corporation tax that nevertheless affected the amount of profits.[18]

This argument could support the conclusion that regardless of the actual denomination and form of the tax, where a tax is levied on profits, it should not matter for the purposes of the condition set in Article 81.1.a) whether or not it is labelled as such and/or has the structure of a corporation tax. This conclusion could be right, but it would – in the

---

15 In such cases tax authorities of any EU Member State could indeed request such information from the third country involved on the basis of the applicable bilateral tax treaty.

16 Surprisingly, the European Parliament did not revise this rate, as occurred in the case of Article 82 for CFC legislation (amendment 29).

17 Accordingly, profits would be an excess of deductible expenses and other deductible items over revenues in a tax year.

18 See for instance ECJ, 8.6.2000, case C-375/98, *Epson Europe* and ECJ, 26.6.2008, case C-284/06, *Burda*.

author's view – fail to match the actual wording of such provision, which specifically mentions corporation tax and its levy at a statutory rate not below 40 per cent of the average statutory corporation tax rate within the EU. After all, one should not forget what can be theoretically acceptable could be extremely difficult to find out, since it would require insight into taxes levied in the non-EU country that would be often difficult to carry out.

From the opposite perspective, one could hold the view that no matter how broad the taxable base of such corporation tax is, no matter how much tax the profits actually bear, the existence and levying of such a tax at a statutory rate of not less than 40 per cent of the average EU rate would be sufficient to meet the conditions set in Article 81.1.a). Although this option may seem *prima facie* rather superficial, it can in fact be more suitable, especially if placed in the actual context of this provision, whose function is possibly to carve out cases in which associated enterprises are resident in countries with similar features of corporation tax as the ones that exist within the EU.

We should now inquire whether the existence of Article 81.1.b) may supplement the weaknesses of Article 81.1.a) and protect the scope of the anti-abuse clause from cases in which nominally high rates of taxes on profits are not matched by their effective tax rates if compared to the levels of taxes applicable within the EU.

The wording of Article 81.1.b) is linked to that of Article 81.1.a), since it covers situations in which special regimes deviate from the statutory tax rates applicable in the non-EU country and make it possible to tax profits at substantially lower levels if compared to the ones that would otherwise apply on the basis of the standard regime. This link between the two provisions catches special regimes, but not all types of advantages that the associated enterprises can have in non-EU countries.

Problems of application could arise in cases of a special regime where the corporation tax is not calculated on the basis of a percentage of the profits, but rather through alternative methods. This can be the case of flat corporation taxes not levied on the basis of rates, but rather of *ad valorem* amounts. This situation would clearly not meet the condition set in Article 81.1.a), but nothing excludes the fact that it would still be relevant for the purpose of the application of the alternative regulated by Article 81.1.b). In this case, such as, more in general, most cases concerning the application of Article 81.1.b) the correct application of this condition requires a thorough analysis of taxes levied on profits of the non-EU country of residence of the associated enterprise that receives the payment. This is of course rather difficult to implement, but possibly indispensable to achieve a balanced and proportionate outcome that reflects the wording and rationale of the provision.

Specific mention should then be made for a situation in which the author believes that a loophole arises from the link between Articles 81.1.a and 81.1.b CCCTB Directive. In particular, if the statutory corporation tax rate is above 40 per cent of the average statutory corporation tax rate applicable in the EU and special regimes bring the actual levels of taxation substantially below the tax that would otherwise be due, Article 81.1.b) can be invoked to disallow the deduction of interest payments to the non-EU associated enterprise. However, if the statutory corporation tax rate is levied on (an even significantly) narrow taxable base at a rate that is above 40 per cent of the average statutory corporation tax rate within the EU and no special regime exists, neither of the alternatives set under Article 81.1 could achieve the disallowance of interest payment. This shows a loophole in the coordination between Article 81.1.a and 81.1.b that creates a potential bias in favour of making interest payments to associated enterprises resident in non-EU countries that exchange information with the EU and are liable to a narrow-based corporation tax on their profits without being eligible for some special regimes that substantially lower the levels of taxation.

This loophole can only successfully be filled insofar as a given structure or payment is regarded as constituting abuse under Article 80 CCCTB Directive and meets the standards of abusive practices corresponding to the interpretation by the ECJ. From this perspective, one should, however, not forget that Article 80.2 CCCTB Directive would clearly allow for structures involving the payment of lower taxes insofar as they can be regarded as having a genuinely commercial purpose,[19] thus requiring a thorough analysis of the transaction involving the associated enterprises situated in the third country. This outcome should not necessarily be seen as a further element contributing to the structural deficiencies of the combination resulting from the application of Article 81.1.a) and 81.1.b).[20] Instead, it should be regarded as securing that the

---

[19] According to Article 80.2 CCCTB Directive, "The first paragraph shall not apply to genuine commercial activities where the taxpayer is able to choose between two or more possible transactions which have the same commercial result but which produce different taxable amounts".

[20] For such a purpose one could consider that in case the CCCTB Directive were introduced by means of the enhanced cooperation procedure, the non-application of Article 81 CCCTB Directive to relations with associated enterprises in non-CCCTB Member States would automatically create a bias in favour of interest payments to such enterprises as opposed to the ones established

need to counter abusive practices and to prevent the formation of tax biases towards the establishment of associated enterprises in some non-EU countries is harmoniously reconciled with the need to provide a competitive tax framework for business carried out within the CCCTB geographical area.

Nevertheless, the author suggests that the two alternatives of the second condition included in Article 81.1 be supplemented (in the final drafting of such provision) by an additional clause. Such a provision could indicate that the disallowance also covers cases of profits taxed at a substantially lower rate (for instance, below 40 per cent of the average statutory corporate tax rate applicable within the EU), due to the existence of a corporation tax that is levied on a much narrower basis than that applicable in the EU under the CCCTB system. The application of this clause would imply a significant effort on tax authorities of the EU MS(s) involved, but at least be appropriate to fill the loophole that has been indicated earlier in this section of the chapter.

A further question could arise as to how evidence of the conditions set by Article 81.1 should be met. In principle, this provision is phrased in a way that requires the right for tax authorities of the EU Member State(s) involved to obtain tax information from the non-EU country of residence of the associated enterprise. For such a purpose, one could consider the case of an official certificate issued by the non-EU country, which has an agreement on exchanging information with the EU Member State(s), and having as object the fact that the associated enterprise meets neither of the two conditions indicated in Article 81.1 as this is an official document duly released by the competent authorities of the non-EU country involved, the author believes that it should put the enterprise in a safe haven, provided that the tax authorities of the EU Member State(s) find this document supported by all the due information that they would need in order to allow for the deduction of interest payment.

---

outside the EU (which would instead fall within the scope of Article 81 CCCTB Directive).

8.4 APPLICATION IN THE ABSENCE OF AN AGREEMENT ON EXCHANGE OF INFORMATION (ARTICLE 81.3)

Article 81.3 CCCTB Directive sets the conditions for allowing deduction of interest in the absence of an agreement on the exchange of information that is comparable to exchange of information on request under Directive 2011/16/EU. From its wording and context, Article 81.3 has a residual function to Article 81.1 within the system. However, the content of Article 81.3 and the conditions for its application do not entirely mirror those indicated under Article 81.1, since the former clause in fact limits the deduction of interest to arm's length,[21] whereby the latter includes no such condition. Furthermore, the two provisions are also drafted in the opposite way: Article 81.1 sees the deduction as the rule, except when its two groups of conditions are met; Article 81.3 sees the right to deduction as a goal that can only be achieved upon the specific conditions expressly indicated therein.

Due to its residual function, one has to preliminarily ascertain whether Article 81.3 is the relevant provision at all in respect of an interest payment to a third-country associated enterprise. For such purposes, one should not just look at whether there is an agreement on exchange of information, but also at whether such an agreement allows for an exchange that is qualitatively comparable to the one that would be possible under Directive 2011/16/EU. As for the application of Article 81.1, one should not carry out such comparison on a solely legal basis, but rather take into account the specific situation and the implications that exchange of information can have in the case at stake.

Accordingly, the point should be whether for a specific interest payment and situation tax authorities can get the same information that is needed for the purpose of carrying out the effective fiscal supervision under the agreement that would be possible under Directive 2011/16/EU. This is clear in theory, but in practice perhaps not as much so, especially insofar as it has to be concretely assessed in advance by the EU taxpayer with a degree of certainty that is required to avoid an exposure to potential corrections and sanctions by tax authorities. The goal of identifying some criteria to determine a safe haven could be pursued by looking at whether in a given situation, on the basis of the information

[21] The author is aware that the wording of Article 81.3 CCCTB Directive refers to "an amount not exceeding that which would be stipulated between independent enterprises".

that the taxpayer has voluntarily supplied to its tax authorities in the EU Member State, such authorities can make use of the exchange of information clause contained in the applicable tax treaty to obtain relevant elements to confirm the genuine nature of the payment and the other persons involved in it. Whether or not such clause will then lead to an effective exchange of information is something that the taxpayers should not be concerned with.

The difficulties in determining whether it is Article 81.1 or 81.3 CCCTB Directive that governs a given case lead the author to suggest that CCCTB taxpayers should be allowed to ask in advance for some kind of technical assistance by a technical body – established at EU level and without binding powers – which could be activated upon request: a kind of technical helpdesk that would set up good practices and strengthen compliance. Its optional nature excludes possible issues related to an additional procedural compliance burden. The nature of such a consultation would be more similar to feedback by a technical helpdesk than to an advance ruling, which would have some kind of binding effect that is in fact difficult to apply in this context.

Besides having a residual function with respect to Article 81.1, Article 81.3 sets three alternative conditions for its application and, as indicated above, a rule concerning the actual amount of interest that can be deductible.

Before dealing with the analysis of the three conditions, the author wishes to make some considerations on the relevance of arm's length under Article 81 CCCTB Directive for deduction purposes. Although only Article 81.3 sets such a limit, settled case law from the ECJ[22] constantly regards arm's length as a safe haven. The author does not believe that such case law automatically considers non-arm's length as a synonym for abusive practices, but acknowledges that alterations in the burden of proof in such context would be justified with a view to understanding the grounds for departing from what is regarded as a widely accepted standard within the EU. The ECJ has never been confronted with the reluctance concerning arm's length and the wide use of non-arm's length methods that still achieve a balanced allocation of taxing powers among States. However, since the reference to arm's length is decisive for understanding the amount of deduction in situations covered by Article 81.3, one should understand the implications that can arise from the asymmetry between Article 81.1 and 81.3 in this respect.

---

[22] See among other ones, ECJ, 13.3.2007, case C-520/04, *Thin Cap GLO* and ECJ, 21.1.2010, case C-311/08, *SGI.*

No major difference would arise in the case of arm's length dealing. However, some critical issues could occur in respect of non-arm's length dealing with associated enterprises that make the interest payment subject to Article 81.3 instead of Article 81.1.

From a legal and policy perspective the author believes that the European Union is certainly free to determine what standards should be followed by its secondary law in respect of the amount of interest to be deducted. However, the author is not as sure whether this can also justify the fact that such a limit is only set under Article 81.3 and not under Article 81.1. The point does not arise much within the European Union,[23] but rather in relations with third countries, since associated enterprises eligible for Article 81.1 and resident in countries endorsing non-arm's length methods would find their enterprises enjoying an advantage as compared to the ones established in countries that make them eligible instead to Article 81.3. For such purposes, the author suggests considering re-establishing the symmetry between the two provisions by adding in Article 81.1 the requirement concerning the amount that may not exceed that which would be stipulated between independent enterprises.

The focus will now be shifted to the three alternative conditions listed in Article 81.3 CCCTB Directive.

Article 81.3.a) includes a reference to Article 82, the provision on controlled foreign companies, opening up the right to deduction in case the amount of interest is included in the tax base as income of the associated enterprise. Besides the already indicated asymmetry with Article 82.2 in respect of EEA controlled foreign companies, the author believes that the condition listed in Article 81.3.a) should operate independently and thus not be subject to the arm's length limitations set under Article 81, since it would otherwise determine some partially compensatory effects of a taxation that has already undergone another clause within the same Directive.

Article 81.3.b) grandfathers interest payments whose amount is certainly driven by the market, and which are often subject to multiple reporting obligations and therefore unlikely to be at stake in abusive practices. This condition is particularly important from the perspective of big groups of companies, since it can be easily and objectively proved in advance with results that can be satisfactory to both parties and do not give rise to major problems.

[23] This refers to the case of a CCCTB passed with enhanced cooperation only within a limited group of EU countries.

By contrast, despite the appreciable drafting efforts, the condition set out in Article 81.3.c) is significantly more complex to administer and apply. This condition is formulated in two sentences, which respectively set its boundaries and defines its meaning for the purpose of the application of Article 81.3. The essence of the condition is found in the idea of the active trade, or active business test, according to which deduction of interest payments is only possible to the extent that the payee of interest carries on an independent economic activity, in other words, pursues profit making and disposes of staff with suitable know-how and activities. This idea perfectly fits within the SAAR function of Article 81 as a whole, but again it leads the author to consider the potential implications that would arise from a comparison between Article 81.3.c and the conditions set under Article 81.1 CCCTB Directive.

For such purposes one could consider a possible example and look at what would happen in respect of an associated enterprise that carries on a profit-based activity, disposes over staff with the suitable know-how, but lacks any sort of premises and/or has unsuitable equipment with which such an activity could be carried on. Insofar as such activity is carried on from a country that has an agreement that allows an exchange of information comparable to that of Directive 2011/16/EU one could conclude that the information could lead the EU principal tax authorities to decide that such features are not sufficient to meet the objective criteria indicated by settled case law of the ECJ to single out abusive practices.[24] Accordingly, interest paid to such associated enterprises would likely not be deducted. Opposite conclusions could instead be reached insofar as Article 81.3 applies to this case, since the presence of Article 81.3.c) would automatically grandfather the case of this associated enterprise due to the existence of a profit-based activity with officers and employees that carry out substantial managerial and operational activities.

This conclusion might not be affected by the relation between Article 81.3.d and Article 80 for at least two reasons. First, the taxpayer would not be obliged to supply that information for the purpose of obtaining the deduction, nor could one in principle understand how tax authorities of the EU State would otherwise get it. Second, even if they succeeded in that respect, problems would arise as to the legitimate expectations that

---

[24] ECJ, 12.9.2006, case C-196/04, *Cadbury Schweppes*, para. 67, which refers to "premises, staff and equipment".

the EU and non-EU associated enterprises would rely on under the wording of Article 81.3.d).

This example possibly explains the perplexities that the author has, in particular with the second sentence of Article 81.3.c). Despite the fact that all attempts to achieve clarity with definitions are in principle welcome, the asymmetries with primary law and the interpretation by the ECJ could create more problems here than such a sentence in fact can solve in advance. For this reason, the CCCTB Directive could either delete it, or formulate it differently and include a reference to Article 80, which brings it more clearly back into the general pattern of abuse. After all, the author does not believe that a specific reference to Article 80 is needed within Article 81.3.c) for such a purpose.

8.5 THE DEFINITION OF INTEREST (ARTICLE 81.2)

An important component of the clause on interest deduction within the CCCTB Directive is the one concerning the definition of interest, which clearly shows the willingness of the drafters to find inspiration in Article 11 OECD MC. This broad correspondence is particularly positive, since the CCCTB looks at interest from the perspective of its deduction in the hands of the EU payer, while tax treaties take the opposite perspective, in other words, the extent to which the payee is liable to tax in the State of source, be it an EU or a non-EU State, and can claim relief for double taxation in the country of residence. Consistency between the two perspectives achieves a balanced and even outcome, which can even go as far as to secure the elimination of economic double taxation at international level. By contrast, inconsistencies can give rise to potential problems and undesirable tax biases to flows of interest between CCCTB groups in the EU and their non-EU associated enterprises. For instance, this can be the case where interest is, on the one hand, deductible in the hands of the EU payer and, on the other hand, not taxable by the EU country of source when paid to a non-EU resident associated enterprise.

Nevertheless, the consistency with the current version of the OECD MC is not necessarily conclusive evidence of a consistency with the applicable bilateral treaty, since the old treaties patterned along the OECD MC may contain a different definition of interest, which can also be found in treaties that mirror the UN Model Tax Convention.[25]

[25] See further on this in Pistone, P., "General Report", in Lang, M., Pistone, P., Schuch, J., Staringer, C. (eds), *The Impact of the OECD and UN Model Conventions on Bilateral Tax Treaties*, Cambridge University Press, 2012, p. 21.

A few more remarks are now needed with a view to comparing the wording of the two provisions and then searching for potential critical points that can arise from the interaction with the applicable tax treaties with third countries.

The wording is by and large identical and only differs in three parts from the current wording of Article 11 under the OECD MC: (i) the missing reference to "government" when mentioning "securities" in its first sentence, (ii) the missing inclusion of an explicit reference to "premiums and prizes attaching to such securities, bonds or debentures" and (iii) the missing indication of the fact that the purposes to which the definition applies.

The first difference indicates that non-governmental securities are also to be included for CCCTB purposes within the scope of the provision that determines the entitlement to deduction under Article 81. The CCCTB regime thus gives entitlement to a deduction that is possibly broader than the scope of tax treaties.

The second difference shows a higher degree of specificity in the definition provided by the OECD MC, which could perhaps be held as implicit in the CCCTB definition and be solved through consistent legal interpretation.

The third difference plays a more limited role, which does not seem to require any specific comment for the purposes of this provision.

8.6 RELATION OF THE CCCTB DIRECTIVE TO DOMESTIC, TREATY AND EU LAW

An analysis of the general issues concerning the relations with the national, international and supranational legal orders is beyond the scope of this chapter, which is limited to the rule concerning the limits to deduction of interest payments to associated enterprises resident in third countries. However, for the specific purpose of understanding such limits, the chapter will now address a selection of problems that arise from the relations of the CCCTB Directive with domestic law, tax treaties and other provisions of primary and secondary Union law.

8.6.1 Relation of the CCCTB Directive to Domestic and Treaty Law

The relations of the CCCTB Directive and domestic law and tax treaties partly raise some common issues, mainly related to the circumstance that, from the perspective of European Union law, both involve the relation with national law of EU Member States. For this reason they will be bundled together in this section. Nevertheless, the analysis will include some separate remarks on each of them in this section whenever needed.

In principle, as the CCCTB Directive is an instrument of Union law, both relations raise an issue of ensuring the supremacy of supranational law over national law. However, insofar as one sees this problem in an exclusive context of relations with third countries, the supremacy issue only arises from the perspective of the EU Member State involved.

The presence of an optional CCCTB regime implies a shift of competences that is subject to the exercise of such an option by the taxpayers. One should therefore differentiate between situations that are not the object of such option, which continue to be governed at the national level, and cases to which the CCCTB regime applies. The latter group of situations shows a total shift in the level of government from the national to the European one, which cannot remain without implications when one is analysing the relations with national law. Although the analysis of the exact boundaries of such a shift does not fall within the purview of this specific chapter on the limits to interest deduction set by Article 81 of the proposed CCCTB Directive, one should consider that Member States would no longer enjoy a freedom to legislate in this domain within the EU, or in relations with third countries, especially taking into account that a large number of provisions are included in the (proposed) CCCTB Directive on such relations.

Accordingly, to the extent that a group of enterprises has opted for CCCTB, domestic law of EU Member States will no longer be applicable and will give way to the CCCTB regime. This is an automatic consequence of the Union *acquis* and of the obligation to secure loyalty to the Union, but also, and more specifically, an effect of the complete shift of taxing powers. This also implies that rules on non-deduction of interest payments with third countries are automatically wiped out by the provision implementing Article 81 CCCTB Directive.

From the perspective of domestic law, the issue specifically arises as to whether this also implies that thin capitalization rules in force in some countries should share the same destiny. Settled case law of the ECJ excludes the compatibility of such rules with fundamental freedoms inside the internal market whenever these are discriminatory, implicitly admitting their application in relations with third countries as being intrinsically linked to the right of establishment, which lacks an external scope. However, their elimination in a domestic and intra-EU context could add a new dimension to the problem, since Member States could be tempted to keep them in relations with third countries, perhaps arguing that they would affect a situation that is not comparable to the one falling under the CCCTB Directive. The author believes that the shift of taxing powers to the Union level should create a new dimension, which no longer raises an issue of compatibility in the exercise of national taxing powers with EU primary law, but rather an issue of preventing a Member State from legislating in an area that, whenever taxpayers opt for treatment under the CCCTB regime, has in fact been shifted to the Union level. This argument comes into play at a logically prior moment to that of the compatibility with fundamental freedoms,[26] since it affects the need to secure an effective and homogeneous common regime throughout the European Union. Accordingly, insofar as Member States were allowed to keep their national rules, companies could seek advantages resulting from the presence or absence of a thin-cap regime, or dependent on how strict the anti-abuse rules are. For this reason the author believes that the obligation of Union loyalty should deprive EU Member States of the right to apply any of their domestic rules on interest deduction, as this topic is regulated at EU level. Such conclusions should not be affected on the basis of arguments concerning the need to counter abusive practices, since the CCCTB Directive contains specific and general rules in this domain.

Thin capitalization rules in relations with third countries could instead survive in cases where there is no option for CCCTB until the ECJ changes its view concerning the compatibility with the fundamental freedoms and, in particular, the relations between the external scope of the free movement of capital and the non-applicable right of establishment in such a context.

From the tax treaty perspective the issue arises with a slightly different shape. In particular, Article 8 CCCTB Directive correctly reminds one that such a regime overrides tax treaties within the European Union. Drafting of legal rules can sometimes raise problems not only because of what the wording of a given rule says, but also because of the implications of what such a rule fails to say. In the specific case one could consider that the failure to mention the relations with third countries could be interpreted from two perspectives, which will be briefly highlighted here.

First, if there was any need for a provision like Article 8 in the Union, the fact that no such provision exists for relations with third countries can imply that treaties keep producing their effects regardless of the Directive, which should therefore not be allowed to override them. Second, from the opposite perspective one can say that Article 8 has a mere

[26] The analysis of such specific issues of compatibility will follow in section 8.6.2 of this chapter.

declaratory function of a principle that is already intrinsic in the system of Union law, according to which treaties concluded by EU Member States must now take into account the effects of the shifting of competences to the EU level, with the consequence that their rules keep their effect only to the extent that is compatible with the existence of secondary Union law in this field. Since the object of this chapter exclusively deals with third countries, the author will not further inquire on the possible implications of this second view. However, the author should also add that from such a perspective one should not make conclusive statements on the basis of what a rule fails to say. Accordingly, it can be argued that this rule simply does not deal with the relations of the CCCTB Directive and treaties involving third countries. This is not an absolute *première* in Union law, since Article 351 TFEU leaves some issues concerning treaties with third countries unanswered and all other directives in the field of direct taxes simply do not regulate such relations. However, the CCCTB Directive clearly produces direct effects in relations with third countries and for this reason the problem of such relations cannot be left unanswered.

The point shall now be analysed from the specific perspective of this chapter, which could raise some issues in the relations between the limits to deduction of interest payments and the deduction non-discrimination clause contained in Article 24.4 of tax treaties patterned along the OECD MC. Relevant elements for interpretation could be based on paragraph 74 of the Commentary on Article 24 (also after the amendments included in 2008), according to which limits to deduction of interest payments can be set in accordance with national thin capitalization rules without infringing Article 24.4 insofar as the application of such rules complies with Articles 9.1 and 11.6 OECD MC. The latter treaty provisions take into account the existence of relations between associated enterprises, which is in essence the type of relations covered by Article 81 CCCTB Directive. Consequently, the author believes that, from the specific perspective of this chapter, no significant problem should arise in the presence of a treaty provision such as Article 24.4 to the extent that is drafted like the one currently contained in the OECD MC and interpreted in conformity with its Commentary. The outcome would not change for treaties based on the corresponding UN provision, but perhaps on the basis of other treaties that do not include any such specific clause (thus following the 1963 OECD MC), or which otherwise regulate the issue.

Despite such a conclusion, the author feels it useful to indicate that – from the perspective of interpretation in conformity with Union law – the second theory illustrated above has more merits than the first one. Union law regards treaties signed by its Member States as legal instruments of national law, thus implying that only the ones signed before entering the EU will not be affected by the evolution of integration within the European Union. Accordingly, the author believes that by no means can the clause of Article 8 be interpreted in a way that prevents the Directive from overriding tax treaties with third countries, since the need to protect the obligations accepted by EU Member States with third countries cannot prevail over the supremacy of Union law for EU Member States.[27]

8.6.2 Relations with Union Law

As an instrument of secondary law, the CCCTB Directive should fit into the pattern of primary European Union law of which it is a concrete development in tax matters. Accordingly, it should also comply with the corresponding requirements and conditions, since any directive would otherwise be automatically deprived of its legal foundation. Furthermore, this section will also inquire as to whether any problem of compatibility can arise with other directives in tax matters. Once more, the analysis of such issues will not be carried out on a general basis, but only to the extent that is specifically required by this chapter with respect to the right to limit interest deduction in relations with third countries.

The compatibility with primary law should mainly be ascertained from the perspective of rules on fundamental freedoms, since rules on state aids apply within the internal market only. However, the author points out that some current developments are also pushing the EU competition rules in the direction of non-EU preferential tax regimes and could soon become relevant as well in the relations between the external scope of the CCCTB Directive with a view to countering a growing phenomenon within international tax planning, which could be defined as smart tax competition.[28]

The analysis of the compatibility with the EU non-discrimination principle should take into account two basic issues that act at two different logical moments, namely the applicable EU freedom and the anti-abuse nature of Article 81 CCCTB Directive. As indicated earlier in this chapter, settled case law of the ECJ indicates that measures targeted

---

[27] Clear examples of this interpretation are included in the *open skies* case law of the ECJ. See, ECJ, 5.11.2002, case C-466/98, *Commission vs. United Kingdom et al. [open skies].*

[28] Such issues fall outside the scope of this chapter. See further on them in Pistone, P., "Smart tax competition and the geographical boundaries of taxing jurisdictions: countering selective advantages amidst disparities", *Intertax* 2/2012, at 85 et seq.

at applying only in situations where a person is in a position to exercise a definite influence over the decisions of a company fall within the scope of the right of establishment only. Consequently, due to the prevalence of such a right over the free movement of capital, case law of the ECJ has concluded that even the non-applicable right of establishment in external relations can prevent the free movement of capital from applying. Although one could *prima facie* consider that all relevant situations falling within Article 81 CCCTB Directive are by their own nature to be regarded as covered by the right of establishment, the author is not persuaded that this conclusion would necessarily apply.

As indicated earlier in this chapter, a precise definition of associated enterprises is included in Article 78. Such a definition includes cases of persons exercising a significant influence over the decisions of the associated enterprise (Article 78.2.c), which is in essence very close to the criterion of definite influence over which the ECJ has based its case law indicated above. However, the very fact that other criteria are indicated in the same provision leads the author to imagine that there could well be situations in which the ECJ could not necessarily be persuaded that an issue with regard to only the right of establishment could arise. For instance, one could think of the situation of a shareholder that owns 20.1 per cent of the capital, but has no voting rights in the associated enterprise. Furthermore, more in general one could wonder whether the very fact of holding 20 per cent of either (or both) the share capital and/or the voting rights should be sufficient to meet the criteria indicated by the ECJ in the *Baars* judgment.[29] For such a reason the author believes that there may be some mismatches between the boundaries of the two freedoms and the application of this measure to associated enterprises, which makes it important to continue the analysis of compatibility at the level of justifications. However, besides such uncertainty, the author has already put in writing his perplexity for the very foundations of this exclusive relevance of a non-applicable freedom and the fact that it can prevent an otherwise applicable freedom from producing its effects.[30]

Accordingly, taking into account the possibility that the free movement of capital and payments can also be relevant for a measure of secondary law limiting the deduction of interest payments to associated enterprises, one should now ascertain whether potential problems arise with the steps

---

[29] See ECJ, 13.4.2000, case C-251/98, *Baars*, para. 22.

[30] Among others see Pistone, P., "The impact of Community law on the relations with third countries in the field of direct taxes", *Intertax* 5/2006, at 234 et seq.

that the ECJ normally follows when applying the justification based on anti-abuse grounds for limiting the exercise of such a freedom. Settled case law of the ECJ has clarified that such a justification cannot be invoked to prevent the occurrence of abusive practices, but rather to counter the actual abusive practices, since it is only in such situations that European Union law cannot be invoked.[31] Therefore, any application of anti-abuse measures beyond such situations would imply a restriction on the exercise of freedoms that goes beyond what is strictly admitted for the purpose of countering actual abusive practices, would run against the principle of proportionality and would not be justified.

Such preliminary remarks make it possible to carry out a technically accurate analysis of compatibility between Article 81 CCCTB Directive and the free movement of capital and payments.

From this specific perspective the main problem arises as to the identification of the relevant benchmark, since no similar problem of abuse can arise within a CCCTB group that would require the disallowance of interest deductions for tax purposes. A possible benchmark could be represented by the rules that govern interest deduction in each country in non-CCCTB situations, in other words, in cases involving associated enterprises that have not opted for the CCCTB tax regime and therefore are in a position in which the special relationship could raise a similar danger of abusive practices. However, the author feels that such benchmark would be rather misleading, since it would entail different conclusions from country to country on a matter where the powers, in the presence of an option for the CCCTB system, have been shifted to the Union level.

The author suggests instead that the solution to this problem concerning the correct benchmark is to be found on the basis of the same reasoning that the ECJ applied when ascertaining the compatibility of national thin-cap rules with the fundamental freedoms. From the *Lankhorst-Hohorst* decision[32] onwards the ECJ has always looked at whether the application of such limits by the home State to cross-border situations only could have dissuasive effects on the exercise of the fundamental freedoms. The author acknowledges that the factual pattern of Article 81 CCCTB Directive does not exactly match that concerning limits to interest deduction existing in respect of thin-cap rules. However, the author believes that limits to interest deductions should not turn into an instrument to give national governments a *carte blanche* as to the

[31] See ECJ, *Emsland-Stärke*, para. 51.

[32] See ECJ, 12.12.2002, case C-324/00, *Lankhorst-Hohorst.*

erection of barriers against the free movement of capital, since this would transform the directive into an instrument to pursue a goal that runs counter to primary Union law.

Accordingly, the author believes that a restriction to deductions of interest could only be allowed under Article 81 CCCTB Directive not just for the mere fact that objective factors indicate the actual danger of abusive practices, but rather in the presence of the need to counter an actual abusive practice.

The mechanism of Article 81 CCCTB Directive can, in the author's view, be held to have some general dissuasive effects in the movements of capital and payments with associated enterprises established outside the European Union. However, besides the need for specific amendments indicated earlier in this chapter, the author believes that the general problems of compatibility concerning the interpretation and application of Article 81 CCCTB Directive can be justified on the basis of the settled ECJ case law on anti-abuse grounds when the limit applies to deduction of interest payments to associated enterprises residents in third countries in the presence of actual abusive practices.

When interpreting such a justification, one should duly take into account that Article 81 itself is framed within Chapter XIV of the CCCTB Directive and has a non-mutually exclusive relation with Article 80, in other words, the GAAR of the CCCTB Directive. The existence of such rules implies that the existence of abusive practices should be ascertained regardless of what happens at the national level and thus requires a similar development in direct tax matters as the one that has taken place in VAT with the *Halifax* judgment,[33] which would be entirely and immediately applicable as a relevant judicial precedent in this context. Accordingly, within the boundaries of the CCCTB regime, Member States will therefore no longer enjoy a freedom to determine what constitutes abuse and what should instead be acceptable, and thus be in fact deprived of the right to determine the features of their approach to abusive practices, including the interpretation and application of their GAARs and SAARs, exactly as happens in VAT matters.

To the extent that Article 81 CCCTB Directive will (exclusively) concern relations with non-EU Member States, the author finds it important to also include a second justification that is often applied on a separate basis by the ECJ, namely the one according to which the need to protect an effective fiscal supervision can be invoked in relations with third countries. Mentioning such a specification on a separate basis is

---

[33] ECJ, 21.2.2006, case C-255/02, *Halifax*, paras. 67 et seq.

important from the perspective of primary law despite the fact that from the perspective of the CCCTB Directive Article 81 is explicitly regarded as an anti-abuse measure and is included in a chapter concerning anti-abuse measures. According to settled case law of the ECJ,[34] the need to secure an effective fiscal supervision can justify restrictions on the free movement of capital in relations with non-EU Member States unless tax authorities are allowed to obtain tax information needed and to an extent that is equivalent to the one applicable under the EU Directive on exchange of information. The extent to which this justification applies has so far been disconnected from the principle of proportionality and puts more emphasis on the need to protect the interest of the Revenue against taxpayers that operate outside the EU. From the perspective of this specific justification the author feels that the fact that Article 81.1 subjects the right to deduction to the existence of an agreement with exchange of information is never a problem as such, nor can a problem otherwise arise from the fact that different and more burdensome conditions apply under Article 81.3 to the deduction of interest payments with associated enterprises that are resident in countries having no agreement on exchange of information similar to Directive 2011/16/EU. However, the general possibility of justifying such limits on interest deduction on the basis of the need to secure an effective fiscal supervision only covers the first part of conditions set by Article 81.1 and 81.3. Therefore, one may not conclude that the limits to interest deduction under Article 81 CCCTB Directive would always be justified on the basis of the need to justify an effective fiscal supervision, since the compatibility of the additional conditions set by both Article 81.1 and 81.3 should be reviewed on the basis of anti-abuse grounds.

The author believes that the limits to deduction of interest payments to associated enterprises resident in third countries raise no major problems of compatibility with other secondary law already applicable in direct tax matters. As indicated earlier, the option for CCCTB automatically shifts the competence from the level of EU Member States to that of the Union, depriving the former of their powers to exercise their jurisdiction at the national level. Since this chapter only focuses on the scope of interest payments, it will not inquire into potential general problems that may arise in relations with third countries concerning the application of European international agreements. However, for the very specific purpose of Article 81 one should consider the implications that arise insofar as interest is not deductible. The answer to such a problem depends on

34 See joined cases C-436/08 and 437/08, *Haribo and Salinen*, para. 68.

whether the scope of the applicable freedom under such agreement and its direct effect.

An interesting issue then arises in relations with Switzerland as a consequence of the fact that Article 15 of the EU-Switzerland agreement on taxation of savings applies a zero-rating on outbound payments within groups of companies. The agreement also includes a specific provision on exchange of information limited to cases of tax fraud and the like, in other words, (as indicated by Article 10.1 of the agreement) "including offences with the same level of wrongfulness as is the case for tax fraud under the law of the requested State". Accordingly, while zero-rating can only be limited in such cases, deduction of interest payments by an EU CCCTB to its Swiss associated enterprise can be limited whenever the conditions of Article 81 CCCTB Directive are met. No problem of compatibility, however, seems to arise, but merely the opportunity for Switzerland to consider negotiating the issuing of special rules of coordination with the European Union.

Commentary

Christoph Spengel

WHY IS THERE A NEED FOR HARMONIZED PROVISIONS?

Article 81 of the proposal for a CCCTB Directive (hereafter: CCCTB Directive) introduces special provisions for the deductibility of interest paid by a member of a CCCTB group to an associated enterprise resident in a third country. Ignoring the scope and consequences of Article 81 for the moment, the necessity of harmonized provisions for interest deductibility at the borderline of the EU has to be pointed out first.

The main reason for such a provision is to secure Member States' tax revenues with regard to debt-financing. Since not all Member States have implemented thin capitalization rules or fat capitalization rules[35] or earnings stripping rules, as the case may be, members of a CCCTB group could avoid domestic limitations of interest deductibility by rearranging financing arrangements within their group. An example is provided in Figure 8.1.

X-GmbH (Germany), Z-GmbH (Austria) and Y-Corp. (third country) are members of the same group of companies. First suppose that X-GmbH and Z-GmbH do not form a CCCTB group. If X-GmbH has been granted a loan from Y-Corp., the deductibility of interest payments would be considered under German fat capitalization rules. From this it follows, broadly speaking, that interest is only deductible up to an amount of 30 per cent of the EBITDA of X-GmbH.[36] Now suppose that X-GmbH and Z-GmbH opt for a CCCTB group and rearrange intra-group financing in a way that Z-GmbH takes the loan from Y-Corp and

[35] In contrast to thin capitalization rules, which limit the deductibility of interest paid upon shareholder loans under certain conditions, fat capitalization rules also cover interest payments to third parties such as bank loans, etc.

[36] D. Endres and C. Spengel (eds), *Unternehmensbesteuerung in Deutschland – Corporate Taxation in Germany*, 3rd edition (Düsseldorf: IDW, 2012), p. 114 et seq.

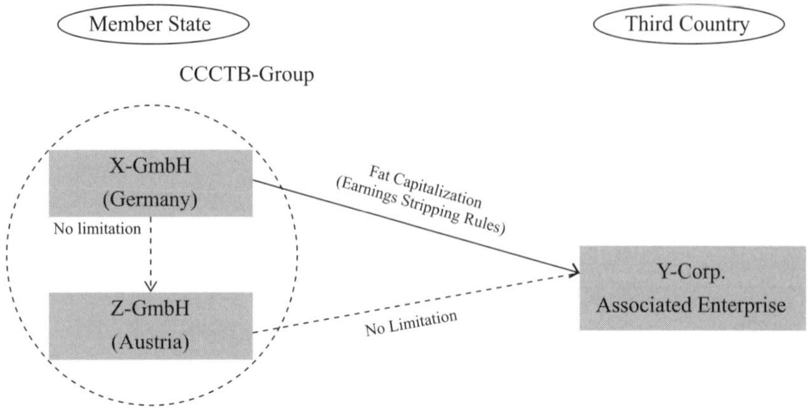

Figure 8.1 Deductibility of interest on intercompany financing arrangements

forwards the loan to X-GmbH. As far as the forwarded loan from Z-GmbH to X-GmbH is concerned, interest payments can be deducted at the level of X-GmbH without any limitation due to the CCCTB regime. Moreover, since Austria, as a general rule, does not apply thin capitalization rules, interest payments from Z-GmbH to Y. Corp. are deductible as well and thus reduce the consolidated CCCTB income through the sharing mechanism (in other words, formula apportionment).

As a result, domestic thin capitalization rules could very easily be circumvented by means of re-routing the interest payment via associated enterprises located in Member States which do not impose restrictions on interest deductibility. It is therefore necessary to implement harmonized thin capitalization rules with respect to third countries under the CCCTB regime.

INTEREST DEDUCTIBILITY ACCORDING TO THE CCCTB DIRECTIVE

Article 81 of the CCCTB Directive sets out the conditions for allowing/disallowing the deduction of interest payments between members of a CCCTB group and associated enterprises located in third countries. Figure 8.2 illustrates the underlying subjective and objective conditions.

As a general rule, all interest paid by a company with a view of obtaining or securing income is deductible from taxable income under the CCCTB Directive (Article 12). Yet, Article 81 limits the deductibility

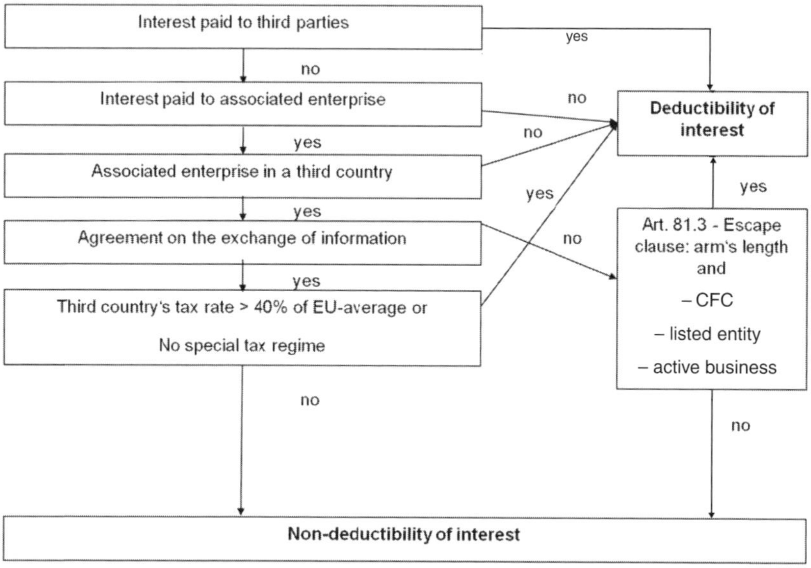

Figure 8.2 Interest deductibility according to Article 81 CCCTB Directive

of interest payments under certain conditions. Accordingly, interest – as defined by Article 81 (2) – paid to an associated enterprise resident in a third country is not deductible where there is no agreement on the exchange of information comparable to the exchange of information on request provided for in Directive 2011/16/EU and where one of the following conditions is met:

1 The general statutory tax rate in the third country is lower than 40% of the average statutory corporate tax rate applicable in the Member States; or
2 The associated enterprise is subject to a special tax regime which allows for a substantially lower level of taxation than that of the general regime.

By way of exception, in the absence of an agreement regarding the exchange of information such interest is still deductible up to the amount which would be stipulated between independent parties (arm's length principle) under the escape clause of Article 81 (3).

Pasquale Pistone's chapter presents and analyses the provisions laid down in Article 81 of the CCCTB Directive in a comprehensive and very accurate matter. In principle, as a commentator of his chapter, I have nothing substantial to add. His analysis in section 8.6 (Relation of the CCCTB Directive to domestic, treaty and EU law) very clearly points out that a CCCTB Directive will override domestic law. Moreover, it is emphasized that due to the optionality of the CCCTB regime domestic provisions limiting interest deductibility (no option is exercised) and Article 81 (option is exercised) are likely to coexist within each Member State. In my view, such a possible coexistence cannot only be traced back to optionality, but is also likely to appear if the CCCTB regime would be mandatory. This would simply be the case for companies which do not qualify for the CCCTB regime at all (stand-alone companies). In addition, the chapter identifies potential conflicts with primary EU law (here: free movement of capital), if domestic law contains no specific provisions limiting interest deductibility.

Referring to these findings, I strongly argue in favour of a harmonized provision for the deductibility of interest payments both under the CCCTB Directive and Member States' domestic law. Figure 8.3 provides an example which illustrates my concerns.

Consider two EU-based corporations – X1, a member of a CCCTB group and X2, a stand-alone company – both of them maintaining loan arrangements with corporations located in third countries. One of them (Y-Corp.) is supposed to be an associated enterprise, the other one (Z-Corp.) is a non-associated enterprise. With regard to loan arrangements concluded by X2 (stand-alone company) the deductibility of interest payments would be considered under domestic law. Depending on the particular Member State, there might be specific limitations or not. On the other hand, the deductibility of interest payments on loan arrangements concluded by X1 (member of a CCCTB group) will no longer be judged by domestic law. Due to the supremacy of supranational law, Article 81 of the CCCTB Directive is relevant in this respect. Therefore, interest paid to non-associated enterprises in third countries would be deductible irrespective of limitations in domestic law. The provisions laid down in Article 81 of the CCCTB Directive would only be relevant for interest payments to associated enterprises. They can be more generous or more restrictive than domestic law.

The coexistence of domestic law and Article 81 of the CCCTB Directive might raise legal, economic and administrative concerns. Legal concerns arise with respect to EU law and the principle of equal treatment of taxpayers as a guiding taxation principle in many jurisdictions: there seems to be no justification for a different treatment of members of a CCCTB group and stand-alone companies with regard to interest deductibility. Referring to economic concerns, it becomes obvious that such coexistence is decisive for exercising the option for the

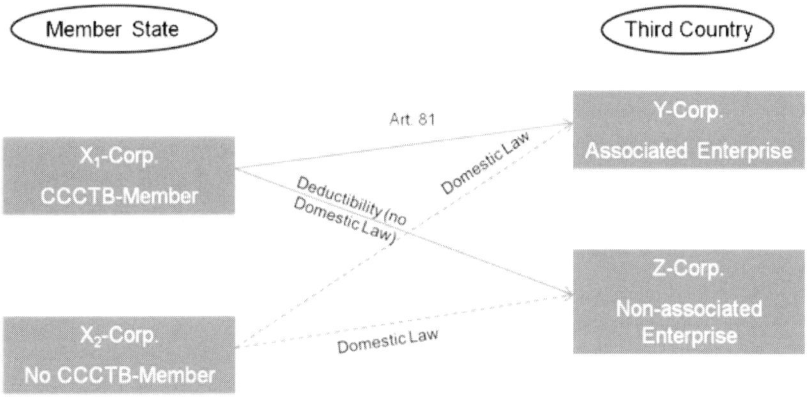

Figure 8.3 Coexistence of domestic law and Article 81 CCCTB Directive

CCCTB regime: should groups opt for a CCCTB if domestic law offers more generous provisions for the deductibility of interest payments compared to Article 81 of the CCCTB Directive? Finally administrative or practical concerns arise with respect to the tax authority being responsible for controls: is it the local domestic tax authority or the superordinate tax authority envisaged for a CCCTB?

To sum up, only a harmonized provision for the deductibility of interest payments both under the CCCTB Directive and Member States' domestic law would eliminate such concerns. In the following, I will argue that the provisions laid down in Article 81 of the CCCTB Directive cannot serve as a blueprint for harmonized action.

MEMBER STATES' PRACTICE

Article 81 of the CCCTB Directive more or less provides an anti-abuse provision. It is far less restrictive than current Member States' practice. Article 81 does not cover third-party loans (for example, loans from the capital market and from non-associated enterprises). Regarding loans from associated enterprises located in third countries, Article 81 does not contain any debt-equity, assets or EBIT(DA) restrictions and offers a generous escape clause.

National practices regarding thin capitalization diverge widely across Member States.[37] As illustrated in Figure 8.4, only eight Member States

[37] Please note that in practice and as highlighted above, thin capitalization rules are often highly complex and usually depend on various conditions.

currently do not apply specific thin capitalization rules, among them Austria,[38] Sweden and the United Kingdom.[39] By contrast, the vast majority of countries have implemented specific thin capitalization rules. Among those, there are significant differences regarding their specific design. Most important, while the thin capitalization or interest limitation rules in Bulgaria, Denmark, Germany, Hungary, Italy, Latvia and Romania extend to related parties and third-party lenders, the majority of countries apply thin capitalization rules – in line with the CCCTB Directive – only to interest payable on debt owed to any related party.

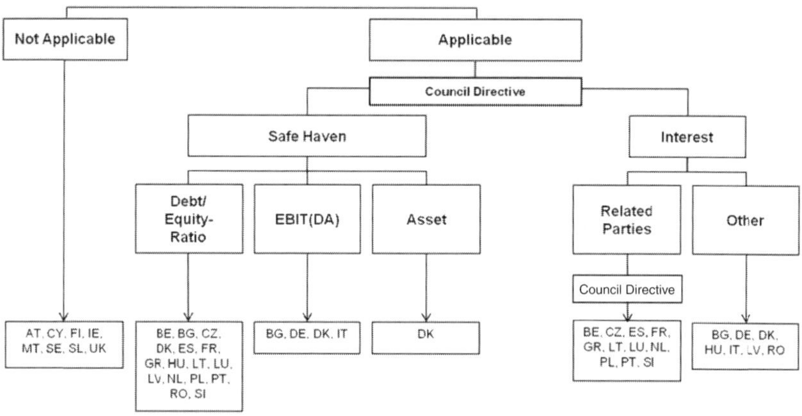

Figure 8.4 Thin-capitalization Rules/Deductibility of interest expenses

In most Member States a corporation is regarded as thinly capitalized if debt exceeds certain prescribed debt to equity ratios. By contrast, in Denmark the total debt of a company may not exceed the aggregate value of certain assets. Moreover, Bulgaria, Denmark, Germany and Italy apply earnings stripping rules which limit the maximum interest deduction to certain EBIT(DA) thresholds. Yet, in line with the CCCTB Directive, almost all countries applying some form of thin capitalization rules

Therefore, the following must be seen as a rough overview of the regulations currently applied in the countries under consideration. For a more detailed overview see A.P. Dourado and R. de la Feria, *Thin Capitalization Rules in the Context of the CCCTB*, Oxford University Center for Business Taxation Working Paper 08/04, 2008.

[38] Please note that courts have established certain guidelines which are used to determine whether a corporation is regarded thinly capitalized.

[39] Please note that the thin capitalization rules are included in the transfer pricing legislation in the United Kingdom.

provide the opportunity to prove that the transactions were at arm's length or provide other escape clauses.

Moreover, it is worth mentioning that Article 81 of the CCCTB Directive has been designed in the overall context of the CCCTB assuming consolidation and allocation of the common tax base across Member States. As shifting profits through interest payments between Member States would be eliminated within a CCCTB group, the regulations laid down in Article 81 are more or less relevant to associated enterprises resident in a third country only. It seems at least questionable whether Member States are willing to follow the less restrictive thin capitalization rules of Article 81 under a CCCTB or whether they continue to protect their national tax base by applying more restrictive national thin capitalization regulations.

In addition, referring to the two secondary conditions mentioned in Article 81 of the CCCTB Directive I do not believe that restrictions to interest deductibility will be effective in reality. According to the first condition, interest paid to a third country is not deductible if the general statutory tax rate in the third country is lower than 40 per cent of the average statutory corporate tax rate applicable in the Member States. As shown in Table 8.1, a third country is only considered as a low-tax jurisdiction if the statutory tax rate is below 9 per cent (8.82 per cent = 40 per cent of the statutory tax rate in the EU Member States as from 1 January 2011).

Finally, with regard to the escape clause laid down in Article 81 (3) of the CCCTB Directive one has to be aware that agreements on the exchange of information exist with many well-known tax havens. Germany, for instance, has concluded such agreements with the Bermudas, Gibraltar, Guernsey, Isle of Man, Jersey and Liechtenstein.

CONCLUSION

With regard to interest deductibility, the provisions laid down in Article 81 of the CCCTB Directive and domestic law would coexist.

This situation is not in line with the idea of a Common Market, since it raises legal concerns (EU law and equal treatment of taxpayers), causes economic distortions (option and companies which do not qualify for the CCCTB regime) and administrative problems.

Therefore, there is a need for a uniform and harmonized provision in the CCCTB Directive and in the domestic law of all Member States.

The provisions laid down in Article 81 of the CCCTB Directive cannot serve as a blueprint for harmonization since they are by far too generous.

Table 8.1 Statutory corporate tax rates in the EU Member States (as from 1 January 2011)

Austria	25.00%	Lithuania	15.00%
Belgium	33.00%	Luxembourg	21.00%
Bulgaria	10.00%	Malta	35.00%
Cyprus	10.00%	Netherlands	25.00%
Czech Republic	19.00%	Poland	19.00%
Denmark	25.00%	Portugal	27.50%
Estonia	21.00%	Romania	16.00%
Germany	15.00%	Slovakia	19.00%
Finland	26.00%	Slovenia	20.00%
France	33.33%	Spain	30.00%
Greece	24.00%	Sweden	26.30%
Hungary	19.00%	UK	26.00%
Ireland	12.50%		
Italy	27.50%	**Average**	**22.04%**
Latvia	15.00%	**40% of Average**	**8.82%**

Member States' tax revenues would be threatened due to an erosion of the corporate income tax base through thin capitalization and earnings stripping.

9. CFC rules within the CCCTB

Christiana HJI Panayi

9.1 INTRODUCTION

On 16 March 2011 the Commission published the eagerly awaited final proposal for a Council Directive on a Common Consolidated Corporate Tax Base ("draft CCCTB Directive")[1] and a detailed impact assessment.[2] The CCCTB is a proposal to provide companies with establishments in at least two Member States with the opportunity to compute their group taxable income according to one set of rules, those of the new consolidated tax base, rather than according to the national tax bases of each Member State. The overall aim of the CCCTB is to reduce the costs of complying with 28 tax regimes, to minimize tax arbitrage and to simplify restructurings. It is also aimed at providing comprehensive consolidation of profits and losses on an EU basis. In other words, the CCCTB is essentially a 29th system.

As the Commission stated in its press release on publishing the draft proposal,[3] the aim of it is to significantly reduce the administrative burden, compliance costs and legal uncertainties that businesses in the EU currently face by having to comply with up to 27 (at the time) different national systems for determining their taxable profits. The Commission extolled the proposal, in that it would offer companies a

[1] European Commission, COM(2011) 121/4, 2011/0058 (CNS); SEC(2011) 316 final. For a detailed analysis, see Christiana HJI Panayi, *The Common Consolidated Corporate Tax Base and the UK* (Institute for Fiscal Studies, 2011); ISBN 978-1-903274-57-6.

[2] Commission, Working Document Impact Assessment Accompanying document to the Proposal for a Council Directive on a Common Consolidated Corporate Tax Base (CCCTB), Brussels, 16.3.2011, SEC(2011) 315 final. Also see Commission Staff Working Paper, Summary of the impact assessment – Accompanying document to the proposal for a Council Directive on a Common Consolidated Corporate Tax Base (CCCTB), SEC(2011) 316 final (hereafter, Summary Report of the Impact Assessment).

[3] IP/11/319, dated 16/03/2011.

"one-stop-shop" system for filing their tax returns, as well as providing consolidation. It was estimated that on a yearly basis the CCCTB would translate into savings in compliance time and costs.[4] It was also claimed that the new system would bring tangible benefits for companies wishing to expand into other Member States.[5] Whether or not under this new system third-country companies would enjoy the same benefits is unclear. The anti-abuse rules of the proposal seem to suggest not.

The author examines one set of anti-abuse rules of the CCCTB proposal: the CFC rules. Before doing so, the general context in which CFC rules arise is analysed.

9.2 THE TAXATION OF CFCS

9.2.1 International Tax Law Issues

Whilst most countries tax their residents on a worldwide basis, invariably, one group company is not taxed on the profits of another group company (whether resident or not), being separate legal entities.[6] Taxation is deferred until the subsidiary's profits are distributed to the parent company or the parent company disposes of its shares in the subsidiary. This deferral is especially beneficial to shareholders of non-resident companies located in low-tax jurisdictions or tax havens. If the non-resident company is located in such a jurisdiction and is controlled by the parent company, then the parent company could effectively avoid paying domestic corporation tax by diverting profits to that subsidiary.

---

[4] The Commission estimated that the CCCTB would save businesses across the EU EUR 700 million in reduced compliance costs, EUR 1 billion in reduced costs to expand cross-border and EUR 1.3 billion through consolidation. It was also estimated that businesses looking to expand cross-border would benefit from up to EUR 1 billion in savings. See press release IP/11/319, dated 16/03/2011. Also see MEMO/11/171, dated 16/03/2011, 2.

[5] As the Commission noted, currently, it costs a large enterprise over EUR 140,000 in tax-related expenditure alone to open a new subsidiary in another Member State. The CCCTB would reduce these costs by EUR 87,000 or 62 per cent. Medium-sized enterprises stand to gain even more, with their average tax-related costs of expanding within the EU dropping from EUR 127,000 to EUR 42,000 (a decrease of 67 per cent). If even just 5 per cent of SMEs were to decide to expand on this basis, overall savings would be of the order of EUR 1 billion. See MEMO/11/171, fn.4, 5.

[6] Some countries have rules that allow consolidation of profits between group companies for tax purposes.

CFC regimes, sometimes called anti-deferral regimes, are often put in place to prevent such arrangements by taxing resident shareholders of CFCs on their pro rata share of some or all of the undistributed income of the CFC.[7] A CFC is typically described as a non-resident company controlled by residents (individuals or companies), which is subject to a much lower level of taxation by being established offshore.[8] Therefore, the main focus of CFC rules was thought to be to prevent or limit the ability of residents of a country to use foreign companies in tax havens to avoid or defer domestic tax (i.e. protection of tax base from tax-haven deferral).[9] However, CFC rules are no longer limited to tax haven deferral. In fact, in recent years, their scope has been extended to include the deflection of income into jurisdictions that may not be tax havens but which have preferential regimes for certain types of income. They are also a means through which tax audits can be facilitated in countries that are reluctant to exchange information or do not exchange information at all. The importance of CFC rules in combating harmful tax competition was reiterated and emphasized by the OECD Committee on Fiscal Affairs in its 1996 report on harmful tax competition[10] and in subsequent reports.

It is often claimed that CFC rules protect capital export neutrality as they attempt to achieve neutrality between investing at home or abroad.[11]

---

[7] For a general overview, see OECD, *Controlled Foreign Company Legislation* (1996); Brian Arnold, *The Taxation of Controlled Foreign Corporations: An International Comparison* (1986) 1 et seq.; Jacques Malherbe and Michael Lang, "Controlled Foreign Corporations in the EU After Cadbury Schweppes" (2007) *Tax Management International Journal*, Vol. 36, No. 12 (12 July); Michael Lang et al., *CFC Legislation, Tax Treaties and EC Law* (Kluwer Law, Vol. 8, 2004). Also see analysis of the topic in Brian Arnold and Patrick Dibout, "Limits on the Use of Low-Tax Regimes by Multinational Businesses: Current Measures and Emerging Trends", General Report, in *Cahier de Droit Fiscal International LXXXVIb* (2001).

[8] See Arnold and Dibout, fn.7, 38 et seq.; Office of Tax Policy, *The Deferral of Income Earned Through US Controlled Foreign Corporations – A Policy Study* (Department of Treasury Office, 2000), chapters 1–2.

[9] See Arnold and Dibout, fn.7, p. 38. Also see Office of Tax Policy Report, fn.8, and how it describes tax-haven deferral (chapter 3).

[10] OECD, *Harmful Tax Competition – An Emerging Global Issue* (1998) report, 40.

[11] Peggy Brewer Richman, *Taxation of Foreign Investment Income, An Economic Analysis* (American Economic Association 1963); Peggy B. Musgrave, *United States Taxation of Foreign Investment Income*, (Harvard Law School 1969), chapter 7; Gary C. Hufbauer, *A Guide to Law and Policy, U.S. Taxation of American Business Abroad* (American Enterprise Institute, Hoover Institution Policy Study No.16 1975).

By taxing investments in a low-tax jurisdiction, it is argued that CFC regimes ensure equality of foreign and domestic investments. Whilst there is some force in this argument,[12] it is somehow difficult to justify how capital export neutrality is attained when the CFC regime contains a business activity exemption. Is passive investment in a low-tax jurisdiction more of an affront to capital export neutrality than active investment in such a jurisdiction? Furthermore, capital export neutrality, a corollary of residence-based taxation,[13] is not universally accepted as the only theory or the best theory maximizing global welfare. Therefore, CFC rules seem to be incongruous with the competing theory of capital import neutrality[14] and on grounds of international competitiveness.[15]

In so far as the technical details and the focus of CFC regimes are concerned, these vary across different countries. There is a diversity of techniques for defining CFCs, encompassing criteria such as control, effective level of taxation, activity and type of income of the CFC. There is also a diversity of methods for the identification of low-taxation regimes, ranging from objective criteria to a system of lists, or both.[16]

In essence, there are two (theoretical) approaches according to which countries frame their rules in taxing the parent company on the (sheltered) profits of its non-resident subsidiary. Under the first approach, the sheltered profits are deemed to have been distributed (the fictive or deemed dividend approach). Under the second approach, the profits are considered to have arisen in the hands of the shareholder/parent company (piercing the corporate veil approach).[17]

---

[12] See, for example, an extensive analysis of how Subpart F rules improve global and US economic welfare, based on capital export neutrality arguments in chapter 3, Office of Tax Policy Report.

[13] Christiana HJI Panayi, *Double Taxation, Tax Treaties, Treaty Shopping and the European Community,* (Kluwer Law 2007), chapter 1.

[14] Pursuant to this theory, a corollary of source-based taxation, there should be equality of resident and non-resident investors so that taxation does not affect the question of *who* invests in a particular country. See analysis in HJI Panayi (supra).

[15] Analysis in HM Treasury, *Reform of Controlled Foreign Companies (CFC): Policy principles document* (July 2009).

[16] Se Arnold and Dibout, fn.7, pp. 29–34.

[17] OECD, "Double Taxation Conventions and the Use of Base Companies" in *Issues in International Taxation No.1, International Tax Avoidance and Evasion, Four related studies* (Paris 1987). In paragraph 24 of this report, three approaches are listed. The third one is that the profits improve the ability of the shareholder to pay taxes as economically these profits are at its disposal. As the report concedes, in practice, counteracting legislation appears to have proceeded

Both approaches raise concerns as to the compatibility of CFC rules with double taxation agreements. One argument is that the attribution-of-income approach, in so far as business income is concerned, is contrary to Article 7 OECD Model, as it breaches the source country's exclusive right to tax the profits of the CFC. Another argument is that the fictive or deemed distribution approach is contrary to Article 10 of the OECD Model, as it leads to taxation of dividends before they are paid, contrary to Article 10(1) of the OECD Model. Also, the taxation of a foreign subsidiary's undistributed profits in the hands of the shareholder is contrary to Article 10(5).

These arguments are often disputed. The Commentary to the OECD Model states that CFC legislation, which is "internationally recognized as a legitimate instrument to protect the domestic tax base",[18] is not contrary to the provisions of it.[19]

As far as incompatibility with Article 7 is concerned, the official position in the OECD Model Commentary is that a contracting state is not restricted from taxing under domestic law its own residents, even though the CFC tax imposed is computed by reference to the profits of a non-resident enterprise that are attributable to the residents' participation in the enterprise.[20] Furthermore, the CFC tax levied by a state on its own residents is not considered to reduce the profits of the non-resident enterprise "and may not, therefore, be said to have been levied on such profits".[21]

As far as incompatibility with the dividends article is concerned, the OECD Model Commentary states that Article 10(5) is confined to taxation at source (i.e. at the state of the CFC) and concerns the taxation of the company, having no bearing on the taxation in the country of residence of the shareholder and the taxation of the shareholder.[22]

These arguments appear to be overtly technical and have been criticized.[23] Whilst in some jurisdictions the risk of conflict between domestic CFC rules and tax conventions has been obviated following judgments

---

in a pragmatic way rather than follow rigidly any of these theoretical approaches.

18 Commentary on Art.1 of the OECD Model, para. 23.

19 *Ibid.*

20 Commentary on Art.7, para. 14.

21 *Ibid.*

22 Commentary on Art 10, para. 37.

23 See, for example, Peter Harris and David Oliver, *International Tax Law* (Cambridge University Press 2010), pp. 304–305; Michael Lang, "CFC Regulations and Double Taxation Treaties", (2003) 57 *Bulletin for International Fiscal Documentation* 251, 51; Michael Lang et al., *CFC Legislation, Tax Treaties and EC Law* (Kluwer Law, Vol. 8, 2004), General Report; Arnold and Dibout, fn.7, p. 81 et seq.

in national courts,[24] in other jurisdictions a finding of treaty override could not be avoided.[25] The question of incompatibility of CFC regimes with tax treaties is still unsettled.[26] This renders the drafting of the CCCTB's CFC rules an even more complicated matter.

9.2.2 EU Tax Law Issues

EU law now also imposes serious constraints on the ability of Member States to draft their CFC regimes. Notwithstanding the rationale of CFC rules (whether legitimate or not), broadly, as a result of their application, the parent company is being penalized for having invested in foreign (low-tax) jurisdictions. As the Commission recognized in its Communication on the application of anti-abuse measures in the area of direct taxation,[27] "[the] main purpose of CFC rules is to prevent resident companies from avoiding domestic tax by diverting income to subsidiaries in low tax countries".[28] This treatment raises issues of discrimination. As the Commission commented in the Communication:

> [u]nder CFC rules, the profits of a subsidiary receive different tax treatment for the sole reason that the subsidiary is resident in another State. That difference in treatment constitutes discrimination unless there is an objective, relevant difference of situation such as to justify it. Equally, the inclusion of the profits of a foreign subsidiary in the taxable profits of the resident parent company constitutes an obstacle to the ability of the latter to establish itself in other [Member States] by way of subsidiaries.[29]

The Court of Justice examined the compatibility of anti-deferral rules with EU law in three important cases and has set out important principles.

---

[24] See English Court of Appeal case, in *Bricom Holdings Ltd. IRC* [1997] STC 1179. Also see case of the Supreme Administrative Court of Finland, KHO 596/2002/26 (2002) 4 ITLR 1009. For commentary, see *inter alia,* Harris & Oliver, *ibid.,* Marjaana Helminen, National Reporter for Finland, in Lang et al., fn.23, 204.

[25] See French Conseil d'Etat case, *Societe Schneider Electric* (2002) 4 ITLR 1077.

[26] Arnold and Dibout, fn.7, 81.

[27] Commission Communication, "*The application of anti-abuse measures in the area of direct taxation – within the EU and in relation to third countries*", 10 December 2008, COM (2007) 785 final.

[28] *Ibid.*, p. 7.

[29] *Ibid.*, p. 7.

In *Cadbury Schweppes*[30] the Court held that for Member State CFC rules to be compatible with EU law, they must specifically relate to *wholly artificial arrangements* intended to circumvent the application of the legislation of the Member State concerned.[31] The specific objective of the restrictive rules must be to prevent conduct involving the creation of wholly artificial arrangements that do not reflect economic reality.[32] As a corollary, CFC rules must exclude from their scope situations whereby, despite the existence of tax motives, the incorporation of a CFC reflects economic reality.

In determining whether or not economic reality exists in addition to the subjective element, which consists of the intention to obtain a tax advantage, objective factors must be taken into account.[33] These objective factors, which have to be ascertainable by third parties, include, in particular, the extent to which the CFC physically exists in terms of premises, staff and equipment.[34] The parent company of the CFC must be given the opportunity to produce evidence that the arrangement is genuine.[35]

---

[30] Case C-196/04 *Cadbury Schweppes* [2006] ECR I-7995, C-196/04. For general commentary, see, *inter alia*, R. Szudoczky, "UK CFC rules breach freedom of establishment unless application limited to wholly artificial arrangements", (2006) 11 *European Taxation* 41; Gerard Meussen, "Cadbury Schweppes: The ECJ significantly limits the application of CFC rules in the Member States", (2007) 1 *European Taxation* 13; Simon Whitehead, "Practical implications arising from the European Court's recent decisions concerning CFC legislation and dividend taxation", (2007) 4 *EC Tax Review* 176.

[31] *Cadbury Schweppes*, fn.30, para. 51.

[32] *Ibid.*, para. 55.

[33] *Ibid.*, paras. 64–65.

[34] *Ibid.*, para. 67. Advocate General Léger had explained in greater detail some relevant criteria in establishing artificiality: first, the degree of physical presence of the subsidiary, in other words, examining whether or not the subsidiary has the premises, staff and equipment necessary to carry out the services provided to the parent company; second, the genuine nature of the activity provided by the subsidiary, in other words, considering the competence of the subsidiary's staff in relation to the services provided and the level of decision-making in carrying out those services; third, the economic value of that activity with regard to the parent company and the entire group, in other words, whether or not the value reflects the exercise of genuine activities in the state of the subsidiary. Case C-196/04 *Cadbury Schweppes,* paras 111-114 (Opinion).

[35] *Cadbury Schweppes*, para.70 (Court of Justice). The fact that the activities which corresponded to the profits of the CFC could just as well have been carried out by the parent company did not warrant the conclusion that this was a wholly artificial arrangement. More was required. See also para. 69.

Cadbury Schweppes was followed in the *CFC GLO* case.[36] In this case, the Court of Justice looked at the UK CFC rules.[37] An important feature of this case was that the Court of Justice found certain compliance requirements (where the resident company sought exemption from taxes already paid on CFC profits) *not* to be prohibited, as long as their aim was to verify that the CFC was actually established and that its activities were genuine and did not entail undue administrative constraints.[38] The Court of Justice also held that the resident company was best placed to establish that it had not entered into wholly artificial arrangements which did not reflect economic reality.[39] It was up to the national court to determine whether the motive test of the UK CFC legislation lent itself to an interpretation which enabled the CFC charge to be restricted to wholly artificial arrangements.

Incidentally, in *Vodafone 2*,[40] in the High Court (Chancery Division), Mr Justice Evans-Lombe found that the UK CFC legislation was incompatible with EU law because the motive test[41] did not ensure that only wholly artificial arrangements would be caught by the CFC regime. Therefore, the UK CFC rules had to be disapplied.[42] This decision was reversed at the Court of Appeal,[43] which held that the CFC rules should be interpreted as if there was a new additional exception applying with retrospective effect.[44] This new exception would apply to companies that are actually established in the EU/EEA area and which carry on genuine economic activities there.[45] The concept of "genuine economic activities" was not defined. For companies established outside the EU/EEA area and

---

36 Case C-201/05 *CFC GLO*, [2008] ECR I-2875.

37 The Court of Justice also looked at the rules on the taxation of inbound dividends.

38 Case C-201/05 *CFC GLO*, fn.36, paras. 82 and 85.

39 *Ibid.*, para. 82.

40 *Vodaphone 2 v. HMRC* [2008] EWHC 1569 (Ch).

41 The motive test, as set out in section 748(3) ICTA, stipulated that the profits of the foreign subsidiary were not to be apportioned to the UK parent "if it is the case that: (a) in so far as any of the transactions … achieved a reduction in United Kingdom tax, either the reduction so achieved was minimal or it was not the main purpose or one of the main purposes of that transaction [and] (b) it was not the main reason or, as the case may be, one of the main reasons for the company's existence in that accounting period to achieve a reduction in United Kingdom tax …".

42 *Ibid.*, para. 90.

43 *Vodaphone 2 v. HMRC* [2009] EWCA Civ 446.

44 This was to be added in either s 748(1) or 748(3) of ICTA 1988.

45 *Vodaphone 2 v. HMRC*, fn.43, para. 39.

for companies established in the EU/EEA area but without genuine economic activities, the normal CFC rules would apply. The case has now been settled.[46]

In 2010 ECOFIN adopted a resolution on the co-ordination of Member States' tax policies with regard to anti-abuse provisions.[47] The resolution recommended that Member States, when applying CFC and thin cap rules within the EU which are not applicable in similar domestic situations, should adopt some guidelines. These guidelines:

> are a political commitment, whose implementation is left to the decision of each Member State, and therefore affect neither the rights or the obligations of the Member States nor the respective competencies of the Member States and of the Union under the Treaty and, in particular, do not require Member States who do not have the types of rules referred to in this Resolution to introduce such rules.[48]

The guidelines included a non-exhaustive list of indicators suggesting that profits may have been artificially diverted to a CFC.[49] The importance of administrative co-operation was also stressed.

It should be noted that one type of CFC legislation, switch-over clauses, appears to be less problematic from an EU perspective. In fact, the Court of Justice has held that these clauses do not restrict

---

[46] See David Stewart, "Vodafone Settles Dispute With HMRC Over Controlled Foreign Corporations", reported in *Tax Analysts* 2010 WTD 142-2.

[47] See Draft Council resolution contained in 10597.10 FISC 58, dated 2 June 2010. The resolution was adopted by ECOFIN on 8 June 2010.

[48] *Ibid.*, p. 3.

[49] The list of indicators read as follows:

a. there are insufficiently valid economic or commercial reasons for the profit attribution, which therefore does not reflect economic reality;
b. incorporation does not essentially correspond with an actual establishment intended to carry on genuine economic activities;
c. there is no proportionate correlation between the activities apparently carried on by the CFC and the extent to which it physically exists in terms of premises, staff and equipment;
d. the non-resident company is overcapitalized, it has significantly more capital than it needs to carry on its activity;
e. the taxpayer has entered into arrangements which are devoid of economic reality, serve little or no business purpose or which might be contrary to general business interests, if not entered into for the purpose of avoiding tax. *Ibid.,* p. 4.

fundamental freedoms. The case in question is *Columbus Container*.[50] In this case, the claimant was a Belgian limited partnership with German resident partners. The activities of the partnership consisted, inter alia, of financing subsidiaries and branches. The partnership's profits and assets were, under German domestic tax law, assessed as foreign branch profits and assets of the German partners. In Belgium the partnership was treated as a company and enjoyed the status of a Belgian Coordination Centre.

According to the Belgium-Germany tax treaty, the profits from the net assets of a Belgian partnership were exempt in Germany. However, German anti-abuse rules provided for a switch from the exemption method to the tax credit method in respect of certain passive branch profits subject to low taxation abroad. The key question was whether or not this switch-over clause (technically a treaty override) was compatible with the freedom of establishment and free movement of capital.

The Court of Justice, contrary to Advocate General Mengozzi's Opinion,[51] held that such clauses did not constitute a restriction to the freedom of establishment or the free movement of capital. The effect of the switch-over clause was that investors who invested in low-tax jurisdictions were brought to the same position as investors who invested in Germany in so far as tax rates were concerned. The German legislation did not make any distinction between taxation of income derived from the profits of partnerships established in Germany, and taxation of income derived from the profits of partnerships established in another Member State which subjects the profits made by those partnerships in that state to a rate of tax below 30 per cent. Accordingly, there was no difference of treatment and no discrimination, as "partnerships such as Columbus [did] not suffer any tax disadvantage in comparison with partnerships established in Germany".[52]

---

[50] C-298/05 *Columbus Container Services BVBA & Co. v. Finanzamt Bielefeld-Innenstadt* [2007] ECR I-10451. For commentary, see generally, Jose Calderon and Andrés Baez, "The Columbus Container Services ECJ case and its consequences: A Lost Opportunity to Shed Light on the Scope of the Non-Discrimination Principle", (2009) *Intertax* 212; Gerard Meussen, "Columbus Container Services – A Victory for the Member States' fiscal autonomy", (2007) *European Taxation* 169.

[51] Advocate General Mengozzi had opined that the German switch-over clause restricted freedom of establishment and the free movement of capital. The Advocate General also devoted most of his Opinion to considering whether or not the restriction was justified – a question ultimately left for the national court. See Opinion dated 29 March 2007.

[52] *Columbus Container*, fn.50, para. 40.

With the hindsight of the issues arising in international and EU tax law, how will the CFC rules of the CCCTB proposal be interpreted? For this question to be addressed, it is important first to look briefly at the general scheme of the CCCTB.

9.3 KEY FEATURES OF THE CCCTB

The CCCTB is a proposal to provide companies with establishments in at least two Member States with the possibility of computing their group taxable income according to one set of rules, those of the new consolidated tax base, rather than national tax bases.[53]

The first salient feature of this proposal is the common tax base. The CCCTB aspires to provide cogent rules for the calculation of the tax base of group members that elect to adopt the CCCTB. The second salient feature is consolidation; i.e. the automatic set-off of profits and losses and the elimination of intra-group transactions for the consolidated group members (if different from the CCCTB group members).

The CCCTB is confined to EU companies (whether or not under ultimate EU ownership).[54] An eligible company must take one of the forms listed in Annex I to the draft CCCTB Directive and must be subject to corporate taxes in a Member State as listed in Annex II or to a similar tax introduced subsequently.[55] A company established under the laws of a third country can also benefit from the directive if the company has a similar form to one of the forms listed in Annex I and the company is subject to one of the corporate taxes listed in Annex II.[56]

Only eligible companies that are tax resident in a Member State[57] and not under the terms of a tax treaty resident in a third country may opt for the system provided for in the directive.[58] A company resident in more than one Member State is considered to be resident in the Member State in which it has its place of effective management.[59] If a company is not tax resident in a Member State, then it may opt for the system provided

---

53 For a detailed analysis of the CCCTB, from the perspective of the UK, see Christiana HJI Panayi, fn.1.

54 Proposal for a Council Directive on a Common Consolidated Corporate Tax Base (CCCTB) COM(2011) Art. 2(1).

55 *Ibid.*, Art. 2(1).

56 *Ibid.*, Art. 2(2).

57 *Ibid.*, Art. 6(1).

58 *Ibid.*, Art. 6(3) and (4).

59 *Ibid.*, Art. 6(4).

for in the draft CCCTB Directive vis-à-vis a permanent establishment maintained by it in a Member State.[60]

The new tax base will not be compulsory.[61] It is only when the option to apply the directive is exercised that eligible taxpayers satisfying a single test will be subject to mandatory consolidation (the all-in, all-out principle). All CCCTB group members will automatically be consolidated.

The starting point is Article 54 of the draft CCCTB Directive, which stipulates who the qualifying subsidiaries can be. These include all immediate and lower-tier subsidiaries in which the parent company holds the following rights: a right to exercise more than 50 per cent of the voting rights;[62] an ownership right amounting to more than 75 per cent of the company's capital or more than 75 per cent of the rights giving entitlement to profit.[63]

In the draft CCCTB Directive it is clarified that a resident taxpayer may form a group with: (a) all its EU permanent establishments; (b) all permanent establishments located in a Member State of its qualifying subsidiaries resident in a third country; (c) all its qualifying subsidiaries resident in one or more Member States; (d) other resident taxpayers that are qualifying subsidiaries of the same company that is resident in a third

---

[60] *Ibid.*, Art. 6(2). A permanent establishment is defined in Art 5 of the draft CCCTB Directive. The definition is almost identical to the definition in Art. 5 of the OECD Model. There are, however, some subtle differences. For example, for the purposes of the draft CCCTB Directive, a taxpayer can only be considered to have a permanent establishment in a state other than the state in which its central management and control is located: Art. 5(1). There is no such stipulation in Art. 5 of the OECD Model. Also, in certain places, the draft CCCTB Directive refers to "taxpayer" or "another person" (see Art. 5(3)(a), Art. 5(3)(c), Art. 5(6) by way of example), rather than enterprise.

[61] *Ibid.*, Art. 6. Also see Explanatory Memorandum to the Directive, p. 5, Commission Communication, *Implementing the Community Lisbon Programme: Progress to date and next steps towards a Common Consolidated Corporate Tax Base (CCCTB) of 5/4/2006,* COM (2006) 157 final, 8.

[62] Art. 54(1)(a) of the draft CCCTB Directive. This is subject to the rule in Art. 54(2)(a) that once the voting-right threshold is reached in respect of immediate and lower-tier subsidiaries, the parent company will be deemed to hold 100 per cent of such rights.

[63] *Ibid.*, Art. 54(1). This is subject to the rule in Art. 54(2)(b) that entitlement to profit and ownership of capital will be calculated by multiplying the interests held in intermediate subsidiaries at each tier. Ownership rights amounting to 75 per cent or less held directly or indirectly by the parent company, including rights in companies resident in a third country, will also be taken into account in the calculation.

country and has a similar form to those listed in Annex I.[64] A non-resident taxpayer may form a group in respect of all its permanent establishments located in Member States and all its qualifying subsidiaries resident in one or more Member States (and their EU permanent establishments).[65]

In any case, once the option to become a CCCTB group and, as a corollary, mandatory consolidation occur, the consolidated tax base will then be subject to apportionment according to a commonly agreed formula. The formula for apportioning the tax base comprises three equally weighted factors: labour, assets and sales.[66]

If the membership/consolidation test is not satisfied, then the taxpayer may still apply the common tax base for the purpose of determining its individual tax base. This will be on a voluntary basis, depending on whether the Member State adopts the CCCTB as an additional rather than as its unique tax base.

Contrary to some opinions, the CCCTB will not affect tax rates. The CCCTB seeks to harmonize the tax base and not the tax rates. In other words, the CCCTB determines the portion of the consolidated tax base that belongs to a Member State. Member States will be entitled to tax the income apportioned to them as they wish. This was reiterated by the Commission on the release of the draft CCCTB Directive.

The adoption of a Union[67] legislative measure such as this Directive will require unanimity[68] among Member States. This is becoming more

---

[64] *Ibid.*, Art. 55(1).

[65] *Ibid.*, Art. 55(2).

[66] *Ibid.*, Art. 86. It is noteworthy that intangible property is excluded from the asset factor and that the sales factor is sales by destination. The draft CCCTB Directive also contains sector-specific formulae for financial institutions, insurance, oil and gas, shipping and airlines. Also see the precursor to the formula, set out in CCCTB/WP060: "CCCTB: possible elements of the sharing mechanism" (10, 11 and 12 December 2007), pp. 7–15, 17.

[67] Following the Lisbon Treaty, the Treaty on European Union (TEU) is amended and the Treaty establishing the European Community (EC Treaty) is amended and renamed as the Treaty on the Functioning of the European Union (TFEU). Thereafter, the "European Union" replaces and succeeds the "European Community".

[68] By contrast to indirect taxes and the explicit tax base for harmonization found in Art. 113 TFEU (ex Art. 93 EC), for direct taxes there were never any express legislative bases in successive European Treaties. The general legislative bases found in Arts. 115 and 352 TFEU (ex Arts. 94 and 308 EC) have been used for direct tax legislation. Unanimity is required under all of these provisions. Art.

and more unlikely.[69] There had already been suggestions to allow a few Member States to adopt the CCCTB under the enhanced co-operation procedure, even before the Commission postponed its work on it in 2008. Therefore, any proposal that is agreed seems likely to be on the basis that the CCCTB is optional at Member State level; i.e. only Member States that wish to adopt it will do so. In other words, there could be non-CCCTB Member States and CCCTB Member States. It also seems most likely that the CCCTB will be elective within Member States.[70] This is because Member States are likely to maintain domestic tax rules alongside the CCCTB, since the only possibility for a single uniform tax base will exist if a Member State adopts the CCCTB rules for its domestic taxpayers as well.[71] It should be noted, however, that in the drafting of the main technical document,[72] as amended by the four papers recently released,[73] the Commission was proceeding on the assumption

---

116 TFEU (ex Art. 96 EC), another general legislative base, only requires qualified majority voting but has never been used to enact direct tax legislation.

[69] See report in *Tax Analysts* explaining the objections raised by some Member States; namely, Poland, Latvia, and Slovakia, Czech Republic and Bulgaria. Most of these Member States refer to the administrative difficulties faced by the authorities and small and medium-sized enterprises, the narrower tax base that would yield lower revenues, formulary apportionment, the elective nature of the scheme and the unclear rules. Charles Gnaedinge, "News Analysis: CCCTB Opponents Stake Out Different Positions", *Tax Analysts International* (21 November 2008). For general commentary see Luca Cerioni, "The Possible Introduction of Common Consolidated Base Taxation via Enhanced Cooperation: Some Open Issues", [2006] 5 *European Taxation* 187. The possibility of enhanced co-operation was referred to, *inter alia*, by Philip Baker and Ioanna Mitroyanni, "The CCCTB Rules and Tax Treaties", and Malcolm Gammie and Christiana HJI Panayi, "Inbound Investment and Thin Capitalization", in Michael Lang, Pasquale Pistone, Josef Schuch and Claus Staringer, *Common Consolidated Corporate Tax Base* (Linde, 2008). For an economic analysis, see Leon Bettendorf, Albert van der Horst, Ruud A. de Mooij and Handrik Vrijburg, "*Corporate tax consolidation and enhanced cooperation in the European Union*", (2009) Oxford University Centre for Business Taxation WP 10/01.

[70] CCCTB40, "Personal scope of the CCCTB".

[71] This would have to include all domestic business entities. If not, then only corporate entities within the scope of the CCCTB proposal would be able to elect to follow the CCCTB. Other business vehicles would remain outside its scope.

[72] CCCTB\WP\057\doc\en: "*CCCTB: Possible Elements of a technical outline*" (hereafter CCCTB57), annotated in December 2008 in CCCTB/WP057annotated\doc\en: "*CCCTB: Possible Elements of a technical outline – Annotated*" (hereafter CCCTB/WP057annotated).

[73] See CCCTB/RD\001\doc\en: "*Eligibility Tests for Companies and Definition of a CCCTB Group*" (hereafter CCCTB/RD\001); CCCTB/RD\002\doc\en:

that *all* Member States would adopt the CCCTB. The draft CCCTB Directive follows that approach.

Overall, the CCCTB proposal aspires to provide a common tax framework for corporate groups. As with the other direct tax directives, its protective and empowering scope is limited to EU group companies only. If eventually Member States opt out of it, then its scope would be limited to companies from CCCTB Member States only. It is not surprising, therefore, that the proposal's anti-abuse rules and more specifically the CFC rules reflect this approach.

9.4 ANTI-ABUSE AND CFC RULES OF THE CCCTB

9.4.1 General Overview

The search for the appropriate anti-abuse rules in the context of the CCCTB has been ongoing.

Prior to the release of a discussion paper on the CCCTB anti-abuse rules in April 2008, the Commission had not really given any detailed suggestions on anti-abuse rules in the context of the CCCTB. Neither had it given a view as to whether any anti-abuse rules would apply in the same way to non-CCCTB Member States and third countries – for obvious reasons. What it had said in a number of earlier reports was that it is desirable to create common rules when the common *consolidated* tax base is directly affected.

Controlled foreign companies, thin capitalization and fat capitalization were mentioned in CCCTB57 as areas in which the CCCTB may need to provide special rules.[74] However, no concrete suggestions were made. Rather, comments were invited.

In April 2008 the Commission released CCCTB65, a discussion paper focusing on anti-abuse rules for the CCCTB.[75] In this paper, the

---

"*Business Reorganisations in the CCCTB*" (hereafter CCCTB/RD\002); CCCTB/RD\003\doc\en: "*Transactions and Dealings between the Group and Entities outside the Group*" (hereafter CCCTB/RD\003); CCCTB/RD\004\doc\en: "*Anti-Abuse Rules in the CCCTB*" (hereafter CCCTB/RD\004).

[74] For CFCs, see CCCTB57, fn.72, paras.127–129; for fat capitalization, see para. 130. Passing reference is made to thin capitalization in footnote 40.

[75] CCCTB/WP065\doc\en: "CCCTB: Anti-Abuse rules" (14-15/04/2008) (hereafter CCCTB65).

Commission referred to its previous (non-CCCTB-related) Communication on anti-abuse measures mentioned above.[76] According to the Commission, the latter Communication provided "a useful framework for the concrete rules of the CCCTB but obviously the CCCTB needs to be more specific and detailed than the Communication".[77]

Within the CCCTB, there could be general or specific anti-abuse provisions, or both. If a general anti-abuse rule was established, then the "taxpayer should always be able to refute this by producing evidence of a commercial justification".[78] Although such a rule would provide Member States with a flexible tool to combat abusive practices, it may be a difficult provision to apply and be interpreted differently within Member States, thus introducing uncertainty.[79]

In CCCTB65 the Commission expressed its preference for a general anti-abuse rule underpinned by specific anti-abuse provisions. Such a combination would "provide tax administrations with easily and straightforward specific rules to combat specific and well known cases of abuse and a general rule could be applied to combat possible abuse that was not foreseen when designing the common rules".[80]

The Commission went on to analyse a number of specific anti-abuse provisions. *Inter alia*, it looked at thin capitalization rules and more general rules restricting interest deductibility, CFC rules and switch-over clauses from exemption to credit, as well as rules to avoid possible double deductions (double dips) in a "sandwich" situation. The Commission also examined rules to re-characterize the sale of shares as *sale of assets* to avoid the abuse of the consolidation rules in connection with the participation exemption. Furthermore, the Commission examined possible rules to avoid the manipulation of the factors in formulary apportionment.

Most of these issues were later on refined in the Commission's discussion document entitled *Anti-Abuse Rules in the CCCTB*.[81] In this document the anti-abuse "shield" of the CCCTB was effectively structured through rules at two levels: namely, through a General Anti-Abuse Rule (GAAR) and through specific anti-abuse rules.

The GAAR was to be triggered when a transaction or a series of transactions were carried out for the sole purpose of avoiding taxation.

---

[76] COM (2007) 785, fn.27.
[77] CCCTB65, fn.75, para. 2.
[78] *Ibid.*, para. 6.
[79] *Ibid.*, para. 8.
[80] *Ibid.*, para. 9.
[81] CCCTB/RD\004, fn.73.

Practices without economic substance were targeted (in accordance with the concept of purely artificial arrangements of the Court of Justice) and artificial steps ignored.[82] There was an escape clause if the taxpayer showed evidence of a commercial justification for its activity, even if the scheme was in essence designed to mitigate tax.[83] The GAAR would only be relevant if the potentially abusive practices were not caught by any of the other specific anti-abuse rules.[84] The specific rules[85] had the function of protecting the consolidated tax base from erosion in relations between the group and the outside world, or in intra-group transactions.[86]

Furthermore, under CCCTB/RD\004, some crucial anti-abuse rules (thin capitalization rule, switch-over clause and CFC rule) were only applicable vis-à-vis third-country companies; i.e. non-Member States.[87] The document did not include any discussion of how these rules were to apply vis-à-vis companies in a Member State that opted out of the CCCTB. Nor was there any discussion on the potential overlap between domestic and CCCTB anti-abuse rules.

The approach in CCCTB/RD\004 has been largely followed in the draft CCCTB Directive though there are some subtle differences. The GAAR, set out in Article 80,[88] is similarly structured to that in CCCTB/RD\004. However, in the draft CCCTB Directive there does not appear to be an express hierarchy between the GAAR and the specific anti-abuse rules. In other words, it is not made clear in the main text of the draft CCCTB Directive whether the GAAR would only apply if the other rules

---

[82] *Ibid.*, para. 6.

[83] *Ibid.*, para. 7.

[84] *Ibid.*, para. 9.

[85] The rules listed were the following: (i) disallowance of third-country source interest deduction; (ii) switch-over from a tax exemption of foreign income to relief by credit; (iii) controlled foreign company legislation; (iv) disallowance of the participation exemption in share disposals; (v) rules to tackle double deductions in "sandwich cases"; (vi) rules to avoid a manipulation of the asset factor.

[86] *Ibid.*, para. 5.

[87] This is understandable given that the consultations submitted to the Commission prior to the December 2007 discussion documents revealed that the business community was less inclined to have CFC rules applied within the EU for the purposes of the CCCTB.

[88] This article provides that artificial transactions carried out for the sole purpose of avoiding taxation will be ignored for the purposes of calculating the tax base. This rule does not apply to genuine commercial activities where the taxpayer is able to choose between two or more possible transactions which have the same commercial result but which produce different taxable amounts.

do not apply. Neither is it made clear in the preamble.[89] Therefore, a tax authority may be tempted to use the GAAR, which is more general and vague, rather than specific anti-abuse rules.

This is exacerbated by the fact that the specific anti-abuse rules, as set out in CCCTB/RD\004, are scattered in the draft CCCTB Directive in such a way that it is not always immediately apparent that they constitute anti-abuse rules. In fact, Chapter XIV of the draft CCCTB Directive, entitled Anti-Abuse Rules, contains only two specific anti-abuse rules (apart from the GAAR); namely, disallowance of interest deductions[90] and controlled foreign companies.[91] Again, it is not clear whether this is an intentional deviation from CCCTB/RD\004, or whether it is a deviation at all. Nevertheless, it may help tilt the balance in favour of tax authorities more frequently than not.

Overall, it would seem that the need for a GAAR remains perplexing. So does its scope and its overlap with other anti-abuse rules. One thing to note is that under the draft CCCTB Directive the application of the GAAR is not restricted to third-country entities. This could have important repercussions, not only for CCCTB companies but also for non-CCCTB EU companies. It could prove to be a means to bridge some of the differences between domestic and CCCTB anti-abuse rules, as well as fill the gaps in the design of CCCTB anti-abuse rules vis-à-vis non-CCCTB EU companies.

Some of these issues are examined in the context of the CCCTB's CFC regime.

9.4.2 The CFC Rules of the CCCTB

It was initially assumed that CCCTB Member States would develop and adopt common CFC rules within the CCCTB. This was a matter of concern to non-CCCTB Member States and third countries, especially if they had low-tax regimes.

In CCCTB57 the Commission admitted that due to the proposed exemption on outbound investment, measures would be required to protect the tax base. Two possibilities were identified, i.e. first, a switch-over to credit if

---

[89] See para. 20 of the preamble, fn.1, which states that "[t]he system should include a general anti-abuse rule, supplemented by measures designed to curb specific types of abusive practices".

[90] *Ibid.*, Art. 81.

[91] *Ibid.*, Art. 82.

exemption was not justified because of low local taxation on the foreign profits and, second, a common CFC regime.[92]

In so far as a switch-over clause was concerned, in CCCTB57 the Commission gave the following example: exemption could be conditional on profits from third countries being subject to not less than 40 per cent of the average statutory corporate income tax rate applicable in their Member State and not being subject to a special regime resulting in a substantially lower level of taxation.[93]

In so far as a common CFC regime was concerned, the Commission invited comments on:

> (i) what types of income such a regime should target; (ii) what ownership threshold should apply; (iii) whether it should apply only in the case of undistributed profits in low rate jurisdictions or should apply generally to certain income types, whether distributed or not; (iv) whether the same or different arrangements should apply to domestic, non-consolidated EU and third country companies; and (v) whether such a regime would be seen as an alternative or an adjunct to a switch-over mechanism.[94]

In the December 2007 (annotated) technical discussion document,[95] the Commission disclosed some of the comments made by Member States on this topic. The Commission noted that, apart from some divergences,[96] most of the Member States agreed that any CFC legislation should primarily cover passive income and should not hinder real economic activities.[97] Consultations from the business sector also showed lack of "appetite" for CFC rules.[98]

---

[92] CCCTB57, fn.72, para. 127.

[93] *Ibid.*, para. 128.

[94] *Ibid.*, para. 129.

[95] CCCTB/WP057annotated, fn.72.

[96] *Ibid.*, p. 32. One Member State suggested that CFC rules should also apply to mobile activities. Another Member State suggested that CFC rules should apply when more than one third of an entity's income was financial.

[97] On the relevant participation to be covered, one Member State recommended making use of a 25 per cent threshold and another a 50 per cent threshold (whether of voting rights or capital or any rights). On the geographic scope of a CFC regime, several Member States wanted CFC measures to apply to any entities not included in the CCCTB group and this would include EU and third-country entities. In addition, one Member State stressed that CFC rules should be complementary to switch-over clauses and should not be applied as an alternative. *Ibid.*

[98] For example, Business Europe Task Force considered that there was no need for CFC rules as the switch-over mechanism sufficed. However, "[s]uch a

Under the more recent discussion paper CCCTB/RD\004, the switch-over clause was preserved as an exception to the general rule of exempting inbound profit distributions, proceeds from share disposals and income earned from third-country-located permanent establishments.[99] These otherwise exempt inflows were made taxable and credit was given for tax already paid at source. The aim was to discourage the inflow of revenues through low-tax third countries.[100]

For the purposes of this provision, according to the Commission, a low-tax third country was one which operated under its general tax regime a statutory corporate tax rate lower than 40 per cent of the average statutory corporate tax rate in the Member States or a special regime allowing for substantially lower tax than its general regime.[101]

The switch-over clause, as set out in Article 73 of the draft CCCTB Directive, adopts the Commission's wording in CCCTB/RD\004. The only difference is that the provision is listed in Chapter XII, entitled Dealings between Group and Other Entities, rather than within the Anti-Abuse Rules chapter. Also, Article 73 further adds that the average statutory corporate tax rate applicable in the Member States will be published by the Commission annually and will be calculated as an arithmetic average.

It would seem that the current drafting of the switch-over clause continues to perpetuate the confusion as to whether such a clause can be applicable to non-CCCTB Member States. It is also unclear whether in finding the average statutory corporate tax rate in the EU only participating Member States will be taken into account. Moreover, the switch-over clause does not have an escape clause in cases of genuine economic activities, which is something already criticized.[102]

---

clause would only apply vis-à-vis third countries and never vis-à-vis EU Member States (even for those which would not participate in the CCCTB)". CCCTB/WP057annotated, fn.72, p. 32. EUROCHAMBRES even proposed the gradual abolition of CFC regimes. Specifically, CFC rules "try to prevent resident companies from avoiding domestic tax by diverting income to subsidiaries in countries with a significantly lower level of taxation and thus tax abuse. There is a need to avoid disproportionate restrictions on cross-border activities which go against Community law and seriously hamper business." EUROCHAMBRES, "Company Taxation – complement the freedoms of the Single Market to foster the growth of European businesses", p. 6.

99 CCCTB/RD\004, fn.73, para. 15.

100 *Ibid.*

101 *Ibid.*, para. 16.

102 Also see criticism by Business Europe Task Force, published in its discussion of the switch-over clause under CCCTB/RD\004. The fact that the

As for the relationship between the switch-over clause and CFC rules, in CCCTB/RD\004 the Commission had stated that the CFC rules of the CCCTB function as an adjunct and not as an alternative to the switch-over clause.[103] By contrast, the draft CCCTB Directive does not refer to the relationship between the two. The fact that one rule is set out in the chapter on dealings between the group and other entities and the other rule is set out in the chapter on anti-abuse rules might even suggest that the two rules have a different function and could be applied simultaneously.

In any case, the new CFC rules, drafted in line with CCCTB/RD\004, provide for the tax base to include the non-distributed income of an entity resident in a third country where the following conditions are met:

(a) The taxpayer, by itself or together with its associated enterprises, controls more than 50 per cent of the voting rights or owns more than 50 per cent of the capital or is entitled to receive more than 50 per cent of the profit.[104]
(b) The CFC is tax resident in a low-tax third country, meaning a country which operates under its general tax regime, a statutory corporate tax rate lower than 40 per cent of the average statutory corporate tax rate in the Member States, or a special regime allowing for a substantially lower level of taxation than the general regime.[105] EEA countries which exchange information to the standard of the Mutual Assistance Directive 2011/16/EU are excluded from the scope of this rule.[106]

---

switch-over clause is not listed with the other Anti-Abuse Rules of the draft CCCTB Directive is unlikely to be sufficient justification, as another anti-abuse provision listed in this chapter (Art. 75: Disallowance of exempt share transfers) contains an escape clause.

103 CCCTB/RD\004, fn.73, para. 17.

104 Art. 82(1)(a) of the draft CCCTB Directive. Also see CCCTB/RD\004,fn.73, paragraph 19(a). In defining "control" in CCCTB65, the Commission thought that although various possibilities existed "probably for the CCCTB the CFC should be considered to be under the control of the resident company if this company controls, direct or indirectly, more than 50 per cent of the voting rights, ownership or capital or entitlement to profits". CCCTB65, fn.75, para. 30. Other possibilities referred to were the rules on related parties (20 per cent of voting rights – see CCCTB57, para. 78) and control as defined in the Parent-Subsidiary Directive. These possibilities should be considered when the >50 per cent threshold is owned by any entities acting in concert.

105 Art. 82(1)(b) of the draft CCCTB Directive and CCCTB/RD\004, fn.73, para.19(b). Also see CCCTB/WP057 annotated, fn.72, para. 128 and CCCTB65,

(c) The CFC's principal class of shares is not regularly traded on a recognized stock exchange.[107]

(d) More than 30 per cent of the income accruing to the CFC is "tainted".[108] The concept includes certain listed types of revenues[109] where more than 50 per cent of this category of income is derived from transactions between the CFC and the taxpayer or its associated enterprises.[110]

CFC rules in the CCCTB only apply to subsidiaries resident in a third country.[111] All non-distributed income of the CFC will be taxable in proportion to the profit entitlement of the taxpayer.[112] Distributed profits and/or proceeds of a share disposal linked to an entity which has already

---

fn.75, para. 30 in that a foreign tax rate would be acceptable if it is not less than 40 per cent of the average statutory corporate tax rate applicable in Member States and not subject to a special regime resulting in a substantially lower level of taxation.

106 *Ibid.*, Art. 82(2).

107 *Ibid.*, Art. 82(1)(d) and CCCTB/RD\004, fn.73, para.19(c).

108 Art. 82(1)(c) and CCCTB/RD\004, para.19(d). Art. 82(1)(c) does not use the term "tainted" income.

109 *Inter alia,* interest, royalties, dividends, income from the disposal of shares, income from insurance, banking and other financial activities, income from movable property or from immovable property. See Art.82(3) of the draft CCCTB Directive. CCCTB/RD\004, fn.73, para. 19(d) had stated that this income would be tainted, unless a tax treaty was in place which provided otherwise.

110 See Art. 82(3) of the draft CCCTB Directive and CCCTB/RD\004, fn.73, para.19(d). This also seems to follow from the discussion in CCCTB65. In this document, in defining a "CFC", there were two suggestions: a CFC ought to be defined, either by taking into account the fact that the CFC does not *engage in any real economic activity* or by considering *the nature of the income earned* by the CFC (in other words, checking if it is mainly passive income). CCCTB65, fn.75, para. 30. The Commission preferred the latter and argued that the CFC should be defined "considering the nature of the income earned by the company: if a certain threshold of the total income earned by the company is passive income (for example 80 per cent) the company would be a CFC". CCCTB65, para. 34.

111 See Art. 82(1) and CCCTB/RD\004, fn.73, para. 20.

112 See Art. 83(2), dealing with computation. Also see CCCTB/RD\004, fn.73, para. 19 which further provided that the non-distributed income of the CFC would be taxable without distinction between active and passive income. This seemed to be contrary to the preference shown by the Commission in CCCTB65 where it was stated that "[o]nce the CFC is identified only the passive income should be integrated in the tax base of the resident company and when

been taxed by the group as a CFC will be deducted from the tax base when calculating the taxpayer's liability to tax on the distributed income.[113] If a CFC is loss-making, the losses will not be incorporated in the tax base of the taxpayer but the CFC will be entitled to carry forward the losses for future years.[114]

This provision is beleaguered by similar drafting limitations as other provisions. Let us take as an example the threshold test. A CFC would be tax resident in a low-tax third country if it is subject to taxation which is lower than 40 per cent of the average statutory corporate tax rate or is subject to a special regime that allows for a substantially lower level of taxation than the general regime. How will this average statutory corporate tax rate be calculated? Will this average be calculated on a yearly basis? Also, how can it be assessed that a special regime is in place that allows for a substantially lower level of taxation? What is the general regime or is it assessed from the perspective of the relevant Member State (i.e. of the principal tax authority) or of Member States in general? The latter would prove impossible to assess. The former would give rise to opportunities for tax arbitrage.

Another issue is the treatment of EEA states. The CFC provision does not apply to CFCs in EEA states if these states exchange information to the standard of the new Mutual Assistance Directive 2011/16/EU. However, it is highly unlikely that EEA States exchange information to such standards, as the new directive contains very extensive provisions for this which go much further than the OECD standard.[115] It is questionable that there should be such reliance and dependence on exchange of information standards.

---

the CFC distributes dividends it would be assumed that the dividends are firstly paid out of the passive income." CCCTB65, fn.75, para. 34.

[113] See Art. 83(4) and (5). Also see CCCTB/RD\004, fn.73, para. 16. This is broadly aligned with the Commission's stance in CCCTB65 in that "there should be relief for the taxes paid abroad and the income that has been taxed in the CFC by being included in the tax base of the resident shareholders should not be double taxed when the dividends are distributed to those shareholders". CCCTB65, fn.75, para. 32. The Commission also argued in paragraph 34 that when the CFC distributed dividends, then it should be assumed that these dividends were firstly paid out of passive income. This is not addressed in CCCTB/RD\003, fn.73.

[114] Art. 83(1) and CCCTB/RD\004, fn.73, para. 20.

[115] For example, from 2014 it provides for mandatory automatic exchange of information on some types of income such as income from employment, directors' fees, pensions, ownership of and income from immovable property and so on. See Art. 8(1). More types of income may be added in this list at a later

Furthermore, the CFC provision does not seem to contain a business activity test or genuine economic activities test or a commercial justification exemption. This seems to contradict the case law of the Court of Justice which only allows national CFC rules if they target wholly artificial arrangements.[116] It may also raise problems as in most domestic CFC regimes, there is some sort of an active trade exemption.

Lastly, an issue that is also relevant to the thin capitalization provision is examined below. Who decides whether the CFC provision applies and how will this be policed? Much will depend on the attitude of the principal tax authority (usually, the tax authority of the parent company's Member State). If they have a lax attitude towards CFCs (or are countries which traditionally have no CFC regimes),[117] then they might not insist on the rigorous application of the rule. This might create an incentive for groups of companies to set up their headquarters in those Member States, therefore leading to intra-EU (or intra-CCCTB) competition. Of course, this will be exacerbated if a business activity test is inserted in the CFC rule, as Member States will have more discretion in applying it. Therefore, it is not certain whether Member States will either apply this anti-abuse rule or apply it in a uniform way.

Furthermore, here, the Commission limits the ambit of the rules to third country CFCs. Therefore, it is uncertain whether the same rules would apply if the controlled foreign company was established in a non-CCCTB Member State. This is understandable given that the Commission has drafted the CCCTB proposal on the basis that all Member States would adopt it. In other words, for the Commission, there could only be CFCs established in third countries – there could never be non-CCCTB CFCs within the EU.

Given the hostility of some Member States towards the CCCTB, this is not a very realistic stance to take and, as mentioned above, enhanced cooperation is likely to be triggered. There may very well be non-CCCTB Member States with low-tax regimes, in which controlled companies may be established. This could create situations of tax arbitrage, which are considered below.

In any case, whichever CFC rules and/or switch-over mechanisms are eventually adopted for the purposes of the CCCTB, their application would still have to comply with the case law of the Court of Justice,

stage. See Art. 8(5). There is also a provision for onward transmission of information from third countries and an MFN clause. See Arts. 24 and 19, respectively.

[116] See below.

[117] For example, Cyprus and Malta.

mentioned below. This point was reiterated by the Commission in CCCTB65.[118] Referring to its Communication on anti-abuse measures, the Commission commented that "[t]o comply with the ECJ law either CFC rules are only to be applied in relation with third countries or CFC rules are also to be applied within the EU but, in this case, the rules should be targeted at wholly artificial arrangements only".[119]

Therefore, any CFC rules in the context of the CCCTB would have to comply with the principles of the case law mentioned above.[120] In other words, they have to be targeted against wholly artificial arrangements, be suitable and proportional. Arguably, *Columbus Container* leaves considerable leeway for the Member States to switch to the credit mechanism when the controlled subsidiary of a domestic company is in a low-tax jurisdiction. Consequently, in contrast to the more general CFC rules for which *Cadbury Schweppes* is highly prescriptive, in principle, a CCCTB regime could incorporate a switch-over mechanism with relative ease.

9.4.3 The CCCTB's CFC Rules and Tax Arbitrage

As mentioned earlier, the fact that the current CFC and switch-over rules are limited to third countries only may lead to opportunities for tax arbitrage.

Let us take as an example Cyprus, which has a 12.5 per cent corporation tax rate. Compared to a CCCTB Member State with a statutory tax rate of >32 per cent, Cyprus may be seen as subjecting CFC profits to less than 40 per cent of the average statutory corporate income tax rate applicable in the Member State of the parent company. If this were a third country, then the CCCTB CFC rules would be triggered following CCCTB/RD\004. However, as this is an EU Member State, then the CCCTB CFC rules are not triggered *ab initio*.

This could mean that intra-EU CFC structures which qualify as a CCCTB group would be insulated from attribution of profits or switch-over clauses, even in situations where domestic CFC rules or CCCTB anti-abuse rules would be triggered. However, it is still unclear whether the GAAR can be used by the Member State of the parent company to apply its stricter version of anti-deferral rules. It is also unclear whether the application of the GAAR would be more or less justified if the CFC

---

118 See para. 29 in CCCTB65, fn.75: "[…] if CFC rules were to be introduced in the CCCTB they should be in line with the recent ECJ rulings".

119 *Ibid.*, citing COM (2007) 785.

120 See 9.2.2 above.

is established in a non-CCCTB Member State rather than a CCCTB Member State.

Another issue arising is whether the non-CCCTB Member State of the parent company of a consolidated CFC in another Member State is obliged to follow the CCCTB anti-abuse rules, as a result of its duties under enhanced co-operation.

Let us assume under the UK CFC rules, that profits of an Irish CFC are attributed to the UK parent company, in situations where profits would not be attributed under the CCCTB. If Ireland is a CCCTB Member State and the CFC is part of a CCCTB group, will the UK be able to apply its domestic CFC rules and attribute profits to the UK parent company or will it be obliged to defer to the CCCTB rules, even if it is not part of it? Again, in such situations, the GAAR could provide a way to prevent or resolve these conflicts.

Furthermore, the issue of deferral and CFCs could arise in a purely domestic setting, given that the threshold for membership and consolidation is relatively high. In such circumstances, there could be non-consolidated controlled group companies within the same CCCTB Member State of one of the consolidated companies.

The following example helps illustrate the point.

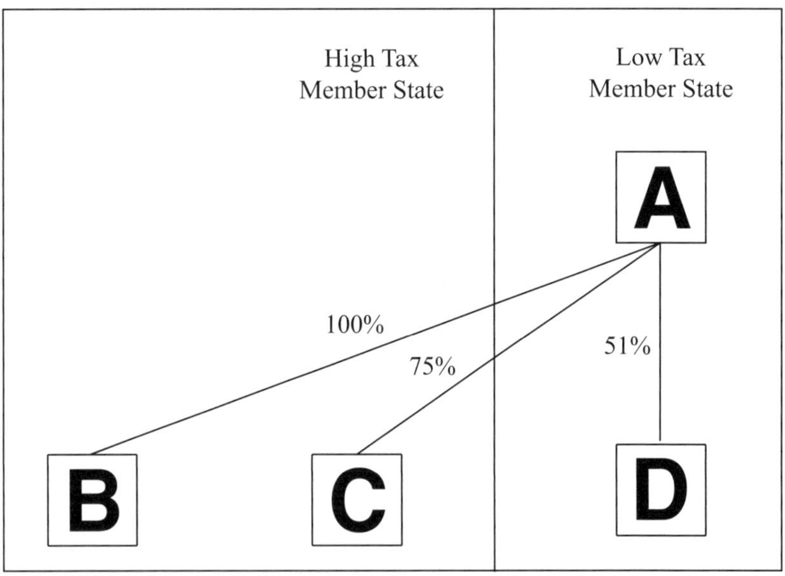

Figure 9.1 Deferral in a domestic scenario

Here, it is assumed that companies A, B and C are consolidated companies. Company D is non-consolidated.[121] Let us assume group profits are artificially diverted to company D, where they are taxed at 10 per cent corporation tax. Had the profits not been diverted away from the consolidated group, then after formulary apportionment, a higher portion of the consolidated tax base could have been allocated to the high-tax Member State.

Arguably, here, there is an issue of deferral of profits through a CFC. Since the consolidated profits represent to an extent a mix of domestic and foreign profits, company D is akin to a controlled *foreign* company, being foreign to the consolidated base and a shelter in which otherwise consolidated profits could find their way.

Therefore, CFC issues[122] are likely to be of concern both to low-tax CCCTB and non-CCCTB Member States.

9.5 CONCLUSION

The taxation of CFCs is a very topical issue due to the changes in regimes in many Member States. In the context of the CCCTB, itself a highly contentious proposal, the taxation of CFCs is even more problematic. This contribution sought to explore the relevant dimensions.

One crucial aspect of the analysis is the Commission's stance in that unless it proceeds on the assumption that all Member States will adopt the CCCTB, then the proposal will not muster enough support or interest to be considered by Member States, even for partial implementation.

---

[121] Company D could voluntarily adopt the new tax base. However, the fact that company D may have to calculate its tax profits on the basis of the CCCTB does not affect the tax rate that would be applied to it. Therefore, mere adherence to the new tax base, without consolidation, is not relevant to this case study.

[122] The same arguments are applicable to thin capitalization structures involving a German borrower company which is a CCCTB company and its foreign lender. If the foreign lender is an associated enterprise in a third country, and there is a commercial justification, then interest may be deductible in situations where it would not have been deductible under the German thin capitalization rules. Similarly, if the lender is a non-CCCTB Member State company, then arguably the CCCTB thin capitalization rules are not applicable and interest may be deductible in situations where it would not have been deductible under the German thin capitalization rules. Again, it is not certain whether the German rules will apply by default or whether the application of the GAAR will result in deference being paid to the domestic rules. See HJI Panayi, fn.1, part 6.3.

Whilst this is an understandable position, as argued elsewhere,[123] it does disservice to the whole project, as it leaves it with large gaps in the analysis.

It has been shown in this chapter that the uncertainty over the scope of the GAAR and the lack of clarity as regards the application of the CCCTB's CFC rules vis-à-vis groups with non-CCCTB Member State companies increases the opportunities for tax arbitrage. This is rather unfortunate, as the underlying aim of the CCCTB proposal was to simplify the tax matrix affecting EU groups and to reduce compliance costs. Without acknowledging the possible existence of non-CCCTB Member States and clearly setting out the rules applicable to them in their relations with CCCTB Member States and third countries, any CCCTB rules, and especially the anti-abuse rules, are likely to generate more obstacles and restrictions to cross-border groups than the current situation.

In the author's opinion, the Commission should release its views on what the legal position of non-CCCTB Member States is likely to be, rather than leave it for later, or worse, leave it to the Court of Justice. As shown, the possible implications of the Member States' obligations under the enhanced co-operation procedure are not insignificant in so far as the application of anti-abuse rules and especially CFC rules are concerned. Non-CCCTB Member States may lose out on the benefits of the CCCTB while being burdened with a (positive) duty not to impede its implementation. It is therefore essential that the Commission draft some complementary rules which will govern the rights and obligations of non-CCCTB Member States. That way, Member States could make informed decisions as to whether it would be more suitable for them to opt in or opt out of the CCCTB. The CCCTB's CFC rules could provide a good starting point.

---

123 HJI Panayi, fn.1, part 7.

Commentary

Walter Hellerstein

The following comments on the proposed CCCTB[124] CFC rules are written from the perspective of a third-country observer who has focused largely on the text of the CFC rules and who professes no familiarity with either their extensive "legislative history"[125] or the European Court of Justice case law that may affect them. Such a limitation on any remarks could be regarded as an interesting "thought experiment" designed to tease out the implications of the plain meaning of the language of the CCCTB CFC rules uninfluenced by "extra-textual" sources. In my case, however, the introductory caveat is more accurately viewed as "truth in advertising", because of my general lack of familiarity with the details of the CCCTB, its legislative history and the relevant EU case law.[126] The restriction on the scope of my comments thus relieves me of the burden of undertaking any inquiry into the thorny questions of how the CFC rules are to be construed with respect to non-CCCTB Member State companies – questions that are better left to others with an intimate understanding of the intra-EU issues raised by the CFC and related rules. Instead, I shall focus my attention exclusively

[124] European Commission, Proposal for a Council Directive on a Common Consolidated Corporate Tax Base (CCCTB), COM(2011) 121/3 (16 March 2011). For ease of exposition, all ensuing references to the proposed CCCTB will be simply to the CCCTB.

[125] By "legislative history", I mean the various CCCTB-related communications and other documents produced by the Commission in connection with the development of the proposed CCCTB.

[126] If my comments had been directed to the CCCTB's apportionment provisions, the statement in the text would need some modification. See Walter Hellerstein, "Formulary Apportionment in the EU and the US: A Comparative Perspective on the Sharing Mechanism of the Proposed Common Consolidated Corporate Tax Base" in Ana Paula Dourado (ed.), *Tax Mobility* (IBFD 2013); Walter Hellerstein, "Tax Planning Under the CCCTB's Formulary Apportionment Provisions: The Good, the Bad, and the Ugly" in Dennis Weber (ed.), *CCCTB: Selected Issues* (Kluwer Law International 2012) 221–252.

on the application of the CCCTB CFC rules as written to corporations resident in third countries.

CFC rules share the widely recognized objective of preventing erosion of the domestic tax base through the deferral of foreign-source income earned by foreign corporations controlled by resident taxpayers under circumstances that are perceived by legislative bodies to be, in some sense, "artificial".[127] The CCCTB CFC rules fall squarely within this description.[128] CFC rules typically seek to achieve their objective by requiring that controlling resident shareholders include in their income their proportionate share of the CFC's undistributed income. Again, the CCCTB CFC rules follow this pattern.[129]

Although they share a common purpose and structural features, CFC rules differ in their particulars from CFC regime to CFC regime.[130] For example, the United States, which was the first country to adopt a CFC regime in 1962, generally requires that resident taxpayers own 10 per cent or more of the voting power of a CFC before they are required to include any portion of the CFC's undistributed income in their tax base.[131] The CCCTB CFC rules, by contrast, appear to have no participation threshold for individual taxpayers, as long as "the taxpayer by itself, or together with associated enterprises" has a more than 50 per cent ownership interest in the voting rights,[132] capital, or profits of the CFC.[133] Furthermore, the US CFC rules require the inclusion of only specifically identified categories of undistributed income, namely low-taxed passive or relatively movable income and income not reflecting "real" economic activity, while leaving untaxed the CFC's undistributed income earned in low-tax jurisdictions but derived from substantial

---

127 See, for example, Georg Kofler, "CFC Rules" in Michael Lang, Pasquale Pistone, Josef Schuch and Claus Staringer (eds), *Common Consolidated Corporate Tax Base* (Linde 2008) 725–749, 727–728.

128 I will break my own rule regarding references to legislative history by citing, for the limited purpose of this generalization, European Commission, CCCTB/RD\004\doc\en: "Anti-Abuse Rules in the CCCTB" (28 October 2010), para. 17.

129 Proposal for a Council Directive on a Common Consolidated Corporate Tax Base (CCCTB)COM(2011) Articles 82, 83.

130 Kofler, fn 127, 725–749, 728.

131 US Internal Revenue Code §§ 951(b), 957(c).

132 Directly or indirectly.

133 Proposal for a Council Directive on a Common Consolidated Corporate Tax Base (CCCTB)COM(2011) Article 82(1)(a).

economic activity.[134] The CCCTB CFC rules, by contrast, draw no distinction between a CFC's "passive" or "active" income that is included in the resident taxpayer's tax base, as long as the CFC meets the requirements identifying it as an entity whose undistributed income will be included in its owners' tax base. This is sometimes characterized as the "entity approach" as distinguished from the "transactional approach" employed in the United States and other countries, which require the inclusion in the controlling owners' tax base only of "tainted income" earned by the CFC.[135]

I now turn to some of the specific issues that the CCCTB CFC rules raise with respect to third countries. The focus will be on the relationship between the CFC rules and the switch-over clause,[136] because an examination of their common and distinct features, as well as their interaction, provides a useful vehicle for exploring some of the key issues raised by the CFC rules. The switch-over clause provides that the CCCTB will "switch over" from the exemption method, which generally applies to received profit distributions, proceeds from disposal of shares, and income of a PE in a third country,[137] to a taxation-with-credit method[138] where the entity that made the profit distribution, or whose shares were sold, or whose income-producing PE is in a third country were subject to a low level of taxation in the entity's country of residence or of its income-producing PE.

The objective of the switch-over clause, like the objective of the CFC rules, is to prevent erosion of the CCCTB tax base by removing the tax benefit of conducting activities in low-tax or no tax jurisdictions.[139] Both the switch-over clause and the CFC rules thus constitute an effort to resolve the tension in the CCCTB, and, indeed, in any system of

---

[134] Charles Gustafson, Robert Peroni and Richard Pugh, *Taxation of International Transactions* (4th edn, West 2011) 489–490.

[135] Kofler, fn 127, 725–749, 746.

[136] Proposal for a Council Directive on a Common Consolidated Corporate Tax Base (CCCTB)COM(2011) Article 73.

[137] Proposal for a Council Directive on a Common Consolidated Corporate Tax Base (CCCTB)COM(2011) Articles 11(c), 11(d), 11(e).

[138] Proposal for a Council Directive on a Common Consolidated Corporate Tax Base (CCCTB)COM(2011) Article 76.

[139] For the second and last time, I will break my own rule regarding references to legislative history by citing, for the limited purpose of this generalization, European Commission, CCCTB/RD\004\doc\en: "Anti-Abuse Rules in the CCCTB" (28 October 2010), para. 15.

international income taxation, between capital import neutrality (exemption) and capital export neutrality (residence-credit). The common purpose of the switch-over clause and the CFC rule is reflected in the fact that they employ an *identical* definition of a low-tax country, which is one of the conditions for the application of either the switch-over clause or the CFC rules, namely, "a general regime" in a "third country" "at a statutory corporate tax rate lower than 40% of the average statutory corporate tax rate applicable in the Member States or, … a special regime that allows for a substantially lower level of taxation than that of the general regime."[140]

At least to an uninitiated reader like myself, the condition on the application of the switch-over and CFC rules – that the third country have "a special regime that allows for a substantially lower level of taxation than that of the general regime" – simply invites uncertainty and controversy. First, unless there is a widely understood concept of "substantially lower level of taxation" in the European Union, a question which I can happily say is outside my self-imposed remit, the concept, like beauty, would seem to lie in the eyes of the beholder. Second, even assuming that one could agree on what "substantially lower" means, there could well be complex issues of administrative implementation if the allegedly preferential special regime bears no relation to the entity's income, for example, it is subject to a per unit tax on natural resource extraction in lieu of an income tax. Third, there is the question of the relationship between the two legs of the definition: are they related or independent?

For example, suppose that the average corporate income tax rate applicable in the Member States is 25 per cent (40 per cent of which is 10 per cent), the statutory rate in the CFC state is 30 per cent, but due to a special tax regime the income of the CFC benefits from a 60 per cent exemption.[141] If the CFC earns income of EUR 1000, the CFC will have EUR 400 of taxable income and will pay a tax of 30 per cent or EUR 120 for an effective tax rate of 12 per cent, which exceeds the 10 per cent floor for low-tax states. Can one nevertheless maintain that the 60 per

[140] Proposal for a Council Directive on a Common Consolidated Corporate Tax Base (CCCTB)COM(2011) Article 82(1)(b); see also Article 73. It is worth observing that the same language is employed in Article 81, which disallows specified interest deductions paid to associated enterprises resident in "low-tax" third countries.

[141] This example is taken from Mario Tenore, "CFC Rule" in Dennis Weber (ed.), *CCCTB: Selected Issues* (Kluwer Law International 2012), 299–311, 307–08.

cent exemption is "a special regime that allows for a substantially lower level of taxation than that of the general regime"?

Despite their common objectives and definitions of low-tax states, there are important differences in the scope and application of the switch-over rule and the CFC rule. First, the switch-over rule applies only to income distributed to or realized by a group member whereas the CFC rules apply only to "non-distributed" income earned by separate legal entities (CFCs). Nevertheless, the differences in their application may be more apparent than real. Undistributed income taxed pursuant to the CFC rules can subsequently become income subject to taxation (rather than exemption), but eligible for a credit, under the switch-over clause. However, the CCCTB credit that applies to income that is taxable under the switch-over clause will *not* apply to distributed income previously taxed pursuant to the CFC rules, because the credit applies only to a *source-based* tax imposed for income that is no longer exempt. It says nothing about a *residence-based* tax imposed on income previously taxed on a residence basis under the CFC rules. The CCCTB CFC rules have properly addressed this problem of double residence taxation, which applies to *any* distributed income previously taxed under the CFC rules (including income subject to tax under the switch-over clause), by providing that "income previously included in the tax base" under the CFC rules "shall be deducted from the tax base when calculating the taxpayer's liability on the distributed income."[142]

The switch-over clause and the CFC rules differ not only in the type of income to which they apply but also in their scope. The switch-over clause is both narrower and broader in its scope than the CFC rules. The switch-over clause applies only to three categories of generally exempt income, but it applies regardless of the nature of the entity that is the source of the income, as long as the country of the entity's residence or where its PE is located meets the low-tax requirement. The CFC rules, by contrast, apply to all of the CFC's undistributed income, active or passive, but only to entities that meet the CFC's rule's various requirements:

- control of CFC (50 per cent voting rights, capital, or profit rights);
- CFC's "tainted" income (more than 30 per cent of CFC's income is from specified categories of mobile income[143] when more than 50

[142] Proposal for a Council Directive on a Common Consolidated Corporate Tax Base (CCCTB)COM(2011) Article 83(4).

[143] Interest, royalties, dividends, movable property, immovable property, and insurance, banking, and other financial institutions. CCCTB Article 82(3). Immovable property is not counted if the taxpayer's Member State would not

per cent of the specified category comes from transactions with the taxpayer or its associated enterprises);

- principal class of CFC's shares not regularly traded on recognized stock exchanges; and
- CFC's low-tax country residence.[144]

There is one final point to be made about the switch-over clause and the CFC rules, which is that neither has a "safe harbour" for active business income. Once the requirements of either provision are satisfied, all the income in question is subject to tax (whether as a switch-over from exempt to taxable with credit or as a deemed distribution) regardless of whether the income is active or passive. To an American observer at least, this is somewhat odd,[145] because, as I have already noted,[146] our CFC provisions are generally viewed as targeting "artificial" arrangements (as well as income that is easy to move from one jurisdiction to another) and "active" income earned by a CFC is generally not taxed until distributed. It is not entirely clear why no "active" business exception was ultimately adopted with respect to the switch-over or CFC rules, although perhaps the explanation is simply that capital export neutrality concerns trumped capital import neutrality concerns. This explanation, however, is difficult to square – at least theoretically – with the exception to the disallowance of interest deductions paid to associated enterprises resident in low-tax third countries when "the interest is paid to an entity engaged, in its country of residence, in the active conduct of a trade or business".[147]

---

have been entitled to tax the income under an agreement with a third country. CCCTB Article 82(3)(e).

[144] There is an exception to the CFC rule where the third country is party to the European Economic Area (EEA) Agreement and there is an information exchange agreement comparable to the agreement that governs EU Member States. CCCTB Article 82(2) (citing Directive 2011/16/EU). There is no exception to the CFC rule, however, where a third country is *not* a party to the EEA Agreement and there is nevertheless an information exchange agreement comparable to the agreement that governs EU Member States.

[145] I note in passing that HJI Panayi, whose excellent chapter on the CFC rules are the *raison d'être* for these brief comments, has also noted the inconsistency between the lack of an "escape clause in cases of genuine economic activities" and earlier views expressed by Member States and the Commission.

[146] See *supra* note 134 and accompanying text.

[147] Proposal for a Council Directive on a Common Consolidated Corporate Tax Base (CCCTB)COM(2011) Article 81(3)(c).

Commentary

Richard Lyal

Although her chapter deals principally with CFC rules, Dr HJI Panayi begins with a brief description of the CCCTB proposal as a whole. That seems a sufficient pretext to include a few general remarks.

It may be recalled that 2011 was the silver jubilee of the "*avoir fiscal*" judgment,[148] and it is worth reflecting on the importance of "*avoir fiscal*" as part of the context for the CCCTB proposal. In that seminal judgment the ECJ not only established the principle that the Treaty freedoms apply in the field of direct taxation just as they do in any other field of national legislation but also laid down the basic logic that it has continued to pursue in subsequent cases. The Court first stated that in general, tax rules must apply in a non-discriminatory manner to domestic and to cross-border situations. It then discussed the justifications which may be advanced for different treatment of these two categories. Much of the later case law may be regarded as little more than a gloss on "*avoir fiscal*", though recent years have seen the development of new theories of justification and a particular emphasis on the concept of balanced allocation of taxing rights.

During the intervening period, and in particular over the last dozen years, a large number of cases on direct tax have come before the ECJ. Most of them concern the application of the Treaty freedoms, and most of the recent cases revolve around the apprehension felt by Member States regarding possible erosion of their tax base. The fear that income may be shifted by artificial or devious means towards countries (whether Member States or not) where the tax burden is lower is a legitimate one. In its case law the Court has by now laid down some relatively clear lines on the measures that Member States may take to protect themselves, but there remains considerable scope for debate, particularly on the issue of proportionality. Two things nevertheless seem beyond dispute: the existing situation results in a non-negligible amount of double taxation, and

[148] Commission v France [1986] ECR 273, Case 279/83.

the efforts of Member States to protect themselves result in complication and increased compliance expense for business.

One of the main virtues of the CCCTB proposal is that it would in principle resolve a substantial proportion of those problems at one stroke. Consolidation and the use of formulary apportionment remove the need for Member States to worry about erosion of their tax base. Companies are unable to lower their tax liability in one (by hypothesis relatively high tax) Member State and increase it in another by using such devices as holding companies or finance subsidiaries. At most, Member States might need to worry about manipulation of the apportionment factors, but an astute choice of factors ought to minimize any such risk. If the CCCTB had been in force over the last ten years, there would have been no reason for the majority of the cases that have come before the ECJ – for example, there would have been no scope for disputes over thin capitalization or CFC rules within the Union. Nor would litigation on stranded losses such as *Marks and Spencer* have been necessary. From the point of view of compliance, the removal of the need to engage in transfer pricing calculations in respect of intra-group transactions would significantly facilitate cross-border business operations. Moreover, elimination of the possibility of exploiting mismatches between the national legislation of different Member States in intra-group transactions is a positive factor for tax administrations. From a practical point of view, therefore, consolidation is probably the most interesting aspect of the proposal.

But it is not the only utility of the proposal. This is a comprehensive scheme that would obviate the need for companies doing business across frontiers to deal with multiple tax systems, multiple rules on accounting for tax purposes, multiple tax returns. That in itself ought to bring about a considerable administrative simplification for business.

At the same time, there is no attempt (or indeed any obvious reason) to harmonize tax rates. Tax competition between Member States can continue. What is new is that this tax competition can take place in an open and transparent manner, because differences in the tax base no longer obscure the calculation.

Dr HJI Panayi begins by describing the context within which the CFC rules contained in the CCCTB proposal must be examined. First, she outlines the reasons for the existence of such rules in national legislation (which are also the reasons for the inclusion of such a rule in the CCCTB proposal). In the following section she discusses the EU law context, which places a number of constraints on the legislator in relation to the taxation of dealings with related companies both in third countries and in Member States.

Those constraints flow from the basic economic freedoms laid down in the Treaty, notably freedom of establishment and free movement of capital.

Dr HJI Panayi refers in particular to the case law of the ECJ on CFC rules, namely the *Cadbury*[149] judgment and the reasoned order in the *CFC GLO*[150] case, and to the *Vodafone 2*[151] case in the English Court of Appeal. The *Cadbury* judgment is well known to tax lawyers. It concerned the CFC rules of the United Kingdom, which were fairly narrowly framed but left considerable discretion to the tax authorities and were based on a rather indefinite concept of intention on the part of the taxpayer to reduce the tax burden. The judgment contains perhaps the clearest statement of the judge-made principle of EU law regarding abuse of law: in order for a restriction on the freedom of establishment to be justified on the ground of prevention of abusive practices, the specific objective of the rule in issue must be to prevent conduct involving the creation of wholly artificial arrangements which do not reflect economic reality, with a view to escaping the tax normally due on the profits generated by activities carried out on national territory.

The focus is thus on the tax base and on the preservation of the right of a Member State to tax profits from activities carried on in its territory, but a clear limit is placed on the types of measures that Member States may deploy in order to protect that tax base. For example, they may not take measures which are based on the premise that if an activity can be carried on in a company's home territory, then it ought to be done there. In the case of CFCs, there can be no presumption that the attribution of tasks to an affiliate in another country – especially in a low-tax jurisdiction – constitutes tax avoidance or evasion. Only where it is quite clear that there is not a valid economic reason for doing things in a certain way, only where there is no real business activity in a low-tax jurisdiction can the Member State ignore the separate legal personality of the foreign subsidiary and tax the profits of the latter in the hands of its own resident company.

The core of the *Cadbury* judgment lies in the question whether a subsidiary carries on real economic activities or is merely an artificial

---

[149] Cadbury Schweppes and Cadbury Schweppes Overseas v Commissioners of Inland Revenue [2006] ECR I-7995, C-196/04.

[150] Test Claimants in the CFC and Dividend Group Litigation v Commissioners of Inland Revenue [2008] ECR I-2875, C-201/05.

[151] Vodafone 2 v Commissioners for HM Revenue and Customs [2009] EWCA Civ 446.

arrangement set up in order to divert taxable income to a low-tax environment.

It is important to note that the *Cadbury* judgment is based on freedom of establishment. That freedom is applicable only within the Union and is of no direct benefit to third-country companies. It would thus become a relevant constraint in relation to CFC rules only in the event that no consensus was found among Member States on the proposal submitted by the Commission, and a group of Member States then asked the Commission to submit a proposal for a measure to be adopted in enhanced cooperation under Article 20 TEU and Articles 326–334 TFEU. Article 82 of the proposal is applicable only in relation to third countries. It is only in the context of enhanced cooperation that the rules laid down in that article could become applicable in relations between Member States – that is to say, between CCCTB Member States and those which decided not to participate.

The only freedom applicable in relations with third countries is the free movement of capital. There has in the past been some uncertainty in the case law over how and where the distinction was to be drawn between the application of the freedoms, assuming indeed that there was to be any such distinction. The debate over this issue goes back to the *Baars*[152] case, where Advocate General Alber proposed in his Opinion that the applicable freedom should normally depend on the centre of gravity of the case (see points 14, 26 and 30). While the Court did not find it necessary in that case to decide on the point, the notion of the centre of gravity has been accepted in subsequent cases (for example, in *Cadbury* – see point 31 of the judgment). That naturally leaves the question of how to determine what the centre of gravity might be. For some time the prevailing view appeared to be that any case concerning a controlling interest in another company was covered by the freedom of establishment, while portfolio interests fell under the free movement of capital. It now seems to be established, however, that the distinction must be based not on the particular circumstances of the case but on the nature of the rule in issue.[153] A rule applicable only in situations of control (CFC provisions are perhaps a paradigmatic example of such a rule) falls

[152] Baars v Inspecteur der Belastingdienst Particulieren/Ondernemingen Gorinchem [2000] ECR I-2787, C-251/98.

[153] See for example Glaxo Wellcome [2009] ECR I-8591 (points 36–51), Case C-182/08; Joined Cases C-436/08 and C-437/08 Haribo, judgment of 10 February 2011, not yet reported, point 35.

within the freedom of establishment; rules which are potentially applicable in all circumstances (for example, rules applicable generally to all distributions of dividends) are matters for the free movement of capital.

It is worth noting here that the other specific anti-abuse rule in the CCCTB proposal, the thin capitalization rule in Article 81, may well be covered by the free movement of capital. There may nevertheless be some uncertainty: there is room for debate over the 20 per cent threshold in the definition of associated companies in Article 78 of the proposal. If that threshold is considered to be intended to reflect the existence of a high likelihood of decisive influence, then the argument can be made that the freedom of establishment must apply.

Having described the context, Dr HJI Panayi gives a brief summary of the key features of the proposal. It would be superfluous, in these brief comments and in the light of the discussion in previous sessions, to discuss that summary. She then presents a very useful concise history of the discussions on possible anti-abuse rules which took place in the period before the proposal was presented. Two points of interest at the end of this section may be mentioned: first, Dr HJI Panayi expresses scepticism regarding the need for a general anti-abuse rule. That is to a large extent a doctrinal issue, and there will certainly be others who share her view, particularly in the light of the case law of the ECJ. Secondly, she notes that there is no clear hierarchy between the GAAR in Article 80 and the specific anti-abuse rules, notably the thin cap rule in Article 81 and the CFC rule in Article 82. It is not clear just how important the absence of such a hierarchy is. The GAAR is a very narrow one, and there is likely to be little scope for its exploitation by tax authorities in preference to the SAARs. Moreover, it is hard to see why a wholly artificial construction which for some reason does not trigger the CFC rule (for example because less than 30 per cent of the controlled entity's income is "tainted" according to the criteria in Article 82(3)) should escape the application of the general rule simply because it may be considered to fall within the general scope of the CFC concept.

Dr HJI Panayi then turns to a discussion of the CFC rules contained in the CCCTB proposal. She includes in this discussion the switch-over clause in Article 73, criticizing the absence of any indication of the relationship between it and the CFC rules contained in Article 82. She further argues that the switch-over clause should contain an escape clause.

The switch-over rule is a rather rough instrument aimed at discouraging profit-shifting. In a certain sense it could thus be regarded as an anti-avoidance rule. But it does not focus on any precise avoidance activity. Instead, it applies systematically every time there is income coming from a [very] low-tax jurisdiction. It could be regarded as constituting in reality a minimum tax requirement attached to an exemption, a measure ensuring that a reasonable amount of tax is paid somewhere.

It could therefore be thought to be a form of intermediate measure, something which diverges from the normal system of taxation but is not strictly speaking a real anti-avoidance measure. In that regard it is interesting to refer to the judgment of the ECJ in *Columbus Container*.[154] In that judgment there is no reference to anti-avoidance. The Court does not need to address that issue because it concludes that there is no restriction, there being no greater tax burden for the taxpayer than in a purely domestic situation. It may well be that *Columbus Container* is something of a special case: though no mention is made of the fact in the judgment, the tax benefit enjoyed by the company was Belgian State aid which was incompatible with the Treaty.[155] Perhaps more importantly, any other result would have required the Court to hold that the two methods of relieving double taxation are not, as a matter of principle, equivalent for the purposes of the application of the Treaty freedoms. This latter point offers a degree of comfort in relation to the switch-over rule in the CCCTB.

That view of the switch-over rule could also provide an answer to the criticism expressed by Dr HJI Panayi and by other commentators regarding the absence of an escape clause. If this is not a true anti-abuse rule but a more general minimum taxation requirement, then the need for an escape clause is less compelling.

Dr HJI Panayi then describes the rather narrowly framed CFC rule contained in Article 82 of the proposal: its criteria are the existence of control, a low-tax regime, the absence of a stock exchange quotation and a high level of passive income, most of it received from related companies.

According to Dr HJI Panayi, the provision is poorly drafted. One example she gives is the criterion used in order to define a low-tax third country, which refers to the average statutory corporate tax rate of the Member States. How, she asks, is this average to be calculated? Is it to be calculated on a yearly basis? The answer to those questions is clear:

---

[154] Columbus Container Services v Finanzamt Bielefeld-Innenstadt [2007] ECR I-10451, C-298/05.

[155] See Commission Decision 2003/757/EC of 17 February 2003 on the aid scheme implemented by Belgium for coordination centres established in Belgium (OJ 2003 L 282, p. 25); Joined Cases C-182/03 and C-217/03 Belgium and Forum 187 v Commission [2006] ECR I-5479.

under the second paragraph of Article 73, the average is published annually by the Commission. She goes on to ask how the existence of a "special" tax regime is assessed – from the perspective of the Member State of the principal tax authority or from that of Member States in general? Again, the answer to that question ought to be clear: neither. Instead, a special regime for this purpose is one which diverges from the normal tax regime of the third country in issue. The purpose of this provision is to cover companies which benefit from exceptional schemes in countries whose normal tax system is unobjectionable.

Dr HJI Panayi expresses concern regarding the treatment of EEA States. Article 82(2) excludes the operation of the CFC rule where one of these States is party to an information exchange agreement comparable to the exchange of information on request provided for in the relevant Union legislation.[156] Since this legislation now provides (or will in the near future provide) for very extensive exchange of information going beyond the scope of the information exchange provision in the OECD Model, she argues that reliance on this standard is undesirable. However, what is important in this context is the ability to obtain information relevant to the assessment of tax. Article 26(1) of the OECD Model is broad in its scope, and should normally cover all the information required by Member State authorities in this context. It should not be forgotten, moreover, that both Iceland and Norway have signed and ratified the OECD/Council of Europe Convention on Mutual Administrative Assistance in Tax Matters as amended by the 2010 Protocol, which contains far-reaching provisions for information exchange.

Some of Dr HJI Panayi's remarks in this section relate to the situation which would obtain in the event that it was found impossible to agree on a CCCTB directive for 27 Member States, and a certain number of Member States decided to proceed with such a measure in enhanced cooperation. As will be explained below, those remarks are premature. However, she is correct to observe that if CFC rules were to be applied within the Union they would need to comply with the *Cadbury* case law (essentially, be confined to artificial arrangements). As the draft presently stands, however, the problem does not arise.

Dr HJI Panayi points out that the fact that the CFC and switch-over rules apply only in relation to third countries leaves scope for tax arbitrage within the Union. She says that it is unclear whether the GAAR could be used in relation to a CFC in, say, Cyprus (assuming that its 10

---

[156] European Commission, Council Directive 2011/16/EU of 15 February 2011 on administrative cooperation in the field of taxation, OJ 2011 L 64, p. 1.

per cent tax rate makes it a low-tax country within the meaning of the CFC rule). Surely, however, there should be no doubt of that, assuming the tax authorities are in a position to demonstrate the existence of an artificial construction.

One of Dr HJI Panayi's comments which is a little difficult to understand is the question whether the non-CCCTB (Member) State of residence of the parent company of a consolidated CFC in another Member State would be obliged to apply the CCCTB anti-abuse rule by virtue of its obligations under enhanced cooperation. Again, as will be explained below, any discussion of the hypothetical position under enhanced cooperation is premature in relation to the proposal which is at present under discussion in the Council. However, assuming her premise – that is, that a CCCTB Directive is at some point adopted in enhanced cooperation – it may well be that in the process of negotiating such a measure provisions governing this matter would be inserted in the text. In the absence of such provisions, it is not clear what obligations for non-participating Member States could flow from the enhanced cooperation procedure. What is clear, conversely, is that the Member State of the parent would be obliged to comply with the *Cadbury* case law.

Dr HJI Panayi notes the potential for arbitrage within a single Member State, and gives the interesting example of a parent company resident in a low-tax Member State which has consolidated subsidiaries in another Member State, one with high tax rates, and a 51 per cent subsidiary (thus under the consolidation threshold set out in Article 54) in its own Member State. Profits are diverted to the domestic subsidiary, which in a sense is a CFC in relation to the CCCTB. There is no scope for the application of Article 82, which applies only to third country CFCs. Is this a flaw in the system? Surely the answer, here again, is the GAAR – and that is how it should be, according to the *Cadbury* case law.

The chapter closes with the complaint that the Commission should in its proposal have explained and provided for the consequences of adoption of the CCCTB by a limited number of Member States under enhanced cooperation. Indeed, Dr HJI Panayi describes the current drafting of the proposal as unrealistic.

That objection is misconceived. The Commission is the executive arm of the EU, and one of its functions is to propose draft EU legislation: that is to say, EU legislation adopted in the normal manner and applicable throughout the Union. It is true that there is now a mechanism in the Treaty for the adoption of measures within the framework of the EU by a reduced group of Member States. However, a certain number of conditions must be complied with before that mechanism of enhanced cooperation can be put into operation. One – perhaps the most important in the context of the present discussion – is that enhanced cooperation is in the first instance an initiative of the Member States concerned: a group of no fewer than nine Member States may request the Commission to make a proposal. If the Commission does make a proposal, the next step is authorization of the process by the Council. The latter institution may authorize enhanced cooperation only "as a last resort, when it has established that the objectives of such cooperation cannot be attained within a reasonable period by the Union as a whole" (Article 20 TEU; see also Articles 326–334 TFEU). In practice, that means that the Commission must first have made a proposal for a normal Union measure governing the same subject matter and that the discussions of that proposal in the Council must have reached stalemate.

Accordingly, it is not legally possible for the Commission to make a hybrid proposal of the kind apparently envisaged by Dr HJI Panayi, incorporating provisions for the functioning of the CCCTB on the assumption that its territorial scope is limited to a group of Member States numbering somewhere between nine and 26. A proposal for legislation applicable within a limited circle of Member States may be advanced only at a later stage and subject to conditions that are not at present met. That is also an answer to some specific criticisms made elsewhere in her chapter, for example the point that the current drafting of the switch-over clause in Article 73 "perpetuates the confusion" regarding the possible application of that clause to non-CCCTB Member States. In the scheme of the CCCTB proposal, there can be no such thing as a non-CCCTB Member State.

Where Dr HJI Panayi is certainly right is where she states that if the CCCTB were adopted by a restricted number of Member States in enhanced cooperation, CFC rules (and indeed any anti-abuse rules) applicable to transactions between related companies within the Union would have to comply with the criteria laid down in the case law of the ECJ, in particular in the *Cadbury* judgment. One could thus envisage rules confined to purely artificial constructions. That is essentially the hypothesis of the GAAR in Article 80, and it could therefore perhaps be said that there would be no need for a separate CFC rule or other SAAR within the Union. One might also bear in mind the solution currently found in Article 82(2) regarding EEA countries: that is to say, if there is no need to apply CFC rules to these countries where there is an agreement on exchange of information equivalent to the rules contained in EU legislation, *a fortiori* there should be no such need in relation to Member States which are actually bound by that legislation. This is naturally pure speculation. All these matters would have to be examined closely if the Commission were requested to make a proposal for enhanced cooperation.

Having regard to the complexity of the subject matter, it will be apparent that the foregoing comments concern relatively peripheral points. Dr HJI Panayi's chapter is thorough, very interesting and thought-provoking.

Index